Acts and the Isaianic
New Exodus

Acts and the Isaianic New Exodus

David W. Pao

WIPF & STOCK · Eugene, Oregon

Wipf and Stock Publishers
199 W 8th Ave, Suite 3
Eugene, OR 97401

Acts and the Isaianic New Exodus
By Pao, David W.
Copyright©2000 Mohr Siebeck
ISBN 13: 978-1-4982-9944-2
Publication date 6/6/2016
Previously published by Mohr Siebeck, 2000

Preface

This book is a revision of a doctoral dissertation submitted to Harvard University in 1998. Many have contributed at the various stages in the writing of this dissertation. First of all, I would like to thank Prof. François Bovon who has been most generous in terms of both time and invaluable insights. His knowledge of all things Lukan became the most valuable resource throughout the development of this dissertation project. Most important of all, he has provided me with an exemplary model of creative and rigorous scholarship. Prof. Helmut Koester, with his expertise in early Christian literature and his sensitivity to methodological issues, has provided me with critical guidance during the course of my research. This study would not be possible without his support and continuous encouragement. Prof. Peter Machinist's insightful comments especially in matters related to the Hebrew Bible have allowed me to dive into the field of Isaianic scholarship with less apprehension.

I would also like to thank my fellow members of the New Testament Dissertation Seminar at Harvard for their encouragement as well as constructive comments. Laura Nasrallah and David Warren deserve special mention for their friendship and help.

This study has also benefited from the support from my own department at Trinity Evangelical Divinity School. Profs. Grant Osborne, Eckhard Schnabel, and Robert Yarbrough have provided helpful advice and tremendous encouragement during the stage of revision. Prof. D. A. Carson, in particular, has read the entire manuscript and offered valuable comments in the midst of his own busy research schedule.

I am indebted to John Vonder Bruegge who helped with proof-reading. Thanks are also due to David Moffitt, my teaching fellow, for his help in indexing and in preparing the manuscript for publication.

I am grateful to Prof. Dr. Martin Hengel and Prof. Dr. Otfried Hofius for accepting this book for publication in the WUNT 2 series. Prof. Dr. Hengel, in particular, has provided incisive comments for the revision of this study. Thanks also to the publishing staff of J.C.B. Mohr (Paul Siebeck) for their patience and efficient work.

Above all, I must thank my wife Chrystal for her sacrifice during the months when I could not separate myself from the computer. Her love and patience became the fuel behind this project.

To my parents, Dr. and Mrs. John Pao, this book is dedicated. They have given me all of themselves. More importantly, they have provided me living examples of faithful "ministers of the word."

David W. Pao

Table of Contents

Chapter 5: The Agent of the New Exodus:
The Word of God...147

Chapter 6: The Lord of the Nations:
The Anti-Idol Polemic...181

Chapter 1

Introduction

1.1 Approaches to the Study of the Acts of the Apostles

More than thirty years after the statement was first made, many are still compelled to begin any study on a particular aspect of the Lukan writings with the quotation of Willem van Unnik who has depicted Luke-Acts as "one of the great storm centers of New Testament scholarship."[1] While the literary unity of Luke-Acts has generally been maintained, the methodological explorations into the two halves of the Lukan writings have traveled different paths. Hans Conzelmann's emphasis on the redactional approach has greatly influenced the study of Luke since the 1950s even though the limitations of this approach have frequently been voiced.[2] With the difficulties surrounding the source-critical issues of Acts, however, the exact methodological focus in the study of Acts remains an unsettled matter.

The different approaches to studying the two volumes of the Lukan writings can best be illustrated by the various ways the travel narratives in both Luke and Acts have been understood. The significance of the travel narratives in both Luke and Acts has long been recognized by scholars.[3] In Luke, the author has transformed the travel report of Mark 10:1–52 into an extensive travel narrative (Luke 9:51–19:44) that occupies more than one third of the entire gospel. The explicit note at the beginning of the journey (9:51) is followed by recurring reminders of its destination (Luke 9:51, 53; 13:22, 33; 17:11; 18:31; 19:11, 28, 41). In Acts, the importance of traveling is even more apparent when apostolic journeys become the single most important organizing principle of its content. The journeys of Philip (Acts 8:4–40),

---

[1] Willem C. van Unnik, "Luke-Acts, a Storm Center in Contemporary Scholarship," in Leander E. Keck and J. Louis Martyn, eds., *Studies in Luke-Acts* (Nashville: Abingdon, 1966) 16.

[2] See, for example, the discussion in Charles H. Talbert, "Luke-Acts," in Eldon J. Epp and George W. MacRae, eds., *The New Testament and Its Modern Interpreters* (Philadelphia: Fortress, 1989) 311–12.

[3] The most significant blocks of travel narrative are present in Luke 9:51–19:44; Acts 12:25–21:16; and 27:1–28:16.

Peter (Acts 9:32–11:18) and Paul (Acts 12:25–28:16) form the framework in which the story of Acts develops.

While a primarily redactional approach to the study of the travel narrative in Luke has produced numerous studies,[4] a detailed study of the nature and purpose of the travel narrative within the structure and arguments of Acts is still lacking. Previous studies on the travel narrative in Acts have failed to explain how the journey motif is essential to the theological program of Acts. Studies by a number of scholars[5] who understand the author of Acts primarily as a historian assume that traveling is emphasized in Acts because the apostles did travel in the middle of the first century. While concentrating on the historical background of such journeys, this approach isolates the travel narrative from other theological themes in Acts. Significant theological emphases such as the relationship between Jews and Gentiles are simply ignored; and the importance of the "word of God" as the subject of the journey(s) remains unnoticed. Furthermore, the designation of the early Christian community as "the Way" becomes a subject unrelated to the travel narrative in Acts.

For those who emphasize the theological contribution of Luke,[6] the travel narrative in Acts is frequently considered to be a framework in which

---

[4] The purpose of the travel narrative in Luke has been understood to be christological (e.g., Hans Conzelmann, *The Theology of St. Luke* [trans. Geoffrey Buswell; 2nd ed.; New York: Harper & Row, 1960]), ecclesiological (e.g., Michi Miyoshi, *Der Anfang des Reiseberichts Lk 9,51–10,24: Eine redaktion-geschichtliche Untersuchung* [AnBib 60; Rome: Biblical Institute Press, 1974]), catechetical (e.g., David H. Gill, "Observations on the Lukan Travel Narrative and Some Related Passages," *HTR* 63 [1970] 199–221), authentication of Christian witness (e.g., William C. Robinson, Jr., "The Theological Context for Interpreting Luke's Travel Narrative [9:51ff.]," *JBL* 79 [1960] 20–31), or representation of the rejection by the Jews (e.g., Helmuth L. Egelkraut, *Jesus' Mission to Jerusalem: A Redaction-Critical Study of the Travel Narrative in the Gospel of Luke, Lk. 9:51–19:48* [Frankfurt am Main/New York: Peter Lang, 1976]). More recently, David Moessner (*Lord of the Banquet: The Literary and Theological Significance of the Lukan Travel Narrative* [Minneapolis: Fortress, 1989]) argues that Luke portrays Jesus, against the background of a Deuteronomistic view of history, as the prophet like Moses who is rejected by the wicked generation.

[5] See, in particular, William M. Ramsay, *St. Paul the Traveller and the Roman Citizen* (London: Hodder & Stoughton, 1897) although he himself recognizes that his study does not aim at exhausting the meaning of the Lukan writings. Other studies that adopt primarily a historical approach without rejecting completely the theological one include Colin J. Hemer, *The Book of Acts in the Setting of Hellenistic History* (WUNT 49; Tübingen: Mohr Siebeck, 1989) and F. F. Bruce, *The Acts of the Apostles* (3rd ed.; Grand Rapids, MI: Eerdmans, 1990).

[6] See Martin Dibelius, *Studies in the Acts of the Apostles* (ed. Heinrich Greeven; trans. Mary Ling; New York: Charles Scribner's Sons, 1956); Ernst Haenchen, "Tradition und Komposition in der Apostelgeschichte," *ZTK* 52 (1955) 205–25; and Conzelmann, *Theology of St. Luke*, 209–18.

theological ideas can be deposited. The travel narrative itself is, therefore, not considered worthy to be the focus of serious theological examination.

Recent studies on the travel narrative in Acts, as illustrated by the works of Richard Pervo[7] and Loveday Alexander,[8] have emphasized the literary affinities of Acts with the ancient Romance novels. While such works rightly emphasize the importance of the "journey plot" in ancient literature,[9] they fail to appreciate the distinctiveness of the theological program of Acts and other major differences between Acts and Greco-Roman Romance novels.[10] Most importantly, the function of Luke-Acts as the foundation story within the early Christian community needs to be emphasized.[11] The same isolation of the travel narrative from the wider theological emphases in Acts can be seen from Pervo's conclusion concerning the travel narrative in Acts: "What we do find in Acts is good guys versus villains. Neither doctrinal issues nor community experience plays a major role."[12] In short, one should question whether these attempts to identify the literary genre of Acts are sufficient to explain fully the purpose of its travel narrative.[13]

---

[7] Richard J. Pervo, *Profit with Delight: The Literary Genre of the Acts of the Apostles* (Philadelphia: Fortress, 1987). This study is carried out under the quest for an identification of the genre of Acts.

[8] Loveday C. A. Alexander, "'In Journeying Often': Voyaging in the Acts of the Apostles and in Greek Romance," in Christopher M. Tuckett, ed., *Luke's Literary Achievement* (Sheffield: Sheffield Academic Press, 1995) 17–49. See also Rosa Söder, *Die apokryphen Apostelgeschichten und die romanhafte Literatur der Antike* (Stuttgart: W. Kohlhammer Verlag, 1932).

[9] See the discussion in Percy Adams, *Travel Literature and the Evolution of the Novel* (Lexington, KY: University Press of Kentucky, 1983) 148–50.

[10] Bryan P. Reardon (*The Form of Greek Romance* [Princeton: Princeton University Press, 1991] 15–17) has listed the three generic characteristics of Greek Romance: 1. action: love at first sight, separation of couple and return of the hero; 2. character: beautiful hapless heroine and a handsome and often rather passive hero; and 3. situation: bourgeois idyll, "with a distinct air of social snobbery about it." The differences between Acts and the Greek Romance are apparent.

[11] See Marianne Palmer Bonz ("The Best of Times, the Worst of Times: Luke-Acts and Epic Tradition" [Th.D. diss., Harvard Divinity School, 1996]) who, drawing on the literary affinities of Virgil's *Aeneid* and Acts, argues that "Luke-Acts was composed as a foundational epic for the newly emerging Christian community, written to confer ancient Israel's religious heritage definitively and exclusively upon the church, to affirm its identity as completely independent of contemporary Israel and its diasporan communities, and to legitimize and empower its missionary mandate, with its promise of salvation for all believers and its universalizing claim to represent the ultimate fulfillment of the true plan of God" (33).

[12] Pervo, *Profit with Delight*, 28.

[13] Here, I am simply arguing that the ancient Romance novels alone are insufficient in providing the key to the understanding of the theological meaning embedded in the travel narrative.

The problems connected with the various approaches to the study of the travel narrative in Acts reflect the problems surrounding the study of Acts in general. The historical approach fails to account for the "historical" function of the text and the "historical" situation of the Lukan community. Those who champion the theological approach fail to reach a consensus as to ways the "theology" of the narrative of Acts can be extracted from both the form and the content of the work. Finally, those who emphasize the literary nature of the text place too much confidence in the literary genre as the key to unlocking the message of Acts. The failure of these approaches to provide a satisfying account of the connections between the "travel narrative" and the earlier chapters in Acts suggests the need for a different starting point in the examination of the narrative of Acts.

Without denying the role of early Christian traditions, form-critical concerns, and the literary models available to Luke in the articulation of his vision, I would emphasize another important pole upon which the Lukan story is constructed. In the Lukan writings, the importance of Scripture has long been recognized.[14] In Acts alone, the author has explicitly quoted twenty passages from the Septuagint.[15] These quotations should not simply be understood as isolated statements that bear no significance beyond their immediate contexts. Furthermore, the importance of Scripture is not limited to the numerous explicit quotations. In this study, I will argue that these scriptural statements point toward a wider story with which the narrative of Acts interacts. While such an interaction necessarily affects the "meaning" of both the scriptural story and the one that the author of Acts tries to construct, for the purpose of this study, I will concentrate on ways the scriptural story illuminates the narrative of Acts. In this sense, the scriptural story can best be understood as providing the hermeneutical framework within which the various individual units find their meaning. Although this study remains primarily a literary one, the theological claim that Luke could use Scripture in such a manner because of the possibility that scriptural promises did find their "fulfillment" in the early Christian movement is an

---

[14] See the discussion in François Bovon, *Luke the Theologian: Thirty-Three Years of Research (1950–1983)* (trans. Ken McKinney; Allison Park, PA: Pickwick, 1987) 78–108.

[15] These are Gen 15:13–14 (Acts 7:6–7); Gen 2:18 (Acts 3:25); Exod 3:12 (Acts 7:7); Exod 22:27 (Acts 23:5); Lev 23:29 with Deut 18:15–19 (Acts 3:23); Ps 2:1–2 (Acts 4:25–26); Ps 2:7 (Acts 13:33); Ps 16:8–11 with Ps 110:1 (Acts 2:25–28); Ps 69:25 (Acts 1:20); Ps 109:8 (Acts 1:20); Ps 118:22 (Acts 4:11); Isa 6:9–10 (Acts 28:26–27); Isa 49:6 (Acts 13:47); Isa 53:7–8 (Acts 8:32–33); Isa 55:3 (Acts 13:34); Isa 66:1–2 (Acts 7:49–50); Joel 2:28–32 (Acts 2:17–21); Amos 5:25–27 (Acts 7:42–43); Amos 9:11–12 (Acts 15:17); and Hab 1:5 (Acts 13:41).

important one and cannot be dismissed as irrelevant for this present exercise.[16]

More specifically, I will argue that the scriptural story which provides the hermeneutical framework for Acts is none other than the foundation story of Exodus as developed and transformed through the Isaianic corpus. The use of the Exodus tradition in Isaiah has long been recognized by scholars.[17] In Isaiah, this story provides an identity for the exilic community during the rebuilding of the community of God's people. Similarly, in the development of the identity of the early Christian movement, the appropriation of ancient Israel's foundation story provides grounds for a claim by the early Christian community to be the true people of God in the face of other competing voices. I will argue that this scriptural story illuminates the meaning of both the early chapters of Acts and the travel narrative that occupies the second half of the story. A survey of past studies on the role of Scripture in the Lukan writings will provide a fitting context for pursuing this reading.

1.2 The Scriptural Story and the Narrative of Acts within the Context of Lukan Scholarship

In this section, I will first discuss the various studies that attempt to examine the role of the Scripture in the Lukan writings. After this general survey, I will examine previous attempts in detecting the Isaianic New Exodus behind Acts.

a. The "Use" of Scripture in the Lukan Writings

Several works provide the foundation upon which recent discussions of the function of Scripture in the Lukan writings stands. The early study by William K. L. Clarke[18] establishes that the text behind the scriptural citations in the Lukan writings should be identified as the LXX[a] text. In those instances where Luke deviates from the LXX, Clarke proffers stylistic variations by the

---

[16] This reflects the theological location of the present writer as one who affirms that the Lukan program is not a construction without corresponding historical basis.

[17] See, for example, Bernhard W. Anderson, "Exodus Typology in Second Isaiah," in B. W. Anderson and W. Harrelson, eds., *Israel's Prophetic Heritage: Essays in Honor of James Muilenburg* (New York: Harper, 1962) 177–95; E. John Hamlin, "Deutero-Isaiah's Reinterpretation of the Exodus in the Babylonian Twilight," *Proceedings: Eastern Great Lakes and Midwest Biblical Societies* 11 (1991) 75–30; and Samuel E. Loewenstamm, *The Evolution of the Exodus Tradition* (trans. Baruch J. Schwartz; Jerusalem: Magnes Press, 1992). A detailed discussion will be provided in chapter two below.

[18] William K. L. Clarke, "The Use of the Septuagint in Acts," in F. J. Foakes Jackson and Kirsopp Lake, eds., *The Beginnings of Christianity* (London: Macmillan, 1922) 2.1.66–105.

author and free quotation from memory as sufficient explanations. While many still follow Clarke's identification of the Lukan LXX text type, recent development in the history of the LXX has disclosed the complexity involved in the identification of relationships between various "versions" of the LXX.[19] Furthermore, the fact that Clarke's study was produced before the 1950s is reflected in his lack of appreciation for the role of the author's theological conviction in the use of various scriptural citations.

The next study that needs to be mentioned is Traugott Holtz's *Untersuchungen über die alttestamentlichen Zitate bei Lukas*,[20] a study which provides a solid foundation for examining individual scriptural quotations in the Lukan writings. Like Clarke, Holtz also identifies the underlying text as the LXX[a] text type, and he does not attribute variations to the theological creativity of the author and the concerns of the community. In an examination of the use of particular books in the LXX, Holtz identifies the Twelve Prophets, Isaiah, and Psalms as the most significant texts for the Lukan writings. Corresponding to this observation, Holtz also makes a strong claim that Luke does not possess the LXX text of the Pentateuch and that he shows no interest in the narratives of Genesis and Exodus. This conclusion reflects the basic methodological weakness in Holtz's study—he concentrates solely on explicit scriptural citations. Lukan interest in the story of Abraham, for example, has been emphasized by many after Holtz;[21] and the importance of Moses and the Exodus tradition simply cannot be denied.[22] François Bovon has also highlighted the important fact that *verbatim* citations do not necessarily reflect the degree of the author's familiarity of the quoted passage or book.[23] Finally, the same criticism that has been directed against Clarke

---

[19] See, in particular, the recent discussion in Wayne Douglas Litke, "Luke's Knowledge of the Septuagint: A Study of the Citations in Luke-Acts" (Ph.D. diss., McMaster University, 1993) 21–24. Most significant is the probability that "Hebraicising" texts were available to Luke; and the divergence from the other versions of the LXX needs to be examined afresh. The question of Semitic influence has been raised in particular by Max Wilcox, *The Semitisms of Acts* (Oxford: Clarendon, 1965). The critique by Earl Richard ("The Old Testament in Acts: Wilcox's Semitisms in Retrospect," *CBQ* 42 [1980] 330–41) does not represent the end of the discussion. The issue of Semitic influence has now focused on issues such as the nature of Septuagintal Greek, the conceptual instead of linguistic influences in Acts, and, as mentioned above, the development of the different text types of the LXX.

[20] Traugott Holtz, *Untersuchungen über die alttestamentlichen Zitate bei Lukas* (TU 104; Berlin: Akademie-Verlag, 1968).

[21] See, for example, Nils A. Dahl, "The Story of Abraham in Luke-Acts," in Leander E. Keck and J. Louis Martyn, eds., *Studies in Luke-Acts: Essays Presented in Honor of Paul Schubert* (Nashville: Abingdon, 1966) 139–59; and Joel B. Green, "The Problem of a Beginning: Israel's Scripture in Luke 1–2," *BBR* 4 (1994) 1–25.

[22] This is also a major thesis of this study. See the discussion in the following section.

[23] Bovon, *Luke the Theologian*, 101.

applies here too, for Holtz can also be accused of underestimating the theological contribution of Luke.

In contrast to Holtz, Martin Rese's work on Lukan Christology highlights Luke's theological contributions.[24] Focusing on the function of individual citations, Rese has been able to situate the discussion within the wider program of Luke. Furthermore, Rese has also provided a categorization of the different uses of scriptural citations in Luke: hermeneutical, scriptural proof, types within the promise-fulfillment framework, and typological. Although Rese has been criticized for overemphasizing the editorial influence of Luke,[25] this work moves beyond the concern surrounding the mechanics of scriptural quotation into an exploration into the theological program of Acts.

These three studies have set the agenda for the discussion of the role of Scripture in the Lukan writings even though some of the conclusions they offer may not be acceptable to all. The topics that continue to dominate the discussion include: the text type behind the Lukan citations of Scripture, the particular Lukan interest in and focus on various portions of Scripture, the different functions of scriptural citations, and the importance and role of the Lukan hand behind such citations.

Two limitations of these studies, and those following similar paths, should however be noted. First, their strong emphasis on christological uses of scriptural citations tends to overshadow concerns for the ecclesiological function of the "evocation"[26] of scriptural traditions in the Lukan writings. While the significance of the question of the nature and identity of the early Christian community is clearly present throughout the narrative of Acts, many works that deal with the use of Scripture in Luke and Acts demonstrate an overly narrow preoccupation with christological issues. This is best represented in the work of Henry J. Cadbury who understands the Lukan use of Scripture as christological proofs;[27] and similar concerns are present in the work of Darrell Bock who ends his examination in Acts 13, the chapter where

---

[24] Martin Rese, *Alttestamentliche Motive in der Christologie des Lukas* (StNT 1; Gütersloh: Gütersloher Verlagshaus, 1969).

[25] The most sustained critique of this particular aspect of Rese's study is offered in Darrell L. Bock, *Proclamation from Prophecy and Pattern: Lucan Old Testament Christology* (JSNTSup 12; Sheffield: Sheffield Academic Press, 1987).

[26] My use of the term "evocation" in this study aims at highlighting the fact that the scriptural traditions recalled in the use of certain key words may be more profound than the content explicitly noted in the scriptural quotations and allusions.

[27] See, for example, Henry J. Cadbury, *The Making of Luke-Acts* (New York: Macmillan, 1927) 303–5. This is followed by Paul Schubert ("The Structure and Significance of Luke 24," in W. Eltester, ed., *Neutestamentliche Studien für Rudolf Bultmann* [Berlin: Alfred Töpelmann, 1954] 165–88) who argues that "proof-from-prophecy theology is Luke's central theological idea throughout the two-volume work" (176).

"Luke's OT christology stops."[28] Rese's own emphasis on the hermeneutical use of Scripture should not be forgotten.[29] Even Hans Conzelmann, who does not deny the apologetic function of Scripture, insists that as the Church becomes the heir of Israel, "Scripture belongs to the Church, for she is in possession of the correct interpretation."[30] A study focusing on the ecclesiological function of scriptural citations in the Lukan writings still needs to be written.[31]

Second, the weight placed on explicit scriptural quotations has not been balanced by examinations of other modes of the "use" of Scripture. This has led to an emphasis on isolated quotations without an awareness of other possible patterns that might exist behind these quotations. As a result, the radical dichotomization of speech and narrative becomes evident. The relationship between the scriptural citations embedded in the Lukan speeches and the development of the narrative's wider plot has frequently gone unnoticed.[32] Recent works that attempt to search for a wider pattern behind individual scriptural citations and allusions have focused primarily on the first

[28] Bock, *Proclamation from Prophecy and Pattern*, 277. An underlying agenda of Bock's study is to show that a Semitic origin should not be dismissed in either linguistic or conceptual form behind the numerous scriptural citations. Nevertheless, the value of Bock's work cannot be dismissed. The detailed exegesis offered in this study as well as the emphasis on the theme of "proclamation from prophecy" instead of the characteristically apologetic theme of "proof from prophecy" deserve further discussion.

[29] See also Martin Rese, "Die Funktion der alttestamentlichen Zitate und Anspielungen in den Reden der Apostelgeschichte," in Jacob Kremer, ed., *Les Actes des Apôtres: Traditions, rédaction théologie* (BETL 48; Leuven: Leuven University Press, 1979) 61–79.

[30] Conzelmann, *Theology of St. Luke*, 162.

[31] John T. Carroll ("The Uses of Scriptures in Acts," *SBLSP* 29 [1990] 522) rightly observes that the christological use of Scripture in Acts "stands in service of an even more crucial theological concern within the narrative, one that has to do with the question, Who are the people of God?" However, it should be further noted that ecclesiology originated from Christology, and one must not deny that Luke also has a unique interest in christological issues.

The particular understanding of proof-from-prophecy as the only paradigm within which the Scripture citations in Luke-Acts can be examined has been successfully refuted by Charles H. Talbert, "Promise and Fulfillment in Lucan Theology," in Charles H. Talbert, ed., *Luke-Acts: New Perspectives from the Society of Biblical Literature Seminar* (New York: Crossroad, 1984) 91–103.

[32] Interestingly, while the important work of C. H. Dodd (*According to the Scriptures: The Sub-Structure of New Testament Theology* [London: Nisbet, 1952]) has highlighted the importance of the context of individual citations, this work has also reinforced the understanding of these quotations as isolated ones that were circulated in certain early Christian circles. While clusters of quotations may have circulated among the churches, the possible use of some of these citations by the author of Luke-Acts together with other citations and allusions in forming the framework within which the narrative of Acts can be understood should prevent one from overemphasizing the citations as isolated statements.

volume of the Lukan writings. These works can be classified into three general categories.

The first group is best represented by John Drury who argues that at least certain portions of the narrative in Luke should be understood as midrash.[33] Drury's identification of midrash as narrative creation that relates historical traditions to texts is questionable. Most follow Earle Ellis in recognizing the presence of midrashic techniques in the gospel without accepting the generic identification for the gospel itself.[34] It should also be noted that in both the Lukan writings and the midrashic literature, the wider context of the source text is assumed.[35]

Related to this approach is one that points to the liturgical function of the gospel text. Michael Goulder, for example, has argued that both Matthew and Luke are to be read as lectionaries for early Christian churches.[36] The lack of evidence for the existence of a lectionary behind the text and the failure to account for the narrative structure of the gospel are problems that proponents of this hypothesis cannot easily dismiss.

The third group is represented by those who argue for the presence of a scriptural pattern behind portions of the narrative of Luke and Acts. Notable examples include the works of Thomas Brodie who suggests that the narrative of Luke and Acts should be understood in light of the Elijah-Elisha cycle.[37] David Moessner, on the other hand, has argued that the journey narrative in

---

[33] John Drury, *Tradition and Design in Luke's Gospel: A Study in Early Christian Historiography* (Atlanta, GA: John Knox, 1976).

[34] See, in particular, the discussion in E. Earle Ellis, *The Old Testament in Early Christianity: Canon and Interpretation in the Light of Modern Research* (WUNT 54; Tübingen: Mohr Siebeck, 1991) 91–105. See also Craig A. Evans and James A. Sanders, *Luke and Scripture: The Function of Sacred Tradition in Luke-Acts* (Minneapolis: Fortress, 1993) 1–13.

[35] In the case of midrash, however, the "wider context" can go beyond the immediate context as one part of the canon can be used to illuminate another. See, in particular, the discussion in James L. Kugel, "Two Introductions to Midrash," in Geoffrey H. Hartman and Sanford Budick, eds., *Midrash and Literature* (New Haven, CT: Yale University Press, 1985) 77–103.

[36] Michael D. Goulder, *The Evangelists' Calendar: A Lectionary Explanation of the Development of Scripture* (London: SPCK, 1978).

[37] See Thomas L. Brodie, "Towards Unraveling the Rhetorical Imitation of Sources in Acts: 2 Kgs 5 as One Component of Acts 8:9–40," *Bib* 67 (1986) 41–67; *Luke the Literary Interpreter: Luke-Acts as a Systematic Rewriting and Updating of the Elijah-Elisha Narrative* (Rome: Pontifical Univ. of Thomas Aquinas, 1987); "The Departure for Jerusalem (Luke 9:51–56) and a Rhetorical Imitation of Elijah's Departure for the Jordan (2 Kgs 1:1–2:6)," *Bib* 70 (1989) 96–109; and "Luke-Acts as an imitation and emulation of the Elijah-Elisha narrative," in Earl Richard, ed., *New Views on Luke and Acts* (Collegeville, MN: Liturgical Press, 1990) 78–85.

Luke needs to be read against the Exodus journey narrative of Deuteronomy.[38] This approach proves to be the most fruitful one when coming to examine the complex relationship between the Scripture of ancient Israel and the Lukan writings. While the importance of the Elijah-Elisha cycle and the Exodus story cannot be doubted, these studies fail to take into account the wider narrative of Acts. More importantly, these approaches ignore the significance of the numerous Isaianic citations and allusions at critical points in the Lukan narrative as well as the distinct Isaianic thematic emphases in the Lukan writings.

In this study, I will demonstrate that the narrative of Acts should primarily be read within the hermeneutical framework of the Isaianic New Exodus. This approach will both recognize the significance of the scriptural story behind the Lukan narrative and highlight the ecclesiological function of Scripture in the construction of the identity claim of the early Christian movement. To situate this study within several recent studies on the relationship between Isaiah and the Lukan writings, a brief discussion of this narrower field of studies is required.

b. Isaianic New Exodus and the Narrative of Acts

A number of recent studies highlight the importance of the Isaianic pattern behind the writings of Luke. A detailed examination of the narrative of Acts in light of the Isaianic New Exodus program is, however, still lacking.

Moving beyond the study of Holtz, some point out the distinctive significance of Isaiah in the Lukan writings. David Seccombe, for example, notes several aspects in which the Lukan interest in Isaiah is evident.[39] First, in addition to the many Isaianic allusions and quotations, Luke includes four lengthy quotations of Isaiah.[40] Second, the emphasis on Isaiah can be seen in Luke 3:4 and 4:17 where the book of Isaiah is explicitly mentioned.[41] Most

---

[38] Moessner, *Lord of the Banquet*. Unlike the earlier work of Christopher F. Evans ("The Central Section of St. Luke's Gospel," in Dennis E. Nineham, ed., *Studies in the Gospels: Essays in Honor of R. H. Lightfoot* [Oxford: Basil Blackwell, 1955] 37–53), Moessner argues for thematic correspondence instead of strict verbal and structural parallelism. See also the work of Jindrich Mánek, "The New Exodus in the Books of Luke," *NovT* 2 (1957) 8–23. Mánek has already suggested that the Lukan portrayal of the life of Jesus should be understood as a New Exodus event. Naturally, his analysis stops at the account of the ascension of Jesus in Acts 1.

[39] David P. Seccombe, "Luke and Isaiah," *NTS* 27 (1981) 252–59.

[40] Luke 3:4–6 citing Isa 40:3–5; Luke 4:18–19 citing Isa 61:1–2; Acts 8:28–33 citing Isa 53:7–8; and Acts 28:25–27 citing Isa 6:9–10. Significantly three of these four passages are found at either the beginning or the end of the two volumes of the Lukan writings.

[41] Luke 3:4a: ὡς γέγραπται ἐν βίβλῳ λόγων Ἡσαΐου τοῦ προφήτου ("as it is written in the book of the words of the prophet Isaiah"); and 4:17a: καὶ ἐπεδόθη αὐτῷ βιβλίον τοῦ προφήτου Ἡσαΐου ("and the scroll of the prophet Isaiah was given to him"). In this study,

significant of all is the question raised by the Ethiopian eunuch concerning the identity of the one mentioned in Isaiah 53 (Acts 8:34). This perceptive interpretive question points to the existence of the wider relationship between Isaiah and the Lukan writings. Seccombe's study has successfully highlighted the importance of Isaiah for the Lukan writings. Nevertheless, he fails to discuss the hermeneutic function of these Isaianic passages in the Lukan theological program. Moreover, he does not discuss the role of the general pattern constructed by the various Isaianic passages for the development of the narrative of Luke and Acts.

In another study on "Isaiah in Luke," James Sanders reflects on the use of Isaiah in Jesus' Nazareth sermon in Luke 4 and probes into "Jesus' hermeneutic in interpreting the Isaiah passage."[42] This study shows how the Lukan Jesus uses Isaiah with full awareness of its context to express his theological concerns. Sander's study represents those who seek to examine the relationship between Isaiah and the Lukan writings primarily through the study of individual explicit quotations. Without denying the importance of this study, it must be stressed that focusing on one passage cannot provide a satisfactory account of the relationship between Isaiah and Luke as the title of the article promises.[43]

Three recent studies which emphasize the role of Isaiah in the construction of the Lukan theological vision demand a more detailed discussion. The first is Mark Strauss' *The Davidic Messiah in Luke-Acts*.[44] This work is not directly aimed at studying the relationship between Isaiah and Luke-Acts. Rather, it focuses on "an examination of one major theme within Luke's christology, Jesus as the coming king from the line of David."[45] From an examination of the Lukan infancy narrative, the Nazareth sermon of Luke 4, the travel narrative occupying the gospel's central section, and three speeches in Acts (2:14–41; 13:16–41; 15:13–21), Strauss suggests that "Luke has a tendency to

---

all English biblical quotations are taken from the New Revised Standard Version (NRSV) unless otherwise noted.

[42] James Sanders, "Isaiah in Luke," *Int* 36 (1982) 153. See also his "From Isaiah 61 to Luke 4," in J. Neusner, ed., *Christianity, Judaism and Other Greco-Roman Cults: Studies for Morton Smith at Sixty* (Leiden: Brill, 1975) 1.75–106.

[43] See, for example, Geoffrey W. Grogan, "The Light and the Stone: A Christological Study in Luke and Isaiah," in Harold H. Rowdon, ed., *Christ the Lord: Studies in Christology Presented to Donald Guthrie* (Leicester: InterVarsity Press, 1982) 151–67. In this study, the author focuses solely on Luke 2:25–35. While Grogan has successfully highlighted the Isaianic context in which the story of Simeon should be understood, the insistence on a strict christological reading of Isaiah is unjustifiable when the wider Isaianic influence is recognized throughout the Lukan writings.

[44] Mark L. Strauss, *The Davidic Messiah in Luke-Acts: The Promise and Its Fulfillment in Lukan Christology* (JSNTSup 110; Sheffield: Sheffield Academic Press, 1995).

[45] Ibid., 9.

introduce Davidic messianism into christological sections which are
introductory and programmatic for his two-volume work."[46]

Moving beyond this focus, Strauss searches for the unity behind the
various christological motifs in the Lukan writings. He argues that behind the
Lukan portrait of Jesus as prophet, servant, and Davidic king lies the Isaianic
texts as "Luke links the Jesus event particularly in the Isaianic portrait of
eschatological salvation, where the messianic deliverer is at the same time
prophet, servant and king."[47] Embedded in his discussion of the Lukan travel
narrative,[48] and in reaction to the works of Evans and Moessner,[49] Strauss
argues that instead of understanding the travel narrative which occupies the
central portion of the gospel as modeled upon the Deuteronomic Exodus, one
should examine this lengthy account in light of the New Exodus of Isaiah.[50]
Therefore, as Rikki Watts has earlier argued for the gospel of Mark,[51] Strauss
points to the significance of the Isaianic New Exodus for the gospel of Luke,
although he considers the Isaianic New Exodus not as "the controlling theme
of Luke's work" but merely as "one of the metaphors Luke uses to describe
the dawn of eschatological salvation."[52]

This work has successfully highlighted the significance of Isaiah especially
in providing a unified context for the diverse christological motifs found in
Luke. Strauss' sound exegesis provides a solid foundation for his discussion of
Lukan christology. However, the limitations of his study, and in particular his
understanding of the Lukan use of Isaiah, should also be noted.[53] First, the
understandable preoccupation with christology prevents Strauss from further
examining the ecclesiological function of the Lukan adaptation of the Isaianic
program. More importantly, his arguments concerning the importance of the
Isaianic New Exodus in Luke are not developed in sufficient detail to show

---

[46] Ibid., 340.

[47] Ibid., 343.

[48] Ibid., 285–305.

[49] See the discussion above.

[50] Strauss (*Davidic Messiah in Luke-Acts*, 302–4) further argues that the New Exodus
does not begin with Luke 9 but has already begun to take place at the beginning of the public
ministry of Jesus.

[51] Rikki E. Watts, *Isaiah's New Exodus and Mark* (WUNT 2.88; Tübingen: Mohr
Siebeck, 1997). Although this work is published after Strauss', the dissertation from which
this book is developed was completed in 1990. I am grateful to the author for making
available the manuscript of this book before it was published.

[52] Strauss, *Davidic Messiah in Luke-Acts*, 304–5. See also Willard M. Swartley,
Israel's Scripture Traditions and the Synoptic Gospels: Story Shaping Story (Peabody, MA:
Hendrickson, 1994). In this study, Swartley argues that the synoptic gospels share common
structural patterns that are rooted in the traditions of Israel's past.

[53] I will limit my comments to Strauss' understanding of the relationship between
Isaiah and Luke. Questions concerning his selective use of texts and overemphasis on the
Davidic messiah motif will not be dealt with here.

that the Isaianic "pattern" should indeed be considered as the framework in which the Lukan narrative develops.[54] Furthermore, although he examines three speeches in Acts in the early part of this study, his discussion of the Isaianic New Exodus paradigm, which appears in the latter part of the study, relates only to the gospel of Luke. The focus of his analysis on the Isaianic influence on Luke can only be justified by taking an approach which is limited to christological issues.

One must agree with Strauss that Jesus' journey to Jerusalem should be understood against the Isaianic theme of the arrival of the salvation of God in Jerusalem. This theme alone, however, does not represent the entire program of the Isaianic New Exodus. Significantly, many of the Isaianic themes critical in the narrative of Acts are absent in Luke. These include the four recurring themes introduced in the Isaianic prologue of Isa 40:1–11: the restoration of Israel, the power of the word of God, the anti-idol polemic, and the concern for the nations.[55] In addition, the Isaianic pattern that can be established behind the narrative of Acts plays much less of a role in the gospel narrative. Therefore, one can only conclude that while Strauss has rightly identified the importance of the Isaianic New Exodus for the gospel of Luke, the fully developed program is found only in the narrative of Acts. The validity of his observation that the Isaianic New Exodus is only "one of the metaphors" used in Luke's work also needs to be modified when the importance of the Isaianic paradigm in the narrative of Acts is taken into consideration. Moreover, when the focus on the people of God in Isaiah 40–55 and the ecclesiological use of the Isaianic program in the Lukan writings are recognized, one is tempted to suggest that the Isaianic New Exodus in Luke can now be considered as the "prelude" to the development of the Isaianic program in Acts where the Isaianic New Exodus takes on a much more critical role in the narrative.[56]

---

[54] Although he has noted that the Isaianic framework is not "*the* controlling framework" of Luke, as mentioned above, his argument against the detailed study of Moessner requires greater elaboration.

[55] Although the word "absent" may be an overstatement, the unique ways in which these Isaianic themes are present in Acts only highlight their "lack of emphasis" in Luke. For a further discussion of these themes, please refer to chapters four to seven below.

[56] This, of course, does not diminish the significance of the foundational event of the Christ-story as presented in the Lukan writings. It is the precise function of this christological focus that needs to be questioned. The mere act of writing a second volume in addition to the gospel alters the theological program of the entire work. If the christological focus of the use of Isaiah and scriptural traditions in general is maintained in the Lukan writings, one is obliged to focus on the narrative in the gospel itself. If the ecclesiological focus is highlighted, however, the identity of the early Christian movement becomes the central issue that is at stake. Although one cannot draw a sharp dichotomy between the two, it seems clear that the christological controversy that occupies the later centuries cannot be considered as the central problem behind Luke-Acts. Rather, the identity of the early Christian community as the true people of God over against those who offer competitive claims seems to be the issue

The acceptance of Strauss' emphasis on the Isaianic New Exodus can be found in Max Turner's *Power from on High*,[57] a book that was published a year after the appearance of Strauss' study.[58] Yet, while Strauss emphasizes Christology, Turner chooses to focus on the role of the Spirit. After a survey of scholarship and a discussion of the understanding of the Spirit in Jewish sources, Turner turns his attention to the "Messiah of the Spirit."[59] In his discussion of the Nazareth Sermon of Luke 4, Turner argues that the quotation from Isaiah 61 should be understood as "part of a more general New Exodus soteriology."[60] Turner uses the term "New Exodus" to refer to the Isaianic New Exodus but he departs from Strauss by also stressing the importance of Moessner's work that highlights certain Deuteronomic motifs behind the central section of Luke such as the Deuteronomic "rejection of the prophet" motif.[61]

More significantly, Turner's work is able to locate the discussion of the Spirit's role within the expectation of the restoration of Israel.[62] This is especially clear in his discussion of the Mosaic allusions of the Pentecost account. He proposes that "the parallels do suggest Pentecost is viewed as part of the fulfillment and *renewal* of Israel's covenant, and so ensure that the gift of the Spirit will have a vital role in Israel's restoration."[63] Moving beyond Acts 2, Turner examines Acts 3:19–25 and 15:12–21 concluding that the risen Lord "continues the task of Israel's restorative cleansing and transformation, which he commenced as one empowered by the Spirit."[64] The other references to the Spirit are dealt with in the final section of his book:

---

that controls the development of the narrative. The same ecclesiological focus can be found in the Isaianic New Exodus. The identity of the "servant" or any other messianic figures is not the central concern. The identity and situation of the exilic community, rather, becomes the focus of the narrative. The utilization of the ancient Israelite tradition of Exodus further confirms this observation. The foundation story of the Israelite community is evoked in a new era where "the people of God" needs to be redefined and reestablished. Therefore, in an examination of the use of the Isaianic New Exodus in the Lukan writings, the ecclesiological concern naturally needs to be examined.

[57] Max M. Turner, *Power from on High. The Spirit in Israel's Restoration and Witness in Luke-Acts* (Sheffield: Sheffield Academic Press, 1996).

[58] Ibid., 144 n. 15: the relationship between the two works is not surprising considering that Strauss was one of Turner's research students.

[59] Ibid., 140–315.

[60] Ibid., 244.

[61] Ibid., 148. Turner's study also emphasizes the significance of other christological motifs although the primacy of the Davidic Messiah motif is affirmed.

[62] The role of the expectation for the restoration of Israel in the Lukan writings has already been suggested although not in connection with the Isaianic New Exodus. See, in particular, Jacob Jervell, *Luke and the People of God* (Minneapolis: Augsburg, 1972).

[63] Turner, *Power from on High*, 289.

[64] Ibid., 314–315.

"The Disciples and the Spirit."[65] Here, Turner demonstrates that "for Luke the Spirit is at least a principal means of God's saving restoration and transformation of Israel."

This significant work on the role of the Spirit in the Lukan writings has again highlighted the importance of Isaiah for the theological program of Luke. While Turner emphasizes the link between the introduction of the Isaianic New Exodus in Luke and the continuation of the restoration program in Acts, the particular Isaianic features of this restoration program need to be explored in greater detail. His examination of the role of the Spirit in the restoration program should be supplemented by other themes present in the Isaianic restoration program although this would go beyond the proper limit of his study. Furthermore, Turner's argument that the restoration program "is largely complete by Acts 15"[66] naturally leads him to ignore other Isaianic themes developed in the second half of the narrative of Acts. As the emphasis of the Spirit is only one aspect of the Isaianic restoration program, the restoration program itself is also only one aspect of the wider Isaianic New Exodus program. Nevertheless, Turner must be commended for introducing the ecclesiological significance of the Isaianic New Exodus especially in the second volume of the Lukan writings.

The final study that needs to be discussed is Rebecca Denova's work on the "prophetic tradition in the structural pattern of Luke-Acts."[67] This study, one that appeared a year after Turner's, is unaware of either Strauss' or Turner's monographs.[68] Arguing against Conzelmann and others who have suggested that the Lukan writings were produced in response to the delay of the parousia,[69] Denova suggests that Luke-Acts was written to demonstrate the fulfillment of the promises made to Israel.[70] Denova rightly argues that the Lukan writings cannot be understood within the paradigm of an apologetic "proof from prophecy." Rather, Luke uses Scripture "to design his structure of the narrative units in the life of Jesus and his followers."[71]

On the use of particular scriptural traditions, Denova points to the significance of Isaiah as well as the Elijah-Elisha narrative for the

---

[65] Ibid., 318–427.

[66] Ibid., 419.

[67] Rebecca I. Denova, *The Things Accomplished Among Us: Prophetic Tradition in the Structural Pattern of Luke-Acts* (JSNTSup 141; Sheffield: Sheffield Academic Press, 1997). See also my comments in "Review of Rebecca Denova, *The Things Accomplished Among Us*," *TLZ* 124.4 (1999) 400–01.

[68] This can be explained by the fact that this study is a revision of the author's 1994 doctoral dissertation at the University of Pittsburgh.

[69] Conzelmann, *Theology of St. Luke*, 146–69.

[70] The dependence upon Jervell's work is noted at the very beginning of the work. See Denova, *Things Accomplished Among Us*, 8.

[71] Ibid., 27.

understanding of the structural pattern of Luke-Acts. Following E. P.
Sanders,[72] Denova highlights the importance of the "Jewish Restoration
Theology" of Isaiah. Following Thomas Brodie,[73] Denova argues that the
relationship between Jesus (Luke) and his disciples (Acts) is modeled upon
the Elijah-Elisha relationship. Concerning the purpose of the use of such
scriptural traditions, Denova argues that Luke is writing "typological-
history"[74] to "persuade other Jews that Jesus of Nazareth was the Messiah
of scripture and that the words of the prophets concerning 'restoration' have
been 'fulfilled'."[75]

This study provides a helpful discussion of the literary devices used in the
narrative of Luke and Acts especially in relation to the Lukan use of Scripture.
Although Denova rightly emphasizes the importance of Scripture behind the
structural pattern of Luke-Acts, a stronger case can be developed in support
of this claim. For example, in the chapter entitled "The 'fulfillment of
Prophecy' in the Acts of the Apostles,"[76] one is surprised to note that only
two passages are examined: the rejection of Stephen in Acts 7 and the
ingathering of the exiles in Acts 2. Instead of demonstrating the scriptural
pattern behind the Lukan writings, Denova allows the larger concern of the
focus on the Jews in the Lukan writings to dominate her discussion.

While Denova recognizes the importance of Isaiah, the appropriation of
the Exodus tradition in Isaiah is not developed. The function of the foundation
story of ancient Israel in both Isaiah and Acts needs to be discussed. Some
further limitations of her work follow partly from her dependence upon three
scholars. In relying on the works of Sanders to characterize the restoration
theology of Isaiah, she does not explore the wider Isaianic program beyond
the theme of restoration. In relying on the works of Brodie, who has rightly
stressed the significance of the Elijah-Elisha narrative in bridging the two
volumes of the Lukan writings, Denova does not emphasize the Isaianic
framework that extends from the Lukan prologue to the end of Acts. Most
importantly, in drawing from the works of Jacob Jervell, she ignores the
transformation of the scriptural pattern and the Isaianic vision in the Lukan
writings. This is most evident in Denova's treatment of the Gentile issue[77]

---

[72] See, for example, E. P. Sanders, *Jesus and Judaism* (Philadelphia: Fortress, 1985)
77–119.

[73] The works of Brodie have already been mentioned above in n. 37.

[74] Denova, *Things Accomplished Among Us*, 230.

[75] Ibid., 231.

[76] Ibid., 155–77.

[77] Ibid., 184–98. See also her unsubstantiated statement concerning Acts 1:8: "There is
no indication that the commission in Acts 1.8 contains any reference to Gentiles or to Rome"
(110). While a reference to Rome may be disputed, further discussion is required to expel the
notion of an at least implicit reference to the Gentiles.

where the criticisms leveled by many against Jervell's work are left unanswered.[78]

From the preceding discussion, it is clear that a systematic study of the use of the Isaianic New Exodus especially in the second volume of the Lukan writings is still lacking. Yet only through such a study can one appreciate the power of the hermeneutic framework Isaiah provides for understanding Luke's theological program.

1.3 The Plan of the Present Study

This study seeks to examine the appropriation of the Isaianic New Exodus in the narrative of Acts. In one sense this can be understood as a kind of "source-critical" study although the main emphasis is not upon the diachronic analysis of the prehistory of the text. The word "intertextuality" can also be used although the exact understanding of this term varies among its recent practitioners.[79] Since this study focuses on the hermeneutical significance of the Isaianic tradition in the development of the narrative of Acts, it should best be considered a "literary-critical" study, understood in the widest sense of the term.[80] The basic assumption behind this approach is that the author should not be considered merely as a collator of sources but also a skilled writer.[81] Sensitivity to the development of the story of Luke in light of the Isaianic program also aligns this approach with the concerns of narrative criticism although modern narratological theories are not considered as primary in this project for the understanding of the Lukan text.

The designation of literary criticism as the general approach of this study does not, however, exclude the use of traditional historical-critical

---

[78] See chapter seven below for a detailed discussion of the issue of the Gentiles in the Lukan writings.

[79] See, in particular, the discussion in Jonathan Culler, *The Pursuit of Signs: Semiotics, Literature, Deconstruction* (Ithaca: Cornell, 1981); and Julia Kristeva, *Revolution in Poetic Language* (trans. Margaret Waller; New York: Columbia University Press, 1984). The utilization of the term "intertextuality" by biblical scholars like Richard B. Hays (*Echoes of Scripture in the Letters of Paul* [New Haven, CT: Yale University Press, 1989]) has been criticized for reducing the term to a study of the literary relationships between two texts.

[80] One is tempted to call this an eclectic method but the designation "literary-critical" highlights the concern for the literary development of the narrative itself.

[81] For a discussion of this aspect of the literary-critical approach, see Norman R. Petersen, *Literary Criticism for New Testament Critics* (Philadelphia: Fortress, 1978); and Richard A. Spencer, ed., *Orientation by Disorientation: Studies in Literary Criticism and Biblical Literary Criticism* (Pittsburgh: Pickwick, 1980).

methodologies within this paradigm.[82] A literary analysis of ancient documents must also be "historical" in the sense that only after fully understanding the documents in their historical and cultural contexts can the texts be examined in literary terms. In one sense, my understanding of literary criticism is therefore not a rejection of traditional methodologies but a natural continuation of them.[83] As Norman Perrin[84] predicted twenty years ago, redaction criticism has developed into "genuine literary criticism" in which the fundamental goals of redaction criticism — careful reading of a complete text and attention to the meaning of the text as a whole — have been further developed.[85] The designation of this study as one that adopts a literary approach is significant, however, in that the issue of historicity is not its focus. The emphasis on the active role of Scripture, one that must not be confused with narrative creation, should not be considered as a challenge to the "historical" character of the text.

In establishing the relationship between Isaiah and the narrative of Acts, several aspects will be discussed. First, the significance of Isaiah at the very beginning of the public ministry of the Lukan Jesus will be noted. Here, I will examine the role of Isa 40:3–5 in Luke together with the terminology of "the Way" in the narrative of Acts. It is in relation to this discussion that I will introduce the unique thematic emphases of the Isaianic New Exodus.[86] Second, the influence of Isaiah in the construction of the narrative framework of the Lukan writings will be investigated in detail.[87] Finally, I will examine the unique Isaianic themes that control the narrative of Acts.[88] This examination will conclude with a chapter on the transformation of the Isaianic vision in Acts. The combination of the analyses of (1) explicit Isaianic citations, (2) the Isaianic influence on the Lukan narrative framework, and (3) the broad Isaianic themes developed in Acts will show that the narrative of

---

[82] Craig A. Evans ("Source, Form and Redaction Criticism: The 'Traditional' Methods of Synoptic Interpretation," in S. E. Porter and D. Tombs, eds., *Approaches to New Testament Study* [Sheffield: Sheffield Academic Press, 1995] 19) rightly notes that "an exegesis that cares little about history and sources is in danger of misunderstanding the text and distorting the distinctive motif the respective evangelists may have wished to convey."

[83] See John R. Donahue, "Redaction Criticism: Has the *Hauptstrasse* Become a *Sackgasse?*" in E. S. Malbon and E. V. McKnight, eds., *The New Literary Criticism and the New Testament* (Sheffield: Sheffield Academic Press, 1994) 27–57.

[84] Norman Perrin, "The Interpretation of the Gospel of Mark," *Int* 30 (1976) 120.

[85] Donahue ("Redaction Criticism," 29) has noted the distinction between the German practice of redaction criticism which has a stronger emphasis on the history of traditions and the American practice of redaction criticism which has a stronger emphasis on the text as a unitary composition with concern for the overarching themes and motifs. It is in the American form of redaction criticism that literary criticism finds its closest ally.

[86] See chapter two below.

[87] See chapter three below.

[88] See chapters four to seven below.

Acts cannot be properly understood apart from the wider context of the Isaianic New Exodus.

In examining the appropriation of Isaianic traditions in the Lukan writings, this study will not adopt the modern designations of First-, Second-, and Third-Isaiah. Recent discussions on the redactional, thematic, and structural unity of the Isaianic corpus have pointed to the possibility that the relationship between the various sections within Isaiah is much more complex than has previously been assumed.[89] More importantly, such modern divisions would not be understandable to the author of Luke-Acts. Therefore, while Luke draws primarily from Isaiah 40–55 in his adaptation of the Isaianic New Exodus, the constant references from beyond these chapters should not be surprising.

The issue concerning the unity of Luke-Acts also needs to be addressed. Many have followed Henry Cadbury's statement that Luke and Acts "are not merely two independent writings from the same pen; they are a single continuous work."[90] The narrative unity of Luke-Acts receives its strongest support in the two-volume work of Robert Tannehill.[91] The challenge to the unity of the Lukan writings has not been silenced, however. In Mikeal Parsons and Richard Pervo's *Rethinking the Unity of Luke and Acts*,[92] the debate is rekindled as they attempt to distinguish the various types of relationship between Luke and Acts. Parsons and Pervo affirm the authorial unity of Luke and Acts while challenging those who argue for the canonical, generic, narrative, and theological unity. While the unity of Luke-Acts will not be the primary concern of this study, it will both be assumed and affirmed especially in light of the common Isaianic story underlying both works.[93] One wonders if "scriptural unity" can be established behind the works of Luke and Acts.

---

[89] For a survey of the current state of scholarship, see the detailed discussion in Hugh G. M. Williamson, *The Book Called Isaiah: Deutero-Isaiah's Role in Composition and Redaction* (Oxford: Clarendon, 1994).

[90] Cadbury, *Making of Luke-Acts*, 8–9.

[91] Robert C. Tannehill, *The Narrative Unity of Luke-Acts: A Literary Interpretation* (2 vols.; Foundations and Facets; Philadelphia: Fortress Press, 1986, 1990).

[92] Mikeal C. Parsons and Richard I. Pervo, *Rethinking the Unity of Luke and Acts* (Minneapolis: Fortress, 1993).

[93] While it seems that Isaianic influence is more evident in Acts, the presence of the common story behind both volumes of the Lukan writings cannot be ignored. For a recent survey of scholarship on the issue of the unity of Luke-Acts, see Joseph Verheyden, "The Unity of Luke-Acts: What Are We Up To?" in J. Verheyden, ed., *The Unity of Luke-Acts* (Leuven: Leuven University Press, 1999) 3–56.

1.4 Historical Plausibility

Before embarking on the journey, a note concerning historical context and
assumptions should be provided. While this is primarily a literary study,
Luke's use of Isaiah needs to be situated within the context of the first
century early Christian movement. In one sense, therefore, the strength of my
case will be enhanced when "historical plausibility" is established.[94] On the
other hand, due to the nature of my investigation, the discussion provided
here can only be considered an outline of the framework within which my case
is built.

I will begin with the introductory questions of authorship and dating.
Then, the availability of Isaiah will be discussed through an examination of its
use in Second Temple Jewish literature as well as early Christian writings.
Admittedly, brief treatment of these topics will not do justice to any of them,
and the tentativeness of this discussion has to be recognized.[95] Nevertheless,
this lengthy digression aims at overcoming the modern dichotomy of historical
and theological concerns.

a. Authorial Context

The significance of questions concerning the historical author for a literary
study lies not in the interest in the individual himself but in the historical
context in which he is writing, his social and rhetorical location, and the
resources available to him.[96] In the case of the third Gospel and Acts,
overwhelming external evidence supports the traditional identification of
Luke, the companion of Paul, as the author. The oldest manuscript of the
gospel ($\mathfrak{P}$75) identifies Luke in the attached title. The roughly contemporary
Muratorian canon, if one is willing to accept the traditional second century
dating,[97] points in the same direction. At the end of the second century,

---

[94] I am borrowing this term from Hays (*Echoes of Scripture*, 30–31). For Hays,
"historical plausibility" is one of the seven tests for the identification of intertextual echoes.
While the question of Luke's literary intention can be approached primarily within a
historical paradigm, what follows is intended to be understood as assumptions underlying
this literary study.

[95] In the discussion of the four Isaianic themes in chapters four to seven, relevant Second
Temple material that will provide the proper context for my discussion will be presented in
the form of excursuses.

[96] The male personal pronoun is used for stylistic reason and also because of the
arguments for Lukan authorship that are to follow.

[97] The challenge to the traditional dating is presented in Albert C. Sundberg, Jr.,
"Canon Muratori: A Fourth-Century List," *HTR* 66 (1973) 1–41; and Sundberg's conclusion
is supported by the study of Geoffrey M. Hahneman (*The Muratorian Fragment and the
Development of the Canon* [Oxford: Clarendon, 1992]). Their conclusion has not been left
unchallenged, however. See Everett Ferguson, "Canon Muratori: Date and Provenance,"

Irenaeus provides the same conclusion,[98] and this is followed by other early Christian authors.[99] Lukan authorship can therefore claim universal support in the early church.

This identification is consistent with the internal evidence in the Lukan writings. The most significant is the "we-passages" in Acts (16:10–17; 20:5–15; 21:1–18; 27:1–28:16) that may point to the author as a companion of Paul. These "we-passages" naturally appear in most discussions of the historical nature of the Lukan account. Several possibilities have been raised in dealing with these passages: (1) Luke, the companion of Paul, writes as an eyewitness to the events recorded;[100] (2) an unknown author of Acts incorporated into his writings eyewitnesses accounts authored by someone else;[101] and (3) the "we-passages" are creations of the author as consistent with practices in related genres such as sea-voyage accounts.[102]

Studia Patristica 18 (1982) 677–83; P. Henne, "La datation du canon de Muratori," *RB* 100 (1993) 54–75; and C. E. Hill, "The Debate Over the Muratorian Fragment and the Development of the Canon," *WTJ* 57 (1995) 437–52.

[98] *Adv. haer.* 3.1.1, 3.3.3. A recent detailed analysis of the significance of Irenaeus can be found in Claus-Jürgen Thornton (*Der Zeuge des Zeugen, Lukas als Historiker der Paulusreisen* [WUNT 56; Tübingen: Mohr Siebeck, 1991] 7–81) who argues that the traditions behind Irenaeus' testimony can be dated to the early second century.

[99] E.g., *Adversus Marcionem* 4.2.2–4; *Stromateis* 5.12. Others include the Monarchian Prologue, Jerome, Ephraem Syrus, Adamantius, Epiphanius and the Prologue of the Latin Vulgate. For further discussion of relevant external evidence, see Joseph Fitzmyer, *The Gospel According to Luke (I–IX)* (AB 28; Garden City, NY: Doubleday, 1981) 37–41.

[100] This is the traditional position affirmed by early Christian writers. Modern defenders include Joseph Fitzmyer, *Luke the Theologian: Aspects of his Teaching* (Mahwah, NJ: Paulist, 1989) 3–16; Hemer, *The Book of Acts in the Setting of Hellenistic History*, 315–21. An extensive defense can be found in Thornton, *Der Zeuge des Zeugen*, 83–367, who deals with both literary and historical issues surrounding the "we-passages."

[101] See, for example, C. K. Barrett, *Luke the Historian in Recent Study* (London: Epworth, 1961) 22: "This means, not necessarily that the author was an eye-witness but that he had some sort of access to some sort of eye-witness material for this part of the narrative." A recent articulation of this position can be found in Stanley E. Porter, "The 'We' Passages," in David W. J. Gill and Conrad Gempf, eds., *The Book of Acts in its First Century Setting* (Grand Rapids, MI: Eerdmans, 1994) 545–74.

[102] Some have argued with an explicit appeal to generic license. See, for example, P. Vielhauer, "On the 'Paulinism' of Acts," in Leander E. Keck and James L. Martyn, eds., *Studies in Luke-Acts: Essays Presented in Honor of Paul Schubert* (Nashville: Abingdon, 1966) 33–34. The most notable argument that Luke utilizes existing generic paradigms in his composition of the "we-passages" is Vernon K. Robbins, "The We-Passages in Acts and Ancient Sea Voyages," *BR* 20 (1975) 5–18. A recent discussion drawing on Jewish material can be found in Jürgen Wehnert, *Die Wir-Passagen der Apostelgeschichte: Ein lukanisches Stilmittel aus jüdischer Tradition* (GTA 40; Göttingen: Vandenhoeck & Ruprecht, 1989). Wehnert argues that (1) Silas was behind the "we-passages" and (2) Dan 6:29–10:1 in particular is the key to understand the coexistence of first and third person voices in a narrative. Both suggestions are questionable. The identification of Silas as the eyewitness and

Most now recognize that the Lukan "we-passages" cannot be full explained by literary conventions. First, convincing parallels are simply lacking in ancient literature.[103] More specifically, first-person plural is not a characteristic feature of sea-voyage accounts.[104] Furthermore, in other Lukan accounts of sailings, one does not find the "we-passages."[105] Finally, as Susan Praeder notes, appeals to generic conventions fail to account for several unique features of the Lukan "we-passages": "the anonymity of the first person narrator, plurality of the first person participants, occurrence of first person narration only in the passages in 16:10–17, 20:5–15, 21:1–18, and 27:1–28:16, and the first and third person sections in the first person passages."[106]

An appeal to eyewitness accounts written by someone other than the author of the rest of the Lukan story is also problematic considering the stylistic unity of the Lukan narrative.[107] In his defense of this hypothesis based on the characteristics of the "we-passages", Stanley Porter admits that his arguments fail to exclude the author of Acts as the one behind the eyewitness accounts.[108] Furthermore, if the author of Acts was as careful a redactor as Porter suggests, the retention of the first-person plural is inexplicable.

This leads one back to the traditional position: Luke himself as the eyewitness narrator. Needless to say, this position has the support of ancient literature where the first person plural reflects the author's participation in the events. The convergence of external and internal pointers cannot be overlooked, and this provides the most plausible reading of the Lukan "we-passages".

---

the subsequent silencing of this eyewitness through anonymity is questionable. Furthermore, the critical feature of the Lukan "we-passages"—the appearance of the first person plural—is absent in the Daniel passage.

[103] Porter's ("The 'We' Passages," 548) statement reflects the consensus of modern scholarship: "no truly suitable literary parallels to these 'we' passages have been found in all of ancient Greek literature." See also Hemer, *Book of Acts in the Setting of Hellenistic History*, 317.

[104] See Colin J. Hemer, "First Person Narrative in Acts 27–28," *TynBul* 36 (1985) 79–109.

[105] Cf. Acts 13–14.

[106] Susan M. Praeder, "The Problem of First Person Narration in Acts," *NovT* 29 (1987) 214.

[107] See the classic statement in Henry J. Cadbury, *The Style and Literary Method of Luke* (New York: Klaus, 1969) 1–39.

[108] Porter, "The 'We' Passages," 573. After listing features of the Lukan "we-passages", Porter himself concludes: "The factors cited above point to an explicit use of a continuous, integral source." This conclusion is acceptable but he fails to present compelling arguments against a more natural reading of the "we-passages": the author himself participated in the described journeys with Paul.

To account fully for the unique features of the Lukan "we-passages", a literary analysis is needed. William Kurz, in taking up the challenge raised by Praeder, provides an admirable analysis of the narrative.[109] While focusing on the level of the implied reader (and implied author), Kurz does not see a clear divorce of the implied author from the historical author. Thus, he concludes that "there seems genuine plausibility to the claims that the author of Acts was a companion of Paul and a peripheral participant during some of Paul's later journeys and experiences."[110] This approach emphasizes the literary function of the "we-passages" and assumes that the implied reader is taking these passages at face value. Convincing arguments have yet to be presented to show that the historical readers did not possess the same understanding.

This eyewitness called Luke can probably be identified as the Luke of the Pauline material (Col 4:14; Phlm 24; 2 Tim 4:11).[111] Some further suggest that Luke was also the eyewitness present behind the Lukan prologue and therefore witness to the ministry of Jesus. Building on the work of Henry Cadbury,[112] John Wenham argues that παρηκολουθηκότι ἀκριβῶς in Luke 1:3 does not mean "investigate" but "follow" and therefore while "it remains doubtful whether παρηκολουθηκότι ἀκριβῶς can be said to mean participation, it could well imply participation."[113] This, however, cannot be substantiated since a natural reading of the prologue separates Luke at least one generation from the ministry of Jesus. Furthermore, a detailed investigation on the phrase παρηκολουθηκότι ἀκριβῶς by David Moessner shows that this is an improbable reading.[114]

---

[109] See William S. Kurz, *Reading Luke-Acts: Dynamics of Biblical Narrative* (Louisville, KY: Westminster/John Knox, 1993) 123–24, who argues for narrative participation as a way to explain the unique features of the Lukan "we-passages" as highlighted by Praeder. The same approach is taken by Tannehill, *Narrative Unity of Luke-Acts*, 2.247; and Steven M. Sheeley, "Getting into the Act(s): Narrative Presence in the 'We' Sections," *PRSt* 26 (1999) 203–20.

[110] Kurz, *Reading Luke-Acts*, 123. A similar conclusion is reached by the literary study of Charles H. Talbert, *Reading Acts: A Literary and Theological Commentary on the Acts of the Apostles* (New York: Crossroad, 1997) 1.

[111] See Thornton, *Der Zeuge des Zeugen*, 199–367 for his discussion of the relationship between the Lukan material and the Pauline material.

[112] See Henry Cadbury, "The Knowledge Claimed in Luke's Preface," *Expositor* 8 (1922) 401–20; and idem, "Commentary on Luke's Preface," in F. J. Foakes Jackson and Kirsopp Lake, eds., *The Beginnings of Christianity, Part I: The Acts of the Apostles* (London: Macmillan, 1922) 2.489–510.

[113] John Wenham, "The Identification of Luke," *EvQ* 63 (1991) 3–44.

[114] David P. Moessner, "The Appeal and Power of Poetics (Luke 1:1-4): Luke's Superior Credentials (παρηκολουθηκότι), Narrative Sequence (καθεξῆς), and Firmness of Understanding (ἡ ἀσφάλεια) for the Reader," in David P. Moessner, ed., *Jesus and the Heritage of Israel: Luke's Narrative Claim upon Israel's Legacy* (Harrisburg, PA: Trinity Press International, 1999) 87–88. Moessner shows that Cadbury is correct in that παρηκολουθηκότι always has the sense of staying abreast of something developing, but the

While details concerning the author are not easily accessible,[115] the understanding that he was Paul's companion is important both for historical concerns and chronological placement. Historically, the possibility of authorial presence allows room for understanding Acts as theological history.[116] Chronologically, this would place the work within the generation of Paul's missionary endeavors.[117] While one may not go so far as to claim that in Acts Paul "is the real goal of the work"[118] and that Luke's work "is a deliberate history of the Pauline mission 'with an extended introduction,'"[119] the author's interest in Paul is consistent with his being the apostle's companion. This intense interest is not widespread in the early development of the Christian movement.

If the Pauline references to Luke are to be accepted as relevant for the identification of the author of Acts, then the tradition that Luke is "the beloved physician" (Col 4:14) may be significant. It is a well known fact that W. Hobart's[120] effort to identify medical language in Luke has been demolished by Cadbury.[121] Recently however, in her examination of the Lukan prefaces, Loveday Alexander has argued for the location of these prefaces within the scientific traditions that include medicine.[122] The conclusion of both Cadbury and Alexander is consistent with the traditional identification of Luke as the "beloved physician."[123] Martin Hengel and Anna Maria Schwemer further show the interests of ancient medical doctors in

---

verb does not mean "to physically follow." See also his "'Eyewitnesses,' 'Informed Contemporaries,' and 'Unknowing Inquirers': Josephus' Criteria for Authentic Historiography and the Meaning of ΠΑΡΑΚΟΛΟΤΘΕΩ," *NovT* 38 (1996) 105–22.

[115] Wenham's ("The Identification of Luke," 5–38) further identification of Luke as one of the seventy and the disciple of Emmaus remains less than convincing.

[116] See Martin Hengel, "Kerygma oder Geschichte," *TQ* 151 (1971) 323–36; F. F. Bruce, "The Acts of the Apostles: Historical Record or Theological Reconstruction?" *ANRW* 2.25.3 (1985) 2569–603; and I. Howard Marshall, *Luke: Historian and Theologian* (2nd ed.; Grand Rapids, MI: Zondervan, 1989).

[117] Please see the following section for a discussion of the dating of Luke-Acts.

[118] Martin Hengel, *Between Jesus and Paul: Studies in the Earliest History of Christianity* (Philadelphia: Fortress, 1983) 2.

[119] Ibid., 55. Luke's interest in Paul cannot be denied. I will further argue in this study, however, that the ecclesiological focus of the Lukan writings and the central role of the word demands closer attention.

[120] W. K. Hobart, *The Medical Language of St. Luke* (Dublin: Hodges, Figgis, 1882).

[121] Cadbury, *The Style and Literary Method of Luke*, 1–72.

[122] Loveday C. A. Alexander, *The Preface to Luke's Gospel: Literary Convention and Social Context in Luke 1.1–4 and Acts 1.1* (SNTSMS 78; Cambridge: Cambridge University Press, 1993).

[123] Ibid., 176: "It will be clear immediately that our reading of the preface accords well with the traditional belief that the author of Luke-Acts was the 'beloved physician' of Col. 4.14."

journeys and the level of education they acquired.[124] These are reflected in the carefully crafted narrative of Acts; and again Luke's literary creativity fits well within this background.[125]

The major objection to the identification of the author of Acts as the companion of Paul is the difference between the Lukan Paul and the one found in the Pauline epistles.[126] The current debate concerning issues at the very core of both the theologies of Paul and of Luke weakens the power of this objection. Various attempts that accept the traditional identification have been made to explain the differences. Some question whether the differences really are so striking,[127] while others consider one the presupposition of the other.[128] After all, the occasional nature of both the Lukan and Pauline material must be noted. Taking a historical approach, one can explain the differences by observing that Luke was only a companion of Paul for a short period of time;[129] and one wonders how often the mind of a profound thinker is clearly and fully reflected in the work of his companions or even disciples.[130] Even recognizing the full weight of this problem, the probability of Lukan authorship remains viable.

---

[124] Martin Hengel and Anna Maria Schwemer, *Paulus zwischen Damaskus und Antiochien: Die unbekannten Jahre des Apostels* (WUNT 108; Tübingen: Mohr Siebeck, 1998) 18–22. See also the epigraphical evidence for itinerant doctors noted in G. H. R. Horsley, *New Documents Illustrating Early Christianity: A Review of the Greek Inscriptions and Papyri published in 1977* (Sydney, Australia: Macquarie University Ancient History Documentary Research Centre, 1982) 19–21. Horsley argues that in light of the available evidence, it seems possible that Luke belonged to this group of itinerant doctors "since Paul worked at his own *techne* to earn his living where he went, it is a most natural inference to draw that those who accompanied him did the same." See also the discussion in W. Marx, "Luke, the Physician, Re-examined," *ExpTim* 91 (1980) 168–72. A more speculative hypothesis can be found in Ben Witherington, III, *Conflict and Community in Corinth* (Grand Rapids, MI: Eerdmans, 1995), 459–64, who argues from the "thorn in the flesh" reference in 2 Cor 12:7 that Luke may have been Paul's personal doctor since Paul's physical condition required constant medical attention.

[125] The important question of the ethnic identity of Luke is intentionally left untreated. This study leaves no doubt that he is familiar with the LXX and possibly other Jewish traditions. Therefore, this Luke is most likely a god-fearer if not himself a Jew.

[126] See the influential statement in Vielhauer, "On the 'Paulinism' of Acts," 33–50.

[127] Marshall, *Luke: Historian and Theologian*, 220.

[128] E.g., Peder Borgen, "From Paul to Luke: Observations toward Clarification of the Theology of Luke-Acts," *CBQ* 31 (1969) 168–82.

[129] See Fitzmyer, *Luke the Theologian*, 3–7; and the discussion on the "we-passages" above.

[130] See the detailed discussion in Stanley E. Porter, *The Paul of Acts: Essays in Literary Criticism, Rhetoric, and Theology* (WUNT 115; Tübingen: Mohr Siebeck, 1999), who concludes that while differences between Luke and Paul cannot be denied, "these are merely the kinds of differences that one could expect to find between virtually any two different yet accomplished authors when writing about the same events" (206).

b. Temporal Context

The earliest possible date for Acts is early in the 60s, the date of Paul's imprisonment recorded in Acts 28, and the latest is mid-second century when the use of Acts is evident among early Christian writers. Suggested dates fall roughly within three groups: pre-70, 80–95, and 115–30.

My discussion on authorship renders a second century dating unlikely, and most recent studies have argued against such a late dating.[131] A second century date is often based on alleged literary dependence on works of late first century and early second writers.[132] A notable example is John Knox who argues that the purpose of Acts was to respond to Marcionite theology.[133] In support of Knox, John Townsend notes that this second century dating is probable in light of the ideological parallels between Acts and early second century Christian writings.[134] This conclusion has not gained wide support. Allusion to Marcion in Acts is absent, and details in support of Knox's argument have been questioned by recent discussions of Lukan theology that fail to confirm a hidden anti-Marcion agenda behind the text.[135] In more general terms, Luke's primitive Christology and ecclesiology make a second century dating unlikely.[136] Luke's emphasis on the Spirit also points one away from labeling Lukan theology as Early Catholicism. Most important of all, the intense Lukan interest in the identity of the Early Christian

---

[131] See the three recent commentaries: Charles K. Barrett, *A Critical and Exegetical Commentary on the Acts of the Apostles* (ICC; Edinburgh: T & T Clark, 1998) 2.xxxiii–liv; Joseph A. Fitzmyer, *The Acts of the Apostles* (AB31; New York: Doubleday, 1997) 51–55; and Jacob Jervell, *Die Apostelgeschichte* (KEK 17; Göttingen: Vandenhoeck & Ruprecht, 1998) 85–6.

[132] Other factors include temporal distance from first century events such as Domitian's persecution or the separation between the church and the synagogue.

[133] John Knox, *Marcion and the New Testament: An Essay in the Early History of the Canon.* (Chicago: University of Chicago Press, 1942).

[134] John T. Townsend, "The Date of Luke-Acts," in Charles H. Talbert, ed., *Luke-Acts: New Perspectives from the Society of Biblical Literature Seminar* (New York: Crossroad, 1984) 47–62; and idem, "The Contributions of John Knox to the Study of Acts: Some Further Notations," in Mikeal C. Parsons and Joseph B. Tyson, eds., *Cadbury, Knox, and Talbert: American Contributions to the Study of Acts* (Atlanta, GA: Scholars Press, 1992) 81–89.

[135] See the evaluation in Joseph B. Tyson, "John Knox and the Acts of the Apostles," in Mikeal C. Parsons and Joseph B. Tyson, eds., *Cadbury, Knox, and Talbert: American Contributions to the Study of Acts* (Atlanta, GA: Scholars Press, 1992) 55–80. A more detailed critique of the individual points of Knox's reconstruction can be found in Leland E. Wilshire, "Was Canonical Luke Written in the Second Century?—A Continued Discussion," *NTS* (1973–74) 246–53.

[136] Martin Hengel (*Acts and the History of Earliest Christianity* [trans. John Bowden; Philadelphia: Fortress, 1980] 65) points to John for a more developed Christology and Matthew for more interest in ecclesiastical matters.

movement and the relationship between Jews and Gentiles points to a first century dating.

The question concerning the exact period of time within the first century is a more difficult one. A pre-70 dating is based primarily on the following observations:[137] (1) the absence of any mention of Paul's death; (2) the lack of comment on Jerusalem's destruction in 70; (3) Luke does not show any awareness of Paul's letters; and (4) the "tone" of the work.

The absence of any mention of the death of Paul at the end of Acts is considered the "objective" fact in favor of a pre-70 dating. This, however, is possible only if Acts is to be understood simply as a biography that focuses on the life of Paul. Some note the well crafted ending of Acts, and convincing attempts have been made showing that the ending is intentional.[138] The commonly raised proposal that Luke's ending represents some form of anti-imperialistic propaganda can still be defended.[139] In light of the abrupt ending of Mark, one should not be surprised by the ending of Acts, both seem to invite continued action and dialogue.[140] Moreover, according to Jacob Jervell, hints of the knowledge of Paul's death can already be detected within the Lukan narrative.[141] In my discussion on the word of God below, I will further show that it is the word of God that should be considered as the central character of the Lukan narrative.

The argument from silence concerning the destruction of Jerusalem is also indecisive. Such silence can be observed in other post-70 works where one would expect some comment. Moreover, this argument may also support a

---

[137] For a detailed defense of a pre-70 dating, see Hemer, *Book of Acts in the Setting of Hellenistic History*, 365–410.

[138] See, in particular, Jacques Dupont, "La conclusion des Actes et son rapport à l'ensemble de l'ouvrage de Luc," in Jacob Kremer, ed., *Les Actes des Apôtres: Traditions, rédaction, théologie* (BETL 48; Leuven: Leuven University Press, 1979) 359–404. See also my discussion in chapter three below.

[139] The representative statement is found in N. T. Wright, *The New Testament and the People of God* (London: SPCK, 1992) 375: "Here at last is a Jew living in Rome itself (i.e. not just hiding in the hills of Galilee), and declaring that, in and through Jesus, Israel's god is the sole king of the word." Concerning the absence of an account of Paul's death at the end of Acts, Wright bluntly states: "Luke has no intention of making Paul as second redeemer, dying for the sins of the world." See recent restatements in Allen Brent, "Luke-Acts and the Imperial Cult in Asia Minor," *JTS* 48 (1997) 411–38; and Carsten Burfeind, "Paulus muß nach Rom. Zur politischen Dimension der Apostelgeschichte," *NTS* 46 (2000) 75–91.

[140] See the recent discussion in Wm. F. Brosend, II, "The Means of Absent Ends," in Ben Witherington, III, ed., *History, Literature, and Society in the Book of Acts* (Cambridge: Cambridge University Press, 1996) 348–62; and Daniel Marguerat, "The Enigma of the Silent Closing of Acts (28:16–31)," in David P. Moessner, ed., *Jesus and the Heritage of Israel: Luke's Narrative Claim upon Israel's Legacy* (Harrisburg, PA: Trinity Press International, 1999) 284–304.

[141] Jervell, *Die Apostelgeschichte*, 85–6.

later date when the effect of the event was no longer as vivid or urgent. Similarly, the absence of references to Paul's letters may point to an early dating but not necessarily as early as before the destruction of Jerusalem.[142] Finally, to argue from the "tone" of Acts is problematic. While some argue for an early dating basing on the sense of "immediacy" in Acts,[143] others point to the sense of "tranquillity" in arguing for a later date.[144]

A post-70 dating is generally based on (1) the apparent Lukan redaction of the Markan apocalypse; (2) dependence on Mark that was probably written in the 60s; and (3) the Lukan prologue assumes a certain distance from other gospel traditions. The Lukan redaction of Mark 13 does provide a more detailed account of the fall of Jerusalem, although Old Testament background and the possibility of prophetic utterances have been noted.[145] Arguments from the date of Mark depend on one's assumptions concerning the synoptic relationship as well as the dating of Mark. If Markan priority is accepted,[146] a post-70 dating of Luke-Acts is likely. Finally, the availability of gospel traditions to Luke also points in the same direction.

Arguments for a pre-70 dating have shown that an early dating is not impossible, while a post-70 dating argues for some distancing from the events recorded. Therefore, it seems wise to state simply that Acts was written

---

[142] However, an awareness of Paul's letters cannot be ruled out with certainty. See William O. Walker, Jr., "Acts and the Pauline Corpus Reconsidered," *JSNT* 24 (1985) 3–23; and L. Aejmelaeus, *Die Rezeption der Paulusbriefe in der Miletrede (Apg. 20:18–35)* (Helsinki: Academia Scientiarum Fennicae, 1987).

[143] Hemer, *Book of Acts in the Setting of Hellenistic History*, 365: "Our study of detail has uncovered much material which is not easily explained as the product of reflective editing. It seems that some considerable weight should be given to this 'immediacy' factor."

[144] See F. F. Bruce, "Chronological Questions in the Acts of the Apostles," *BJRL* 68 (1986) 273: "All that need to be said here about the date of the composition of Acts is that a sufficient time has elapsed for the author to look back in tranquillity over the course of events and present them in a more balanced perspective than would have been possible for one writing *in mediis rebus*." See also Michael Wolter, "Israel's Future and the Delay of the Parousia, According to Luke," in David P. Moessner, ed., *Jesus and the Heritage of Israel: Luke's Narrative Claim upon Israel's Legacy* (Harrisburg, PA: Trinity Press International, 1999) 307–24.

[145] See C.H. Dodd, "The Fall of Jerusalem and the 'Abomination of Desolation'," *JRS* 37 (1947) 47–54. Nevertheless, some who accept the prophetic nature of Jesus' speech consider the Lukan manner of portrayal points to a post-70 date. See, for example, Bruce, *Acts of the Apostles*, 12–18. Reading Luke's account by itself, however, does not show clear signs of reporting/redaction after-the-fact.

[146] This is the assumption of this study. My analysis of Lukan passages may also add weight to this assumption. I do recognize, however, that this remains a working assumption. For a recent survey of scholarship, see, among others, Arthur Bellinzoni, ed., *The Two-Source Hypothesis: A Critical Appraisal* (Macon, GA: Mercer, 1985).

"towards AD 70."[147] This provides a clearer context in which to situate Luke's program, and the following discussion on the parallel use of Isaiah in literature around this period of time adds support to this conclusion.

c. Literary Context

The use of Isaiah in Luke needs to be situated within the wider context of the use of Isaiah in the Second Temple period. While even a sketchy outline is not possible at this point, the goal of this section is merely to show that my reconstruction of the Lukan use of Isaiah is indeed "plausible" within its literary context.

Jewish exegesis in the Second Temple period resists reductionistic treatment. The later Rabbinic rules of interpretation should not be the primary guide in an attempt to understand the use of scripture during this period of time. Recent studies prefer to speak of "assumptions" and "functions" rather than strict exegetical rules. A helpful study by David Brewer provides a window into the complex world of pre-70 Jewish interpretative enterprises.[148] While many have argued from Rabbinic material that the wider context of a verse/passage is insignificant for the Jewish interpreter in this period, Brewer shows that this cannot be asserted in an unqualified manner. As far as pre-70 scribal exegesis is concerned, Brewer concludes: "Every single scribal exegesis examined could be quoted as an example to show that Scripture was interpreted according to its context. This is true from the plainest Pesht to the most ingenious Ultra-literal or Derash interpretation."[149] While Lukan exegesis does not fit the exact category of "scribal exegesis," Brewer's study corrects previous assumptions on the role of context in different exegetical traditions.

In another recent study, James Kugel attempts to get at the basis of Second Temple Jewish interpretive traditions.[150] He suggests that there are four assumptions behind "all ancient interpreters": (1) Scripture is a fundamentally cryptic document; (2) it is a relevant text; (3) it is perfectly harmonious; and (4) it is divinely sanctioned.[151] This list serves to highlight how the presence of Isaiah in the Lukan narrative might have been understood. Luke's use of Isaiah, however, goes beyond these general assumptions. As in other early Christian works, Luke does not simply regard his work as yet

---

[147] So I. Howard Marshall, *The Gospel of Luke: A Commentary on the Greek Text* (NIGTC; Grand Rapids, MI: Eerdmans, 1978) 48.

[148] David Instone Brewer, *Techniques and Assumptions in Jewish Exegesis before 70 CE* (TSAJ 30; Tübingen: Mohr Siebeck, 1992).

[149] Ibid., 167. For non-scribal exegetical traditions, however, this may not always be the case. Cf. James L. Kugel, "Two Introductions to Midrash," 77–103.

[150] James L. Kugel, *Traditions of the Bible: A guide to the Bible As It Was at the Start of the Common Era* (Cambridge, MA: Harvard University Press, 1998).

[151] Ibid., 14–19.

another "application" of the sacred text. The events included in his narrative are placed in a historical framework in which the past is "fulfilled" in the sense that the climax of history is realized.[152] The primacy of the salvation-historical nature of the "events" themselves and the hermeneutical use of scripture to interpret these events should not be overlooked.

Beyond these general comments, the use of Isaiah in the Second Temple period deserves further attention. A comprehensive survey on the use of Isaiah is yet to appear, but a few points can be made.[153] These can serve as a contrast to the early Christian use of Isaiah. The continuing unfulfilled promises in Isaiah occupied the mind of the ancient interpreters. This leads to the expectation of (1) the coming of the salvation of God; and (2) the judgment on the nations. These two seem to be the two major areas in which one finds Isaianic quotations or allusions appearing in Second Temple material.

The expectation of the coming of the salvation of God centers on both the arrival of the blessed state and the appearance of the agent of God's salvation. The continuing condition of the exilic condition that leads to the expectation of the blessed stated is noted below.[154] The expectation of the coming ruler centers around passages such as Isa 11:1–9, and the influence of this expectation can be traced in numerous works.[155] Unlike the case of the early

---

[152] One can point to the Qumran material as a parallel case but the historical framework is not as evident. See, for example, the comparison of Matthew and Qumran material in Krister Stendahl, *The School of St. Matthew and its Use of the Old Testament* (2nd ed.; Philadelphia: Fortress, 1968); and the cautious note in John J. Collins, "Prophecy and Fulfillment in the Qumran Scrolls," *JETS* 30 (1987) 257–78. For the particular understanding of fulfillment language in the New Testament, see C. F. D. Moule, "Fulfillment-Words in the New Testament: Use and Abuse," *NTS* 14 (1967–68) 293–320. Moule points to the wider paradigm of promise-fulfillment that transcends the narrower scheme of prediction-fulfillment.

[153] Even the following collection of essays does not completely fill this gap: Craig C. Broyles and Craig A. Evans, eds., *Writing and Reading the Scroll of Isaiah: Studies of an Interpretive Tradition, vol. 2* (Leiden: Brill, 1997).

[154] See the excursus at the end of chapter four. The proclamation of the coming of the salvation of God is evoked primarily through the formulaic statement in Isa 40:3. See the discussion of the use of this verse in Second Temple Jewish traditions in section 2.3 below.

[155] Michael A. Knibb ("Isaianic Traditions in the Apocrypha and Pseudepigrapha," in Craig C. Broyles and Craig A. Evans, eds., *Writings and Reading the Scroll of Isaiah: Studies of an Interpretive Tradition, vol. 2* [Leiden: Brill, 1997] 633) notes the following passages: *Pss. Sol.* 17.23–24, 29, 35–37; 18.7–8; *1 En.* 46.3; 49.1–4; 62.2–3; *2 Esd* 13.10; *T. Levi* 18.7; *T. Jud.* 24.5–6. See also the discussion in George W. E. Nickelsburg, *Resurrection, Immortality, and Eternal Life in Intertestamental Judaism* (HTS 26; Cambridge, MA: Harvard University Press, 1972) 74; John J. Collins, *The Scepter and the Star: The Messiahs of the Dead Sea Scrolls and Other Ancient Literature* (New York: Doubleday, 1995) 49–73; Turner, *Power from on High*, 114–118; Michael A. Knibb,

Christian use of Isaiah, however, Isaiah 53 does not play a significant part in the construction of the vision of the coming Messiah.[156] The judgment of the nations theme is expressed through the affirmation of the sovereignty of Yahweh and the demolition of idols. The existence of one God and his power over the creation are themes that "run from Deutero-Isaiah right through the whole literature of Second Temple Judaism."[157] The influence of the Isaianic anti-idol polemic is discussed below.[158] Both themes reappear as significant motifs in the Lukan narrative of Acts.[159]

In discussing the use of Isaianic material in Second Temple traditions, it is the themes that do not reappear as frequently that demand attention. Most notable are the passages that promise salvation to the Gentiles. The optimistic tone reflected in these passages is not apparent in Jewish texts after Isaiah.[160] More importantly, the wider program of the Isaianic New Exodus is not systematically integrated into any Second Temple non-Christian material. The expectation of the new creation of God remains unfulfilled.[161]

More relevant for the development of my claim of historical plausibility is the use of Isaiah in early Christian material. The pervasive use of Isaianic material in early Christian literature encourages one to look behind the Lukan narrative to examine a comparable use of the same material. In the early church, Isaiah was considered the "Fifth Gospel", and forty five of the sixty-six chapters of Isaiah appear in some form in the text of the New Testament.[162] The significance of Isaiah is also reflected in the fact that the key term εὐαγγέλιον finds its root primarily in Isaiah 40–55.[163]

"Isaianic Traditions in the Book of Enoch," in John Barton and David J. Reimer, eds., *After the Exile: Essays in Honour of Rex Mason* (Macon, GA: Mercer University Press, 1996) 222.

[156] See George W. E. Nickelsburg, "Reading the Hebrew Scriptures in the First Century: Christian Interpretations in Their Jewish Context," *WW* 3 (1983) 238–50.

[157] Richard Bauckham, *God Crucified: Monotheism and Christology in the New Testament* (Grand Rapids, MI: Eerdmans, 1999), 12. Among the listed passages are: Wis 12.13; Jdt 8.20; 9.14; Bel 41; Sir 24.24; 36.5; 4Q504[4QDibHamᵃ] 5.9; Bar 3.36; and *4 Ezra* 6.38.

[158] See the excursus at the end of chapter six below.

[159] Other Isaianic themes that reappear in Second Temple texts include the power of the word of God. See the excursus at the end of chapter five below.

[160] The issue of universalism and nationalism is discussed in chapter seven below, and an excursus on the issue of Jews and Gentiles in Second Temple material is included.

[161] The use of Isa 40:3 in numerous texts and especially in the Qumran material should be considered as exceptions. Nevertheless, even in these cases, the climactic moment in history still lies in the future; and the systematic construction of the identity of the people of God within the paradigm of Isaianic New Exodus is lacking.

[162] See John F. A. Sawyer, *The Fifth Gospel: Isaiah in the History of Christianity* (Cambridge: Cambridge University Press, 1996) esp. 30.

[163] Peter Stuhlmacher, *Die paulinische Evangelium, vol. 1: Vorgeschichte* (FRLANT 95; Göttingen: Vandenhoeck & Ruprecht, 1968) 109–79, 218–25. Stuhlmacher points to 40:9; 41:27; and 52:7 as important for the New Testament usage of εὐαγγέλιον. Otto Betz

Scholarly interest frequently focuses on the use of the servant song of Isa 52:13–53:12 in the construction of early Christology.[164] Various aspects of the significance of this servant song have been explored.[165] A more aggressive proposal is presented by Richard Bauckham who finds "the convergence of Paul, Revelation and the Fourth Gospel in the inclusion of Jesus in Deutero-Isaianic monotheism."[166] Bauckham argues that these works include Jesus in the "identity of God" when Jesus is identified as "the Servant of the Lord of Deutero-Isaiah whose humiliation and exaltation together reveal the identity of the one God."[167]

Beyond the focus on Isaiah 53, a wider pattern of the use of Isaiah appears in early Christian interpretations of the significance of Jesus' ministry. This focus on the message of Isaiah provides a fruitful angle into the use of the Isaianic "story" behind various early Christian works. Isaianic themes of the dawn of salvation and the presence of the kingdom can already be found in the message of Jesus, despite questions about the details of his

---

("Jesus and Isaiah 53," in William H. Bellinger, Jr., and William R. Farmer, eds., *Jesus and the Suffering Servant: Isaiah 53 and Christian Origins* [Harrisburg, PA: Trinity Press International, 1998] 75) further states: "It is my contention that it [εὐαγγέλιον] was derived *from* Isaiah 53:1, and from that source only." For a different view of the origin of the term, see Helmut Koester, *Ancient Christian Gospels: Their History and Development* (Philadelphia: Trinity Press International, 1990) 3, who argues for a Roman imperial background.

[164] Morna D. Hooker (*Jesus and the Servant: The Influence of the Servant Concept of Deutero-Isaiah in the New Testament* [London: SPCK, 1959]), among others, challenges the use of Isaiah 53 in the earliest stages of Christological reflections. Hooker concludes that this use of Isaiah 53 cannot be dated to before First Peter. Recently, however, Hooker showed a willingness to revise her thesis when she argued that evidence of the use of Isaiah 53 can now be traced back to Paul. See her "Did the Use of Isaiah 53 to Interpret His Mission Begin with Jesus?" in William H. Bellinger, Jr., and William R. Farmer, *Jesus and the Suffering Servant: Isaiah 53 and Christian Origins* (Harrisburg, PA: Trinity Press International, 1998) 88–103.

[165] For a survey of the issues involved, see the two recent collections of essays: Bernd Janowski and Peter Stuhlmacher, *Der leidende Gottesknecht: Jesaja 53 und seine Wirkungsgeschichte, mit einer Bibliographie zu Jes 53* (FAT 14; Tübingen: Mohr Siebeck, 1996); and William H. Bellinger, Jr., and William R. Farmer, *Jesus and the Suffering Servant: Isaiah 53 and Christian Origins* (Harrisburg, PA: Trinity Press International, 1998). See also T. N. D. Mettinger, *A Farewell to the Servant Songs: A Critical Examination of an Exegetical Axiom* (Scripta Minora; Lunk: CWK Gleerup, 1983) who cautions against examining the servant songs apart from their contexts.

[166] Bauckham, *God Crucified*, 51.

[167] Ibid., 56. Other aspects of early Christian Christology can of course be noted. Beyond the theme of suffering and glorification, the Markan emphasis on Jesus as "a ransom for many" can also be traced back to Isaiah 53. See Seyoon Kim, *The Son of Man as the Son of God* (WUNT 30; Tübingen: Mohr Siebeck, 1983) 53–61.

vision.[168] This message is developed in the gospel traditions. Rikki Watts highlights the wider Isaianic story in the narrative of Marks as already introduced in the Markan prologue;[169] and this is confirmed by an independent study carried out by Joel Marcus.[170] The same use of Isaiah can be found in Matthew. Adrian Leske, for example, argues that "the hope for restoration expressed particularly in 2 and 3 Isaiah and how these hopes were developed in later prophetic writings were the basis of the message of Jesus as presented in Matthew's Gospel."[171]

The closest parallel to Luke's ecclesiological interest in Isaiah in the understanding of early Christians as the people of God can be found in Paul. Richard Hays, building upon his work on Paul's use of scripture,[172] provides a brief analysis of Paul's reading of Isaiah.[173] Paul's special interest in Isaiah is noted, and he argues that one should move beyond the focus on christological uses of Isaiah to appreciate the ecclesiological emphasis in

---

[168] See Bruce D. Chilton, *God in Strength: Jesus' Announcement of the Kingdom.* Freistadt: Plöchl, 1979; and W. Grimm, *Weil ich dich liebe: Die Verkündigung Jesu und Deuterojesaja* (ANTJ 1; Frankfurt am Main: Peter Lang, 1981).

[169] Watts, *Isaiah's New Exodus and Mark.*

[170] Joel Marcus, *The Way of the Lord: Christological Exegesis of the Old Testament in the Gospel of Mark* (Louisville, KY: Westminster/John Knox, 1992). Watts' study is, however, wider in scope. His study focuses on the entire narrative of Mark emphasizing the role of the Isaianic emphasis of Yahweh as a warrior. This emphasis is explicitly denied by Joel Marcus, "Mark and Isaiah," in A. B. Beck, A. H. Bartelt, P. R. Raabe, and C. A. Franke, eds., *Fortunate the Eyes that See: Essays in Honor of David Noel Freedman in Celebration of His Seventieth Birthday* (Grand Rapids, MI: Eerdmans, 1995) 465: "Isaiah is, of course, not the key to everything in Mark. For example, the book of Isaiah lacks a developed demonology, while Mark's picture of Jesus as the holy warrior against Satan and the unclean spirits is a vital element in his Gospel." See now also the recent work of R. Schneck, *Isaiah in the Gospel of Mark, I–VIII* (Bibal Dissertation Series 1; Berkeley: Bibal, 1994).

[171] Adrian M. Leske, "Isaiah and Matthew: The Prophetic Influence in the First Gospel: A Report on Current Research," in William H. Bellinger, Jr., and William R. Farmer, *Jesus and the Suffering Servant: Isaiah 53 and Christian Origins* (Harrisburg, PA: Trinity Press International, 1998) 152–69, here 156. See also his "The Influence of Isaiah on Christology in Matthew and Luke," in William R. Farmer, ed., *Crisis in Christology: Essays in Quest of Resolution* (Livonia, MI: Dove, 1995) 241–69. Leske has, however, overstated his case when he argues that the same intense interest in Isaiah cannot be found in Mark and Luke because "Matthew was written for a Jewish Christian audience and Mark and Luke primarily for gentile Christians, who would not always appreciate the many allusions to the prophetic literature" ("Isaiah and Matthew," 169). My discussion below provides a significant qualification to this conclusion.

[172] Hays, *Echoes of Scripture in the Letters of Paul.*

[173] Richard Hays, "'Who Has Believed Our Message?' Paul's Reading of Isaiah," *SBLSP* 37 (1998) 205–25.

Paul's appropriation of Isaianic material.[174] In Paul, one finds Isaiah's story of Israel's exile and restoration, as well as the mission to the Gentiles. The gospel message is not accepted by all, but God will act again at then on behalf of his people. This story lies behind the theology of Paul and is constructed through the use of Isaiah.[175] Paul himself sees his role within the Isaianic program as one who proclaims salvation to the Gentiles.

This brief study is supported by a detailed examination of the use of Isaiah in Romans by Ross Wagner.[176] Wagner provides a detailed study of Isaianic quotations and allusions in Romans 9–11 and concludes that the Isaianic story can be plotted in Romans when the theme of Gentile inclusion in Israel's restoration appears together with that of Israel's unresponsiveness. This conclusion can also be found in a recent study of Paul's use of Isaiah by Florian Wilk.[177] Again, it is shown that Paul's self-understanding as an apostle to the Gentiles, and the question of Israel within the context of the Christian proclamation forms the center of Isaiah's message in Paul. This same ecclesiological use of Isaiah also shows up in Acts when Luke focuses on the themes of the Gentile mission and Israel's rejection in his construction of the identity claim for the early Christian movement.[178] This serves as a contrast with other uses found in Second Temple Jewish traditions where these two themes understandably do not play as significant a role.[179] The fact that Luke was the companion of Paul may provide a historical link to such

---

[174] Ibid., 219: "the Christian fixation on christological proof texts may have caused readers to zero in on texts like Isaiah 53 and to overlook Paul's concern for explaining the mission to the Gentiles and the fate of Israel in relation to Scripture." Hays also notes that with one possible exception in Rom 9:32–33, "Paul does not resort to christological typology in his interpretation of Isaiah" (223).

[175] Ibid., 221–23.

[176] J. Ross Wagner, Jr., "'Who Has Believed Our Message?': Paul and Isaiah 'In Concert' in the Letter to the Romans." Ph.D. diss., Duke University, 1999. This dissertation was written under the supervision of Richard Hays.

[177] Florian Wilk, *Die Bedeutung des Jesajabuches für Paulus* (FRLANT 179; Göttingen: Vandenhoeck & Ruprecht, 1998).

[178] This focus is most prominent in first century writings. In the later Christian writings, literary efforts center around the identification of details in the life of Christ with the prophetic statements in Isaiah. See Sawyer, *Fifth Gospel*, 42–64.

[179] The use of Isaiah in the Book of Revelation, a work usually dated after Luke-Acts, provides another case for contrast. Instead of focussing on Gentile inclusion and Israel's rejection, the Isaianic allusions in Revelation center around Christological depictions, judgment against the nations, and the salvation of the people of God. The extensive use of Isaiah shows, however, that Isaiah is available to another early Christian author. For a further discussion, see Jan Fekkes, III, *Isaiah and Prophetic Traditions in the Book of Revelation: Visionary Antecedents and their Development* (JSNTSup 93; Sheffield: Sheffield Academic Press, 1994).

literary connections, although Luke's use of Isaiah is neither identical with nor limited to Paul's program.[180]

The prominence of Isaiah in early Christian circles and the availability of Isaiah to early Christian authors such as Luke is now established.[181] Whether the real audience is able to appreciate fully his program remains uncertain although the "implied readers" are certainly familiar with the LXX. The probability of audience literacy can be hypothesized based on the following factors: (1) the prevailing use of Isaiah in other early Christian works as shown above; (2) the Lukan focus on synagogues and therefore the possibility of his audience being God-fearers; (3) the Lukan text itself reflects the training of Christian converts in Israel's scripture;[182] and (4) the pervasive use of scriptural quotations, allusions, and patterns in the narrative itself. Moreover, if we assume that Luke had a wider audience in mind,[183] the possibility that at least some of them would be able to recognize his use of the Isaianic New

---

[180] Craig A. Evans ("From Gospel to Gospel: The Function of Isaiah in the New Testament," in Craig C. Broyles and Craig A. Evans, eds., *Writing and Reading the Scroll of Isaiah: Studies of an Interpretive Tradition, vol. 2* [Leiden: Brill, 1997] 687) may be correct in stating that "the function of Isaiah in Acts reflects Luke's theology more than it does Paul's," but the connection between the two cannot be denied. A comparison of the use of Isaiah in the two works can only be done in a separate study.

[181] The "physical accessibility" of Isaiah to Luke is a question that cannot be determined with any certainty. As in other cases of the use of Old Testament material, several possibilities can be noted. First, quotations from memory cannot be ruled out. In the Lukan writings, however, lengthy block quotations may call for an alternative explanation. Consensus on criteria for determining what should or should not be considered as derived from memory are still lacking. See Christopher D. Stanley, *Paul and the Language of Scripture* (SNTSMS 74; Cambridge: Cambridge University Press, 1992) chapter three. Second, the use of excerpts provides easy access to biblical material. This possibility is tied with the testimony hypothesis although one does not have to assume the existence of any standard form of testimony material used by various authors. The existence of such collections of texts can be found in the Qumran documents. See Christopher D. Stanley, "The Importance of 4QTanhumim (4Q176)," *RevQ* 15 (1992) 589–92. Third, access to actual scrolls of Isaiah may have been possible especially given Luke's interest in synagogues, assuming however that at least some synagogues had scriptural scrolls in their possession. See A. Seager, "Ancient Synagogue Architecture: An Overview," in J. Gutmann, ed., *Ancient Synagogues: The State of Research* (Chico, CA: Scholars Press, 1981) 39–43. Finally, the relationship between Luke and Paul may also relevant. With his educational background, Paul's knowledge of scripture can be assumed. Luke's dependence on Paul may be possible although their writings do not betray any explicit direct literary relationship in their use of Isaiah.

[182] See, for example, Acts 17:10–15 and 18:24–28.

[183] See the recent discussion in Richard Bauckham, ed., *The Gospels for All Christians: Rethinking the Gospel Audiences* (Grand Rapids, MI: Eerdmans, 1998). E. Earle Ellis, *The Making of the New Testament Documents* (BibInt 39; Leiden: Brill, 1999) further suggests the possibility of "corporate authorship" in understanding the relationship between the author and the wider Christian movement.

Exodus paradigm may be sufficient reason to motivate him to carry out this task. Nevertheless, my reading of Luke's reappropriation of Israel's foundation story does not depend on knowledge of the real audience.

This discussion on "historical plausibility" provides a context in which to examine the literary relationship between Isaiah and the Lukan narrative. Literary exercises take place at a particular moment in history, and it is my hope that my study of the Lukan use of the Isaianic New Exodus paradigm will in turn shed light on the historical issues surrounding the study of the Lukan writings.

Chapter 2

Continuity and Discontinuity:
The Significance of Isa 40:1–11 in the Lukan Writings

2.1 Introduction

Isa 40:3–5 in Luke 3:4–6 has long been treated as an isolated quotation from Isaiah introducing the ministry of John the Baptist. I will, however, show that the importance of this citation reaches beyond the early chapters of Luke. It functions as a hermeneutical lens without which the entire Lukan program cannot be properly understood. I will also argue that one of the main functions of Isaiah in the Lukan writings is to establish the identity of the early Christian movement in the midst of competitive claims. Luke accomplished this by evoking a text from Isaiah that has a long history before its appearance in the writings of Luke. The citation itself presupposes the knowledge of the wider context of Isaiah 40–55. The prominent themes in Isaiah 40–55 become the organizing principles for the second volume of the Lukan writings.

One significant implication of this discussion that will reappear throughout the rest of this study is the highlighting of the limitations of the narrow scheme of "prediction-fulfillment." I will show that this understanding of the passive role of Scripture does not adequately lead one to appreciate the constructive role Scripture played in the process of the "presentation" of early Christian traditions.[1] I will further argue that Luke evokes the wider Isaianic program to provide meaning for the various episodes in the narrative of Acts.

I will begin by examining the text of Isa 40:3–5 in Luke 3:4–6. Then, I will discuss why this Isaianic passage is selected and the significance it carries. Third, the various components of the Isaianic New Exodus program that are already embedded in Isa 40:1–11 and reappear throughout the narrative of Acts will be presented. Finally, I will examine the way Isa 40:3–5 and the wider Isaianic program are evoked through the ὁδός-terminology in Acts.

---

[1] The use of the term "presentation" here points to the organization and construction of a story based on both available (oral and/or written) sources and plausibly eyewitness accounts.

2.2 The Presentation of the Isaianic Program in Luke-Acts

Luke 3:1–6 forms the introduction to a new period with a complete synchronism, a prophetic formula of the coming of the word of God, and a reference to Scripture. This pericope defines how the rest of the narrative of Luke-Acts should be understood since it provides the definition of the nature of Luke's history. With the traditions concerning the beginning of the ministry of Jesus and the text of Mark before him, Luke begins the process of the reinterpretation of the story of Jesus and his apostles as well as the Scripture of Israel.

Within this pericope lies a scriptural quotation that forms the hermeneutical key for the Lukan program. I will begin by examining the text of Isa 40:3–5 as it appears in Luke 3:4–6:

ὡς γέγραπται ἐν βίβλῳ λόγων Ἡσαΐου τοῦ προφήτου, Φωνὴ βοῶντος ἐν τῇ ἐρήμῳ, ἑτοιμάσατε τὴν ὁδὸν κυρίου, εὐθείας ποιεῖτε τὰς τρίβους αὐτοῦ. πᾶσα φάραγξ πληρωθήσεται καὶ πᾶν ὄρος καὶ βουνὸς ταπεινωθήσεται, καὶ ἔσται τὰ σκολιὰ εἰς εὐθείαν καὶ αἱ τραχεῖαι εἰς ὁδοὺς λείας· καὶ ὄψεται πᾶσα σὰρξ τὸ σωτήριον τοῦ θεοῦ.

As it is written in the book of the words of the prophet Isaiah, "The voice of one crying out in the wilderness: 'Prepare the Way of the Lord, make his paths straight. Every valley shall be filled, and every mountain and hill shall be made low, and the crooked shall be made straight, and the rough ways made smooth; and all flesh shall see the salvation of God.'"

This citation is taken from the LXX with four changes. First of all, as in Mark and Matthew, instead of τοῦ θεοῦ ἡμῶν Luke has αὐτοῦ. Luke probably follows his (Markan or Q) source here[2] and the change can be understood as an attempt to apply the passage to Jesus himself.

Second, the omission of πάντα before τὰ σκολιά can also be detected in certain LXX traditions.[3] It is uncertain whether those with the omission are earlier (since the Hebrew text does not contain the equivalent of πάντα) or later when the original reading was corrected to conform to the Hebrew reading. The change in itself does not affect the meaning of this text. A similar change can also be found in Luke's use of the plural αἱ τραχεῖαι instead of

---

[2] Traugott Holtz, *Untersuchungen über die alttestamentlichen Zitate bei Lukas* (TU 104; Berlin: Akademie-Verlag, 1968) 37. This change also appears in some of the later LXX manuscripts but this is most likely a result of the influence of the gospel traditions. See Joseph Ziegler, *Isaias* (3rd ed.; Septuaginta 14; Göttingen: Vandenhoek & Ruprecht, 1983) 267.

[3] Ziegler, *Isaias*, 267. See, for example, A and V.

the singular ἡ τραχεῖα. This again may represent a reading from some variant LXX traditions attempting to conform to the Hebrew text.[4]

Finally, Luke omits καὶ ὀφθήσεται ἡ δόξα κυρίου of Isa 40:5. The omission is most likely Lukan although the exact reason cannot be determined with any certainty. The omission may be due to the presence of a similar idea in the next phrase καὶ ὄψεται πᾶσα σὰρξ τὸ σωτήριον τοῦ θεοῦ, a phrase that seems to reflect a central idea in the Lukan writings.

The function of this Isaianic passage in Luke can now be discussed through an examination of the ways Luke presents his story with his knowledge of the traditional material.[5] For some time scholars have recognized that Luke cites a longer version of the Isaianic quotation to emphasize the universalistic message (i.e., καὶ ὄψεται πᾶσα σὰρξ τὸ σωτήριον τοῦ θεοῦ). However, this redactional reading concentrates solely on the differences between Luke and his Markan source and thus fails to appreciate the dynamic role the Isaianic text plays in providing meaning and coherence for the Lukan narrative. The Lukan addition does not simply add one more item to the quotation but shifts its focus entirely.[6] Therefore, the examination of this Lukan passage should be carried out in light of the entire Lukan program.

Luke's inclusion of the phrase καὶ ὄψεται πᾶσα σὰρξ τὸ σωτήριον τοῦ θεοῦ within the citation in Luke 3:4–6 points to the wider Isaianic program lying behind the narratives of both Luke and Acts. The insertion does not function merely to highlight the importance of the Gentile mission for Luke; rather, it signifies the unity of the Lukan writings on the basis of the scriptural tradition that Luke evokes. The narrative of the apostles becomes part of the story in which one also finds the narrative concerning Jesus. Luke-Acts together therefore represent an entirely different agenda from that of the other gospels.[7] This will become important in the redefinition of the people of God as one in which the Gentiles will play an important role.

The presence of this extended quotation also points to the fact that the rest of the Lukan narrative should not be read apart from the wider context of

---

[4] Ibid., 267.

[5] François Bovon, *Das Evangelium nach Lukas: 1. Teilband Lk 1,1–9,50* (EKK III/1; Zürich: Benziger Verlag, 1989) 165–66 suggests that Mark, Q, and other traditions can be detected behind this pericope. Cf. W. D. Davies and Dale C. Allison, Jr., *The Gospel According to Saint Matthew* (ICC; Edinburgh: T. & T. Clark, 1988) 1.294.

[6] It is entirely possible that Isa 40:3 is linked with John's desert ministry in early Christian traditions (see Krister Stendahl, *The School of St. Matthew and Its Use of the Old Testament* [2nd ed.; Philadelphia: Fortress, 1968] 48). This, however, should not be assumed to be the primary function of Isa 40:3–5 within the Lukan context.

[7] Although this may be an overstatement, it seeks to balance the effects achieved by the canonical division of Luke and Acts with the result that Luke is considered as one of the four gospels while Acts becomes a book often considered apart from Luke.

Isaiah 40–55. The hermeneutical function of this citation can be seen in the allusion that already appears in Luke 2:30 in the phrase uttered by Simeon: εἶδον οἱ ὀφθαλμοί μου τὸ σωτήριόν σου ("my eyes have seen your salvation"),[8] The same text is also alluded to at the very end of the Lukan writings in Acts 28:28 in a phrase referring explicitly to the Gentiles: τοῖς ἔθνεσιν ἀπεστάλη τοῦτο τὸ σωτήριον τοῦ θεοῦ ("this salvation of God has been sent to the Gentiles"). The connections between these two allusions and the Isaianic quotation in Luke 3:5–6 are confirmed by the fact that the neuter form of the noun σωτήριον appears only in these three instances in the Lukan writings.[9] These two allusions presuppose some knowledge of Isa 40:3–5; and the constant recalling of the Isaianic context provides meaning for the development of the story.

Other echoes of Isa 40:3–5 can be found in the Lukan writings. In Luke 1:17, the phrase ἑτοιμάσαι κυρίῳ λαὸν κατεσκευασμένον ("to make ready a people prepared for the Lord") contains an allusion to Isa 40:3. Similarly, in 1:76, the phrase προπορεύσῃ γὰρ ἐνώπιον κυρίου ἑτοιμάσαι ὁδοὺς αὐτοῦ ("for you will go before the Lord to prepare his ways") should also be read against the background of Isa 40:3. Furthermore, in Acts 13:23–26, the ministry of John the Baptist is mentioned together with the sending forth of the word of this salvation (ἡμῖν ὁ λόγος τῆς σωτηρίας ταύτης ἐξαπεστάλη, lit.: "to us the word of this salvation has been sent"). This passage cannot be understood apart from the context of Isa 40:3–5.

It is therefore unjustifiable to understand this Isaianic quotation simply as a "proof-text" that the ministry of John the Baptist "fulfills." It has already been pointed out that in Luke, John is not portrayed primarily as a messenger of salvation.[10] This is consistent with the understanding that a wider application is intended as the significance of the Isaianic quotation is not limited to the early chapters of Luke. The importance of this citation that extends beyond its immediate context can also be seen through another deviation from the Markan text. In Mark 1:2, a quotation of Malachi 3:1 precedes the Isaianic quotation. Luke, however, probably following the order in Q, separates the quotation from Malachi concerning the sending of the messenger from the Isaianic quotation and moves it to Luke 7:27. The separation of Malachi 3:1 from Isa 40:3 together with the addition of Isa

---

[8] Note also the appearance of παράκλησις in Luke 2:25. The significance of this term in the Isaianic New Exodus and especially in Isa 40:1–11 points to the presence of the Isaianic context behind Luke 2:25–32.

[9] Outside the Lukan writings, this word reappears only in Eph 2:3.

[10] Heinz Schürmann, *Das Lukasevangelium* (HKNT 3; Freiburg: Herder, 1969) 1.161. Interestingly, on the basis of this observation, Schürmann concludes that this quotation should not be taken as a Lukan one. This reading, however, misses the wider ecclesiological application of the quotation in the Lukan writings.

40:4–5 force one to look beyond the ministry of John the Baptist for the meaning of this quotation.[11]

Before moving to the discussion of the significance of Isa 40:3–5 for the construction of the narrative of Acts, the question of why Luke evokes Isaiah 40 at all needs to be addressed.

2.3 The Evocative Power of Isa 40:3–5: The New Act of God

An examination of Isa 40:3–5 within the context of Second Temple Jewish traditions helps one appreciate its function in Luke 3:4–6.[12] Such an examination alerts one of the connotative power evoked by Luke's reference to the Isaianic passage in Luke 3:4–6.

Isa 40:3–5 is situated within the unit (Isa 40:1–11) that forms the prologue to Isaiah 40–55. This section begins with the declaration coming forth from the divine council: נחמו נחמו ("Comfort, Comfort").[13] It signifies the beginning of a new period that is characterized by the salvific work of God in history; and this divine command "has placed Israel at a historical turning point."[14] Isa 40:3–5 forms the center of this message of comfort; and "the Way of the LORD" (Isa 40:3) becomes a phrase that points to the coming salvation of God. Significantly, in the context of Isaiah 40–55(66), Isa 40:3–5 stands as a promise for the arrival of the new era yet to take place.[15] This futuristic aspect paved the way for the eschatological interpretation of this particular passage in subsequent interpretive traditions.

In the LXX, an eschatological reading is not yet apparent, although two changes to the text are present at this early stage in the development of the

---

[11] But see Luke 1:17 that connects the ministry of John the Baptist with Isa 40:3.

[12] A discussion of the themes embedded in Isa 40:1–11 and the wider context of Isaiah 40–55 is reserved for the next section.

[13] Here, I am following the conclusion of Frank M. Cross, "The Council of Yahweh in Second Isaiah," *JNES* 12 (1953) 274–77; and idem, *Canaanite Myth and Hebrew Epic: Essays in the History of the Religion of Israel* (Cambridge, MA: Harvard University Press, 1973) 186–90. Some have challenged the identification of the divine council as the context for Isa 40:1–11. For example, Klaus Kiesow (*Exodustexte im Jesajabuch: Literarkritische und motivgeschichtliche Analysen* [Göttingen: Vandenhoeck & Ruprecht, 1979] 54) has argued that the plural refers not to the heavenly audience but to a circle of prophets. For a further discussion and a defense for the reading that affirms a divine council context, see Christopher R. Seitz, "The Divine Council: Temporal Transition and New Prophecy in the Book of Isaiah," *JBL* 109 (1990) 229–47.

[14] Paul D. Hanson, *Isaiah 40–66* (IBR; Louisville, KY: John Knox, 1995) 20.

[15] For a discussion of the inherent conception of the futuristic aspects of Isaiah 40–55, see Rikki E. Watts, "Consolation or Confrontation? Isaiah 40–55 and the Delay of the New Exodus," *TynBul* 41 (1990) 31–59.

tradition that evolved from this text. In the LXX, the tone of comfort is
further highlighted by the insertion of παρακαλέσει in both 40:2 and 40:11.
More significantly, in the LXX, the phrase τὸ σωτήριον τοῦ θεοῦ has been
inserted in 40:5 to define the object of the sight of all flesh. This further
encouraged the use of Isa 40:3–5 as an icon signifying the coming of the
salvation of God in history.

Within the Hebrew Bible, Mal 3:1 provides an interpretation of Isa 40:3:

> See, I am sending my messenger to prepare the way before me,
> and the Lord whom you seek will suddenly come to his temple.
> The messenger of the covenant in whom you delight—
> indeed, he is coming, says the LORD of hosts.

The verse that follows highlights the eschatological character of this passage:
"But who can endure the day of his coming, and who can stand when he
appears" (Mal 3:2). Instead of the coming of salvation in Isa 40:3, the arrival
of judgment is announced.[16] The Way of the Lord also takes on a
metaphorical tone as it moves away from a literal reference to the return of the
exiles from Babylon.

Beyond the Hebrew Bible,[17] one already finds allusions to Isa 40:3–5 in
Baruch's description of the anticipated return of the exiles (Bar 5.6–9).[18] The
allusion is most clear in Bar 5.7: "For God has ordered that every high
mountain and the everlasting hills be made low and the valleys filled up, to
make level ground, so that Israel may walk safely in the glory of God." As in
Isa 40:3–5 the author's concern centers upon the literal return of the exiles and
the subject of God himself.

An ironic use of Isa 40:3 can be found in *Pss. Sol.* 8.17 where Pompey
becomes the one whose arrival the people prepare for: "They graded the
rough roads before his coming; they opened the gates to Jerusalem, they
crowned her city walls." In *Pss. Sol.* 11, however, one finds a similar use of
Isa 40:4 as that which appears in Baruch. The return of the exiles is again the
concern of the author and the activity of God is described: "He flattened high

---

[16] Robert A. Bascom ("Preparing the Way — Midrash in the Bible," in Philip C.
Stine, ed., *Issues in Bible Translation* [London: United Bible Societies, 1988] 227) further
suggests: "Not fully developed here, a crack is nevertheless opened through which the full
force of the apocalyptic 'day of the Lord' will later pass." For a discussion of the relationship
between Malachi 3:1 and the Isaianic New Exodus, see also Rikki E. Watts, *Isaiah's New
Exodus and Mark* (WUNT 2.88; Tübingen: Mohr Siebeck, 1997) 67–76.

[17] For the discussion of the transformation of traditions, see Klyne R. Snodgrass,
"Streams of Tradition Emerging from Isaiah 40:1–5 and their Adaptation in the New
Testament," *JSNT* 8 (1980) 24–45; and Carl Judson Davis, *The Name and Way of the Lord:
Old Testament Themes, New Testament Christology* (JSNTSup 129; Sheffield: Sheffield
Academic Press, 1996) 61–102. I am indebted to these studies in my discussion of the
various passages here.

[18] Baruch has been dated between 200 and 60 BCE.

mountains into level ground for them; the hills fled at their coming .... So that Israel might proceed under the supervision of the glory of their God" (*Pss. Sol.* 11.4, 6). Many see a literary relationship between these two works.[19]

In the *Testament of Moses* the same imagery is applied to the coming of the kingdom of God.[20] *T. Mos.* 10.1 introduces the promise of the coming of the kingdom of God: "Then his kingdom will appear throughout his whole creation." The specific allusion to Isa 40:4 in this context comes in *T. Mos.* 10.4: "And the earth will tremble, even to its end shall it be shaken. And the high mountains will be made low. Yea, they will be shaken, as enclosed valleys will they fall." The eschatological interpretation of Isa 40:3–5 reaches its fully developed form here as the arrival of the eschatological era replaces the hope for the return of the exiles as the center of these interpretive traditions.

The same eschatological use of Isa 40:3–5 is also present in *1 Enoch*.[21] In the first chapter, the coming of God is described; and a reference to Isa 40:4 is behind 1.6: "Mountains and high places will fall down and be frightened. And high hills shall be made low; and they shall melt like a honeycomb before the flame." The idea of judgment is explicitly stated in 1.7: "And earth shall be rent asunder; and all that is upon the earth shall perish. And there shall be a judgment upon all (including) the righteous." This text probably belongs to the same tradition that extends from Mal 3:1 to *T. Mos.* 10.4.

The eschatological use of Isa 40:3 also plays an important role in the Qumran literature. Literary dependence upon *1 Enoch* cannot be ruled out as an awareness of the text of *1 Enoch* is obvious (cf. 4QEnᵃ). An additional element is introduced in that the Isaianic program is evoked in the delineation of the eschatological community from the wider society. Isa 40:3 is explicitly quoted (see 1QS 8.13–16; 9.16–21). More importantly, the self-designation דרך (1QS 9.9, 16–21; 10.21) appears in various contexts and is apparently derived from Isa 40:3 as a description of the identity of the community. The

---

[19] See R. B. Wright, "Psalms of Solomon," in James H. Charlesworth, ed., *The Old Testament Pseudepigrapha* (Garden City, NY: Doubleday, 1985) 2.647–68. Wright suggests that the "Psalms of Solomon emerge from the tradition of a Jewish community in the last century before the turn of the era" (641). In this study, English translation of passages from pseudepigraphical works are taken from Charlesworth, ed. *Old Testament Pseudepigrapha, 2 vols.*, unless otherwise noted.

[20] The *Testament of Moses* has been dated to the first century CE. See J. Priest, "Testament of Moses," in James H. Charlesworth, ed., *Old Testament Pseudepigrapha*, 1.920–21.

[21] *1 Enoch* 1–5 can be dated to roughly the same period as the *Testament of Moses*, if not earlier. See E. Isaac, "1 (Ethiopic Apocalypse of) Enoch," in James H. Charlesworth, ed., *Old Testament Pseudepigrapha*, 1.6–7.

wilderness locality provides further connection with the Isaianic context.[22] The centrality of Isa 40:3 in the self-understanding of the Qumran community reflects the significance this passage held in the Second Temple Jewish eschatological traditions.[23]

Finally, the use of Isa 40:3 in Mark should also be noted. In Mark, Isa 40:3 is used together with Exod 23:20 and Mal 3:1 even though the formula καθὼς γέγραπται ἐν τῷ Ἠσαΐᾳ τῷ προφήτῃ is used for the entire quotation.[24] Here, the appearance of the quotation from Isaiah to introduce the eschatological event is consistent with what one finds in other Jewish interpretive traditions.[25] Isa 40:3 therefore became a signal for the arrival of the salvific work of God.

The preceding discussion does not intend to show that Luke had knowledge of some or all of the mentioned texts.[26] It does, however, show the connotative value attached to Isa 40:3–5. The contexts in which phrases from Isa 40:3–5 appear show that a wider Isaianic context is presupposed and evoked merely by quoting a phrase. Within these Jewish traditions, the appearance of symbols taken from Isa 40:3–5 signified the arrival of a new age of salvation, and the events themselves became understandable only through this symbolic framework. These symbols instilled meaning into events that may have had various interpretive possibilities. The primary function of the Isaianic citation is, therefore, not simply to note the "fulfillment" of particular correspondent events, but to show how the entire narrative should be understood. To an audience familiar with these scriptural traditions, the

---

[22] See, in particular, the discussion in George J. Brooke, "Isaiah 40:3 and the Wilderness Community," in George J. Brooke, ed., *New Qumran Texts and Studies: Proceedings of the First Meeting of the International Organization for Qumran Studies, Paris 1992* (STDJ 15; Leiden: Brill, 1994) 117–32; and James H. Charlesworth, "Intertextuality: Isaiah 40:3 and the Serek ha-Yahad," in Craig A. Evans and Shemaryahu Talmon, eds., *The Quest for Context and Meaning: Studies in Biblical Intertextuality in Honor of James A. Sanders* (Leiden: Brill, 1997) 197–224.

[23] For a further discussion, see section 2.6 below.

[24] Joseph Fitzmyer (*Essays on the Semitic background of the New Testament* [Missoula, MT: Scholars Press, 1974] 62–63) has noted: "Possibly a collection of texts existed that dealt with 'preparing the way,' and in the course of time it was thought that all the passages were from Isaiah." See, however, Robert H. Gundry, *The Use of the Old Testament in St. Matthew's Gospel* (NovTSup 18; Leiden: Brill, 1967) 125, concerning the practice of using the name of one author in a composite quotation.

[25] Robert Gundry (*Mark: A Commentary on His Apology for the Cross* [Grand Rapids, MI: Eerdmans, 1993] 35) rightly notes that "Mark puts the quotation in the superscription that precedes the narrative rather than at the close of the narrative, where quotations indicating correspondence would naturally appear. As a result, the emphasis falls not so much on correspondence at the time of John as on God's planning things out long before the time of John."

[26] The same eschatological reading of Isa 40:1–5 is present in Rabbinic literature. See, for example, *Pesiq. Rab.* 29.30A.

mentioning of Isa 40:3–5 in Luke 3 evoked the wider program of Isaiah 40–55; and the isolated events described in the rest of the Lukan writings concerning Jesus and his apostles would naturally have been interpreted through this particular hermeneutical key.

2.4 Isaianic Themes in the Lukan Construction of an Identity Claim

Moving beyond the evocative value of Isa 40:3–5, I will now show that the entire prologue of Isa 40:1–11 and the larger text that this prologue points to are presupposed in the construction of the Lukan narrative of Acts. While the previous section discusses "why" the Isaianic quotation is cited, this section will discuss "what" the passage evokes. In Acts, Isa 40:3–5 is evoked in two different ways. First, the various themes dominating the narrative of Acts find their source and meaning in Isa 40:1–11. These themes not only give structure to the narrative of Acts, they also become keys for understanding the meaning of the narrative. Second, the use of the ὁδός terminology in an ecclesiological *way* sense is also dependent upon the context of Isa 40:3–5; and it is used to evoke the Isaianic tradition to establish the identity of the early Christian movement. In this section, I will first discuss the themes embedded in Isa 40:1–11 that provide direction for the narrative of Acts. This will further clarify the import of Isa 40:3–5 as a hermeneutical lens for the Lukan writings.

As mentioned above, Isa 40:1–11 functions as the prologue to Isaiah 40–55. It sets the stage for the development of the various themes in Isaiah 40–55; and together with 55:1–13 it provides unity to the diverse themes developed in the intervening chapters.[27] Isa 40:1–11 itself consists of four distinct parts (vss 1–2, 3–5, 6–8, 9–11)[28] and these parts become thematic

---

[27] The thematic unity of Isaiah 40–55 has been repeatedly affirmed although the precise organizational structure is widely debated. See Roy F. Melugin, *The Formation of Isaiah 40–55* (BZAW 141; Berlin/New York: Walter de Gruyter, 1976) 77–82; and Hendrik C. Spykerboer, *The Structure and Composition of Deutero-Isaiah: With Special Reference to the Polemics against Idolatry* (Franeker, Netherlands: T. Wever, 1976) 2–29.

[28] So Claus Westermann, *Isaiah 40–66: A Commentary* (trans. David M. G. Stalker; OTL; Philadelphia: Westminster, 1969) 32–46; John L. McKenzie, *Second Isaiah* (AB 20; Garden City: Doubleday, 1968) 16; Melugin, *Formation of Isaiah 40–55*, 82–86; Spykerboer, *Structure and Composition of Deutero-Isaiah*, 182–84; Kiesow, *Exodustexte im Jesajabuch*, 24–26; and Reinhard Gregor Kratz, "Der Anfang des Zweiten Jesaja in Jes 40,1f. und seine literarischen Horizonte," *ZAW* 105 (1993) 400–19. Isa 40:9–11 should, however, be understood as both the conclusion of Isa 40:1–11 and the introduction to the next section. Thematically, it forms an *inclusio* with Isa 40:1–2 on the announcement of the arrival of the new era. Some have excluded it from the main body of the prologue of Isa 40:1–8 although a

introductions to the various emphases of Isaiah 40–55.[29] I will briefly discuss these four parts and argue that these themes correspond to the ones controlling the narrative of Acts. Luke's conscription of these Isaianic themes to construct the narrative of Acts allows him to make a theological claim concerning the identity of the early Christian movement.

a. Isa 40:1–2: The Restoration of the People of God

The opening section in Isa 40:1–2 begins with a call from God from the heavenly council:

> Comfort, O comfort my people, says your God.
> Speak tenderly to Jerusalem, and cry to her
> that she has served her term, that her penalty is paid,
> that she has received from the LORD's hand
> double for all her sins.

Here, the call to comfort (נחם) is further defined and explained by the end of the period of punishment for God's people (cf. 40:11).[30] In the context of Isaiah 40–55, the promise of "comfort" entails an act of God on behalf of his people.[31] This recurrent theme appears in 49:13 in connection with the end of the era of suffering: "Sing for joy, O heavens, and exult, O earth; break forth, O mountains, into singing! For the LORD has comforted his people, and will have compassion on his suffering ones."

This call for comfort also implies a promise to restore Jerusalem/Zion. This is explicitly stated in 51:3 ("For the LORD will comfort Zion; he will comfort all her waste places, and will make her wilderness like Eden, her desert like the garden of the LORD;" cf. 51:12) and 52:9 ("Break forth together into singing, you ruins of Jerusalem; for the LORD has comforted his people, he has redeemed Jerusalem"). This idea reappears in the parallel passage in the epilogue of Isaiah 40–55 with the promise of "an everlasting covenant" (55:3) with his people. The dawn of the era of salvation and the deliverance of the

---

significant connection is not denied. See, for example, David McLain Carr, "Isaiah 40:1–11 in the Context of the Macrostructure of Second Isaiah," in Walter R. Bodine, ed., *Discourse Analysis of Biblical Literature* (Alpharetta, GA: Scholars Press, 1996) 52–64.

[29] See also the concise statement in Watts, *Isaiah's New Exodus and Mark*, 76–78.

[30] Westermann, *Isaiah 40–66*, 35: "The echo of the glad tidings that Israel's physical hardships in enforced exile are now at an end is to recur on every page of the chapters that follow."

[31] For an examination of the semantic field of the term "consolation" that points to a correspondence between divine deliverance and the human call to the release of debt, see Klaus Baltzer, "Liberation from Debt Slavery After the Exile in Second Isaiah and Nehemiah," in Patrick D. Miller, Jr., Paul D. Hanson, and S. Dean McBride, eds., *Ancient Israelite Religion: Essays in Honor of Frank Moore Cross* (Philadelphia: Fortress, 1987) 477–84.

people of God and Jerusalem/Zion forms the principle underlying Isaiah 40–55.

This same idea of the consolation of Israel is announced in the Lukan prologue (Luke 1–2) where Simeon is described as one who eagerly awaited "the consolation of Israel" (παράκλησιν τοῦ 'Ισραήλ, Luke 2:25; cf. Isa 40:11), a phrase derived from Isaiah 40.[32] This idea of divine consolation points to the promise of the restoration of Israel (cf. Isa 49:5–6, 8–26). This theme is central in the narrative of Acts and will be treated in chapter four of this study.

b. *Isa 40:3–5: Universal Revelation of the Glory/Salvation of God*

Isa 40:3–5 calls for the transformation of the desert into the way for the return of the Lord,[33] a glorious return that will be witnessed by all:

> A voice cries out:
> "In the wilderness prepare the way of the LORD,
> make straight in the desert a highway for our God.
> Every valley shall be lifted up,
> and every mountain and hill be made low;
> the uneven ground shall become level,
> and the rough places a plain.
> Then the glory of the LORD shall be revealed,
> and all people shall see it together,
> for the mouth of the LORD has spoken."

These verses form a response to the divine call in 40:1–2. The carrying out of the promise to "comfort" begins with the preparation of "the Way" on which Yahweh will travel.[34]

While the coming of Yahweh has already been announced in 40:1–2, the universal manifestation of the glory of God is highlighted in vs 5, a statement that serves as the center of the poem.[35] The universalistic emphasis found

---

[32] In the LXX, the idea of comfort only occurs in Isaiah as a description of the coming salvation of God. See Isa 35:4; 40:1, 11; 49:10, 13; 51:3, 12; 57:18; 61:2; 66:10–13. In Jewish traditions, the idea of consolation as introduced in Isa 40:1–11 becomes one that embraces the entire program of eschatological salvation. See Otto Schmitz and Gustav Stählin, "παρακαλέω, παράκλησις," *TDNT* 5 (1967) 792–93.

[33] The exact identity of the speaker does not affect my analysis here although the prophet himself seems to be a likely candidate. It is a well-known fact that the presence of the prophet is not frequently felt in Isaiah 40–55.

[34] The Babylonian background of the royal highway has frequently been noted as providing the context to these verses. A more fundamental source of the imagery of "the Way of the Lord" is, however, the Exodus pattern that plays an important role in Isaiah 40–55. This will be discussed in detail in section 2.5a below.

[35] See David Noel Freedman, "The Structure of Isaiah 40:1–11," in Edgar W. Conrad and Edward G. Newing, eds., *Perspectives on Language and Text: Essays and Poems in Honor of Francis I. Andersen's Sixtieth Birthday* (Winona Lake, IN: Eisenbrauns, 1987)

here is recognized as one of the distinctive features of Isaiah 40–55. The recurrent statement in 52:10 is sufficient to illustrate this emphasis: "The LORD has bared his holy arm before the eyes of all the nations; and all the ends of the earth shall see the salvation of God" (cf. 42:4, 23; 49:6; 51:4–6). This theme reemerges in the epilogue of Isaiah 40–55: "See, you shall call nations that you do not know, and nations that do not know you shall run to you" (55:5).[36]

With the explicit quotation of Isa 40:3–5 in Luke 3:4–6 and the development of the narrative of Acts, the universalistic emphasis of Luke cannot be denied. Together with the restoration of Israel, the concerns for the nations/Gentiles become part of the central program of Isaiah 40–55. In chapter seven of this study, the distinctive emphasis on the role and fate of the nations in Acts will be examined through the hermeneutical paradigm that Isaiah 40–55 provides.

c. Isa 40:6–8: The Power of the Word of God and the Fragility of the People

The third element of the Isaianic program is the power of the word of God. These verses (Isa 40:6–8) introduce the critical element in the accomplishment of the promise as announced in Isa 40:1–2 and also 40:3–5:

> A voice says, "Cry out!"
> And I said, "What shall I cry?"
> All people are grass,
> and their constancy is like the flower of the field.
> The grass withers, the flower fades,
> when the breath of the LORD blows upon it;
> surely the people are grass.
> The grass withers, the flower fades,
> but the word of our God will stand forever.

This passage establishes the power of the word of God as a fundamental principle of Isaiah 40–55.[37] The supremacy of the word of God resurfaces throughout the text and this is most clearly seen in 45:23: "By myself I have sworn, from my mouth has gone forth in righteousness a word that shall not

---

169, who provides sufficient evidence to show that vs 5 is the "centerpiece" of the entire poem.

[36] The phrase "all flesh" seems to include both the nations and the people of God. It should also be taken as the subject of the plural imperative verbs of vss 1–3. Freedman ("The Structure of Isaiah 40:1–11," 188) further notes that "there is a considerable number of second masculine plural imperative verbs in chapters 34, 35, 40 and 41. It is our claim that the subjects remain the same throughout."

[37] Gerhard von Rad (*Old Testament Theology, vol. II: The Theology of Israel's Prophetic Traditions* [trans. D. M. G. Stalker; New York: Harper and Row, 1965] 93) notes that the treatment of the word of God in Isaiah 40–55 "is prophecy's most comprehensive statement about the word of Jahweh and its effects."

return: 'To me every knee shall bow, every tongue shall swear.'"[38] This is again highlighted in the epilogue of Isaiah 40–55:

> For as the rain and the snow come down from heaven,
> and do not return there until they have watered the earth,
> making it bring forth and sprout,
> giving seed to the sower and bread to the eater,
> so shall my word be that goes out from my mouth;
> it shall not return to me empty,
> but it shall accomplish that which I purpose,
> and succeed in the thing for which I sent it. (Isa 55:10–11)

In the Acts of the Apostles, the power of the word of God is also critical in the development of the narrative.[39] In chapter five, I will argue that the word of God should be understood as the main character in the narrative of Acts. This word is to accomplish the divine plan "with power" (κατὰ κράτος, Acts 19:20).[40]

In Isa 40:6–8, the contrast in which the supremacy of the word is set should also be noted. Unlike the word of God, the people are grass that withers "when the breath of the LORD blows upon it" (40:7). In the context of Isaiah 40–55, the power of God (and his word) is contrasted in particular with the impotence of the idols (e.g., 40:18–20; 41:5–7; 44:9–20; 46:5–7). In Exod 12:12, Yahweh declares that "on all the gods of Egypt I will execute judgments." This is picked up in the early Isaianic traditions in which it is promised that "the idols of Egypt will tremble at his presence" (Isa 19:1). The contrast between Yahweh and the idols becomes explicit in the passage that immediately follows Isa 40:1–11. In 40:12–31, the incomparability of Yahweh is emphasized;[41] and within this passage one reads:

> To whom then will you liken God,
> or what likeness compare with him?
> An idol? — A workman casts it,
> and a goldsmith overlays it with gold,
> and casts for it silver chains.
> As a gift one chooses mulberry wood
> — wood that will not rot —
> then seeks out a skilled artisan
> to set up an image that will not topple. (Isa 40:18–20)

---

[38] The relationship between the power of the word in Isaiah 40–55 and the statement in Isa 2:3 will be discussed in chapter five below.

[39] François Bovon (*Luke the Theologian: Thirty-Three Years of Research (1950–1983)* [trans. Ken McKinney; PTMS 12; Allison Park, PA: Pickwick, 1987] 403) notes that "the Book of Acts does not tell primarily the history of the Church, or the Holy Spirit's either. It situates in the foreground the diffusion of the Word of God."

[40] NRSV: "mightily."

[41] The incomparability of God is illustrated through the themes of creation and redemption. See Hanson, *Isaiah 40–66*, 26–32.

The emphasis on the impotence of idols is therefore used in highlighting the sovereignty of Yahweh. This important theme of anti-idol polemic, often neglected in the study of the Lukan writings, also plays a significant role in the narrative of Acts. Together with the theme of the power of the word of God, the overcoming of the power of idols and false gods remains a constant theme in Acts providing structure and meaning to the development of the narrative. In chapter six, therefore, I will present an extensive discussion of the role of idols as the "enemies" of the word.

d. Isa 40:9–11: The Restoration of the People of God

Isa 40:9–11 does not introduce a new theme but forms the link between Isa 40:1–8 and 40:12–31. It concludes the prologue to Isaiah 40–55 and introduces a new section dealing with the sovereignty of Yahweh:

> Get you up to a high mountain, O Zion, herald of good tidings;
> lift up your voice with strength, O Jerusalem, herald of good tidings.
> lift it up, do not fear; say to the cities of Judah, "Here is your God!"
> See the Lord God comes with might, and his arm rules for him;
> his reward is with him, and his recompense before him.
> He will feed his flock like a shepherd; he will gather the lambs in his arms,
> and carry them in his bosom, and gently lead the mother sheep.

While 40:1–8 can be understood as an independent unit that contains the prophetic call report,[42] the parallel between Isa 40:1–2 and 9–11 points to the unity of Isa 40:1–11.[43] Both vss 1–2 and 9–11 contain imperatives and the content of the command. In both one finds the theologically important appellation "your God" (אלהיכם, vss 1, 9);[44] and both statements are concerned with Jerusalem. The two sections (vss 1–2, 9–11) therefore form the framework for the prologue to Isaiah 40–55. Moreover, the command to speak in vs 1 is not carried out until vss 9–11.[45] These connections between vss 1–2 and 9–11 can also be seen by the fact that there is no direct address in

---

[42] I.e., the call to proclaim, a question or an objection, and the reassurance from Yahweh. See Horst Dietrich Preuss, *Deuterojesaja: Eine Einführung in seine Botschaft* (Neukirchen: Neukirchener Verlag, 1976) 41–42; and Carr, "Isaiah 40:1–11 in the Context of the Macrostructure of Second Isaiah," 60–61.

[43] See Kiyoshi Kinoshita Sacon, "Isaiah 40:1–11: A Redactional-Critical Study," in Jared J. Jackson and Martin Kessler, eds., *Rhetorical Criticism: Essays In Honor of James Muilenburg* (PTMS 1; Pittsburgh: Pickwick, 1974) 99–116; and Kiesow, *Exodustexte im Jesajabuch*, 38–41.

[44] The occurrence of this form in both vss 1 and 9 is important as the noun with the second person plural suffix occurs nowhere else in Isaiah 40–55.

[45] Freedman ("The Structure of Isaiah 40:1–11," 175–77) has pointed out that vs 2 contains not the content of the speech but its rationale.

vs 2 although one would expect that from the imperative in vs 1; and apart from vss 1–2 there is no introduction to the speech in vss 9–11.[46]

The theme of this closing section of the prologue is again the restoration of the people of God. This understanding of the thematic unity of vss 1–2 and 9–11 is confirmed by the combination of ideas from both sections in Isa 52:7–10. Isa 40:9–11 does, however, emphasize the centrality of Jerusalem/Zion in the new era of salvation as the one who brings good tidings (LXX: ὁ εὐαγγελιζόμενος) to Zion is called to go up to the mountain to deliver the good news to the surrounding cities (vs 9). Together with the idea of the spread of the word of God, the centrality of Zion is emphasized in Isa 2:3, a passage that has long been recognized as exhibiting literary and theological affinity with Isaiah 40–55:[47]

> Many peoples shall come and say,
> "Come, let us go up to the mountain of the LORD,
> to the house of the God of Jacob;
> that he may teach us his ways and that we may walk in his paths."
> For out of Zion shall go forth instruction,
> and the word of the LORD from Jerusalem.

The same use of Jerusalem as the center from which the word of God will go forth is also crucial to the development of the narrative of Acts. This point will be more thoroughly discussed in my examination of the power of the word of God in chapter five.

Finally, the way that God will restore his people is set in a military context. The prophet declares that Yahweh will come with power (בחזק, vs 10) and he will rule with his arm (וזרעו משלה, vs 10; cf. vs 11). This language evokes the Exodus paradigm in which God delivers and restores his people. The Exodus paradigm provides the basis for the development of the various themes discussed above. Therefore, since the Isaianic tradition serves as the hermeneutical key to the narrative of Acts, the Exodus paradigm that underlies the Isaianic tradition should also be examined.

2.5 Isaiah 40–55: The Redefinition of the People of God and the Evocation of the Foundation Story of Ancient Israel

In depicting the restoration of the people and the formation of the new community, the Exodus paradigm is evoked and transformed in the context of

---

[46] Ibid., 177: "If it were not for the separation in space between vss 2 and 9, we would have no hesitation in connecting the verbs in vs 2 with the speech in vss 9–11."

[47] See, in particular, Hugh G. M. Williamson, *The Book Called Isaiah: Deutero-Isaiah's Role in Composition and Redaction* (Oxford: Clarendon, 1994) 146.

Isaiah 40–55.[48] I will begin by examining the use of the Exodus tradition in the prologue in Isa 40:1–11. This will be followed by a discussion of the transformation of the Exodus paradigm in Isaiah.

a. Isa 40:1–11 and the Introduction of the Exodus Paradigm

Immediately following the declaration that announces the coming of a new era, the people of God are called to prepare the "Way" (דרך) of the Lord in 40:3. In this context, the way-terminology evokes the foundation story of ancient Israel.

In the Exodus narrative, one finds a description of the presence of Yahweh in the travel account of the people of Israel. In Exod 13:21–22, the presence of the Lord is clearly noted: "The LORD went in front of them in a pillar of cloud by day, to lead them along the 'Way' (דרך), and in a pillar of fire by night, to give them light, so that they might travel by day and by night." This emphasis reappears in Exod 23:20: "I am going to send an angel in front of you, to guard you on the 'Way' (דרך) and to bring you to the place that I have prepared." This verse is important because, in Mark, part of this verse is combined with Isa 40:3, and they are both attributed to the prophet Isaiah. The existence of the connection between Isa 40:3 and Exod 23:20 therefore strengthens the possibility that the former is dependent upon the latter.

The terminology of the way becomes a key theme in the reformulation of the Exodus paradigm in Isaiah 40–55.[49] "The Way" symbolizes the presence of God in the ancient Exodus story as well as the anticipated eschatological event. As in the past, "the LORD will go before you, and the God of Israel will be your rear guard" (Isa 52:12; cf. Exod 23:20). This connection between the

---

[48] See, for example, Bernhard W. Anderson, "Exodus Typology in Second Isaiah," in B. W. Anderson and W. Harrelson, eds. *Israel's Prophetic Heritage: Essays in Honor of James Muilenburg* (New York: Harper, 1962) 177–95; idem, "Exodus and Convenant in Second Isaiah and Prophetic Tradition," in F. M. Cross, W. E. Lemke, and P. D. Miller, Jr., eds., *Magnalia Dei: The Mighty Acts of God* (New York: Doubleday, 1976) 339–60; Joseph Blenkinsopp, "Scope and Depth of the Exodus Tradition in Deutero-Isaiah, 40–55," *Dynamism of Biblical Tradition* (Concilium 20; New York: Paulist, 1967) 41–50; Carroll Stuhlmueller, *Creative Redemption in Deutero-Isaiah* (Rome: Pontifical Biblical Institute, 1970); Dale A. Patrick, "Epiphanic Imagery in Second Isaiah's Portrayal of a New Exodus," *HAR* 8 (1984) 125–41; Watts, "Consolation or Confrontation? Isaiah 40–55 and the Delay of the New Exodus," 31–59; E. John Hamlin, "Deutero-Isaiah's Reinterpretation of the Exodus in the Babylonian Twilight," *Proceedings: Eastern Great Lakes and Midwest Biblical Societies* 11 (1991) 75–80; and George Wesley Buchanan, "Isaianic Midrash and the Exodus," in Craig A. Evans and James A. Sanders, eds., *The Function of Scripture in Early Jewish and Christian Tradition* (JSNTSup 154; Sheffield: Sheffield Academic Press, 1998) 89–109.

[49] See, especially, Frank M. Cross, *Canaanite Myth and Hebrew Epic: Essays in the History of the Religion of Israel* (Cambridge, MA: Harvard University Press, 1973) 112–44.

past and the future is most clearly illustrated in Isa 43:16–19 where the contrast between "former things" and "a new thing" is made:[50]

> Thus says the LORD,
> who makes a way (דרך) in the sea, a path in the mighty waters,
> who brings out chariot and horse, army and warrior;
> they lie down, they cannot rise, they are extinguished, quenched like a wick:
> Do not remember the former things, or consider the things of old.
> I am about to do a new thing; now it springs forth, do you not perceive it?
> I will make a way (דרך) in the wilderness and rivers in the desert.

The same contrast between the Old Exodus and the New can be found in Isa 44:26–27 in which the Lord "who says of Jerusalem, 'It shall be inhabited,' and of the cities of Judah, 'They shall be rebuilt, and I will raise up their ruins'" is also the one "who says to the deep, 'Be dry — I will dry up your rivers.'" Again in 51:9–11, the drying of the Red Sea and the making of "the depths of the sea a way (דרך)" is linked with the New Exodus in which the people will return to their homeland.[51] Through these contrasts, the author depicts the continuous activity of God; and at times such continuity blurs the distinction between the past and the present (e.g., Isa 43:1–3).

The fact that "the Way" signifies the salvific act of God on behalf of his people explains why "the Way" is prepared for both Yahweh and his people. In 40:3, "the Way" is prepared for the coming of Yahweh. In passages such as 42:16, 43:16–19, and 49:11–12, however, "the Way" is prepared by Yahweh for his people.[52] "The Way" therefore functions to point to the coming of Yahweh for his people as well as the return of the people from captivity.[53] John McKenzie has rightly noted that "there seems to be no room for a distinction between the road of Yahweh and road of Israel, for Yahweh travels with his people, as he did in the Exodus."[54]

---

[50] For the discussion of the use of this polarity, see Antoon Schoors, "Les choses antérieures et lest choses nouvelles dans les oracles deutéro-isaïens," *EThL* 40 (1964) 19–47; and Richard J. Clifford, *Fair Spoken and Persuading: An Interpretation of Second Isaiah* (New York: Paulist, 1984) 43–44.

[51] Anderson ("Exodus Typology in Second Isaiah," 193) notes that here one finds the "historification of mythological motifs" as the victory of the chaos monster is linked with the Exodus event.

[52] This usage has already appeared in Isaiah 35. In 35:4, the coming of God is announced; and in vss 8–10, a way (דרך) is prepared for the people to return. Such a usage reappears in Isaiah 56–66 (57:14; 62:10). The relationship between Isaiah 35 and 40–55 has long been recognized by scholars. See, for example, the early statement in R. B. Y. Scott, "The Relation of Isaiah, Chapter 35, to Deutero-Isaiah," *AJSL* 52 (1935–36) 178–91.

[53] Here, it should be noted that the word דרך is also used in other ways in Isaiah 40–55 (see, for example, 40:14, 27; 42:24; 53:6). The use of the term in the prologue as well as its appearance in the context of the Exodus paradigm, however, contributes to the development of a unique use of the term.

[54] McKenzie, *Second Isaiah*, 17.

Not only does the term "Way" evoke the Exodus tradition; the phrase
"make straight in the desert a highway (מסלה) for our God" (Isa 40:3) should
also be understood as an allusion to the Exodus tradition. In Isa 11:16, the
return of the people from exile is compared to the travel of Israel from Egypt:
"so there shall be a highway (מסלה) from Assyria for the remnant that is left
of his people, as there was for Israel when they came up from the land of
Egypt."[55] The wilderness locale also situates this phrase in the Exodus
traditions; and the transformation of the wilderness as described in Isa 40:4 is
a sign for the coming of the New Exodus. This is clear in the last phrase in the
text quoted above (43:16–19) for one now finds "rivers in the desert" (43:19).
The allusion to God's provision in the wilderness journey of old (cf. Exod
17:2–7)[56] and the interpretive value of this allusion is clearly seen in
48:20–21:

> Go out from Babylon, flee from Chaldea,
> declare this with a shout of joy, proclaim it,
> send it forth to the end of the earth;
> say, "The LORD has redeemed his servant Jacob!"
> They did not thirst when he led them through the deserts;
> he made water flow for them from the rock;
> he split open the rock and the water gushed out.[57]

This blending of the past and the present is typical of the act of re-enacting
the Exodus event in Isaiah 40–55; and to understand this simply as a
"typology" does not fully explicate the complex nature of the relationship
between the two. Moreover, the "former" act apparently becomes the basis
without which the "latter" would not be possible.

As in the "ancient" event of the Exodus, the glory of God will again be
revealed (Isa 40:5). The refrain "you/they shall know that I am the LORD your
God" appears throughout the Exodus account.[58] In the context of the New
Exodus (52:7–12), the new act of God is revealed "before the eyes of all the
nations; and all the ends of the earth shall see the salvation of our God"
(52:10). The cosmic impact of this New Exodus becomes an emphasis that
underlies the Isaianic program.

Together with the imagery of "the Way" in 40:3–5, the final section of the
prologue (40:9–11) confirms the importance of the Exodus paradigm in both

---

[55] See also Isa 40:13 and 49:11; cf. 35:6–7.

[56] Significantly, the combination of the themes of provision of water in the desert and
the turning of mountains into the "Way" (דרך) can be found in 49:10–11.

[57] The perfect tense of גאל ("he redeemed") does not necessarily indicate that the work
of redemption is a thing of the past. Westermann (*Isaiah 40–66*, 205) suggests that this is an
"eschatological" hymn of praise to be heard throughout the earth as "Israel's answering
exaltation assumes that God's final act has already taken place."

[58] E.g., Exod 6:7; 7:5, 17; 10:2; 14:4, 18; 16:12; 29:46; 31:13; cf. 8:22; 9:14, 29;
11:7; 16:6.

the prologue and throughout Isaiah 40–55. In 40:10, it is declared that "the Lord God comes with might, and his arm rules for him." The combination of the way-imagery and the imagery of the strength of the arm of Yahweh as in 40:1–11 is also found in Isa 51:9–10 where the Exodus tradition is explicitly evoked:

> Awake, awake, put on strength, O arm of the LORD!
> Awake, as in days of old, the generations of long ago! . . .
> Was it not you who dried up the sea, the waters of the great deep;
> who made the depths of the sea a way for the redeemed to cross over?

The portrayal of Yahweh as the mighty warrior has already appeared in the Song of Moses (Exod 15) where it is explicitly stated, "The LORD is a warrior" (אִישׁ מִלְחָמָה, 15:3).[59] Similarly, the Yahweh of Isaiah 40–55 who is going to deliver his people is also "like a warrior" (כְּאִישׁ מִלְחָמוֹת, 42:13). Moreover, the imagery of the shepherd and his flock as it appears in 40:11 is applied to the Exodus paradigm beyond Isaiah 40–55.[60]

The various themes presented in Isa 40:1–11 are thus tied together by the appropriation of the Exodus paradigm. In the reorganization and restoration of the people of God, the founding moment of Israel's history is evoked.

b. The Transformation of the Exodus Paradigm in Isaiah 40–55

The question as to why the Isaianic New Exodus paradigm is evoked in the Lukan writings should also be approached through a discussion of the transformation of the Exodus paradigm in Isaiah 40–55,[61] a question that has not been adequately dealt with in many treatments of the use of the Exodus

---

[59] The "right hand" of Yahweh (Exod 15:6) plays a significant role in both the Exodus tradition and Isaiah 40–55 (cf. 50:2). In any discussion of the transformation of the Exodus traditions, the importance of the imagery of the hand/arm needs to be emphasized. See David Rolph Seely, "The Image of the Hand of God in the Exodus Traditions" (Ph.D. diss., University of Michigan, 1990). See also his "The Raised Hand of God as an Oath Gesture," in Astrid B. Beck, Andrew H. Bartelt, Paul R. Raabe, and Chris A. Franke, eds., *Fortunate the Eyes That See: Essays in Honor of David Noel Freedman in Celebration of His Seventieth Birthday* (Grand Rapids, MI: Eerdmans, 1995) 411–21.

[60] E.g., Ps. 77:20; 78:52–53. See the discussion in Antoon Schoors, *I am God Your Saviour* (VTSup 24; Leiden: Brill, 1973) 101–2.

[61] This will also explain why the Isaianic New Exodus and not the original Exodus paradigm is the primary one that lies behind the Lukan writings. The failure to recognize the importance of this New Exodus paradigm is the major weakness of previous proposals concerning the nature of the New Exodus in Acts. See, for example, Jindrich Mánek, "The New Exodus in the Books of Luke," *NovT* 2 (1957) 8–23, who, examining the Lukan writings through the Moses typology, covers only the events up to the ascension of Jesus in Acts 1. The remaining part of Acts could not be fully incorporated into this Exodus framework.

paradigm in Isaiah.[62] In this section, I will limit my discussion to the "why" question; the more difficult question of "how" the Isaianic program functions in Acts will be dealt with in the remaining chapters of this study.

In a most striking fashion, the Exodus paradigm has been "eschatologized" in Isaiah.[63] This eschatological reworking of traditions explains the fact that the text can be and has been repeatedly evoked in Jewish traditions. This is accomplished through two major means. First, the "Exodus" becomes a future event promised on the basis of God's action in the past.[64] Isa 40:3–5 itself paradigmatically points forward to a future act of Yahweh and was understood as such in Jewish traditions. This futuristic emphasis is most clearly seen in the repeated contrast between the "former things" and the "new things" (e.g., 42:9; 43:18–19). These "new things" will come to fruition because of the promise of Yahweh: "My purpose shall stand, and I will fulfill my intention" (46:10).

The second way the Exodus paradigm is "eschatologized" is the reformulation of the original Exodus story with the cosmogonic one, thus emphasizing the (new) Exodus as a creative event.[65] The Exodus event is understood against the creation myth of the cosmic defeat of Rahab and the sea (50:2; 51:9–11); and the creative act of God is repeatedly evoked (40:12–31; 42:5; 44:24; 45:9–18; 48:12–13; 51:12–16). The Exodus tradition of provision in the desert (41:17–20; 43:19) becomes a promise in which Yahweh will "make her wilderness like Eden" (51:3). The creative act of Yahweh is transposed to the future event of the New Exodus through the understanding of the Exodus event as a creative event.[66] Therefore, the new

---

[62] I am not suggesting that the old Exodus pattern is systematically reworked and consciously applied in Isaiah 40–55 in a purely mechanical fashion. Isolated symbols and themes provide meaning for the running narrative. The transformation of certain themes in the formation of the message is not a static one.

[63] The term "eschatology" refers to events in the future times that are anticipated in the construction of the ideal world. My use of the term here does not presuppose an apocalyptic framework in which the expectation of an otherworldly reality plays a critical role. The phrase "prophetic eschatology," on the other hand, points to the fulfillment of certain expectations within history; and this phrase can be used in characterizing the eschatology of Isaiah 40–55.

[64] Watts, "Consolation or Confrontation? Isaiah 40–55 and the Delay of the New Exodus," 15: "While Israel may look back to its origins in the first Exodus, it was Isaiah who had *par excellence* transformed it into a future hope."

[65] One is justified in understanding this within the paradigm of *Endzeit wird Urzeit*. See Paul D. Hanson, *The Dawn of Apocalyptic* (rev. ed.; Philadelphia: Fortress, 1979) 131–32 n.84.

[66] So Blenkinsopp, "Scope and Depth of the Exodus Tradition in Deutero-Isaiah, 40–55," 48: "By means of this mythical language the exodus is given the status of a primordial event in which the inherent *dynamis* is, in accordance with the functionality of mythical thinking, transferred to the present moment." See also Bernard F. Batto, *Slaying the*

events "are created now" (48:7); and the radical transformation is expressed in the command: "Do not remember the former things" (43:18). This anticipation for such an eschatological act of God provides fuel for the continuing reappropriation and transformation of the Exodus paradigm.

In ancient Israelite traditions, however, the Exodus narrative is not understood as being entirely distinct from the Creation story; and a strict separation between the two should not be made.[67] Richard Clifford correctly notes that the two (the historic and the cosmogonic) are expressions of a single national story; and "there is interpenetration of the two ideal types."[68] The central concern of both is the formation of the people of God. This is most clearly reflected in the identification of Yahweh as "the Creator of Israel" (43:15) in the context of the Exodus paradigm (43:16–21). Therefore, in the evocation of both the Exodus and Creation traditions, the concern with the creation of a new people of God is highlighted. It is this redefinition and reformulation of the conception of the people of God that plays an important part in the Lukan program in Acts.

The eschatologization of the Exodus paradigm naturally leads to the development of a universalistic emphasis in the salvific program of the New Exodus; and this transformation has already appeared in Isa 40:5. This kind of universalism is developed not through the abolition of the particularistic understanding of election but primarily through the extension of the recognition of the universal sovereignty of the God of Israel and the role of Israel as God's servant in his manifestation as the universal ruler.[69] Going beyond the theme of the restoration of the people of God in the ancient Exodus traditions, the message of salvation is promised to those throughout the created order:

> It is too light a thing that you shall be my servant
> to raise up the tribes of Jacob and to restore the survivors of Israel;
> I will give you as a light to the nations,
> that my salvation may reach to the end of the earth. (Isa 49:6)

Dragon: Mythmaking in the Biblical Tradition (Louisville, KY: Westminster/John Knox, 1992) 110.

[67] Cf. Exod 15; Deut 32:7–14; Pss 74:12–17; 77:12–20; 89:5–37; and 114.

[68] Clifford, *Fair Spoken and Persuading*, 18. He also notes that in modern understanding, "the historic type is called redemption and the cosmogonic type is called creation. They are however the same event — the emergence of Israel as a people before Yahweh" (23).

[69] Hamlin ("Deutero-Isaiah's Reinterpretation of the Exodus in the Babylonian Twilight," 76) has pointed out that while ארץ is used in the Exodus traditions in reference to the promised land of Israel, in Isaiah 40–55 the term almost always acquires a universal sense as it refers to the whole created earth.

Although the exact nature of the universalism of Isaiah 40–55 is still a debated issue,[70] Luke has found it necessary to appeal to the Isaianic paradigm in his discussion of the Gentile issue in Acts.[71]

Embedded in the emphasis of universalism and also the promise of deliverance for "Israel" is the issue of the redefinition of the people of God. As the author of Isaiah 40–55 announces the coming of a new era for the remnant of the people of God, the exact nature of the reconstitution of the community is left open. The comment concerning the new apportionment of the land (49:8) that will take place provides a hint of an understanding of a restructuring of the community. Therefore, while "Jacob-Israel"[72] is called to return, the identity of the "true Israel" becomes an issue of primary importance. Such ambiguity, arising out of an attempt to reuse the traditional story anew, allows for the use of Isaiah 40–55 in various communities to establish the identity of their group as the "true Israel."

Moreover, the evocation of the Exodus paradigm at all in Isaiah 40–55 reflects an attempt to lay claim to the foundation story in a situation where the question of the identity of the exilic community and its continuity with the past is raised. The dramatic reenactment of the Exodus events is the central element of the early cult[73] and it provides the "canon" that binds the community together.[74] This canon of Israel can be defined as one that is "adaptable to the varying fortunes of the people who found their identity in it."[75] In the case of Isaiah, the evocation of the ancient story provides the language in which the renewal and restructuring of a community can be understood. As God created a people in the past, his creative act can also be felt in this historical moment. One should not be surprised, therefore, that Isaiah 40–55 is evoked in Acts precisely when the question of the identity of the people of God is raised. The tension between the continuity with the past

---

[70] This will be discussed in chapter seven below.

[71] The way the Isaianic program is transformed in Acts is also an important topic that will be dealt with in the following chapters (especially chapter seven) of this study.

[72] This is the term used in addressing the exiles in Isaiah 40–55. See, especially, Isa 41:8; 44:1; and 46:3.

[73] See, in particular, Cross, *Canaanite Myth and Hebrew Epic*, 84.

[74] For a discussion of the relationship between story and identity, see Helmut Koester, "Writings and the Spirit: Authority and Politics in Ancient Christianity," *HTR* 84 (1991) 353–72.

[75] James A. Sanders, *From Sacred Story to Sacred Text* (Philadelphia: Fortress, 1987) 19. For a (modern) sociological analysis of the formative influence of the founding moment on a community's self-understanding, see also Watts, *Isaiah's New Exodus and Mark*, 29–47.

and the discontinuity that symbolizes a new creative act is one that characterizes both Isaiah and Acts.[76]

Finally, with the transformation of the redemptive story, the means through which Yahweh accomplishes his goals are also redefined. In the past the arm/hand of Yahweh delivers his people through various mighty acts. In the New Exodus, the word becomes the agent of the new creative act. As discussed above, this emphasis on the word appears in both the prologue and epilogue of Isaiah 40–55. Such an emphasis can be understood as a step forward in the transformation of the Exodus paradigm although the relation with the creation traditions cannot be ignored. While the divine word did play an important role in the Exodus tradition, the word becomes an active and major force in Isaiah 40–55.[77] This emphasis on the word provides the basis for Luke to develop his doctrine of the word in the context of the preaching of early Christians. As the powerful word is the mighty force in Isaiah 40–55, so in Acts κατὰ κράτος τοῦ κυρίου ὁ λόγος ηὔξανεν καὶ ἴσχυεν ("the word grew mightily and prevailed," 19:20).

The preceding discussion provides a foundation on which the significance of the Isaianic New Exodus for the narrative of Acts can be further examined. In the final section of this chapter, I will show that Isa 40:1–11 and the Isaianic New Exodus are evoked through the ὁδός-terminology in Acts.

2.6 Who is the "True Israel"? ʿ Οδός-Terminology as an Identity Claim in Acts

It has long been noted that the "most unusual of the names for Christianity found in Acts is the unmodified ὁδός."[78] This absolute use of the term as a designation of the early Christian movement appears in Acts 9:2; 19:9, 23; 22:4; 24:14 and 22; and a clear parallel cannot be found in early Christian literature apart from Acts and the writings dependent upon it.

---

[76] In Isaiah, this tension is best represented by both the command to "remember the former things of old" (46:9) and the command to "not remember the former things, or consider the things of old" as God is "about to do a new thing" (43:18–19).

[77] One significant parallel can be found in Wis 18:13–15 in which the word becomes the one who "leaped from heaven" and killed the firstborns of the Egyptians. See the discussion in the excursus at the end of chapter five.

[78] Henry J. Cadbury, "Names for Christians and Christianity in Acts," in F. J. Foakes-Jackson and Kirsopp Lake, eds., *The Beginnings of Christianity* (London: Macmillan, 1933) 5.391.

Previous studies[79] on the way-terminology have concentrated on two areas: (1) the source and background of this term; and (2) the exact referent of and meaning embedded in this term. First, those who are preoccupied with the source and background of the term have identified numerous conceptual fields. These include the eschatological use in the Qumran literature,[80] the two-way tradition in Hellenistic Judaism,[81] the Greco-Roman use as a metaphor to knowledge and behavior,[82] and the moral traditions in early Christianity.[83] Those who are concerned with the exact referent of the term, however, concentrate on the discussion of "the Way" as a reference to Jesus,[84] the Christian manner of life,[85] the entire plan of salvation history,[86] and the church as a whole.[87]

While the value of these studies cannot be questioned, a significant aspect has often been neglected: the literary function of the way-terminology in Acts. Moving beyond the two traditional approaches that are concerned primarily with the source and referent of the term, I will argue that one should start by examining the function of the way-terminology as it appears in the various passages in Acts. This approach will uncover the rhetorical role of the way-terminology in the narrative of Acts. In examining the literary context of these particular passages, I will show that the way-terminology is used in polemical contexts where the identity of the "true" people of God is at stake. The way-

---

[79] For the history of scholarship concerning the absolute use of the term "Way" in Acts, see, Bovon, *Luke the Theologian*, 321–23.

[80] E.g., Selby Vernon McCasland, "The Way," *JBL* 77 (1958) 222–30; E. Repo, *Der 'Weg' als Selbstbezeichnung des Urchristentums* (Helsinki: Suomalainen Tiedeakatemia, 1964); and Joseph A. Fitzmyer, "Jewish Christianity in Acts in Light of the Qumran Scrolls," in Leander E. Keck and J. Louis Martyn, eds., *Studies in Luke-Acts* (Nashville: Abingdon, 1966) 240–41.

[81] E.g., Heinz-Werner Neudorfer, *Die Apostelgeschichte des Lukas* (Neuhausen-Stuttgart: Hänssler, 1986) 196–97; and Luke Timothy Johnson, *The Acts of the Apostles* (Collegeville, MN: Liturgical Press, 1992) 162.

[82] E.g., Werner Jaeger, *The Theology of the Early Greek Philosophers* (Oxford: Clarendon, 1947) 99–101; and Reinhard Göllner, "Der 'Weg' christlichen Glaubens Perspektiven lukanischer Theologie," in Michael Albus, ed., *Der dreieine Gott und die eine Menschheit* (Wein: Herder, 1989) 204–5.

[83] E.g., Max Wilcox, *The Semitisms of Acts* (Oxford: Clarendon, 1965) 105–6.

[84] E.g., Repo, *Der 'Weg' als Selbstbezeichnung des Urchristentums*, 182–84; and Stanislas Lyonnet, "'La Voie' dans les Actes des apôtres," *RechSR* 69 (1981) 149–64.

[85] Bruce J. Malina and Jerome H. Neyrey, "First-Century Personality: Dyadic, Not Individualistic," in Jerome H. Neyrey, ed., *The Social World of Luke-Acts: Models for Interpretation* (Peabody, MA: Hendrickson, 1991) 92.

[86] E.g., William C. Robinson, Jr., "The Way of the Lord: A Study of History and Eschatology in the Gospel of Luke" (Dr.Theol. diss., University of Basel, 1960) 61–69; and Wilhelm Michaelis, "ὁδός," *TDNT* 5 (1967) 89.

[87] This position is adopted by most commentators although usually further qualified by one of the above categories.

terminology is therefore utilized in establishing the church as the true heir of the ancient traditions of Israel. I will further argue that it is with this understanding of the function of the term in Acts that one can begin to appreciate the connections of this term with the Isaianic New Exodus.

Unlike any other ecclesiological designations in Acts, in all the passages in which one finds the absolute use of the way-terminology, the context is one of conflict and challenge to the early Christian movement. In these passages, the identity of the Christians becomes the focus as they are forced to define themselves against other groups.[88] The absolute use of the way-terminology first appears at the beginning of the story of the Lukan Paul in Acts 9:1–2;[89] and this passage defines the meaning of the term for the rest of the narrative:

Ὁ δὲ Σαῦλος, ἔτι ἐμπνέων ἀπειλῆς καὶ φόνου εἰς τοὺς μαθητὰς τοῦ κυρίου, προσελθὼν τῷ ἀρχιερεῖ ᾐτήσατο παρ' αὐτοῦ ἐπιστολὰς εἰς Δαμασκὸν πρὸς τὰς συναγωγάς, ὅπως ἐάν τινας εὕρῃ τῆς ὁδοῦ ὄντας, ἄνδρας τε καὶ γυναῖκας, δεδεμένους ἀγάγῃ εἰς Ἰερουσαλήμ.

Meanwhile, Saul, still breathing threats and murder against the disciples of the Lord, went to the high priest and asked him for letters to the synagogues at Damascus, so that if he found any one who belonged to the Way, men or women, he might bring them bound to Jerusalem.

First, it should be noted that this passage introduces the plan of Saul in his dealings with the Christians. The phrase ἐμπνέων ἀπειλῆς καὶ φόνου denotes the zealous action of Saul on behalf of his own Jewish community and the threats that fell upon the Christian community in Damascus. Those who belonged to "the Way" are here defined as the disciples of the Lord. Significantly, while in 8:3 Saul ravages "the church" (τὴν ἐκκλησίαν) and drags men and women to prison, in 9:2 Saul goes into "the synagogues" (τὰς συναγωγάς) of Damascus. The term "synagogue" is ambiguous at this stage in the narrative since it is obvious that both Christian Jews and non-Christian Jews participate in the synagogue worship. Saul's mission is, therefore, to purify the synagogue and restore it as the place of worship for the proper party. The distinction between these two kinds of "people" is the motivating principle behind this passage. It is in this context that the term "the Way" is

---

[88] This has been briefly noted in Paul Minear, *Images of the Church in the New Testament* (Philadelphia: Westminster Press, 1960) 149, although the connections with Isa 40:3 have not been explored and the reason why the way-terminology is used at all is not discussed.

[89] It is significant that the way-terminology initially appears in Acts 9. First, it follows the persecution of Stephen in which the Jewish opposition to the early Christian movement is becoming more explicit. Second, it is the beginning of the story of the Lukan Paul whose call is to take the gospel to the Gentiles in the midst of Jewish opposition. Therefore, Acts 9:2 can be understood as the point where the distinction is established between the early Christian movement and those that the non-believing Jews represent. Cf. Jack T. Sanders, *The Jews in Luke-Acts* (London: SCM, 1987) 72.

used by the Christians as an attempt to define themselves against the other "community." The way-terminology is therefore a significant identity marker that functions through the exclusion of and rejection by "the other."

This relationship between commitment to the Jewish tradition and action against "the Way" is further clarified in another Lukan account of the Damascus experience of Paul. This appears in the context of Paul's defense against the charges of the Jews in Acts 22:

Ἐγώ εἰμι ἀνὴρ Ἰουδαῖος, γεγεννημένος ἐν Ταρσῷ τῆς Κιλικίας, ἀνατεθραμμένος δὲ ἐν τῇ πόλει ταύτῃ, παρὰ τοὺς πόδας Γαμαλιὴλ πεπαιδευμένος κατὰ ἀκρίβειαν τοῦ πατρῴου νόμου, ζηλωτὴς ὑπάρχων τοῦ θεοῦ καθὼς πάντες ὑμεῖς ἐστε σήμερον· ὃς ταύτην τὴν ὁδὸν ἐδίωξα ἄχρι θανάτου, δεσμεύων καὶ παραδιδοὺς εἰς φυλακὰς ἄνδρας τε καὶ γυναῖκας, ὡς καὶ ὁ ἀρχιερεὺς μαρτυρεῖ μοι καὶ πᾶν τὸ πρεσβυτέριον·

I am a Jew, born in Tarsus in Cilicia, but brought up in this city at the feet of Gamaliel, educated strictly according to our ancestral law, being zealous for God, just as all of you are today. I persecuted this Way up to the point of death by binding both men and women and putting them in prison, as the high priest and the whole council of elders can testify about me. (Acts 22:3–5)

In this passage, the full credentials of Paul as a Jew as well as the authority of the Jewish high priest and the council of elders are evoked to set up the contrast with "the Way." The difference in emphasis between Acts 9:1–2 and 22:3–5 should not be missed, however. First, unlike 9:1–2, the persecution mentioned in 22:3–5 centers around the Jerusalem area; but in both cases the zeal of Paul is mentioned and the Christians are identified as those who belonged to "the Way." Therefore, the term "the Way" in Acts 22:4 is also used in a context in which the Christian movement is identifying itself vis-à-vis the Jewish tradition.

Furthermore, the development of the argument contained in the defense speech in 22:3–21 should not be overlooked. The primary purpose for recalling Paul's Jewish credentials is to underscore the continuity between "the Way" and the ancient Jewish traditions. This emphasis is best reflected in the identification of the voice of Jesus as the voice of "the God of our ancestors" (ὁ θεὸς τῶν πατέρων) in 22:14. Paul thus links his ancestral traditions with the understanding that "the Way" is their true legitimate heir. Embedded in this claim is an assertion directed against those who do not belong to "the Way."

Moving away from the accounts of Paul's persecution of the Christians, one finds in the Lukan summary statement of Acts 19:8–9 another absolute use of the way-terminology in a context where opposition against Paul can be felt:

Εἰσελθὼν δὲ εἰς τὴν συναγωγὴν ἐπαρρησιάζετο ἐπὶ μῆνας τρεῖς διαλεγόμενος καὶ πείθων [τὰ] περὶ τῆς βασιλείας τοῦ θεοῦ. ὡς δέ τινες ἐσκληρύνοντο καὶ ἠπείθουν κακολογοῦντες τὴν ὁδὸν ἐνώπιον τοῦ πλήθους, ἀποστὰς ἀπ' αὐτῶν ἀφώρισεν τοὺς μαθητάς, καθ' ἡμέραν διαλεγόμενος ἐν τῇ σχολῇ Τυράννου.

He entered the synagogue and for three months spoke out boldly, and argued persuasively about the kingdom of God. When some stubbornly refused to believe and spoke evil of the Way before the congregation, he left them, taking the disciples with him, and argued daily in the lecture hall of Tyrannus.

As in Acts 9:2, the term "Way" appears in a synagogue setting where the Christians are being challenged. The rhetorical function of "the Way" as an identity marker is apparent. First, the separation of the Christians from the synagogue is in itself a significant symbolic event that distinguishes the two groups. The question why the separation takes place in vss 8–9 and not earlier during the ministry of Apollos in 19:1–7 is left unanswered.[90] What is clear, however, is that the way-terminology appears precisely in the pericope when the separation becomes realized. In addition, the use of the term τινές in reference to those who opposed "the Way" is also significant. Hans Conzelmann notes that the term "belongs to a widespread style of polemical language" and "in this way the believing Jews are indirectly characterized as the true Jews."[91] "The Way" therefore becomes the term that signifies the true people of God who were not "hardened" (ἐσκληρύνοντο, vs 9).

In Acts 19:23, once again, the absolute use of the term "Way" appears in a Lukan summary statement: Ἐγένετο δὲ κατὰ τὸν καιρὸν ἐκεῖνον τάραχος οὐκ ὀλίγος περὶ τῆς ὁδοῦ ("About that time no little disturbance broke out concerning the Way"). The term "the Way" here is also connected with acts of persecution and unrest. While the pericope (19:23–41) may appear at first glance to be primarily concerned with the conflict between Christians and the Ephesian worshippers of Artemis, the curious appearance of the Jew called Alexander at the center of the pericope forces one to reconsider its function:[92]

ἐκ δὲ τοῦ ὄχλου συνεβίβασαν Ἀλέξανδρον, προβαλόντων αὐτὸν τῶν Ἰουδαίων· ὁ δὲ Ἀλέξανδρος κατασείσας τὴν χεῖρα ἤθελεν ἀπολογεῖσθαι τῷ δήμῳ. ἐπιγνόντες δὲ ὅτι Ἰουδαῖός ἐστιν φωνὴ ἐγένετο μία ἐκ πάντων ὡς ἐπὶ ὥρας δύο κραζόντων, Μεγάλη ἡ Ἄρτεμις Ἐφεσίων.

---

[90] For the discussion of the various possibilities, see Ernst Haenchen, *The Acts of the Apostles: A Commentary* (trans. R. McL. Wilson; Oxford: Basil Blackwell, 1971) 560.

[91] Hans Conzelmann, *Acts of the Apostles: A Commentary on the Acts of the Apostles* (trans. James Limburg, A. Thomas Kraabel, and Donald H. Juel; Hermeneia; Philadelphia: Fortress, 1987) 163. A detailed discussion of the polemical use of "some" from Paul to Ignatius can be found in Martin Dibelius and Hans Conzelmann, *The Pastoral Epistles* (trans. Philip Buttolph and Adela Yarbro Collins; Hermeneia; Philadelphia: Fortress, 1972) 71.

[92] Haenchen (*Acts of the Apostles*, 574) considers these verses an "old *crux interpretum.*" See also the discussion in Rick Strelan, *Paul, Artemis, and the Jews in Ephesus* (Berlin/New York: Walter de Gruyter, 1996) 202.

> Some of the crowd gave instructions to Alexander, whom the Jews had pushed forward.
> And Alexander motioned for silence and tried to make a defense before the people. But
> when they recognized that he was a Jew, for about two hours all of them shouted in
> unison, "Great is Artemis of the Ephesians!" (Acts 19:33–34)

Most commentators understand Alexander as a Jew who, pushed forward by
the Jews, represents the Jewish community in an attempt to dissociate
themselves from the Christians (i.e., "the Way").[93] Many have also noted that
the primary meaning and function of these verses remain unclear. Apparently
both the Jews and the Christians opposed the worship of idols. The fine
distinction between them does not appear to be relevant in this episode.[94]
Conzelmann has gone as far as suggesting the possibility that Luke may "no
longer understand his source here."[95]

One possibility is that these two verses appear at the center of the
pericope precisely because of Luke's concern for the relationship between the
(unbelieving-)Jews and the Christians. As in all the previously discussed
passages concerning the use of the way-terminology, the function of this
passage may have to do with the refusal of the Jews to recognize anyone
belonging to "the Way" as one of them. Acts 19:33–34 shows that for non-
Jews a distinction between "the Way" and the Jews cannot or should not be
made, at least as far as their position concerning idol-worship is concerned.[96]
To the Jews, however, the distinction has to be made. Even if one is to
understand the role of Alexander the Jew as one who aims at defending "the
Way," the fact that he is rejected solely because of his Jewishness raises the
same issue concerning the relationship between "the Way" and the Jews. It is
within this discussion of the identity of the Christians over against the
identity of the non-believing Jews that the absolute use of ὁδός appears. This
explains the apparent awkwardness of these two verses, and it is consistent
with the usage of the way-terminology elsewhere in Acts. The identity of
those who belong to "the Way" lies behind the appearance of vss 33–34
within a story that appears otherwise to be a typical mob scene.[97]

---

[93] See, for example, Haenchen, *Acts of the Apostles*, 574; and Gerhard Schneider, *Die Apostelgeschichte* (Freiburg: Herder, 1982) 2.277.

[94] So F. F. Bruce, *The Acts of the Apostles* (3rd ed.; Grand Rapids, MI: Eerdmans, 1990) 419.

[95] Conzelmann, *Acts of the Apostles*, 166.

[96] In his study of this passage within the context of the social world of Jews and Gentiles in the first century, Robert Stoops ("Riot and Assembly: The Social Context of Acts 19:23–41," *JBL* 108 [1989] 73–91) has rightly noted the political interest of Luke in his apologetic attempt to class the early Christians within the broader category of the Jews. His analysis that concentrates on Luke's apologetic claim against the Greco-Roman world does not, however, deal adequately with the tension between "the Way" and the wider "Jewish" world.

[97] This is consistent with the observation of Stoops ("Riot and Assembly: The Social Context of Acts 19:23–41," 80) who suggests that "the reports of anti-Jewish riots present in

Significantly, it is always in the context where the Christians are trying to establish their identity in relation to the Jewish community that the way-terminology appears.

Finally, the definitive passage concerning the function of the way-terminology in Acts appears in Acts 24:10–23. In Paul's speech before Felix, there is a succinct statement concerning "the Way":

> ὁμολογῶ δὲ τοῦτό σοι ὅτι κατὰ τὴν ὁδὸν ἣν λέγουσιν αἵρεσιν οὕτως λατρεύω τῷ πατρῴῳ θεῷ, πιστεύων πᾶσι τοῖς κατὰ τὸν νόμον καὶ τοῖς ἐν τοῖς προφήταις γεγραμμένοις.

> But this I admit to you, that according to the Way, which they call a sect, I worship the God of our ancestors, believing everything laid down according to the law or written in the prophets. (Acts 24:14)[98]

In this statement, the use of the way-terminology as an identity marker is made explicit. First, the contrasting view of the Christian community is presented. While the Christians called themselves "the Way," they were considered a "sect" (αἵρεσιν) by the Jews (cf. vs 9). The word "sect" does not necessarily carry a negative sense in Acts (cf. 5:17; 15:5),[99] but it is used in contexts in which a negative connotation cannot be denied (cf. 24:5; 28:22). No matter how one wishes to understand the word "sect" in 24:14, it is set up as a contrast to the self-understanding of the Christians as "the Way." "The Way" becomes a term that asserts the identity of the early Christians over against the claims of the Jews.

Moreover, the evocation of the "God of our ancestors" and the ancestral traditions in "the law" and the "prophets" should again be understood as a challenge to the competitive claims of the non-believing Jews. The Christian God is the God of the Israelite tradition. With this assertion, the Christians claim to be the true people of God and the true continuation of the ancestral traditions.

From the preceding discussion, one can appreciate the unique function of the way-terminology in the narrative of Acts. The term is not a remnant of Luke's source accidentally appearing in Acts (and nowhere else in early Christian literature). In the narrative of Acts, it is a term that functions as a symbol that defines the identity of the early Christian movement over against the competing claims of the majority culture. Only with this understanding can the conceptual context of this term be examined.

---

historical and apologetic works of Josephus and Philo offer the closest parallels to the riot story in Acts 19."

[98] The way-terminology in 24:22 occurs within the same pericope and derives its meaning (and connotation) from 24:14. Therefore, I will not discuss 24:22 separately.

[99] This is a common word used in reference to the various philosophical schools. See Heinrich Schlier, "αἵρεσις," *TDNT* 1 (1964) 180–84.

The use of this term should be understood against the background of the Isaianic New Exodus. As mentioned above,[100] the term "Way" (דרך) in Isaiah 40–55 became a term that evoked the Exodus tradition and signaled the presence of the new salvific act of God. Furthermore, Isa 40:3 in particular has been evoked in contexts that anticipate the coming of the new age in which God will restore his people.[101] This use originated from the transformation of the Exodus paradigm in Isaiah 40–55 that evokes the national story of Israel in the redefinition of the people of God.[102]

This redefinition in the context of Isaiah should also be understood as an identity claim including some while excluding others in the reconstitution of the "true Israel." In the Lukan writings, therefore, one finds the Isaianic New Exodus tradition used in precisely the same way. The introduction of the new period of salvation history by Isa 40:3–5, which introduces the way-terminology, suggests the Isaianic tradition functions as a hermeneutical principle for the narrative of Luke-Acts. In the narrative of Acts, the absolute use of the way-terminology again evokes the Exodus tradition in an attempt to (re)define the people of God and to establish the identity of the early Christian movement against the competing claims of the other party that also claims to share the ancestral tradition of Israel.[103] This conclusion can be supported by a number of observations.

First, a similar use of the way-terminology as an identity marker in the Qumran literature should now be noted. It has already been suggested that in the Qumran literature one also finds an absolute use of the way-terminology. An often neglected fact, however, is that in both Acts and the Qumran literature, the way-terminology functions as an identity marker; and in the Qumran literature the term's use is also derived from Isa 40:3.[104] In the most often cited passage (1QS 9.16–21) one reads:

---

[100] See section 2.5a above.

[101] See section 2.3 above.

[102] See section 2.5b above.

[103] The differences in the uses of the term "Jews" and "Israel" in the Lukan writings underscore this point. In the Lukan writings, the term "Jews" increasingly becomes one that refers to a group that opposes "the Way." The term "Israel," on the other hand, emphasizes the continuing act of God on behalf of his people (cf. Luke 1:55; Acts 5:31; 28:20). See the discussion in Graham Harvey, *The True Israel: Uses of the Names Jew, Hebrew and Israel in Ancient Jewish and Early Christian Literature* (Leiden: Brill, 1996) 238–45.

[104] For example, while McCasland ("The Way," 222–30) and others have noted the absolute usage of the term "Way" in the Qumran literature, the "function" of the term has not been the focus of these studies. Methodologically, one should begin by examining how the term is used in Acts before identifying the existence of parallels in other traditions. The importance of the Qumran literature lies not in the possibility that it might have been the source text for Acts but in the fact that the usage of the term as an identity marker is present in Jewish literature beyond the text of Acts.

But one must not argue nor quarrel with the men of the pit, so that the counsel of the Torah might be concealed in the midst of the men of deceit. One must argue with true knowledge and righteous judgment (only with) the chosen of the Way, each according to his spirit and according to the norm of the Endtime .... This is the time to prepare the way to the wilderness. He shall instruct them (in) all that is found to be performed in this time. He shall separate himself from each man who has not turned his way from all deceit.[105]

The contrast between the "men of deceit" and "the chosen of the Way" highlights the opposition between the two groups. Those who belong to the community belong to "the Way."[106] In addition, in the same passage, one finds the phrase "preparation of the way into the wilderness," a phrase that alludes to Isa 40:3 that is explicitly cited in 1QS 8.13–16.[107] In the Qumran literature, the way-terminology is again used as an identity marker;[108] and this usage is taken from Isaiah.

In the Qumran literature, however, to belong to "the Way" is to study the law. This should be understood as a further development from the text of Isa 40:3. As in the case of Isaiah, the study of the law is not connected with the way-terminology in Acts. It is neither necessary nor justifiable, therefore, to argue that Acts is dependent upon Qumran in its use of the way-terminology.[109] A more likely hypothesis is that both are dependent on Isa 40:3 and both testify to the fact that the term is used as an identity marker in the Jewish traditions of the late Second Temple period at least in certain marginal groups that attempt to defend themselves against the majority culture.

The recurrence of Isa 40:3–5 throughout the Lukan writings further confirms the dependence of the way-terminology on Isa 40:3. Allusions to Isa

---

[105] In this study, the English translation is taken from James H. Charlesworth et al., eds. *The Dead Sea Scrolls: Hebrew, Aramaic, and Greek Texts with English Translations* (2 vols.; Tübingen: Mohr Siebeck, 1994, 1995), unless otherwise noted.

[106] See also CD 1.11–13: "And he informed the latter generations that which he did in the last generation among the congregation of traitors, who are those who depart from the Way." Cf. CD 2.5–7.

[107] Many have argued that 1QS 9.19–21 should be taken together with 1QS 8.12–16 as reflecting the same redactional layer of the text. Brooke ("Isaiah 40:3 and the Wilderness Community," 125) has further noted that this is confirmed by 4QSᵉ frg. 1 "in which the equivalent of 1QS 9:12–20 follows directly after the equivalent of 1QS 8:11–15."

[108] See Shemaryahu Talmon, "The Community of the Renewed Covenant: Between Judaism and Christianity," in Eugene Ulrich and James Vanderkam, eds., *The Community of the Renewed Covenant* (Notre Dame, IN: University of Notre Dame Press, 1994) 3–24, who argues that the examination of both the continuity and discontinuity of the self-understanding of the Qumran community with the past should commence with the fact that "the Covenanters identify their community as the sole legitimate representative of biblical Israel" (12).

[109] *Contra* McCasland, "The Way," 230; and Fitzmyer, "Jewish Christianity in Acts in Light of the Qumran Scrolls," 241.

40:3–5 beyond Luke 3:4–6 have already been noted above. One additional text should also be mentioned here. In Acts 13:10, the one who opposes the Christians (i.e., "the Way") is one who is "making crooked the straight paths of the Lord" (διαστρέφων τὰς ὁδοὺς τοῦ κυρίου τὰς εὐθείας), a phrase that alludes to Isa 40:3. Again, Isa 40:3 is used to distinguish those who belong to the people of God from those who do not.

Isa 40:3 can no longer be considered merely as the "background" or "source" behind the absolute usage of the way-terminology in Acts. "The Way" functions as a symbol evoking the transformed foundation story of Israel found in Isaiah 40–55 in the construction of the identity of the community. The symbol signifies the movement's continuity with the past as well as its distinctiveness. Luke uses Isaiah 40–55 to articulate the nature of the community in terms of its relationship with and development from Jewish ancestral traditions.

Understanding "the Way" as an identity marker helps explain the diverse referents it embodies. The term cannot be separated from the ethic and teaching that characterizes the community.[110] Naturally the identity of the church is connected with the figure Jesus[111] and has to be understood within the wider plan of salvation history.[112] Nevertheless, the primary meaning of the term is an ecclesiological one for it is used in the definition of the community as the true heir of the ancestral traditions.[113]

---

[110] Cf. Acts 18:25–26. Despite the textual difficulties of these two verses, the term ὁδός with the qualifier τοῦ κυρίου is not used as a designation of the community and therefore is not an exact parallel to the other uses that are discussed above. Nevertheless, the connection with Isa 40:3 is again evident especially in vs 25. See also Hans Kosmala, *Hebräer — Essener — Christen* (SPB 1; Leiden: Brill, 1959) 333; and Schuyler Brown, *Apostasy and Perseverance in the Theology of Luke* (Rome: Biblical Institute Press, 1969) 138–9.

[111] Cf. Acts 9:2; 22:4; and 26:9. In Luke, the Way of the Lord is the ὁδός of Jesus. In Acts, the parallel is not the traveling of the Apostles but the traveling of the "word" that offers salvation. The relationship between the absolute use of the ὁδός terminology in Acts and the more general use of the term is a complex issue that goes beyond the limit of this chapter.

[112] The connection between traveling and the way-terminology will be explored more fully in chapter five that deals with the conquest of the word of God. More specifically, the carrying out of the divine plan and the extension of the domain of the acts of God will be considered. Although Brown (*Apostasy and Perseverance in the Theology of Luke,* 141) might be right in arguing that the way-terminology is not primarily related to the journey motif in Acts, he goes too far in suggesting that in the use of this term in Acts "all connection with external geographical movement is abandoned."

[113] In Isa 40:3, the call for the preparation of the Way of the Lord is also the call for the preparation of the people (cf. Luke 1:76–77).

2.7 Conclusion

In this chapter, I have shown how Luke used Isa 40:3–5 in the formulation of the identity of the early Christian community. This is carried out through the presentation of the story of the early Christian community according to the thematic framework provided by Isa 40:1–11; a point that will become more clear in the following chapters of this study. The Isaianic program is also evoked through the uses of the symbol "the Way" in the description of the community. Both the Isaianic themes and the way-terminology argue for the understanding of the early Christian community as the true heir of the Israelite traditions. This parallels the use of the Exodus traditions in Isaiah 40–55 that attempts to redefine the identity of the people of God for the exilic communities. It is the formative power of the foundation story of Israel that ties the Isaianic program and the narrative of Acts together for both are concerned with the issue of continuity and discontinuity.

Chapter 3

Isaiah and the Hermeneutical Framework of Acts: Statements that Frame the Narrative

3.1 Introduction

In the previous chapter, I discussed the importance of Isa 40:1–11 in the Lukan writings for the portrayal of the identity of the early Christian movement. Before examining the various prominent Isaianic themes that reappear in Acts,[1] I will show how specific Isaianic statements are used at critical points in the narrative of the Lukan writings to provide meaning for the development of the story in Acts. I will concentrate on five passages often considered programmatic for the development of the Lukan story in Acts. I will show that the Isaianic New Exodus tradition is evoked in all five passages to depict the significance of the new movement in light of its claim of continuity with the past.

While many recognize the appearance of isolated Isaianic quotations in the Lukan writings, most fail to see the importance of Isaiah in the construction of the structure of the story as well as its function in the establishment of the Lukan claim concerning the identity of the community.[2] Behind this study is the assumption that the Lukan writings reflect and participate in the struggles and concerns of a community at the intersection between a past it tries to claim and a future it attempts to create.

3.2 Luke 4:16–30

Many follow Martin Dibelius[3] and Rudolf Bultmann[4] in identifying Mark 6:1–6 (par. Matt 13:53–58) as the basic source from which Luke constructs his synagogue scene in Nazareth. Both passages locate the scene in a

---

[1] These will be presented in chapters four to seven below.

[2] See the survey of scholarship in chapter one above.

[3] Martin Dibelius, *From Tradition to Gospel* (New York: Scribner, 1965) 110.

[4] Rudolf Bultmann, *The History of the Synoptic Tradition* (trans. John Marsh; New York: Harper & Row, 1963) 31–32, 386–87.

synagogue in Nazareth on a Sabbath. Both contain a question in regard to Jesus' origin, and both report Jesus' reply with a proverb concerning the rejection of a prophet in his own hometown.[5] Beyond this framework (Luke 4:16, 22–24, 28–29), however, there are elements that suggest a non-Markan origin.[6] While some have suggested that influences from Q may be detectable behind this pericope,[7] others argue that Luke has other traditional sources at his disposal.[8] Most, however, agree that Luke reshaped the material he inherited to express his particular theological concerns.

All Lukan scholars recognize the significance of Luke 4:16–30; and as Jack Sanders aptly notes: "This scene is 'programmatic' for Luke-Acts, as one grows almost tired of reading in the literature of the passage ...."[9] In this section, I will discuss the function of this Isaianic quotation and the way Luke interprets the quotation through the accompanying interpretive context. First, the text of the Isaianic quotation itself should be noted.

a. The Text of the Isaianic Quotation in Luke 4:18–19

As many have shown, a chiastic structure can be identified in Luke 4:16–21.[10] The parallelism cannot be denied: the mentioning of the synagogue (vss 16, 20); Jesus standing and sitting down (vss 16, 20); Jesus being given and giving

---

[5] For a detailed comparison of the two passages, see Gabriel K.-S. Shin, *Die Ausrufung des endgültigen Jubeljahres durch Jesus in Nazareth: Eine historisch-kritische Studie zu Lk 4,16–30* (Europäische Hochschulschriften 23.378; Frankfurt am Main/New York: Peter Lang, 1989) 322–34. For a review of the discussion concerning the source-critical issues surrounding this pericope, see also Christopher J. Schreck, "The Nazareth Pericope: Luke 4:16–30 in Recent Study," in Frans Neirynck, ed., *L'Évangile de Luc — The Gospel of Luke* (BETL 32; Leuven: Leuven University Press, 1989) 403–27.

[6] The most obvious is the episode about Elijah and Elisha which Bultmann (*History of the Synoptic Tradition*, 31) himself also considers as deriving from an Aramaic tradition.

[7] See, for example, Heinz Schürmann, *Das Lukasevangelium* (HKNT 3; Freiburg: Herder, 1969) 1.227–28, 241–42; Christopher M. Tuckett, "Luke 4,16–30, Isaiah and Q," in J. Delobel, ed., *Logia: Les Paroles de Jésus — The Sayings of Jesus. Mémorial Joseph Coppens* (BETL 59; Leuven: Leuven University Press, 1982) 347–8, and the critique of these proposals in Max M. Turner, "The Spirit and the Power of Jesus' Miracles in the Lucan Conception," *NovT* 33 (1991) 150–52.

[8] Cf. Bruce D. Chilton, "Announcement in Nazara," in R. T. France and David Wenham, eds., *Gospel Perspectives II* (Sheffield: JSOT Press, 1981) 164; and Max M. Turner, *Power from on High. The Spirit in Israel's Restoration and Witness in Luke-Acts* (Sheffield: Sheffield Academic Press, 1996) 219. François Bovon (*Das Evangelium nach Lukas: 1. Teilband Lk 1,1–9,50* [EKK III/1; Zürich: Benziger Verlag, 1989] 206–8) also argues that Luke found in Q or Luke's *Sondergut* a version of the story in which certain non-Markan elements had already been incorporated.

[9] Jack T. Sanders, *The Jews in Luke-Acts* (London: SCM, 1987) 165.

[10] See, for example, Donald R. Miesner, "The Circumferential Speeches of Luke-Acts," *SBLSP* 14 (1978) 2.223–4; and David L. Tiede, *Prophecy and History in Luke-Acts* (Philadelphia: Fortress, 1980) 103–7.

back the book (vss 17, 20); and Jesus opening and closing the book (vss 17, 20). At the center of this chiastic structure is the reading from Isaiah (vss 18–19):[11]

Πνεῦμα κυρίου ἐπ ' ἐμέ, οὗ εἵνεκεν ἔχρισέν με εὐαγγελίσασθαι πτωχοῖς, ἀπέσταλκέν με κηρύξαι αἰχμαλώτοις ἄφεσιν καὶ τυφλοῖς ἀνάβλεψιν, ἀποστεῖλαι τεθραυσμένους ἐν ἀφέσει, κηρύξαι ἐνιαυτὸν κυρίου δεκτόν.

The Spirit of the Lord is upon me, because he has anointed me to bring good news to the poor. He has sent me to proclaim release to the captives and recovery of sight to the blind, to let the oppressed go free, to proclaim the year of the Lord's favor.

This quotation (Isa 61:1–2 with 58:6) is most certainly taken from the LXX with four changes:[12] First, the clause ἰάσασθαι τοὺς συντετριμμένους τῇ καρδίᾳ (Isa 61:1c) is omitted in Luke 4:18. Second, a clause from Isa 58:6 is inserted in Luke 4:18: ἀποστεῖλαι τεθραυσμένους ἐν ἀφέσει.[13] Third, instead of καλέσαι (Isa 61:2) Luke 4:19 has κηρύξαι. Fourth, the Isaianic quotation in Luke 4:19 stops at κηρύξαι ἐνιαυτὸν κυρίου δεκτόν without including the next phrase that appears in Isa 61:2 (καὶ ἡμέραν ἀνταποδόσεως).

It has been suggested that the clause ἰάσασθαι τοὺς συντετριμμένους τῇ καρδίᾳ (Isa 61:1c) might have been deleted in the early textual traditions and should be included as part of the Lukan citation of Isaiah.[14] This inclusion is supported by some manuscripts[15] but the external evidence[16] still favors its omission in Luke 4:18.[17] It is difficult in any case to explain why Luke would omit the phrase. Bruce Chilton[18] attributes this quotation (with the omission)

---

[11] This study is more concerned with the narratological significance of the Isaiah quotation and not the historical background of the synagogue reading. For a discussion of the traditional character of the Isaiah reading, see L. C. Crockett, "Luke iv 16–30 and the Jewish Lectionary Cycle: A Word of Caution," *JJS* 17 (1966) 45; Charles Perrot, *La lecture de la Bible dans la synagogue: Les anciennes lectures palestiniennes du Shabbat et des fêtes* (Hildesheim: Gerstenberg, 1973) 195–204; Chilton, "Announcement in Nazara," 164; and Michael Prior, *Jesus the Liberator: Nazareth Liberation Theology (Luke 4:16–30)* (Sheffield: Sheffield Academic Press, 1996) 132.

[12] For the text of the LXX, I am relying on Joseph Ziegler, *Isaias* (3rd ed., Septuaginta 14; Göttingen: Vandenhoek & Ruprecht, 1983).

[13] The LXX of Isa 58:6 has ἀπόστελλε instead of ἀποστεῖλαι.

[14] See, for example, Bo Reicke, "Jesus in Nazareth — Lk 4, 14–30," in Horst Baly and Siegfried Schulz, eds., *Das Wort und die Wörter. FS Gerhard Friedrich* (Stuttgart: W. Kohlhammer, 1973) 48–49; and Schürmann, *Lukasevangelium*, 1.229.

[15] A Θ Ψ 0102 f¹ 𝔐 f vg^cl sy^p.h bo^mss.

[16] ℵ B D L W Ξ f¹³ 33. 579. 700. 892* pc lat sy* co.

[17] In addition, it is difficult to explain why the phrase is deleted especially when its inclusion seems to support Luke's theological program. For a further discussion, see Shin, *Die Ausrufung des endgültigen Jubeljahres durch Jesus in Nazareth*, 21.

[18] Bruce D. Chilton, *A Galilean Rabbi and His Bible: Jesus' Use of the Interpreted Scripture of His Time* (Wilmington, DE: Michael Glazier, 1984) 181.

to a traditional source while Traugott Holtz[19] suggests that the clause was misplaced in Luke's copy of the LXX Isaiah. One can only conclude that the omission is probably not due to any apparent theological reasons.[20]

The inclusion of the clause ἀποστεῖλαι τεθραυσμένους ἐν ἀφέσει from Isa 58:6, however, needs further examination. The connection with Isa 61:1–2 seems to be made with ἄφεσις, a word that appears in both Isa 58:6 and 61:1.[21] The clause from Isa 58:6 is identical with the LXX reading except for the change from the imperative ἀπόστελλε to the aorist infinitive ἀποστεῖλαι to conform to the other subordinate infinitives. The connection of the two Isaianic passages through the word ἄφεσις should be understood as an example of "deliberate exegesis."[22] The clause may have been inserted to emphasize the idea of release and therefore the connection with the Jubilee of Isa 61:1.[23] More importantly, this insertion highlights Jesus not only as one who proclaims the arrival of the Jubilee but also as one who is appointed to accomplish the inbreaking of the new era through his power to bring about ἄφεσις.[24]

The change from καλέσαι to κηρύξαι in Luke 4:19 may be the result of the influence from the widespread Christian usage of the term κηρύσσω.[25] Moreover, κηρύσσω is a term that appears frequently in Luke and Acts and thus a favorite term of the author himself.[26]

---

[19] Traugott Holtz, *Untersuchungen über die alttestamentlichen Zitate bei Lukas* (TU 104; Berlin: Akademie-Verlag, 1968) 125.

[20] But see Martin Rese, *Alttestamentliche Motive in der Christologie des Lukas* (StNT 1; Gütersloh: Gütersloher Verlagshaus, 1969) 145, who suggests that Luke does not want to emphasize the healings of Jesus to highlight the prophetic emphasis. This, however, is not supported by the Lukan context (cf. Luke 4:23, 27).

[21] Cf. Darrell L. Bock, *Proclamation from Prophecy and Pattern: Lucan Old Testament Christology* (JSNTSup 12; Sheffield: Sheffield Academic Press, 1987), 106–7.

[22] Bart J. Koet (*Five Studies on Interpretation of Scripture in Luke-Acts* [SNTA 14; Leuven: Leuven University Press, 1989] 30) understands these texts as combined by a hermeneutical rule that is the forerunner of *gezerah shavah* (verbal analogy between verses).

[23] Robert B. Sloan, *The Favorable Year of the Lord: A Study of Jubilary Theology in the Gospel of Luke* (Austin, TX: Schola Press, 1977) 36–37: "This word [ἄφεσις] represents doubtless the primary theological and verbal connection, and reference to, the levitical proclamation of jubilee." The combination of Isa 61:1 with 58:6 can also be found in Second Temple Jewish traditions. See Bovon, *Das Evangelium nach Lukas*, 1.211–12.

[24] This term acquires a sense of "forgiveness" in the rest of the Gospel and especially in Acts.

[25] Bock, *Proclamation from Prophecy and Pattern*, 106. The LXX manuscripts that also adopt the reading with κηρύξαι may be due to influence from Luke 4:19. See Ziegler, *Isaias*, 348.

[26] This seems to be a better explanation than the one suggested by Holtz (*Untersuchungen über die alttestamentlichen Zitate bei Lukas*, 40) who argues that the author has made a simple error in reduplicating the word κηρύξαι from the previous verse (Luke 4:18).

Finally, the omission of the rest of Isa 61:2 is probably an attempt to highlight the phrase κηρύξαι ἐνιαυτὸν κυρίου δεκτόν in Luke 4:19 as the climax of the reading of Scripture. This is confirmed by the importance of the adjective δεκτός (vs 24) in the narrative that follows.[27]

b. The Evocation of Isa 61:1–2: The New Age for the People of God

In evoking this Isaianic passage, which occurs only here among the synoptic gospels, Luke introduces the framework in which his writings should be understood. The various isolated events now signify the coming of a new age that is in continuity with the ancient Israelite traditions. This is embodied in the statement in Luke 4:21: Σήμερον πεπλήρωται ἡ γραφὴ αὕτη ἐν τοῖς ὠσὶν ὑμῶν ("Today this Scripture has been fulfilled in your hearing").

The various components expressed in the Isaianic quotation provide categories for the organization of events in the Jesus traditions: (1) to bring good news to the poor; (2) to proclaim release to the captives; (3) to restore sight to the blind; (4) to let the oppressed go free; and (5) to proclaim the year of the Lord's favor. Max Turner[28] has argued that the first four phrases express the same concern: the oppressed situation of Israel, the people of God. All five, therefore, are concerned with the salvation of Israel from her low estate. This theological and political reading is confirmed by the reference to "the poor" in a non-social sense in Luke 2:34. One may also add that all five clauses refer to the same arrival of the salvation of God in the context of Isaiah.[29] In light of Luke 7:22, however, a literal sense cannot be totally excluded although the broader meaning of the message should be retained. These clauses should therefore be understood as the manifestations of the arrival of salvation for Israel.

Such categorization allows Luke to emphasize his understanding of the new era as a legitimate continuation of the history of the people of God. The same scheme that is provided by Isaiah resurfaces in the Lukan writings precisely in places where the identity of the early Christian movement is being questioned. In Luke 7:18–20, a question is raised concerning the exact nature and meaning of Jesus' ministry. Jesus' response alludes again to Isa 61:1 where the arrival of the new era is characterized as one in which "the blind receive their sight, the lame walk, the lepers are cleansed, the deaf hear, the dead are raised, the poor have good news brought to them" (τυφλοὶ

---

[27] It is not impossible that the theme of judgment is intentionally omitted in this programmatic statement (Joseph Fitzmyer, *The Gospel According to Luke (I–IX)* [AB 28; Garden City, NY: Doubleday, 1981] 533); but this is unlikely since the theme of judgment has already been introduced in Luke 2:34–35 and 3:7–17 and it reappears in the rest of Luke-Acts.

[28] Turner, *Power from on High*, 250.

[29] The vocabularies of εὐαγγελίζω and πτωχοῖς and the metaphors of sight/blindness and freedom/captivity play an important role in Isaiah.

ἀναβλέπουσιν, χωλοὶ περιπατοῦσιν, λεπροὶ καθαρίζονται καὶ κωφοὶ ἀκούουσιν, νεκροὶ ἐγείρονται, πτωχοὶ εὐαγγελίζονται, Luke 7:22). While this passage is most likely taken from Q (cf. Matt 11:4–5),[30] its connection with the Lukan Nazareth pericope cannot be dismissed. The reappearance of the Isaianic scheme reflects the hermeneutical importance of Isaiah 61 for the identity of the early Christian movement.

Concern with the question of the identity of the early Christian movement is most clear in Acts 10:35–38 where Isa 61:1 is again evoked. This text explicitly notes that the message of Isa 61:1 is addressed "to the people of Israel" (τοῖς υἱοῖς Ἰσραήλ, Acts 10:36). The linguistic parallels between Acts 10:35–38 and the Nazareth synagogue scene have been well established.[31] The words λόγον ὃν ἀπέστειλεν[32] in vs 36 remind one of ἀπέσταλκέν με in Luke 4:18 (Isa 61:1),[33] and the participle εὐαγγελιζόμενος recalls εὐαγγελίσασθαι in Luke 4:18 (cf. Luke 7:22).[34] Acts 10:37 provides the setting for the following verse by the phrase ἀρξάμενος ἀπὸ τῆς Γαλιλαίας μετὰ τὸ βάπτισμα ὃ ἐκήρυξεν Ἰωάννης ("beginning in Galilee after the baptism that John announced"), a phrase that most naturally reminds one of the setting of Luke 4 (esp. vs 14). The reference to Nazareth in Acts 10:38 is also significant for this is the only reference to Nazareth in Acts. Moreover, the previous instance that makes reference to Nazareth in Luke-Acts is in Luke 4:16.[35] Finally the following statement that Jesus was "anointed" (ἔχρισεν) by God can be considered a conscious reference back to Luke 4:18 in which one finds at the beginning of the quotation from Isa 61: "The Spirit of the Lord is upon me, because he has anointed (ἔχρισεν)[36] me." Here, one begins to see that the explicit quotation

---

[30] So Fitzmyer, *Gospel According to Luke (I–IX)*, 662–63; Schürmann, *Lukasevangelium*, 1.413, 418; and Bovon, *Das Evangelium nach Lukas*, 1.369. The wordings in the phrase from Isaiah that appears in Matt 11:5 and Luke 7:22 are almost identical. The only difference is the three additional καί that appear in the Matthean text.

[31] See, especially, Max M. Turner, "Jesus and the Spirit in Lucan Perspective," *TynBul* 32 (1981) 22–23; and idem, *Power from on High*, 262.

[32] See Charles K. Barrett, *A Critical and Exegetical Commentary on the Acts of the Apostles* (ICC; Edinburgh: T & T Clark, 1994) 1.521–22 concerning the grammatical issues surrounding this phrase.

[33] This verse may also have been influenced by Ps 106:20 LXX.

[34] It should also be noted that both phrases (εὐαγγελιζόμενος εἰρήνην [Acts 10:36] and εὐαγγελίσασθαι πτωχοῖς [Luke 4:18; cf. 7:22]) are derived from Isaiah (52:7 and 61:1). The two are connected also in 11QMelch 16–18. See Turner, *Power From on High*, 262.

[35] The Semitic form Ναζαρά is used in Luke 4:16 while Ναζαρέθ is used elsewhere in Luke-Acts (Luke 1:26; 2:4, 39, 51; Acts 10:38). It is uncertain whether this indicates that a Semitic source is behind Luke 4. See Fitzmyer, *Gospel According to Luke (I–IX)*, 526–27, 530.

[36] The only other occurrence of the same verb in the Lukan writings is in Acts 4:27 where it is also used with the anointment of Jesus. It is curious that in spite of the clear

of Isaiah and the various allusions that follow become tools with which Luke is able to construct his theological claim.

Luke's concern for the identity of the community shows that a narrow christological reading of the Nazareth pericope is unjustifiable. The debate concerning the exact identity of Jesus as reflected in Luke 4:16–30 does not seem to be a primary concern of Luke. It is the introduction of the wider Isaianic program concerning the people of God that is central to the Lukan narrative.[37]

This ecclesiological reading is affirmed by the ambiguous nature of the identity of Jesus in Luke 4:16–30. Many have argued concerning whether Jesus is portrayed as a prophetic[38] or a messianic[39] figure in this Nazareth pericope. This debate is misformulated and resembles discussions concerning the identity of the Servant in Isaiah 40–55.[40] A brief discussion of the issue concerning the identity of the Isaianic servant may be helpful here. First, the connections between Isaiah 61 and the Servant Songs in Isaiah 40–55 have to be noted. Like the figure in Isaiah 61, the servant of Isaiah 40–55 also has the "spirit" that the Lord laid upon him (42:1) and knows that he was "sent" by the Lord with his Spirit (48:16). The use of infinitives to designate the tasks of the figure in Isaiah 61 also reminds one of the description of the servant in 40–55. This is most clear in the first Servant Song when the Lord sends his Servant "to open the eyes that are blind, to bring out the prisoners from the dungeon" (42:7). The exact nature of the "imprisonment" is further elaborated and interpreted in Isa 61:1–2. It is in this sense that Isaiah 61 has been understood as an "interpretation of Isaiah 40–55."[41] One is also able to find

---

linguistic and thematic parallels between Luke 4 and 10:38 especially in reference to the verb χρίω, Barrett (*Acts of the Apostles*, 1.524) still ignores the connection between the two. His argument for the reference back to Lukan Baptismal scene needs to be qualified.

[37] Here, the identity of Jesus as the prophet is important primarily as it relates to the question of his rejection by the Jews; and this should be understood in light of the eventual development of the Gentile-majority community of Luke.

[38] See, for example, John Nolland, *Luke* (WBC 35; Dallas, TX: Word, 1989) 1.196; and Paul F. Feiler, "Jesus the Prophet: The Lucan Portrayal of Jesus as the Prophet like Moses" (Ph.D. diss., Princeton Theological Seminary, 1986).

[39] Schürmann, *Lukasevangelium*, 1.229; and Mark L. Strauss, *The Davidic Messiah in Luke-Acts: The Promise and Its Fulfillment in Lukan Christology* (JSNTSup 110; Sheffield: Sheffield Academic Press, 1995) 230–33.

[40] See the discussion on this issue from Christopher R. North, *The Suffering Servant in Deutero-Isaiah: An Historical and Critical Study* (London: Oxford University Press, 1948) to Gordon P. Hugenberger, "The Servant of the Lord in the 'Servant Songs' of Isaiah: A Second Moses Figure," in P. E. Satterthwaite, R. S. Hess, and G. J. Wenham, eds., *The Lord's Anointed* (Carlisle: Paternoster, 1995) 105–40.

[41] See W. A. M. Beuken, "Servant and Herald of Good Tidings. Isaiah 61 as an Interpretation of Isaiah 40–55," in J. Vermeylen, ed., *The Book of Isaiah — Le Livre d'Isaïe. Les oracles et leurs relectures. Unité et complexité de l'ouvrage* (BETL 81; Leuven: Leuven

parallels to the idea of the "acceptable year" in 40:2 and 49:8.[42] It is therefore justifiable to conclude that the figure in 61:1 is modeled upon (if not identical with) the servant figure in 40–55.[43]

Once the connections between Isaiah 61 and the Servant Songs in 40–55 have been established, the identity of the Servant in Isaiah 40–55 becomes relevant for the discussion of the identity of Jesus in Luke 4:16–30.[44] As the Isaianic servant encompasses both prophetic and messianic characteristics, the Lukan Jesus also displays both prophetic and messianic features.[45] Both christological emphases have already been united in the figure of the Isaianic servant. Therefore, the focus of the examination of Luke 4:16–30 should not be upon the debate concerning the precise christological identity of Jesus.

Moving away from the atomistic examination of particular Isaianic quotations in the Lukan writings, one will recognize that the nature of the Isaianic program for the new era is at least as important as the christological focus. The significance of the Isaianic quotation in Luke 4:16–30 lies in the introduction of the Isaianic New Exodus with the claim that the Christians are now the legitimate heirs of the ancient Israelite traditions.[46] Many have highlighted the importance of the connections between Jesus' proclamation in Luke 4 and the Jubilee,[47] but more important for the rest of the Lukan writings are the connections with the wider program of the Isaianic New Exodus.[48]

University Press, 1989) 411–42. Beuken also notes that the reinterpretation of the concept of captivity that appears frequently in Isaiah 40–55 can already be found in Isa 61:1–2 that takes on the sense of "internal imprisonment" (418). This seems to have paved the way for the further spiritualization of the concept of captivity in the Lukan writings.

[42] For a more detailed discussion of the numerous parallels, see Norman H. Snaith, "Isaiah 40–66: A Study of the Teaching of the Second Isaiah and Its Consequences," in N. H. Snaith and H. M. Orlinsky, eds., *Studies on the Second Part of the Book of Isaiah* (VTSup 14; Leiden: Brill, 1967) 139–41.

[43] One should again be reminded that the ancient readers (including Luke) do not operate under the understanding of the multiple-Isaiahs.

[44] Note that Jesus is explicitly identified as the Servant of Isaiah 53 in Acts 8:34.

[45] This is also the conclusion of Strauss, *Davidic Messiah in Luke-Acts*, 244–49.

[46] Please also refer to chapter two above.

[47] See, especially, Sloan, *Favorable Year of the Lord;* and Prior, *Jesus the Liberator.*

[48] Cf. Robert C. Tannehill, *The Narrative Unity of Luke-Acts: A Literary Interpretation* (Foundations and Facets; Philadelphia: Fortress Press, 1986–1990) 1.68: "While it seems clear that Isa 61:1–2 develops themes from the Jubilee year, it is not so clear that the author of Luke-Acts was aware of the connection between this passage and the law of Jubilee." Similarly, Turner, *Power from on High*, 244: "While Luke's source may have presented Jesus as inaugurating an Isaianic messianic Jubilee, Luke himself does not draw attention to distinctively Jubilee language or ideas in his writings."

c. The Reinterpretation of Isa 61:1–2: The Lukan Redefinition of the People of God

The significance of the Nazareth pericope lies not only in the Isaianic quotation but more importantly in the Lukan interpretation and qualification of this quotation. Here, the issues concerning (1) the rejection by the people of God (i.e., Jews) and (2) the reconstitution of the people of God with the inclusion of the Gentiles become the focus of Luke's reappropriation of the Nazareth scene and also of his reinterpretation of the Isaianic tradition. These issues become directly relevant in the claim of the early Christians to be the people of God. The presence of these concerns in Luke 4 shows that the Lukan Nazareth pericope is also programmatic for the narrative of Acts.

The beginning of the Lukan story in the hometown of Jesus dramatizes the theme of the rejection of the prophet of God by his own people. In Mark (6:1–6; cf. Matt 13:52–58), the Nazareth pericope is located in the midst of Jesus' ministry in Galilee. In Luke, however, this story has been moved to the very beginning of Jesus' ministry and therefore contains Jesus' first statement concerning his public ministry. The fact that Luke is aware of the Markan chronology is evident from the statement in Luke 4:23 where Jesus' ministry in Capernaum is mentioned.[49] This stands in contrast to Luke 4:31 where Capernaum is introduced for the first time. These references can be explained only against the background of the Markan framework.[50] This interpretation of the Markan story highlights the relationship between the early Christian movement and others who also claim to be the people of God.

A further discussion of the theme of rejection necessarily involves the question of the inner coherence of the Lukan Nazareth scene and the reason for the negative attitude expressed by the crowd. Whereas it does not seem plausible that the audience was provoked by the omission of the mentioning of God's vengeance on the Gentiles in the quotation of Isa 61:1–2 in Luke 4:18–19 and expressed in the reaction of the audience in Luke 4:22,[51] it appears that the turning point should be located somewhere between Jesus' mentioning of the proverb in Luke 4:23 and the usage of the examples of Elijah

---

[49] The appeal to the summary statement in Luke 4:15 as containing the Capernaum ministry is unconvincing. Cf. William L. Lane, *The Gospel According to Mark* (NICNT; Grand Rapids, MI: Eerdmans, 1974) 201.

[50] For a further discussion of the theological relationship between Nazareth and Capernaum in Luke, see Jean-Noël Aletti, "Jésus à Nazareth (Lc 4, 16–30): Prophétie Écriture et Typologie," *À Cause de l'Évangile: Études sur les Synoptiques et les Actes: Offertes au P. Jacques Dupont, O. S. B. à l'occasion de son 70ᵉ anniversaire* (Paris: Cerf, 1985) 438–39.

[51] This is suggested by Joachim Jeremias, *Jesus' Promise to the Nations* (trans. S. H. Hooke; Philadelphia: Fortress, 1982) 44–6. See the critique of Jeremias' position in John Nolland, "Words of Grace (Luke 4:22)," *Bib* 84 (1984) 52; and Shin, *Die Ausrufung des endgültigen Jubeljahres durch Jesus in Nazareth*, 197–204.

and Elisha in Luke 4:25–27.[52] First, Classical and Rabbinic parallels show that the proverb "Doctor, cure yourself!" (Luke 4:23a) may imply a question concerning Jesus' ability or a challenge for Jesus to prove his claim.[53] The request for Jesus to do in his hometown (ἐν τῇ πατρίδι σου) what he did in Capernaum in 4:23b highlights the distinction between native and foreign Lands. The comment about how the prophet is not welcome (δεκτός)[54] in his own land in 4:24 further identifies Jesus as the prophet and indicates that his rejection is imminent. Luke 4:24 also highlights the motif of rejection by those who are ἐν τῇ πατρίδι αὐτοῦ.[55] The contrast between the native and the foreign becomes especially clear in the usage of the stories of Elijah and Elisha in 4:25–27. The response of the Jews in 4:28–29 can thus be understood against the background of the contrast between the Jews and the Gentiles.[56] Even if one concludes that the hostility from the audience is "insufficiently motivated,"[57] one has to admit that this pericope does successfully highlight two important Lukan themes: the rejection by the Jews and the issue of the contrast between the Jews and the Gentiles. One can only agree with John Drury when he observes that Luke 4:16–30 "is the prototype of similar scenes in Acts where Christians will preach the gospel and meet with a

---

[52] To attempt to locate the turning point of the narrative in one single point of the narrative as many have tried may be a fruitless effort. Henry Cadbury (*The Making of Luke-Acts* [New York: Macmillan, 1927] 334) correctly notes that "some obscurity may be intentional" and that "mob scenes at Nazareth, Corinth and Ephesus are not explained as logical performances." For a useful survey of the various scholarly positions on this issue, see Schreck, "The Nazareth Pericope: Luke 4,16–30 in Recent Study," 427–36.

[53] See John Nolland, "Classical and Rabbinic Parallels to 'Physician, Heal Yourself' (Lk. IV.2)," *NovT* 21 (1979) 193–209. This, of course, requires one to understand σεαυτόν in an individual sense as referring back to Jesus himself. For a corporate reading of σεαυτόν and therefore an understanding of the proverb in the sense of "Doctor, heal those who are around you," see Sijbolt J. Noorda, "'Cure Yourself, Doctor!' (Luke 4:23). Classical Parallels to an Alleged Saying of Jesus," in J. Delobel, ed., *Logia: Les Paroles de Jésus — The Sayings of Jesus. Mémorial Joseph Coppens* (BETL 59; Leuven: Leuven University Press, 1982) 463.

[54] Against the background of Isaiah, Koet (*Five Studies on Interpretation of Scripture in Luke-Acts*, 42–43) argues that δεκτός may take the sense of "pleasing" in the Lukan context and therefore Jesus is indicating that a prophet does not exist to please his fellow citizens. This interpretation draws attention to the contrast between the native and the foreign in 4:24 but does not alter too much the overall emphasis of the whole pericope.

[55] John C. O'Neill, "The Six Amen Sayings in Luke," *JTS* 10 (1959) 1, notes that the word ἀμήν is used in Luke to highlight key points of Jesus' teaching in the development of the narrative.

[56] It seems justifiable to argue that while the term πατρίς in 4:23 only refers to Nazareth (as over against Capernaum), it acquires a broader meaning in 4:24. In 4:27, it seems clear that the distinction between Jews and Gentiles is present.

[57] Robert L. Brawley, *Luke-Acts and the Jews: Conflict, Apology, and Conciliation* (SBLMS 33; Atlanta, GA: Scholars Press, 1987) 17.

hostile, even violent response,"[58] although the particular issue of "Jewish" opposition should also be considered.

It is only within this discussion of the theme of rejection that the identity of Jesus as the prophet can be explicated. The connection between the two is made explicit in Jesus' statement in Luke 4:24: "Truly I tell you, no prophet is accepted in the prophet's hometown." In addition, the examples of the prophets Elijah and Elisha in vss 25–27 confirm this understanding.[59] This portrayal of Jesus as the prophet is confirmed in the rest of the Lukan writings,[60] and Luke explicitly identifies Jesus as the "prophet like Moses" in Acts 3:22–23. Most significant of all is that, in the context of an allusion back to Isa 61:1 in Luke 7:22, Jesus is identified as "a great prophet" (προφήτης μέγας, Luke 7:16). Alongside such christological identification is the inherently related theme of rejection by the prophet's own countrymen.

This qualification of the jubilant message of Isa 61:1–2 serves to make sense out of the significant opposition of the Jews against both the early Christian movement and its "founder." It also explains the existence of a group claiming to be the people of God but not necessarily constituted by a Jewish majority. Given the recurring rejection of the prophet of God within the Israelite tradition, Luke can justify the existence of a movement that claims to be the people of God but is at the same time rejected by many making the same claim. This theme of rejection unites the narratives in both Luke and Acts.

The second theme that Luke emphasizes in his reinterpretation of Isa 61:1–2 is the inclusion of the Gentiles. The discussion of this issue in Luke 4 shows how the Isaianic New Exodus functions as a hermeneutical key to both Luke and Acts. While some have attempted to limit the significance of the stories of Elijah and Elisha in 4:25–27 to an illustration of the rejection of God's prophet,[61] most see in 4:25–27 at least a hint of the future Gentile mission that will play a prominent role in Acts.[62] The former position fails to

---

[58] John Drury, *Tradition and Design in Luke's Gospel: A Study of Early Christian Historiography* (Atlanta, GA: John Knox, 1976) 87.

[59] One can also find the identification of Elijah as the New Moses in the Jewish traditions of the Second Temple period. See Turner, *Power from on High*, 238–40.

[60] Cf. Luke 7:16, 39; 13:33–34; 16:31; Acts 7:52.

[61] See, especially, Koet, *Five Studies on Interpretation of Scripture in Luke-Acts*, 46–47; and Brawley, *Luke-Acts and the Jews*, 26. Cf. Nolland, *Luke*, 1.201.

[62] See, for example, Stephen G. Wilson, *The Gentiles and the Gentile Mission in Luke-Acts* (SNTSMS 23; Cambridge: Cambridge University Press, 1973) 40–41; I. Howard Marshall, *The Gospel of Luke: A Commentary on the Greek Text* (NIGTC; Grand Rapids, MI: Eerdmans, 1978) 188; Jacques Dupont, "La conclusion des Actes et son rapport à l'ensemble de l'ouvrage de Luc," in Jacob Kremer, ed., *Les Actes des Apôtres: Traditions, rédaction, théologie* (BETL 48; Leuven: Leuven University Press, 1979) 400; Tannehill, *Narrative Unity of Luke-Acts*, 1.71; Joseph Tyson, "The Gentile Mission and the Authority of Scripture in Acts," *NTS* 33 (1987) 619–31; Bovon, *Das Evangelium nach Lukas*, 1.215;

appreciate the significance of the juxtaposition of the Isaianic quotation in 4:18–19 and the Elijah/Elisha examples in 4:25–27. Jeffrey Siker has rightly suggested that 4:25–27 is the interpretive key to the whole story as the themes of προφήτης, δεκτός, and πατρίς, which were anticipated in 4:16–24, are developed and resolved. [63] Siker has further argued that the Lukan theme of reversal can also be detected in Luke 4:16–30.[64] First, in regard to the recipients of the message of salvation, the Nazareth/Capernaum reversal is further developed into the Israel/Gentiles reversal in 4:25–27. Second, the locus of Jewish life (i.e., synagogue) ironically becomes the setting for the announcement of the inclusion of the Gentiles. Third, the reversal is also accomplished by redefining προφήτης, δεκτός, and πατρίς through the application of 4:25–27 to 4:18–19, and 21b. Therefore, not only is the theme of Gentile inclusion present in Luke 4:16–30, Luke uses this very occasion "exactly to proclaim Gentile inclusion as *part* of the gospel message."[65]

In addition to the consideration of the juxtaposition of Luke 4:18–19 and 4:25–27, with the two appearances of the phrase οὐδεμίαν/οὐδεὶς αὐτῶν ... εἰ μὴ ... (4:26, 27), a contrast between the two groups of people is established. Therefore, one can only conclude that the theme of the Gentile mission is embedded in the narrative of 4:16–30. The view that Luke does not develop the theme of Gentile mission further in his Gospel but reserves that part of the story to the narrative of Acts is well established.[66] This is confirmed by the reappearance of the term δεκτός in Acts 10:35 where it is applied to the topic of Gentile inclusion.[67] This parallel is all the more striking when one recognizes that this is the only other use of the adjective in the Lukan writings besides Luke 4:19 and 24. Here, one can see that a theme that is introduced in Luke 4:16–30 finds its full development in Acts.

The theme of the inclusion of the Gentiles is also expressed through several parallels between the Nazareth synagogue scene and the synagogue scenes of the Pauline mission among the Gentiles. These parallels point to the fact that the Gentile mission is an essential part of the wider program behind the early Christian movement and that the focus on the identity of the people of God is a major concern of Luke 4:16–30. First, the synagogue setting itself is significant. The combination of the verb εἰσέρχομαι with the phrase εἰς

Schreck, "The Nazareth Pericope: Luke 4:16–30 in Recent Study," 449; and, Strauss, *Davidic Messiah in Luke-Acts*, 223.

[63] Jeffrey S. Siker, "'First to the Gentiles': A Literary Analysis of Luke 4:16–30," *JBL* 111 (1992) 83.

[64] Ibid., 84–85.

[65] Ibid., 74.

[66] For a recent statement of this observation, see Rebecca I. Denova, *The Things Accomplished Among Us: Prophetic Tradition in the Structural Pattern of Luke-Acts* (JSNTSup 141; Sheffield: Sheffield Academic Press, 1997) 147–48.

[67] This is noted in Tannehill, *Narrative Unity of Luke-Acts*, 1.71

τὴν συναγωγήν (Luke 4:16) reappears only once in the rest of Luke (6:6), but can be found frequently in the description of the Pauline mission in Acts (13:14; 14:1; 18:19; 19:8; cf. 17:10). More significant, however, is the phrase κατὰ τὸ εἰωθός (Luke 4:16). This phrase has been recognized as a Lukan redactional construction[68] and it reappears only in Acts 17:2 in the description of the Pauline custom of entering the synagogue.[69] Finally, the phrase ἡμέρᾳ τῶν σαββάτων that appears in Luke 4:16 also reappears only in the Pauline mission in Acts (13:14; 16:13). The parallel between the apostolic mission and that of Jesus cannot be missed.

Second, the content of the Nazareth speech also parallels that of the synagogue sermons in Acts. This Nazareth sermon is a Lukan speech[70] and should be examined with the other speeches in Acts. As it has been noted, "the Jesus of Luke's special tradition (vss 18, 19) preaches, not the proximity of the kingdom, but precisely what the Church preaches (cf. Acts 3:20; 4:27; 10:38): his own anointing."[71] His call to evangelize (εὐαγγελίσασθαι, 4:18)[72] is likewise the call of the apostles (Acts 5:42; 8:4, 12; 10:36; 11:20; 13:32; 14:7, 15, 21 .... etc.). Furthermore, the word ἄφεσις that appears twice in Luke 4:18 in the quotations of Isa 61:1 and 58:6 did not play an important role in the narrative of Luke[73] but is a theologically significant term in Acts.[74]

Third, as in the narrative of Acts, the emphasis of the "word" (λόγος) as the locus of power plays a role in the Nazareth pericope. In Luke 4:22 the people "were amazed at the gracious words" (ἐθαύμαζον ἐπὶ τοῖς λόγοις τῆς χάριτος) while the Markan parallel (6:2; cf. Matt 13:54) simply states they were "astounded" (ἐξεπλήσσοντο). The designation λόγοις τῆς χάριτος is not merely a reference to the eloquence of Jesus.[75] In the Lukan writings, χαρίς can be understood within the semantic range of the word "power" (δυνάμις).[76] This is most clearly reflected in Acts 6:8 with the parallel construction between grace and power in the description of Stephen:

---

[68] See, for example, Schürmann, *Lukasevangelium*, 1.227 n.45; Chilton, "Announcement in Nazara," 152; and Bovon, *Das Evangelium nach Lukas*, 1.210.

[69] In both instances the subject is in the dative case.

[70] See Henry J. Cadbury, "The Speeches in Acts," in Kirsopp Lake and Henry J. Cadbury, eds., *The Beginnings of Christianity* (London: Macmillan, 1933) 5.417, 422.

[71] Chilton, "Announcement in Nazara," 161.

[72] "To evangelize the poor" (Luke 4:18) can be understood as the focus of Jesus' ministry while the following description merely serves to explain the meaning of this phrase. See Ernst Bammel, "πτωχός, πτωχεία, πτωχεύω," *TDNT* 6 (1968) 906; Nolland, *Luke*, 1.196.

[73] This word does reappear in Luke 24:47 but only in a statement that anticipates the future apostolic ministry in Acts.

[74] See Acts 2:38; 5:31; 10:43; 13:38; and 26:18.

[75] So Fitzmyer, *Gospel According to Luke (I–IX)*, 534.

[76] See, especially, Nolland, "Words of Grace (Luke 4:22)," 44–60. Cf. M. Cambe, "La χάρις chez saint Luc," *RB* 70 (1963) 193–207.

Στέφανος δὲ πλήρης χάριτος καὶ δυνάμεως ἐποίει τέρατα καὶ σημεῖα μεγάλα ἐν τῷ λαῷ ("Stephen, full of grace and power, did great wonders and signs among the people").[77] Therefore, it is in reaction to the power of his word that people were amazed and began to question Jesus' origin. The "word" that came from Jesus' mouth is the prophetic word that is able to accomplish the promises that it contains.[78] Luke's emphasis upon the power of the word (λόγος) can be seen throughout the narrative of Acts and especially in the summary statements that describe the growth of the word (Acts 6:7; 12:24; 19:20). This emphasis reaches its height in Acts 19:20 where the growth of the word is described with the phrase κατὰ κράτος.[79]

Finally, the active role of the Spirit also ties the Nazareth pericope with the Lukan narrative in Acts. In the first few chapters of Luke one sees the active work of the Holy Spirit.[80] The definitive statement of the work of the Holy Spirit in Jesus is given in Luke 4:18 in the citation of Isa 61:1: πνεῦμα κυρίου ἐπ' ἐμέ. Curiously the work of the Holy Spirit is not highlighted again in the rest of the Gospel. Not until the beginning of the narrative in Acts, in which the Holy Spirit plays an important role, does emphasis return to the Holy Spirit. While William Shepherd may be correct in noting that in Luke 4 "Luke has now established the basic plot-function of the Holy Spirit in the narrative" and that "Luke omits further mention of the Spirit during most of the rest of the Gospel, for there is little need to remind the reader of the relationship between Jesus and Spirit,"[81] it is equally important to point out that the narrative of the Spirit continues in Acts. Therefore, Luke 4 should be understood together with the narrative of Acts.

Luke-Acts emphasizes both rejection by the Jews and inclusion of the Gentiles by interpreting and qualifying an Isaianic quotation. Both themes play an important role in Acts, and both are concerned with the Christian claim to be the true people of God. Significantly, explicit Isaianic quotations will be further introduced in Acts (13:47; 28:26–27) to justify these two

---

[77] See also Luke 2:40; Acts 13:43; and 20:24. Similarly, Hans-Helmut Esser ("χάρις," *NIDNT* 2 [1986] 119) suggests that "in Acts grace is that power which flows from God or from the exalted Christ, and accompanies the activity of the apostles giving success to their mission."

[78] See also Schürmann, *Lukasevangelium*, 1.234–35; and, Leo O'Reilly *Word and Sign in the Acts of the Apostles: A Study in Lucan Theology* (AnGr 82; Rome: Editrice Pontifica Universita Gregorians, 1987) 37. For the discussion of the following phrase ἐκπορευομένοις ἐκ τοῦ στόματος αὐτοῦ ("that came from his mouth") that confirms the prophetic character of the verse, see also Ignace de la Potterie, "The Anointing of Christ," in Leo J. O'Donovan, ed., *Word and Mystery: Biblical Essays on the Person and Mission of Christ* (New York: Newman, 1968) 162.

[79] For a further discussion of the word of God in Acts, see chapter five below.

[80] See, for example, Luke 1:15, 35, 41, 67; 2:25–7; 3:16, 22; and 4:1, 14.

[81] William H. Shepherd Jr. *The Narrative Function of the Holy Spirit as a Character in Luke-Acts* (SBLDS 43; Atlanta, GA: Scholars Press, 1994) 137.

qualifications. With the introduction of Isa 61:1–2, therefore, a new era is announced for the people of God. Through these two significant qualifications, the peculiar development of the people of God is identified with the growth of the early Christian movement throughout Gentile areas in the midst of Jewish opposition.

3.3 Luke 24:44–49

Luke 24:44–49 belongs to the larger unit of 24:36–53 that is considered to be "the climax" of the appearance of the risen Jesus in Luke.[82] The commission account in Luke 24:44–49 is probably derived from a tradition that also lies behind the Matthean account in Matt 28:18–20 (and possibly also the Markan appendix in Mark 16:15–16).[83] The Lukan hand, however, can be felt throughout 24:44–49; and it is reflected in the themes of μετάνοια, ἄφεσις ἁμαρτιῶν, and μάρτυς.[84] This passage provides the foundation for the development of the narrative of Acts.

a. The Allusion to Isa 49:6 in Luke 24:46–47

While the evocation of the Isaianic program in the beginning chapters of Luke provides the framework in which the various events of Jesus' ministry are to be understood, at the end of Luke another Isaianic phrase provides a link between the story of Jesus and that of the apostles:

καὶ εἶπεν αὐτοῖς ὅτι Οὕτως γέγραπται παθεῖν τὸν Χριστὸν καὶ ἀναστῆναι ἐκ νεκρῶν τῇ τρίτῃ ἡμέρᾳ, καὶ κηρυχθῆναι ἐπὶ τῷ ὀνόματι αὐτοῦ μετάνοιαν εἰς ἄφεσιν ἁμαρτιῶν εἰς πάντα τὰ ἔθνη ἀρξάμενοι ἀπὸ Ἰερουσαλήμ·

And he said to them, "Thus it is written, that the Messiah is to suffer and to rise from the dead on the third day, and that repentance and forgiveness of sins is to be proclaimed in his name to all nations, beginning from Jerusalem." (Luke 24:46–47)

---

[82] Paul Schubert, "The Structure and Significance of Luke 24," in W. Eltester, ed., *Neutestamentliche Studien für Rudolf Bultmann* (Berlin: Alfred Töpelmann, 1954) 175.

[83] Fitzmyer, *Gospel According to Luke (X–XXIV)*, 1580. For the connection between this passage and John 20:19–23, see Raymond E. Brown, *The Gospel According to John XIII–XXI* (AB 29a; Garden City, NY: Doubleday, 1970) 1028–29, who considers the two as drawing upon the same Jerusalem narrative of the appearance of Jesus to his disciples.

[84] For a further discussion of the Lukan redaction, see Fitzmyer, *Gospel According to Luke (X–XXIV)*, 1580–81; Nolland, *Luke*, 3.1217–18; and Marie-Émile Boismard and Arnaud Lamouille, *Les Actes des deux Apôtres, III: Analyses Littéraire* (Paris: Gabalda, 1990) 29–30. Helmut Koester (*Ancient Christian Gospels: Their History and Development* [Philadelphia: Trinity Press International, 1990] 348) suggests that the stories in Luke 24 were added to "form the link to the second part of the work which begins with the repetition of the story of the ascension (Acts 1:6–11)."

The quotation formula γέγραπται in Luke 24:46 is followed by three infinitive clauses. In Luke 24:44–45 the Lukan Jesus gives notice that he is about to refer to Scripture, but the content of what follows in 24:46–47 apparently is not an explicit and literal quotation from Scripture. This is probably due to the Lukan conception that the totality of Scripture is behind the story of Jesus.[85] Nevertheless, throughout the Lukan writings, Luke does have particular passages in mind when he discusses scriptural references to the suffering and resurrection of Jesus.[86] Given my interest in the programmatic nature of Luke 24:44–49 for the narrative of Acts, I will examine the third infinitive clause in vs 47 concerning the mission to the nations/Gentiles. For it is the third infinitive clause that adds something new to the Lukan story that has been developing up to the point of Luke 24.

The discussion of the scriptural allusion behind Luke 24:47 can proceed through the study of the parallels between Luke 24:47 and Acts 1:8, on the one hand, and the parallels between Luke 24:47 and Acts 26:23, on the other. First, in both Luke 24:44–49 and Acts 1:8 there is an address to the "witnesses" to wait for the coming of the "power" so that they can go from "Jerusalem" to "the nations/the ends of the earth." These parallels serve to unite the two volumes and the reader is expected to read one in light of the other. As Jacques Dupont[87] has noted, Luke 24:47 refers to Scripture but the terms do not recall any particular text. Acts 1:8 does not, however, explicitly refer to any scriptural passage but it does contain a phrase that alludes to a particular text. In Acts 1:8 the apostles were called to be Jesus' witnesses "to the ends of the earth" (ἕως ἐσχάτου τῆς γῆς).[88] In the LXX, the phrase ἕως ἐσχάτου τῆς γῆς appears five times, and four of those five times are in Isaiah (Isa 8:9; 48:20; 49:6; 62:11).[89] The closest in context to Acts 1:8 is Isa 49:6,[90] and this is precisely the verse that is explicitly quoted in Acts 13:47

---

[85] So Fitzmyer, *Gospel According to Luke (x–xxiv)*, 1581.

[86] Luke has explicitly used Isaianic passages as he makes references to the suffering and resurrection of Jesus. Here, one may recall the explicit use of Isa 53:7–8 in Acts 8:32–33 in reference to the suffering of Jesus. Concerning the resurrection, see the use of Isa 55:3 in Acts 13:34; and Ps 16:8–11 in Acts 2:25–28. See also the use of Ps 16:10 in Acts 13:35. Cf. the use of Ps 110:1 in Acts 2:34–35.

[87] Jacques Dupont, "La portée christologique de l'évangélisation des nations d'après Lc 24,47," in Joachim Gnilka, ed., *Neues Testament und Kirche: Für Rudolf Schnackenburg* (Freiburg: Herder, 1974) 136.

[88] I am following NRSV here in using the plural "ends" to interpret the singular ἐσχάτου although this translation is questionable. Cf. Ps 135:7 (NRSV).

[89] The only other appearance is in *Pss. Sol.* 1.4, a work that is not quoted at all in the Lukan writings (cf. a similar phrase used in 1 Macc 3:9).

[90] See Ernst Haenchen, *The Acts of the Apostles: A Commentary* (trans. R. McL. Wilson; Oxford: Basil Blackwell, 1971) 143 n.9; *contra* Barrett (*Acts of the Apostles*, 1.80) who sees this as a stock phrase. The difference between the singular and plural form of the word ἐσχάτον has been missed by Barrett.

(τέθεικά σε εἰς φῶς ἐθνῶν τοῦ εἶναί σε εἰς σωτηρίαν ἕως ἐσχάτου τῆς γῆς, "I have set you to be a light for the Gentiles, so that you may bring salvation to the ends of the earth"). Therefore, if one accepts the parallels between Acts 1:8 and Luke 24:47,[91] one should also understand the scriptural reference behind Luke 24:47 as Isa 49:6.[92]

This conclusion is also supported by the parallels between Luke 24:46–47 and Acts 26:23. The same three elements occur in both passages: (1) the suffering and (2) resurrection of Christ; and (3) the mission to the Gentiles/nations. The third element is, however, phrased differently in Acts 26:23. In Acts 26:23 the mission of the Gentiles is characterized as "a light ... to the nations" (φῶς ... τοῖς ἔθνεσιν). This is most likely an allusion to a similar characterization (φῶς ἔθνων)[93] found in Isa 42:6, 49:6, and 51:4. Again, of these three passages, the only passage that Luke has explicitly cited is Isa 49:6.[94] Therefore, it is likely that Isa 49:6 forms the background for the description in Acts 26:23, the passage that parallels Luke 24:47. This confirms my earlier conclusion that Isa 49:6 is indeed behind Luke 24:47.[95]

b. Isaiah and the Extension of the Markan Story of Jesus

In interpreting the Markan story, Luke has made one significant change: the extension of the story beyond its original ending. This move contains an implicit criticism of earlier writings that stop with the end of the story of Jesus. As I have shown in the previous chapter, this extension is accomplished by the introduction of the Isaianic New Exodus program in the early chapters of Luke; and it is motivated by the concerns of Luke's community in which the question of self-identity becomes an issue. Luke's focus on the wider story of the continuation of the people of God now replaces a narrower concentration on the story of Jesus. Here, the Isaianic program is evoked to provide a foundation on which the story of Jesus and that of the early Christian community can be united. This hermeneutic move allows Luke to provide an angle from which the question of the Gentiles can be discussed. Luke 24:44–49, therefore, functions as a link connecting the

---

[91] Even if one is not willing to accept the link between Acts 1:8 and Luke 24:47, a direct connection can be established between Luke 24:47 and Acts 13:46–47 through the use of the same phrase εἰς ... τὰ ἔθνη in both Luke 24:47 and Acts 13:46.

[92] This is further supported by the fact that in both Luke 24:47 and Acts 13:47, the verse is presented as a command of Jesus. Cf. Jacques Dupont, "La portée christologique de l'évangélisation des nations d'après Lc 24,47," 138.

[93] Cf. Luke 2:32: φῶς εἰς ἀποκάλυψιν ἐθνῶν ("a light for revelation to the Gentiles").

[94] See Pierre Grelot, "Note sur Actes, XIII, 47," *RB* 88 (1981) 370.

[95] Another Isaianic allusion can be detected in the phrase ἀρξάμενοι ἀπὸ Ἰερουσαλήμ ("beginning from Jerusalem") in Luke 24:47 as it may be an allusion to Isa 2:3 and 51:4. Since these verses are not explicitly cited in Luke-Acts, I will not discuss them here. I will return to these verses in my discussion of the word of God in chapter five below.

eventual move to the Gentiles with both the story of Jesus and the ancient Israelite traditions.

In Luke 24:44–49, in an act of interpreting Scripture, the risen Jesus explains the totality of the message from the Law of Moses, the Prophets, and the Psalms (Luke 24:44).[96] The message itself contains three infinitive clauses (παθεῖν ... ἀναστῆναι ... κηρυχθῆναι) that reflect the distinctively Lukan fusion of the events of the suffering and resurrection of Jesus with the mission of the apostles as commanded by the risen Jesus with a reference to the fulfillment of Scripture.[97] This unique juxtaposition of the ministry of Jesus and that of the apostles secures the continuity between the two Lukan volumes. Furthermore, as Dupont has emphatically suggested, the extension of the message of salvation to the Gentiles now becomes part of the christological program.[98] This is most clear when Luke 24:44 notes that all the prophecies were περὶ ἐμοῦ (i.e., Jesus). This serves to explain the reappearance of the term ἄφεσις in Luke 24:47 to characterize the message of early Christians, the same term last used to characterize the message of Jesus in Luke 4:18.

The unity and continuity between the ministry of Jesus and that of the apostles is also emphasized by the wider scheme of the divine plan. First, the theologically significant term δεῖ (Luke 24:44) evokes the Lukan notion of the divine plan.[99] Second, the word πληρόω[100] and the whole idea of prophecy-fulfillment provide continuity not only with the ancient writings but also

---

[96] It seems best to understand these three phrases together as referring to the entire Scripture. The tripartite division can be found in the Prologue to Sirach (line 8–10) and Philo, *Contempl.* 25. See Gottlob Schrenk, "γραφή," *TDNT* 1 (1964) 756.

[97] The unity of the three phrases and their interrelationship is discussed in Richard J. Dillon, "Easter Revelation and Mission Program in Luke 24:46–48," in Daniel Durken, ed., *Sin, Salvation, and the Spirit: Commemorating the Fiftieth Year of The Liturgical Press* (Collegeville, MN: Liturgical Press, 1979) 240–70.

[98] Dupont, "La portée christologique de l'évangélisation des nations d'après Lc 24,47," 126: "Il est parfaitement clair ici que l'annonce du salut à tous les peuples appartientà la mission du Christ, telle qu'elle est définie par l'Ancien Testament." It is not certain, however, if Dupont (*op. cit.*, 133) is correct in arguing that this move reflects the Lukan attempt to transform the apocalyptic program into an historical one and therefore includes it within the historical work of Christ (cf. Mark 13:10).

[99] For the use of the divine δεῖ in Luke-Acts, see Cadbury, *Making of Luke-Acts*, 303–5; Hans Conzelmann, *The Theology of St. Luke* (trans. Geoffrey Buswell; New York: Harper & Row, 1960) 153–4; and Charles H. Cosgrove, "The Divine ΔEI in Luke-Acts: Investigations into the Lukan Understanding of God's Providence," *NovT* 26 (1984) 168–90. It is possible that the significance of δεῖ has originated from eschatological discourse. For example, Walter Grundmann ("δεῖ, δέον ἐστί," *TDNT* 2 [1964] 23) has suggested that the term "expresses the necessity of the eschatological event." Cf. Mark 8:31.

[100] Cf. Luke 1:20; 4:21; 9:31; 21:24; 22:16; Acts 1:16; 3:18; and 13:27.

among the Lukan writings themselves.[101] Third, the formula γέγραπται (Luke 24:46) unites isolated events into the unified divine will as expressed in the ancient writings. The use of the cluster of these three terms[102] connects the two stages of development of the Lukan narrative. More importantly, the use of Isaiah here in Luke 24:47 and at the beginning of the ministry of Jesus provides the continuity critical to Luke's program. In the previous chapter, I have shown that the quotation from Isa 40:3–5 evokes the Isaianic New Exodus program for the Lukan writings. In Luke 4:16–30, a quotation from Isaiah sets the stage for the ministry of Jesus while anticipating the mission of the apostles. In Luke 24:44–49, another reference from Isaiah explicitly extends the ministry of Jesus beyond the traditional conceptual boundary of the people of God. Behind these quotations lies the wider Isaianic program that holds together the various isolated events.

With the end of the Jesus-story, the continuation of the story of salvation is to be carried out by his followers. In Luke 24:44–49, one can also detect an attempt to justify the authority of the apostles. Here, the context in which vs 47 is located is important as vss 48–49 already point beyond the text of Luke to the narrative in Acts 1. The term "witnesses" (μάρτυρες, Luke 24:48), which appears only twice in Luke,[103] becomes a significant designation for the apostles in Acts (Acts 1:8, 22; 2:32; 3:15; 5:32; 10:39, 41; 13:31; 22:15, 20; 26:16). The command to stay in the city (i.e., Jerusalem) to wait for τὴν ἐπαγγελίαν τοῦ πατρός μου (lit.: "the promise of my father," Luke 24:49) is repeated in Acts 1:4, and the use of the term δύναμις ("power," Luke 24:49)[104] in relation to the Holy Spirit also appears in Acts 1:8.

Furthermore, Luke 24:44–49 also contains the essence of apostolic preaching as presented in Acts. In a number of studies, Dupont has highlighted the parallels between Luke 24:44–49 and Acts 26:16–23.[105] As

---

[101] Bovon ("The Effect of Realism and Prophetic Ambiguity in the Works of Luke," *New Testament Traditions and Apocryphal Narrative* [trans. Jane Haapiseva-Hunter; PTMS 36; Allison Park, PA: Pickwick, 1995] 97–104) has emphasized the complexity of the phenomenon of prophecy and its theological function in Luke and Acts. Furthermore, Charles Talbert ("Promise and Fulfillment in Lucan Theology," in Charles H. Talbert, ed., *Luke-Acts: New Perspectives from the Society of Biblical Literature Seminar* [New York: Crossroad, 1984], 94) has noted that the scheme of prophecy-fulfillment can also be found within the Lukan writings and not only with reference to the Hebrew Bible.

[102] One may also mention the term ἐπαγγελίαν (Luke 24:49), but this verse does not function in the same way as those in the complex of Luke 24:44–47 that emphasize the unity of the missions of Jesus and the apostles.

[103] Luke 11:48 and 24:49.

[104] The phrase ἐξ ὕψους δύναμιν reflects the common circumlocution that refers to divine origin and can thus be translated as "the power of God" (cf. Luke 1:35). See Shepherd, *Narrative Function of the Holy Spirit as a Character in Luke-Acts*, 148.

[105] See Jacques Dupont, "La portée christologique de l'évangélisation des nations d'après Lc 24,47," 125–43; *The Salvation of the Gentiles: Studies in the Acts of the Apostles*

mentioned above, they are most clearly reflected at the end of the speech before Agrippa (Acts 26:23) when the Lukan Paul summarizes his own teaching which contains: (1) it was necessary that the Christ should suffer, and (2) having risen from the dead (3) he would proclaim light both to his people and to the Gentiles. All three themes can be found in Luke 24:47. Furthermore, in both passages the scriptural foundation is mentioned (Luke 24:44; Acts 26:22); and in both the mission to the Gentiles is attributed to the work of Christ.[106] Finally, "forgiveness" (ἄφεσις, Luke 24:47)[107] and "repentance" (μετάνοια, Luke 24:47)[108] are also terms that frequently appear in the speeches in Acts that were proclaimed "in his name" (ἐπὶ τῷ ὀνόματι αὐτοῦ, Luke 24:47).[109] All these serve to locate the authority of the apostles in the words of the risen Christ.

The continuation of the story of the people of God is central to the Lukan program. It is therefore difficult to agree with Mikeal Parsons when he concludes that "Luke goes to great lengths to provide a sense of closure to this story about Jesus."[110] Although it may be true that the gap between Luke and Acts "is greater than any crack within either narrative,"[111] the continuity between the two cannot be downplayed.

c. Isaiah and the Justification of the Gentile Community: The Lukan Characterization of the Early Christian Movement

Significantly, the direction of the entire narrative of Acts is depicted as a move to the Gentiles in Luke 24:47. The evocation of the Isaianic phrase justifies this move in the redefinition of the people of God. After reviewing the ministry of Jesus, Luke 24:44–49 pushes the Isaianic program as announced in Luke 4:16–30 a step forward with the introduction of the theme of the

---

(trans. J. R. Keating; New York: Paulist, 1979) 28; and "La Mission de Paul d'après Actes 26.16–23 et la Mission des Apôtres d'après Luc 24.44–9 et Actes 1.8," in M. D. Hooker and S. G. Wilson, eds., *Paul and Paulinism: Essays in Honor of C. K. Barrett* (London: SPCK, 1982) 290–301.

[106] The themes expressed in Luke 24:47 can also be detected in other Lukan speeches in Acts. See Ulrich Wilckens, *Die Missionsreden der Apostelgeschichte. Form- und traditionsgeschichtliche Untersuchungen* (WMANT 5; Neukirchen: Neukirchener Verlag, 1974) 97; and Richard J. Dillon, *From Eye-Witnesses to Ministers of the Word: Tradition and Composition in Luke 24* (AnBib 82; Rome: Pontifical Biblical Institute, 1978) 188.

[107] Cf. Acts 2:38; 5:31; 10:43; 13:38; 26:18.

[108] Cf. Acts 5:31; 11:18; 13:24; 19:4; 20:21; 26:20.

[109] Cf. Acts 2:38; 3:6; 4:7, 10, 17–18, 30; 5:28, 40; 8:12; 16; 9:16, 27–28; 10:43, 48; 15:14, 26; 16:18; 19:5, 13, 17; 21:13; 22:16; 26:9.

[110] Mikeal C. Parsons, "The Unity of the Lukan Writings: Rethinking the *Opinio Communis*," in Naymond H. Keathley, ed., *With Steadfast Purpose: Essays in Honor of Henry Jackson Flanders* (Waco, TX: Baylor University Press, 1990) 43.

[111] Idem, "The Narrative Unity of Luke and Acts," in Mikeal C. Parsons and Richard I. Pervo, *Rethinking the Unity of Luke and Acts* (Minneapolis, MN: Fortress, 1993) 81.

Gentiles. While the Isaianic program is introduced in Luke 4:18–21 with a qualification from the examples of Elijah and Elisha (Luke 4:25–27), the concern for the Gentiles is now made explicit by a scriptural reference to Isaiah in Luke 24:47. This theme of the inclusion of the Gentiles plays an important role in Luke's evocation of the program of the Isaianic New Exodus for it has already been highlighted in the quotation of Isa 40:3–5 in Luke 3:4–6.

In addition, the pattern that is developed later in Acts concerning the specific order for delivering the gospel message, "Jews first ... then Gentiles," can already be detected in Luke 24:47 with the context of Isa 49:6 in mind. First, the proposition ἀπό should be understood in an inclusive sense. Therefore the phrase should be translated as "beginning in Jerusalem."[112] Furthermore, the phrase ἀρξάμενοι ἀπὸ Ἰερουσαλήμ should not be understood merely as a geographical reference.[113] With the contrast between τὰ ἔθνη and Jerusalem, one can almost see a contrast between the Gentiles[114] and the Jews, although a strict scheme of periodization in geographical terms is not present.[115] This provides the foundation for the further declaration in

---

[112] Giuseppe Betori ("Luke 24:47: Jerusalem and the Beginning of the Preaching to the Pagans in the Acts of the Apostles," in Gerald O'Collins and Gilberto Marconi, eds., *Luke and Acts* [trans. Matthew J. O'Connell; New York: Paulist, 1993], 106) notes the parallel use of the phrase in Acts 10:37: ἀρξάμενος ἀπὸ τῆς Γαλιλαίας ("beginning in Galilee"). Betori also notes that in Luke-Acts the verb ἄρχομαι "never expresses an action different from that of the verb with which it is linked" (110).

[113] Nevertheless Conzelmann (*Theology of St. Luke*, 133) is correct in noting that Jerusalem is the link between the history of Jesus and that of the church.

[114] Against Jacob Jervell's proposal (see, for example, Jacob Jervell, "The Church of Jews and God-fearers," in Joseph B. Tyson, ed., *Luke-Acts and the Jewish People: Eight Critical Perspectives* [Minneapolis: Augsburg, 1988] 11–20), it must be noted that τὰ ἔθνη in its plural form is never used as a reference that includes the Jews in the Lukan writings. In addition, to limit the term τὰ ἔθνη to refer only to the "God-fearers" is not justifiable. See Jack T. Sanders, "Who is a Jew and Who is a Gentile in the Book of Acts?" *NTS* 37 (1991) 434–55. The question of the relationship between Jews and Gentiles in the Lukan writings will be dealt with in chapter seven below.

[115] This is again confirmed by the parallel in Acts 26:23 where the distinction between "the people" (ὁ λαός) and "the Gentiles" (τὰ ἔθνη) is being made. Betori ("Luke 24:47: Jerusalem and the Beginning of the Preaching to the Pagans in the Acts of the Apostles," 107–114) has overstated his case when he argues that the contrast between the Gentiles and the Jews cannot be established in Luke 24:47. Such an argument is not convincing considering the numerous parallel statements in Acts. His discussion of the unique importance of Jerusalem in Luke-Acts and the role it plays in the Pentecost account does not contradict my contention that the contrast between Jews and Gentiles is at least implicitly present in Luke 24:47.

Acts 13:46 that the message of salvation must be proclaimed to the Jews "first" (πρῶτον).[116]

The allusion to Isaiah thus provides a succinct statement concerning the direction of the narrative of Acts. Such an allusion provides continuity with the past history of the people of God while at the same time justifying the move to the Gentiles and the eventual redefinition of the people of God.

3.4 Acts 1:8

Moving from Luke to Acts, I will discuss the function of several programmatic statements within the narrative of Acts itself. The most obvious starting point is Acts 1:8. Acts 1:8 belongs to the unit that begins with the specifically Lukan phrase οἱ μὲν οὖν (1:6); and 1:8 should be considered as a response to the question raised in 1:6. This unit in turn belongs to the larger unit of 1:1–11[117] that serves as the prologue to Acts, a prologue that recapitulates that which has already been recorded at the end of Luke. The Lukan hand can again be felt throughout this pericope.[118]

a. Allusions to Isaiah in Acts 1:8

The programmatic nature of Acts 1:8 is recognized by most. Acts 1:8 is considered as providing the "groundplan"[119] for the narrative of Acts. The text of Isaiah is also behind this programmatic statement:

---

[116] One must resist, however, the urge to see behind Luke 24:47 rejection by the Jews as the sole or primary cause of the move to the Gentiles. *Contra* Dillon, *From Eye-Witnesses to Ministers of the Word*, 214–5.

[117] *Contra* Barrett (*Acts of the Apostles*, 1.61) who argues that the whole of vss 1–14 is paralleled in Luke and the new section only starts in vs 15. In response, it should be noted that Acts 1:2 seems to outline the final work of Jesus and that which is mentioned in 1:2 is completed in 1:11. Acts 1:12, on the other hand, signifies the beginning of the apostolic history with the main character transferring from Jesus to the apostles. In addition, the final section that includes vss 6–11 provides an outline for the book the fulfillment of which begins in vs 12.

[118] Barrett, *Acts of the Apostles*, 1.62.

[119] Haenchen, *Acts of the Apostles*, 143 n.9; Hans Conzelmann, *Acts of the Apostles: A Commentary on the Acts of the Apostles* (trans. James Limburg, A. Thomas Kraabel, and Donald H. Juel; Philadelphia: Fortress, 1987) 7; and Jacques Dupont, "Le salut des gentils et la signification théologique du livre des Actes," *NTS* 6 (1959–60) 140–1. See also Charles H. Talbert, *Reading Acts: A Literary and Theological Commentary on The Acts of the Apostles* (New York: Crossroad, 1997) 27, who argues that the 1:8 conforms to Mediterranean literary practice in having the plot of the narrative unfold as the fulfillment of prophecy.

ἀλλὰ λήμψεσθε δύναμιν ἐπελθόντος τοῦ ἁγίου πνεύματος ἐφ' ὑμᾶς, καὶ ἔσεσθέ
μου μάρτυρες ἔν τε Ἰερουσαλὴμ καὶ [ἐν] πάσῃ τῇ Ἰουδαίᾳ καὶ Σαμαρείᾳ καὶ ἕως
ἐσχάτου τῆς γῆς.

But you will receive power when the Holy Spirit has come upon you; and you will be
my witnesses in Jerusalem, in all Judea and Samaria, and to the ends of the earth.

The reference to Isa 49:6 behind the phrase ἕως ἐσχάτου τῆς γῆς has
already been established and is recognized by most commentators.[120] This
significant phrase, which in the New Testament appears only in the Lukan
writings, connects the Lukan program to the Isaianic writings. A further
discussion of Isa 49:6 will be presented in the discussion of Acts 13:46–47.
The Isaianic influence on 1:8 is not limited to this phrase, however.

In Acts 1:8, one reads that the witnesses will receive power "when the
Holy Spirit has come upon you" (ἐπελθόντος τοῦ ἁγίου πνεύματος ἐφ'
ὑμᾶς). This promise of the Spirit recalls the phrase in Isa 32:15 in which the
desolation will continue until "a spirit from on high is poured out on us" (ἕως
ἂν ἐπέλθῃ ἐφ' ὑμᾶς πνεῦμα ἀφ' ὑψηλοῦ).[121] The part that does not
appear in 1:8 (ἀφ' ὑψηλοῦ) can be found in a similar phrase in the parallel
passage in Luke 24:49 (ἐξ ὕψους).[122] This parallel further confirms the
Isaianic background behind Acts 1:8. The allusion to Isa 32:15 is significant in
that the Isaianic context suggests that the coming of the Spirit will signify the
end of the desolation of Judah and introduce the coming of the new age. This
is echoed in the first Servant Song in Isa 42:1 and also in Isa 61:1–2 that has
already appeared in Luke 4:18–19. Here, one can only agree with Marvin
Sweeney who, in his recent study of Isaiah 1–39, claims that the placement of
Isaiah 32 "prior to the materials from Deutero-Isaiah indicates that this
chapter played an important role in defining the expectations expressed in chs.
40–55 (60–62)."[123] The connections between Isaiah 32 and the anticipated

---

[120] Among others, see Haenchen, *Acts of the Apostles*, 143, n.9; Gerhard Schneider, *Die Apostelgeschichte* (Freiburg: Herder, 1980) 1.203; Rudolf Pesch, *Die Apostelgeschichte* (EKK 5; Zürich: Benziger Verlag, 1986) 1.70; and Josef Zmijewski, *Die Apostelgeschichte* (Regensburg: Pustet, 1994) 59.

[121] While influence from other Isaianic passages may well be possible (e.g., Isa 11:2; 42:1; 61:1), none rivals Isa 32:15 in its parallels with Acts 1:8. Although this reference to Isa 32:15 has been noted by some, the significance of the Isaianic context escapes most. See Conzelmann, *Acts of the Apostles*, 7.

[122] For further discussion of the link between Luke 24:49 and Isa 32:15, see Fitzmyer, *Gospel According to Luke (X–XXIV)*, 1585; and Craig A. Evans, "Jesus and the Spirit: On the Origin and Ministry of the Second Son of God," in Craig A. Evans and James A. Sanders, *Luke and Scripture: The Functions of Sacred Tradition in Luke-Acts* (Minneapolis: Fortress, 1993) 31.

[123] Marvin A. Sweeney, *Isaiah 1–39 with an Introduction to the Prophetic Literature* (FOTL 16; Grand Rapids, MI: Eerdmans, 1996) 419–20.

coming of the message of salvation in Isaiah 40–55 cannot be missed. The coming of the Spirit thus signifies the dawn of the Isaianic New Exodus.

Finally, the call to the apostles, "you will be my witnesses" (ἔσεσθέ μου μάρτυρες), finds its closest parallels in Isa 43:10 (γένεσθέ μοι μάρτυρες) and Isa 43:12 (ὑμεῖς ἐμοὶ μάρτυρες; cf. 44:8). In the context of Isaiah, the people of God will become witnesses to the salvation of God when the new age arrives. This stands in contrast to Isa 42:18–25 where the deafness and blindness of Israel are noted. Isa 43:10–12 therefore signifies the presence of a reversal,[124] one that is possible through the introduction of the new work of the God of Israel.

b. Isaiah and the Groundplan of Acts: Isaianic New Exodus as the Hermeneutical Grid for the Story of Acts

Many have considered Acts 1:8 as providing three geographical categories in describing the growth of the early Christian movement. In this section, I will argue that Acts 1:8 should not be understood simply in geographical terms. Instead, it depicts the three stages in the program of the Isaianic New Exodus. In his selection of traditional material, Luke constructs the development of the early Christian movement within the framework of the Isaianic New Exodus in order to lay claim to the ancient Israelite tradition.

I will begin by discussing the exact reference behind the phrase ἕως ἐσχάτου τῆς γῆς. There are those who argue that the phrase refers to Ethiopia,[125] the Land of Israel,[126] or Diaspora Jews in general.[127] Others, however, have suggested that the phrase refers to Rome,[128] Spain,[129] the whole inhabited world,[130] or the entire ethnic group "Gentiles."[131]

---

[124] For a further discussion of this reversal, see Paul D. Hanson, *Isaiah 40–66* (Interpretation; Louisville, KY: John Knox, 1995) 66–70.

[125] See, for example, Henry J. Cadbury, *The Book of Acts in History* (New York: Harper and Brothers, 1955) 15; and T. C. G. Thornton, "To the End of the Earth: Acts 1:8," *ExpTim* 89 (1977–78) 374–75.

[126] Etienne Trocmé, *Le 'Livre des Actes' et l'histoire* (Paris: Presses Universitaires de France, 1957) 206; and Schwartz, "The End of the ΓΗ (Acts 1:8): Beginning or End of the Christian Vision?" *JBL* 105 (1986) 669–676.

[127] Karl H. Rengstorf, "The Election of Matthias," in W. Klassen and G. F. Snyder, eds., *Current Issues in New Testament Interpretation: Essays in Honor of Otto A. Piper* (New York: Harper, 1962) 186–87.

[128] Among others, see Floyd V. Filson, "The Journey Motif in Luke-Acts," in W. Ward Gasque and Ralph P. Martin, eds., *Apostolic History and the Gospel: Biblical and Historical Essays Presented to F. F. Bruce on his 60th Birthday* (Grand Rapids, MI: Eerdmans, 1970) 75–76.

[129] E. Earle Ellis, "'The End of the Earth' (Acts 1:8)," *BBR* 1 (1991) 123–32.

[130] Willem C. van Unnik, "Der Ausdruck ΕΩΣ ΕΣΧΑΤΟΥ ΤΗΣ ΓΗΣ (Apostelgeschichte I 8) und sein Alttestamentlicher Hintergrund," *Sparsa Collecta: The Collected Essays of W. C. van Unnik* (NovTSup 30; Leiden: Brill, 1973) 386–401.

In determining the meaning of the phrase ἕως ἐσχάτου τῆς γῆς, it must be noted that it appears only twice in the Lukan writings (and the entire New Testament): Acts 1:8 and 13:47; and the connection between these two verses has already been discussed. In 13:47 this phrase appears in the quotation of Isa 49:6. In the contexts both of Acts 13[132] and Isaiah 49, this particular phrase is used as a reference to the Gentiles. This alone allows one to rule out the first group of possible references.[133]

Furthermore, the suggestion that this is a "stock phrase" used widely in the Greco-Roman world should also be rejected,[134] since the exact form of the phrase (with the singular ἐσχάτου) appears only five times in the LXX,[135] twice in the Lukan writings, and nowhere else in ancient Greek literature not influenced by either Isaiah or Acts.[136] This further highlights the importance of the Isaianic quotation in Acts 13:47 as the background to the phrase.[137] With this in mind, one can conclude that the primary reference is to the Gentiles. This ethnic understanding of the phrase does not exclude the geographical reference to Rome (in which Acts ends) and even to the whole inhabited world[138] since both represent Gentile territories, although the primary reference should probably not be understood in geographical terms.

A significant implication is that it is therefore possible to understand the entire programmatic statement in Acts 1:8 in theopolitical and not geographical terms. First of all, in the first part of 1:8 one finds a reference to a city and two regions. The final phrase ἕως ἐσχάτου τῆς γῆς, which does not exactly refer to a city or a region, adds to the confusion. A possible

---

[131] Wilson, *Gentiles and the Gentile Mission in Luke-Acts*, 94 n.1; and Dupont, *Salvation of the Gentiles*, 18–19.

[132] See especially the appearance of εἰς τὰ ἔθνη in vs 46 that forms the parallel to the phrase in vs 47.

[133] The fact that the phrase refers to the gentile world rules out "the Land of Israel" and "diaspora Jews" as possible referents. The reappearance of the parallel phrase in Acts 13 also rules out "Ethiopia."

[134] *Contra* Barrett, *Acts of the Apostles*, 1.80; and Talbert, *Reading Acts*, 27.

[135] Four of which appear in Isaiah and the fifth in *Pss. Sol.* 1:4. See the discussion in section 3.3a above.

[136] This has already been noted by van Unnik, "Der Ausdruck 'ΕΩΣ 'ΕΣΧΑΤΟΥ ΤΗΣ ΓΗΣ (Apostelgeschichte I 8)," 399–401; and confirmed by Tannehill, *Narrative Unity of Luke-Acts*, 2.17.

[137] It is of course possible that Luke is aware of a similar phrase in *Pss. Sol.* 8:15 (ἀπ' ἐσχάτου τῆς γῆς) where the phrase is used to refer to Rome. Although a reference to Rome is possible, this cannot be established through *Pss. Sol.* 1:4 alone in light of the presence of an explicit Isaianic quotation in Acts 13:47 and the fact that there is no conclusive evidence that Luke is familiar with the *Psalms of Solomon* in his writings.

[138] There is no evidence in Acts that one should understand the phrase as a reference to Spain. Evidence from Greco-Roman literature does not provide an exact parallel to this phrase.

solution is to see the four items as representing three theopolitical categories. The theological significance of Jerusalem in Luke-Acts needs no proof as it has become the locus of the anticipated act of salvation. The second category that includes Judea and Samaria, two terms that have already been linked together by the phrase ἐν πάσῃ τῇ,[139] may evoke the theopolitical connotations of the two regions. As for the final phrase, its theological significance has already been established through the reference to Isa 49:6. Taken together, then, the three categories correspond to the three stages of the Isaianic New Exodus which signifies the arrival of the new era: (1) the dawn of salvation upon Jerusalem; (2) the reconstitution and reunification of Israel;[140] and finally (3) the inclusion of the Gentiles within the people of God.[141] While further discussion is not possible at this point,[142] this understanding is strengthened by the presence of the numerous references to Isaiah in Acts 1:8 as discussed above.

c. The Use of the National Story of Israel: The Establishment of the Kingdom of the People of God

Examining Acts 1:8 in light of its immediate context, one can also see that it is a response to the question raised in Acts 1:6: "Lord, is this the time when you will restore (ἀποκαθιστάνεις) the kingdom to Israel?" In vs 7 one finds the response by Jesus concerning the timing of the restoration raised by the question. The fact of the restoration, however, is not denied; and the disciples were not rebuked for their question.[143] Conzelmann has rightly noted that "it is not the hope of this that is rejected, but only the attempt to calculate when it will happen."[144]

Acts 1:8 therefore becomes the second part of the response to the question in that it confirms the beginning of the process of the restoration of

---

[139] The omission of ἐν in some manuscripts does not significantly affect my discussion here since πάσῃ τῇ by itself seems to qualify both of the following nouns. For a discussion of the textual problem surrounding this verse, see Metzger, *A Textual Commentary on the Greek New Testament*, 244.

[140] Cf. Acts 1:15–26 and the reconstitution of the Twelve. See the discussion in chapter four below.

[141] The understanding of Acts 1:8 as providing the "groundplan" of Acts also needs to be qualified. Acts 1:8 is programmatic for providing a theological framework for understanding Acts but it should not be understood as providing a strict formal outline of the book dividing it into three separate and distinct parts.

[142] Please refer to chapter two above.

[143] An understanding that suggests that the disciples totally misunderstood the nature of the kingdom must be rejected in light of Acts 1:3. See, especially, Anthony Buzzard, "Acts 1:6 and the Eclipse of the Biblical Kingdom," *EvQ* 66 (1994) 197–215. *Contra* Robert Maddox, *The Purpose of Luke-Acts* (Edinburgh: T. & T. Clark, 1982) 106.

[144] Conzelmann, *Theology of St. Luke*, 163.

Israel.[145] This process of restoration is portrayed through the model of the Isaianic New Exodus in which the salvation of the Gentiles becomes part of the program of the reconstitution of Israel. While it must not be denied that the futuristic aspect is present in the Lukan conception of the restoration of Israel,[146] the beginning of the process in Acts has to be acknowledged.[147] Therefore, one should not ignore the role of Isaiah in the depiction of this process and in the redefinition of such a program into one that is concerned not merely with Israel but also with the Gentiles.

3.5 Acts 13:46–47

Naturally, the next passage that demands one's attention is Acts 13:46–47, the passage that finds its parallels in Luke 24:47 and Acts 1:8. These two verses are located in the larger narrative concerning the work of Paul and his companions in Pisidian Antioch (Acts 13:13–52). Acts 13:46–47 contains the reactions of Paul and Barnabas to the negative response of the Jews; and it provides direction for the narrative that follows.

a. The Text of the Isaianic Quotation in Acts 13:47

Isa 49:6, a text that has already been alluded to several times in both Luke and Acts, appears in an explicit quotation in Acts 13:47:

οὕτως γὰρ ἐντέταλται ἡμῖν ὁ κύριος, Τέθεικά σε εἰς φῶς ἐθνῶν τοῦ εἶναί σε εἰς σωτηρίαν ἕως ἐσχάτου τῆς γῆς.

For so the Lord has commanded us, saying, "I have set you to be a light for the Gentiles, so that you may bring salvation to the ends of the earth."

---

[145] So David L. Tiede, "The Exaltation of Jesus and the Restoration of Israel in Acts 1," *HTR* 79 (1986) 278–86.

[146] David Ravens, *Luke and the Restoration of Israel* (Sheffield: Sheffield Academic Press, 1995) 93–95, argues for a "two-stage eschatology" that affirms both the present and future aspects of the restoration of Israel. Cf. John T. Carroll, *Response to the End of History: Eschatology and Situation in Luke-Acts* (SBLDS 92; Atlanta, GA: Scholars Press, 1988) 124–28.

[147] In examining the parallels between Acts 2:38 and 3:19–20, William L. Lane ("Time of Refreshment: A Study of Eschatological Periodization in Judaism and Christianity [Acts 3.19s]" [Th.D. diss., Harvard Divinity School, 1962] 167–71) notes that "the time of refreshment" of 3:19 refers to the coming of the Holy Spirit. Although Acts 2 probably does not exhaust the meaning of the phrase, the restoration of Israel is nevertheless tied with the coming of the Holy Spirit. This fulfills the programmatic statement of 1:8.

This quotation of Isa 49:6 is taken from the LXX[148] with two changes. First, the omission of ἰδού (cf. Isa 49:6 LXX) in the Lukan text is probably the result of a stylistic change to situate the text better in the Lukan context. Given the appearance of the same word in Acts 13:46, the omission in 13:47 may also simply reflect an attempt to avoid using the same word twice in such proximity.[149] In any case, the meaning of the quotation is not affected.

The omission of εἰς διαθήκην γένους ("for the covenant of the race") that appears in Isa 49:6 between τέθεικά σε and εἰς φῶς deserves special attention.[150] While the omission of the phrase may be due to the Lukan interest in the Gentile mission,[151] it is also possible that Luke is aware of the Hebrew text of Isa 49:6 that has no equivalent of εἰς διαθήκην γένους.[152] More importantly, however, the phrase is also omitted in the Alexandrian group of the LXX.[153] The phrase may have been inserted into the text of Isa 49:6 under the influence of Isa 42:6 which includes this particular phrase.[154] If this is the case, then it is possible that the Isaianic quotation in Acts 13:47 reflects the Alexandrian tradition that may even have provided the original reading for this verse in Isaiah. Therefore, the attempt to find a theological reason for the omission of the phrase εἰς διαθήκην γένους may be misguided.

One can therefore conclude that the Isaianic text that lies behind Luke 24:47 and Acts 1:8 finally appears without significant alteration in Acts 13:47.

---

[148] For a discussion of the hypothesis that sees a Semitic background behind this and other Lukan quotations, see Earl Richard, "The Old Testament in Acts: Wilcox's Semitisms in Retrospect," *CBQ* 42 (1980) 330–41.

[149] So, Barrett, *Acts of the Apostles*, 1.657. See also J. H. Ropes, *The Beginnings of Christianity: The Text of Acts* (ed. F. J. Foakes Jackson and Kirsopp Lake; London: Macmillan, 1926) 3.128.

[150] It should be noted that D and the Greek manuscript of Cyprian read ἰδού φῶς τέθεικά σε τοῖς ἔθνεσιν instead of τέθεικά σε εἰς φῶς ἐθνῶν. This should probably be understood as a case of stylistic improvement in the Western texts. See Holtz, *Untersuchungen über die alttestamentlichen Zitate bei Lukas*, 33.

[151] See, for example, Barrett, *Acts of the Apostles*, 1.657.

[152] Cf. F. F. Bruce, *The Acts of the Apostles: The Greek Text with Introduction and Commentary* (3rd ed.; Grand Rapids, MI: Eerdmans, 1990) 315.

[153] I.e., A, Q, 26, 86, 106, 710. For this observation, I am indebted to Wayne Douglas Litke, "Luke's Knowledge of the Septuagint: A Study of the Citations in Luke-Acts" (Ph.D. diss., McMaster University, 1993) 142.

[154] Joseph Ziegler (*Isaias*, 305) has adopted the Alexandrian reading that does not contain the phrase as original. See also the discussion in Joseph Ziegler, *Untersuchungen zur Septuaginta des Buches Isaias* (AltAb 12.3; Münster: Aschendorffschen, 1934) 76.

b. The Transformation of the Isaianic New Exodus: The Accomplishment of the Lukan Redefinition of the People of God

In the Lukan reinterpretation of the Isaianic New Exodus in Luke 4:16–30, a contrast between the Jews and the Gentiles has already been suggested. This reinterpretation finds its climax here in Acts 13:46–47 as an Isaianic phrase is utilized in shifting the focus of the Isaianic New Exodus program. Acts 13:46–47 is significant not only because of the move to the Gentiles that has already been highlighted through the programmatic statements in Luke 24:47 and Acts 1:8. Acts 13:46–47 is also significant because of its claim that the response of the Jews is the force behind the move to the Gentiles. Acts 13:46 therefore becomes a striking reinterpretation of the Isaianic New Exodus program that had not itself anticipated the move of the "locus" of salvation to the Gentile communities. The significance of the juxtaposition of vss 46 and 47 does not, therefore, lie in its presentation of the exact "cause" of the move to the Gentiles[155] but in the fact that it signifies the beginning of a period when the Gentiles will become the majority. The reappearances of Isa 49:6 throughout the Lukan writings (cf. Luke 2:32) reflect the concern of the early Christian movement; and through a radical Lukan reinterpretation Isa 49:6 provides a tool for affirming the identity of a people of God that moves beyond the people of Israel.[156]

I will begin by analyzing the context of this quotation from Isaiah in Acts. Acts 13–14 represents the first sustained effort carried out by Christian missionaries to bring the gospel to the various regions beyond the Land of Israel. The significance of this move is marked by the commission scene in 13:1–3,[157] which contains a description of the ecclesiological leadership of the church of Antioch (προφῆται καὶ διδάσκαλοι, "prophets and teachers") with a list of names, the command of the Holy Spirit, and the formal rites of commissioning (νηστεύσαντες καὶ προσευξάμενοι καὶ ἐπιθέντες τὰς χεῖρας αὐτοῖς ἀπέλυσαν, "after fasting and praying they laid their hands on them and sent them off"). Recognizing the importance of Acts 13–14 in the development of the narrative of Acts, Philippe Menoud rightly argues that

---

[155] Throughout the narrative of Acts, the priority of the mission to the Jews is recognized (Acts 13:46); and the turn to the Gentiles is based not only upon the rejection of the message of salvation by the Jews but primarily upon the scriptural pattern one finds in Isaiah. It is with this understanding that one can understand why the Lukan Paul continues preaching to the Jews (cf. 14:1) immediately after his stay in Pisidian Antioch and also after making a similar claim in 18:6: ἀπὸ τοῦ νῦν εἰς τὰ ἔθνη πορεύσομαι ("From now on I will go to the Gentiles," cf. 18:19).

[156] A detailed discussion of the transformation of the Isaianic New Exodus in the Lukan writings is provided in chapter seven below.

[157] Barrett, *Acts of the Apostles*, 1.598: "This short paragraph marks a major departure in Luke's story."

these two chapters provide the theological paradigm in which the other travel narratives of Paul are to be understood.[158]

Within the narrative of Acts 13–14, the episode at Pisidian Antioch is widely recognized as the climax that provides meaning for the rest of the narrative.[159] It provides the first public sermon of Paul (13:16–41),[160] and this serves as a sample for the other synagogue sermons that are not described in detail, namely, those that appear both within Acts 13–14 and beyond (13:5, 14; 14:1; 17:1–3, 10, 17; 18:4, 19, 26; 19:8–10). This parallels the function of the Nazareth synagogue sermon (Luke 4:16–30), since both serve to introduce the content of the preaching of a main character in the setting of a synagogue.

More importantly, however, is the paradigmatic statement concerning the reaction of the Jews and the response one finds in Acts 13:46–47. As discussed above, the theme of rejection plays an important role in the Nazareth scene of Luke 4:16–30, and the theme of the rejection of the prophet (and his disciples) helps hold the Lukan writings together.[161] The phrase στρεφόμεθα εἰς τὰ ἔθνη ("we are now turning to the Gentiles," 13:46) is echoed in the phrase ἀπὸ τοῦ νῦν εἰς τὰ ἔθνη πορεύσομαι ("from now on I will go to the Gentiles," 18:6) and finds its climactic expression in the conclusion of the narrative: γνωστὸν οὖν ἔστω ὑμῖν ὅτι τοῖς ἔθνεσιν ἀπεστάλη τοῦτο τὸ σωτήριον τοῦ θεοῦ· αὐτοὶ καὶ ἀκούσονται ("Let it be known to you then that this salvation of God has been sent to the Gentiles; they will listen," 28:28). One can reasonably argue, therefore, that 13:46 is strategically placed at a critical point in the narrative. The explicit quotation from Isaiah together with the significant interpretative statement in Acts 13:46 make clear for the first time in the Lukan narrative the connections between the two important themes of Luke and Acts: the rejection by the Jews and the offer of the salvation to the Gentiles.[162] The use of Isa 49:6 also situates the rest of the narrative in Acts within the third stage of the programmatic proclamation of Acts 1:8: the mission to the Gentiles. For the

---

[158] Philippe H. Menoud, "Le Plan des Actes des Apôtres," *NTS* 1 (1954) 47.

[159] See Matthäus Franz-Josef Buss, *Die Missionspredigt des Paulus im pisidischen Antiochien: Analyse von Apg 13, 16–41 im Hinblick auf die literarische und thematische Einheit der Paulusrede* (Stuttgart: Verlag Katholisches Bibelwerk, 1980) 17. See also Edwin S. Nelson ("Paul's First Missionary Journey as Paradigm: A Literary-Critical Assessment of Acts 13–14" [Ph.D. diss., Boston University, 1982] 52) who has suggested that a chiastic pattern can be detected behind Acts 13–14 with the narrative scene of Pisidian Antioch at the center.

[160] This is also the place where Paul becomes the main character of the travel narrative. The others are now depicted as those around/with him (οἱ περὶ Παῦλον, 13:13).

[161] See, especially, Jerry Lynn Ray, *Narrative Irony in Luke-Acts: The Paradoxical Interaction of Prophetic Fulfillment and Jewish Rejection* (New York: Edwin Mellen, 1996).

[162] A further discussion of the relationship between these two themes will be provided in chapter seven below.

Lukan community, however, this is not simply another stage of the
development of the early Christian movement. It signifies the establishment of
the identity of the people of God in contradistinction from the ethnic nation
of Israel.

*c. The Ecclesiological Focus of the Isaianic Program: From the Stories of
Jesus and the Apostles to the Story of the Community*

Throughout the previous discussion, I have emphasized that Isaiah is not used
in a narrow christological sense. Instead, it serves to construct the identity of
the early Christian movement. This can again be seen in the use of Isaiah in
Acts 13:46–47. One of the most surprising aspects of the use of Isa 49:6 in
Acts 13:47 is the transference of the servant role from Jesus to the early
Christian missionaries. In the beginning of the Lukan writings, one already
encounters the phrase φῶς εἰς ἀποκάλυψιν ἐθνῶν ("a light for revelation to
the Gentiles," Luke 2:32), there applied to Jesus. The Isaianic background of
this verse is widely recognized[163] and an allusion to Isa 42:6 and especially
49:6 cannot be disputed.[164] In the narrative of Acts, Jesus' identity as the
servant of God is made clear (Acts 3:13, 26; 4:27, 30), and he is explicitly
identified as the one to whom the Isaianic Servant Songs point (Acts
8:32–35).

While some, such as Pierre Grelot,[165] have suggested that Christ is still the
referent of the φῶς of Isa 49:6 in Acts 13:47, most remain unconvinced and
see Isa 49:6 applied to the apostles.[166] A christological reading of the term
φῶς is improbable in light of the use of the pronoun ἡμῖν in the introductory
formula (vs 47), which refers to Paul and Barnabas.[167] Furthermore, although

---

[163] See, for example, Bovon, *Das Evangelium nach Lukas*, 1.115; and Fitzmyer, *Gospel According to Luke (I–IX)*, 428.

[164] Nolland (*Luke*, 1.120) is probably correct in understanding εἰς ἀποκάλυψιν as an explanatory gloss to φῶς ... ἐθνῶν.

[165] Pierre Grelot, "Note sur Actes, XIII, 47," 368–72: "Ce n'est pas Paul et Barnabé qui sont établis comme lumière des nations: c'est le Christ en gloire, comme le laisse entendre à demi-mot *Act.*, XXVI, 23 et comme c'est proclamé clairement dans la composition typiquement lucanienne de *Lc*, II, 32" (371). Cf. Dupont (*Nouvelles Études sur les Actes des Apôtres* [LD 118; Paris: Cerf, 1984] 345–49) who sees the apostles as representatives of Christ and therefore the light still refers to Christ but is also applicable to the apostles.

[166] See Haenchen, *Acts of the Apostles*, 414 n.3; Schneider, *Apostelgeschichte*, 2.146 n.29; Conzelmann, *Acts of the Apostles*, 417; Zmijewski, *Apostelgeschichte*, 519; and Thomas J. Lane, *Luke and the Gentile Mission: Gospel Anticipates Acts* (Frankfurt am Main/New York: Peter Lang, 1996) 177.

[167] The use of the singular pronoun σε in the quotation itself may be due to Luke's faithfulness to the text. In the context of Isaiah, however, the pronoun σε may refer to the servant who is the representative of Israel. The collective understanding of σε, therefore,

an understanding of ὁ κύριος (Acts 13:47) as referring to God (and not Jesus)[168] is not inconsistent with my reading of the Isaianic quotation, it seems more likely that a christological reference for ὁ κύριος is intended.[169] This is supported by the parallel with Luke 24:47 in which the risen Christ is the one who utters the words that contain an allusion to Isa 49:6. The Lukan accounts of the calling of Paul by Jesus (Acts 9:5; 22:8; and 26:15) also offer another set of parallels that support a christological understanding of the subject of the call. Therefore, the word φῶς should be understood as referring to the apostles.

The continuity between the ministries of Jesus and that of the apostles is thus symbolized by the repeated appearances of Isa 49:6 in the Lukan-writings. The debate concerning the subject of the Isaianic quotation should alert us to the ambiguous nature of the text.[170] This intentional ambiguity forces one to shift one's preoccupation with a christological focus to an appreciation of the wider program this Isaianic text denotes. In the context of Isaiah, Isa 49:6 signifies an important step in the Isaianic New Exodus in which the Gentiles are included in the program.

3.6 Acts 28:25–28

Acts 28:25–28 falls within the larger episode of Paul's activity in Rome (28:11–31) and functions as the climax to his preaching activity among the Jews (28:17–28). Disagreement among the Jews led to Paul's final statement with an explicit quotation from Isaiah. The Lukan hand can again be felt throughout the narrative of this final episode in Acts.[171] An examination of this passage provides a fitting conclusion to my discussion of the programmatic statements for the Lukan writings.

---

should not be ruled out with Paul and Barnabas being the representatives of the early Christian movement.

[168] So Haenchen, *Acts of the Apostles*, 414 n.5; and Koet, *Five Studies on Interpretation of Scripture in Luke-Acts*, 113.

[169] Gert Jacobus Steyn, *Septuagint Quotations in the Context of the Petrine and Pauline Speeches of the Acta Apostolorum* (CBET 12; Kampen: Pharos, 1995) 197.

[170] Buss (*Missionspredigt des Paulus im pisidischen Antiochien*, 138) has already noted that the dichotomy between Jesus and Paul/Barnabas is misconstrued as far as Acts 13:47 is concerned.

[171] See the discussion in Jacques Dupont, "La conclusion des Actes et son rapport à l'ensemble de l'ouvrage de Luc," 363; and Gerd Lüdemann, *Early Christianity according to the Traditions in Acts: A Commentary* (trans. John Bowden; Minneapolis: Fortress, 1989) 263–64. Cf. Haenchen, *Acts of the Apostles*, 726–32.

a. The Text of the Isaianic Quotation in Acts 28:25–28

The importance of the Isaianic quotation is highlighted by the fact that the quotation itself and the comment on it by Paul (28:26–28) are placed after the action of the audience in 28:25. In 28:25 one reads that the people began to leave "after" Paul had uttered his final statement contained in 28:26–28.[172] Such a displacement places emphasis on the quotation from Isaiah in Acts 28:26–27:

Πορεύθητι πρὸς τὸν λαὸν τοῦτον καὶ εἰπόν, Ἀκοῇ ἀκούσετε καὶ οὐ μὴ συνῆτε, καὶ βλέποντες βλέψετε καὶ οὐ μὴ ἴδητε· ἐπαχύνθη γὰρ ἡ καρδία τοῦ λαοῦ τούτου, καὶ τοῖς ὠσὶν βαρέως ἤκουσαν, καὶ τοὺς ὀφθαλμοὺς αὐτῶν ἐκάμμυσαν· μήποτε ἴδωσιν τοῖς ὀφθαλμοῖς καὶ τοῖς ὠσὶν ἀκούσωσιν καὶ τῇ καρδίᾳ συνῶσιν καὶ ἐπιστρέψωσιν, καὶ ἰάσομαι αὐτούς·

Go to this people and say, You will indeed listen, but never understand, and you will indeed look, but never perceive. For this people's heart has grown dull, and their ears are hard of hearing, and they have shut their eyes; so that they might not look with their eyes, and listen with their ears, and understanding with their heart and turn — and I would heal them.

This quotation of Isa 6:9–10 is again based on the LXX.[173] With the LXX, this quotation in Acts differs from the Masoretic Hebrew text by toning down the effect (and agent) of the hardening process.[174] First, the Hebrew imperatives שמעו and ראו become the future indicatives ἀκούσετε and βλέψετε in the LXX. Second, the aorist passive ἐπαχύνθη is used to translate the imperative השמן and thus tones down the emphasis on God as the agent. Similarly, the hiphil imperatives הכבד and השע become the indicatives [βαρέως] ἤκουσαν and ἐκάμμυσαν. Finally, the insertion of γάρ at the beginning of 6:10 also shifts the focus away from God as the

---

[172] I am taking ἀπολύοντο as denoting an action that occurs after the aorist participle εἰπόντος that can be translated as a temporal circumstantial participle: "after (Paul) uttered .... " Cf. Bruce, *Acts of the Apostles*, 538; and Charles B. Puskas, "The Conclusion of Luke-Acts: An Investigation of the Literary Function and Theological Significance of Acts 28:16–31" (Ph.D. diss., St. Louis University, 1980) 60–62. Puskas further notes that "Luke never has Paul address no audience" (60).

[173] Among others, see William K. L. Clarke, "The Use of the Septuagint in Acts," in F. J. Foakes Jackson and Kirsopp Lake, eds., *The Beginnings of Christianity* (London: Macmillan, 1922) 2.1.88; Haenchen, *Acts of the Apostles*, 724; Schneider, *Apostelgeschichte*, 2.418; Conzelmann, *Acts of the Apostles*, 227; and Litke, "Luke's Knowledge of the Septuagint," 146.

[174] I am here assuming that the LXX provides an interpretative translation of the Hebrew text. It is also possible, however, that the LXX reflects a Hebrew text that differs from the Masoretic text.

agent.[175] All these changes from the Hebrew text are also present in the Isaianic quotation in Acts 28:26–27.

The Isaianic quotation in Acts 28:26–27 differs from the LXX in two places. First, instead of πορεύθητι καὶ εἶπον τῷ λαῷ τούτῳ, Acts has πορεύθητι πρὸς τὸν λαὸν τοῦτον καὶ εἰπόν.[176] The change does not seem to alter the overall meaning of the verse; and the exact reason for this change remains uncertain.[177] It is possible that Luke has other textual witnesses that are lost to us but this remains pure speculation.[178]

The second change is the omission of αὐτῶν after ὠσίν in the quotation in Acts. This omission is noteworthy in that it is also missing in the majority of the witnesses of Matt 13:15.[179] This change in both documents may reflect the use of a group of texts that also omit αὐτῶν. This is confirmed by the presence of some LXX manuscripts in which αὐτῶν is also missing[180] and by the fact that the omission does not alter the text in terms of either content or style.[181]

One can therefore conclude that the Isaianic quotation in Acts 28:26–27 is taken from the LXX without any significant change of the text.

---

[175] Nevertheless, as Hans Wildberger (*Isaiah 1–12: A Commentary* [trans. T. H. Trapp; Minneapolis Fortress, 1991] 273) has pointed out, the wider context in Isaiah (cf. 9:7ff) shows that the role of Israel in the hardening process is already present in the Hebrew text.

[176] Some LXX manuscripts also have πρὸς τὸ λαὸν τοῦτον but this reading is probably secondary due to the influence of Christian scribes. See Ziegler, *Isaias*, 144.

[177] Holtz, *Untersuchungen über die alttestamentlichen Zitate bei Lukas*, 36.

[178] Litke ("Luke's Knowledge of the Septuagint," 146) suggests that this may be due to Luke's free citation from memory since the relative infrequency of the locative dative in the Greek of the first century CE may have caused the substitution of a prepositional phrase. This, however, is unlikely since in the LXX the phrase τῷ λαῷ τούτῳ is related to the verb εἶπον and not πορεύθητι and therefore the dative in the LXX is not necessarily a locative dative but can be taken as a dative of indirect object.

[179] Major exceptions that include the pronoun αὐτῶν can be found in: ℵ C 33 892 1241 it vg^mss sy^s.c.p.

[180] Most notable is the original reading of Sinaiticus and Symmachus. See Ziegler, *Isaias*, 144.

[181] Some (e.g., J. R. Harris, *Testimonies* [Cambridge: Cambridge University Press, 1920] 2.65, 74, 137; C. H. Dodd, *According to the Scriptures: The Sub-Structure of New Testament Theology* [London: Nisbet, 1952] 36–38; and Bruce, *Acts of the Apostles*, 540) have suggested that a Christian *testimonium* lies behind both the Matthean and Lukan citations of Isa 6:9–10. This is unlikely in light of the unique Lukan use of the citation here in Acts 28. For a further discussion of this theory, see Holtz, *Untersuchungen über die alttestamentlichen Zitate bei Lukas*, 35; and Krister Stendahl, *The School of St. Matthew and Its Use of the Old Testament* (Second Edition. Philadelphia: Fortress, 1968) 132.

b. Isaiah and the Lukan Justification of the Rejection of the Prophetic Movement: The Development of the Competitive Claim concerning the People of God

In this final chapter of Acts, the theme of the rejection of the Christian message by the Jews reaches its climax with yet another quotation from the text of Isaiah. With an Isaianic quotation, Luke is able to distinguish the community from the Jewish majority while at the same time claiming to be true to the ancient Israelite tradition concerning the development of the people of God. This is not the first appearance of the theme of rejection, but its position at the end of the narrative reflects the importance of this theme in Luke's program. As in Acts 13:46–47 and other similar episodes, in 28:25–28 there is again a turning to the Gentiles after an unfavorable response from the Jews.[182] In both 13:46–47 and 28:25–28 there is a Lukan speech with Paul being the main speaker. In both, a quotation from Isaiah occupies the center of the speech; and both are characterized by an unfavorable response from the Jewish audience. While Acts 13:46–47 belongs to an episode at the center of Paul's earlier ministry,[183] 28:25–28 forms the end of the ministry of the Lukan Paul. The connections between Acts 13 and 28 are further secured by two brief references in 18:6 and 19:9 that relate the theme of Jewish rejection to the decision to turn to the Gentiles. These two brief references serve as links that transform the announcement at 13:46–47 into a recurrent theme and a basic principle throughout the second half of the narrative of Acts.

Not only should the parallels between Acts 13:46–47 and 28:25–28 be noted; the climactic nature of the final episode also needs to be highlighted. The relative length of Paul's statement in Acts 28:25–28 reflects its importance in the work of Luke. Even more, the invocation of the authority of the Holy Spirit (τὸ πνεῦμα τὸ ἅγιον) and the prophet Isaiah (διὰ Ἡσαΐου τοῦ προφήτου) in the final word (ῥῆμα ἕν) of Paul underscores the significance of the passage.[184] This is further supported by the fact that while the Jews rejected the message of Paul in earlier passages, in this final statement the rejection is taken farther, in that it is proclaimed that the Jews

---

[182] Among others who see a link among Acts 13:46–47; 18:6; and 28:25–28, are Haenchen, *Acts of the Apostles*, 729; and Conzelmann, *Acts of the Apostles*, 227. Dupont, "La conclusion des Actes et son rapport à l'ensemble de l'ouvrage de Luc," 384–86, adds the episode in Ephesus (Acts 19:9).

[183] See the discussion in section 3.5 above.

[184] See François Bovon, "'How well the Holy Spirit Spoke Through the Prophet Isaiah to Your Ancestors!' (Acts 28:25)," *New Testament Traditions and Apocryphal Narrative* (trans. Jane Haapiseva-Hunter; PTMS 36; Allison Park, PA: Pickwick, 1995) 47–50.

will "never understand" (οὐ μὴ συνῆτε) and "never perceive" (οὐ μὴ ἴδητε).[185] The importance of Isaiah in the final statement of the Lukan writings is also reflected in the absence of an explicit Isaianic quotation from the discussion of the purpose of parables within the pericope on the parable of the sower (Luke 8:4–15).[186] In Luke 8:10 one finds the phrase taken from Isa 6:9: "looking they may not perceive, and listening they may not understand." This is most likely a summary of the longer statement in Mark 4:12. Unlike Matt 13:14–15, however, an explicit quotation from Isaiah is not presented in Luke 8. Rather, this quotation is moved to the very end of the narrative of Acts. Since it seems likely that Luke is aware of the use of an explicit Isaianic quotation in the discussion of the purpose of parables,[187] the omission in Luke 8 and its transposition to Acts 28 becomes even more significant. This transposition also allows Luke to highlight the contrast between the jubilant message of Luke 3 and the pessimistic conclusion concerning the Jews in Acts 28. It is to this contrast that I must now turn.

c. From Luke 3 (Isaiah 40) to Acts 28 (Isaiah 6): The Dramatic Reversal of the Isaianic Program

In the context of Isaiah, chapter six provides an account of the call to Isaiah to preach to his people. Instead of opening the hearts of the people to the message of God, the prophet Isaiah is called to proclaim a message that hardens the heart of the people.[188] While the LXX version of Isa 6:9–10

---

[185] No matter what position one takes concerning the issue of Jews and Gentiles in Luke-Acts, the narratological finality of this climactic statement cannot be denied. Considering the use of the hardening motif elsewhere in the Biblical corpus, however, one should avoid concluding that this signals the absolute end of the Jewish mission in the Lukan scheme. See Koet, *Five Studies on Interpretation of Scripture in Luke-Acts*, 138; John L. McLaughlin, "Their Hearts were Hardened: The Use of Isaiah 6,9–10 in the Book of Isaiah," *Bib* 75 (1994) 1–25; Vittorio Fusco, "Luke-Acts and the Future of Israel," *NovT* 38 (1996) 1–17; and Michael Wolter, "Israel's Future and the Delay of the Parousia, According to Luke," in David P. Moessner, ed., *Jesus and the Heritage of Israel: Luke's Narrative Claim upon Israel's Legacy* (Harrisburg, PA: Trinity Press International, 1999) 307–24. Cf. Haenchen, *Acts of the Apostles*, 723–24, 729; Wilson, *Gentiles and the Gentile Mission*, 226; Conzelmann, *Acts of the Apostles*, 227–28; and Sanders, *Jews in Luke-Acts*, 296–99. Bovon ("'How well the Holy Spirit Spoke Through the Prophet Isaiah to Your Ancestors!'" 47) has also suggested the possibility of reading the phrase καὶ ἰάσομαι αὐτούς independently of μήποτε (vs 27) and thus implying a last hope for Israel.

[186] Concerning the source of this pericope, one may assume that Luke has Mark and other written (or oral) sources at his disposal. See the discussion in Bovon, *Das Evangelium nach Lukas*, 1.405.

[187] This is suggested by the fact that both Matthew and Acts use the same form of the quotation. See the discussion of the text of Isa 6:9–10 above.

[188] Otto Kaiser (*Isaiah 1–12: A Commentary* [trans. John Bowden; 2nd ed.; Philadelphia: Westminster, 1983] 118–21, 131) has rightly pointed out that Isa 6:9–10 is

emphasizes the role of the people in the process of hardening, the rebellious nature of the people had already appeared in the Hebrew text of Isaiah 1–5. Indeed, as early as Isaiah 1, one encounters the important theme of the rebellious nature of Israel and her turning away from her God. This theme continues in 2:5–22 with the mentioning of the punishment that will come to Jerusalem because of pride and idolatry. The emphasis on judgment goes on through Isaiah 5. The passage in Isa 6:9–10 is therefore the culmination of charges against the people of God, for the rebellious nature of Israel is already an established fact.[189]

In Isa 6:9–10, the metaphors of vision and audition are used in the indictment of the people of God. Gregory Beale[190] has highlighted the ironic use of these metaphors in relation to the people of God. He notes that a similar use of such metaphors can be found in Pss 115:5b–6 and 135:15–17; but in those contexts the point is that those who worship idols will become idols themselves: "Those who make them and all who trust them shall become like them" (Ps 135:18; cf. 115:8). The metaphors of "hearing but not understanding ... seeing but not perceiving" are therefore typical anti-idolatry language and are applied to the people of God in Isa 6:9–10. This is confirmed by both the wider context of Isaiah 6 (especially vss 8–13) and the recurrence of these metaphors in Isaiah 40–55, where they are applied explicitly to the idols.[191] In Acts 28, therefore, the same anti-idol polemic language is used against the people of God.[192]

More important, however, is the focus upon the situation of the people of God in the book of Isaiah. In Isaiah, the indictment of Isa 6:9–10 is not the final statement on the people of God.[193] The coming of the salvation of God in Isaiah 40–55 represents a situation in which the people of God will regain the chance to be the recipients of the salvation of God. Here, the similarities as well as contrasts between Isaiah 6 and 40 demand one's attention. A number of scholars who recognize the transformation of traditions within the Isaianic corpus itself have already highlighted the thematic relationship between these two chapters. First, the generic affinity between Isaiah 6 and

---

less concerned with the message of the prophet than the effect of the proclamation of the prophetic message upon the people. As I have discussed above, this is softened in the LXX through the various changes made to the text. The pessimism of the prophetic ministry remains, however.

[189] Although the theme of salvation is most prominent in Isaiah 40–55, it is already present in 2:1–4 and 4:2–6.

[190] Gregory K. Beale, "Isaiah vi 9–13: A Retributive Taunt Against Idolatry," *VT* 41 (1991) 257–78.

[191] See Isa 42:16–20; 43:8–12; 44:8–20; 47:5–11.

[192] I will argue that anti-idol polemic plays a significant role in both the Isaianic New Exodus and the narrative of Acts. See chapter six below.

[193] Wildberger, *Isaiah 1–12*, 271.

40 should be noted. Frank Cross has already established that Isa 40:1–11 depicts the commission scene from the heavenly council.[194] He has also pointed out that Isa 40:1–11 "is a remarkable parallel to Isaiah 6:1–12."[195] Cross' suggestion concerning the genre of the two passages has been picked up by Robert Fisher,[196] who notes that Isa 40:1–11 is modeled upon Isa 6:1–12 for in Isaiah 40 one also finds the cries of the heavenly beings (cf. 40:3, 6), the protest of weakness and unworthiness (cf. 40:6–7), and the prophet's commission by Yahweh (cf. 40:9). The interrelationship between Isa 6:1–12 and 40:1–11 has been noted by many[197] and it has been recognized that both are pivotal in their respective parts of the book (i.e., Isaiah 1–39 and 40–55).

The similarities between Isa 6:1–12 and 40:1–11 highlight the one critical contrast between the two passages. In Isa 6:1–12, emphasis is placed upon the themes of judgment and destruction and the impossibility of the people of God to respond to the message of the prophet. In Isaiah 40, however, a dramatic reversal of the previous indictment is introduced. This is a section written by one who has "the task of proclaiming salvation, and nothing but salvation, to his people."[198] In 40:1–11, there is the unequivocal announcement proclaiming the dawn of salvation and the reversal of the previous oracles of doom.

---

[194] Frank M. Cross, "The Council of Yahweh in Second Isaiah," *JNES* 12 (1953) 274–77; and idem, *Canaanite Myth and Hebrew Epic: Essays in the History of the Religion of Israel* (Cambridge, MA: Harvard University Press, 1973) 186–90. See also Christopher R. Seitz, "The Divine Council: Temporal Transition and New Prophecy in the Book of Isaiah," *JBL* 109 (1990) 229–47.

[195] Cross, *Canaanite Myth and Hebrew Epic*, 188.

[196] Robert W. Fisher, "The Herald of Good News in Second Isaiah," in Jared J. Jackson and Martin Kessler, eds., *Rhetorical Criticism: Essays In Honor of James Muilenburg* (PTMS 1; Pittsburgh: Pickwick, 1974) 117–32. He concludes that "it might legitimately be said that Isa 40.1–11 is the call of Isaiah translated into terms of Second Isaiah's idiom and represents that phenomenon in both the life and the book of the latter" (126). See also Roy F. Melugin, *The Formation of Isaiah 40–55* (BZAW 141; Berlin/New York: Walter de Gruyter, 1976) 83–84.

[197] In addition to the studies mentioned above, see, for example, the recent studies of Rolf Rendtorff, "Zur Komposition des Buches Jesaja," *VT* 34 (1984) 295–320; idem, "Jesaja 6 im Rahmen der Komposition des Jesajabuches," in J. Vermeylen, ed., *The Book of Isaiah — Le Livre d'Isaïe. Les oracles et leurs relectures. Unité et complexité de l'ouvrage* (BETL 81; Leuven: Leuven University Press, 1989) 73–82; McLaughlin, "Their Hearts were Hardened: The Use of Isaiah 6,9–10 in the Book of Isaiah," 20; and Christopher R. Seitz, "How is the Prophet Isaiah Present in the Latter Half of the Book? The Logic of Chapters 40–66 within the Book of Isaiah," *JBL* 115 (1996) 219–40. For the wider relationship between Isaiah 6 and 40–55, see Bernard Gosee, "Isaïe 52,13–53,12 et Isaïe 6," *RB* 98 (1991) 537–43; and Benjamin D. Sommer, *A Prophet Reads Scripture: Allusion in Isaiah 40–66* (Stanford, CA: Stanford University Press, 1998) 95.

[198] Claus Westermann, *Isaiah 40–66: A Commentary* (trans. David M. G. Stalker; OTL; Philadelphia: Westminster, 1969) 9.

Only with this understanding of the relationship between Isa 6:1–12 and 40:1–11 can one begin to appreciate the significance of the Isaianic quotation in Acts 28:25–28. Immediately after the Lukan prologue, one finds an extended quotation from Isa 40:3–5 in Luke 3:4–6. In the previous chapter I have established the significance of this Isaianic quotation in defining the whole Lukan program. At the end of the Lukan writings, however, there is a quotation from Isa 6:9–10. As in the Isaianic corpus, both Isaiah 6 and 40 play a significant role in the composition of the narrative. The most striking fact is, however, the dramatic reversal of the original Isaianic scheme. The Isaianic scheme of "judgment-salvation" as represented by Isaiah 6 and 40 has been reversed. In the very beginning of the Lukan program, salvation is announced through the use of Isa 40:3–5. At the end of the Lukan writings, however, the theme of judgment is climactically announced through the use of Isa 6:9–10. In the Lukan writings, therefore, instead of "judgment-salvation" one finds the proclamation of the scheme of "salvation-judgment" upon the people of God.[199] This reversal is highlighted by the use of the vision metaphor in Luke 3:6 (Isa 40:5) and Acts 28:27 (Isa 6:10). Whereas in Luke 3:6 there is the announcement that all will "see" the salvation of God, in Acts 28:27 one reads that the eyes of the people of God are closed. Here, one finds an example of a dramatic reversal of the "dramatic reversal" presented in the wider Isaianic context.

This dramatic reversal is further confirmed by a comparison between Isa 61:1–2 as it appears in Luke 4:18–19 and Isa 6:9–10 in Acts 28:26–27. As in the case of Isaiah 40, Isa 61:1–2 represents a use of the vision metaphor in that in the new era the prophet is sent to proclaim sight to the blind (κηρύξαι ... τυφλοῖς ἀνάβλεψιν). This reverses the situation of judgment in Isa 6:9–10 in which the people of God could not see for their eyes were closed. In the Lukan writings, the order of the two passages is again inverted.[200] While the ministry of Jesus begins with a note that brings sight to

---

[199] One should note that an important tie between Luke 3:4–6 and Acts 28:25–28 is the use of the word σωτήριον. As Dupont (*Salvation of the Gentiles*, 15) has pointed out, the neuter form of this noun only appears four times in the New Testament, three of which are in the Lukan writings (Luke 2:30; 3:5; Acts 28:28). It is curious to note, however, that while many see the connections between Luke 3 and Acts 28, the dramatic reversal accomplished by the two Isaianic quotations at the beginning and end of the Lukan writings is consistently missed. See, for example, Dupont, "La conclusion des Actes et son rapport à l'ensemble de l'ouvrage de Luc," 402; Puskas, "The Conclusion of Luke-Acts," 90; and Tannehill, *Narrative Unity of Luke-Acts*, 349.

[200] The vision metaphor plays an important role in both Isaiah and Luke-Acts. See the discussion in Dennis Hamm, "Sight to the Blind: Vision as Metaphor in Luke," *Bib* 67 (1986) 457–77; idem, "Paul's Blindness and its Healing: Clues to Symbolic Intent (Acts 9, 22 and 26)," *Bib* 71 (1990) 63–72; Ronald E. Clements, "Patterns in the Prophetic Canon: Healing the Blind and the Lame," in Gene M. Tucker, David L. Petersen, and Robert R. Wilson, eds., *Canon, Theology, and Old Testament Interpretation: Essays in Honor of*

the people, the Lukan writings end with a note that the people of God have closed their eyes (τοὺς ὀφθαλμοὺς αὐτῶν ἐκάμμυσαν, Acts 28:27). This confirms that the Isaianic quotation in Acts 28:26–27 cannot be examined in isolation from other Isaianic quotations in Acts.[201] Through the use of both Isa 40:3–5 and Isa 6:9–10 and their reversal of the order in Isaiah, the significance of the rejection of the message of salvation by the Jews is skillfully highlighted. With such an appreciation of the Isaianic New Exodus behind the Lukan writings, one can begin to notice the critical deviation from the Isaianic scheme at the very end of the narrative. Throughout the narrative of Acts, there is an attempt to restore the people of God as well as to include the Gentiles within this message of salvation. The success of the Gentile mission remains an open question but the mission to the Jews is now characterized by their rejection. This rejection is ironically noted by yet another quotation from the Isaianic corpus (Isa 6:9–10).

3.7 Conclusion

In this chapter, I have established the importance of Isaiah in all the programmatic statements that control the narrative of Acts. All five of these programmatic statements (Luke 4:16–30; 24:44–49; Acts 1:8; 13:46–47; 28:25–28) fulfill the criteria set by Tannehill as they all provide: previews and reviews, repeated or highlighted scriptural references, commission statements, and interpretive statements by a reliable character.[202] In all these statements, an allusion or explicit quotation to Isaiah can be identified.

In Luke 4:16–30, the dawn of the new age as characterized by the Isaianic New Exodus is announced. This is, however, qualified by two Lukan themes that will be developed further in the narrative of Acts: the rejection of the prophetic movement and the inclusion of the Gentiles. In Luke 24:44–49; Acts 1:8; and 13:46–47, the inclusion of the Gentiles is justified by the use of Isa 49:6. In Acts 28:25–28, the rejection of the prophetic movement by the Jews is noted by a lengthy quotation from Isaiah 6. Through such evocation

---

Brevard S. Childs (Philadelphia: Fortress, 1988) 189–200; and Kenneth T. Aitken, "Hearing and Seeing: Metamorphoses of a Motif in Isaiah 1–39," in Philip R. Davies and David J. A. Clines, eds., *Among the Prophets: Language, Image and Structure in the Prophetic Writings* (JSOTSup 144; Sheffield: JSOT Press, 1993) 12–41.

[201] This is the major weakness of the work of Craig A. Evans (*To See and Not Perceive: Isaiah 6:9–10 in Early Jewish and Christian Interpretation* [Sheffield: Sheffield Academic Press, 1989]) who attempts to trace the development of the use of Isa 6:9–10 through early Jewish and Christian literature. Such narrow diachronic exercise fails to recognize fully the different roles the passage plays in different literary contexts.

[202] Tannehill, *Narrative Unity of Luke-Acts*, 1.21–22.

of the Isaianic traditions, Luke is able to emphasize both the continuity of his community with the ancient Israelite traditions and the distinctive identity of the community as the people of God. The Isaianic program becomes, therefore, the hermeneutical framework in which isolated events can be interpreted. This holistic reading of the narrative against the text of Isaiah allows one to uncover the dramatic reversal placed at the very end of the narrative.

Chapter 4

The True People of God:
The Restoration of Israel

4.1 Introduction

In chapter two above, four themes were highlighted as ones that control the program of both Isaiah and Acts: the restoration of Israel, the word of God, the anti-idol polemic, and the salvation offered to the nations/Gentiles. While the final three can be considered as themes that provide the most distinguishing features of the Isaianic (as well as the Lukan) program, the emphasis on the restoration of Israel is the foundational one upon which the other three can be developed.[1] An examination of the restoration of Israel should, therefore, be the starting point of the discussion.

In the Lukan writings, the theme of restoration is one that occupies the early chapters of Acts. The rhetorical function of the adaptation of the language of "restoration" should first be noted. The claim of restoration does not simply point towards the arrival of a certain historical point of time. The claim of restoration as unfolding within the development of a certain community, albeit as yet an incomplete process, constitutes an attempt to provide a normative definition concerning the nature of the eschatological Israel. The identity of the Christian community therefore again becomes an issue that accompanies the declaration of the arrival of a certain significant period of time, one that has long existed within the prophetic traditions of the hope of restoration.

In this chapter, I will first provide a discussion of the hope of restoration in the Isaianic New Exodus program. Then, the various themes that appear also in Acts will be examined. This approach allows one to appreciate the significance of the emphasis placed on the restoration of Israel in the first half of the narrative of Acts. It is upon such foundation that the rest of the narrative is built.

---

[1] The presence of the theme of restoration in other writings both within the Hebrew Bible and those that are developed in the Second Temple period should not undermine the significance of the theme in the Isaianic program.

4.2 Isaiah and the Restoration of Israel

In the Isaianic New Exodus program, several interrelated themes are tied to the hope of the restoration of Israel. These can be found throughout the text of Isaiah although they are most concentrated in Isaiah 40–55.

a. The Reconstitution of Israel

First and foremost in the vision of restoration is the focus on the reconstitution of Israel. This emphasis is the immediate consequence of the declaration of Yahweh in the prologue to Isaiah 40–55 where the message of comfort is announced: "Comfort, O comfort my people, says your God" (40:1). The people of Israel can rejoice because "the Lord God comes with might, and his arm rules for him" (40:10). It is in this new era that Yahweh "will have compassion on his suffering ones" (49:13).

As the Lord acts, his people will become whole again. The concern for the reconstitution of Israel is manifested in two related expectations. First, during Israel's reconstitution the twelve tribes will come together as in the days of old. In a passage that has already been shown to play a critical role in the Lukan narrative,[2] the mission to the nations is preceded by the reconstitution of Israel as Yahweh declares:

> It is too light a thing that you should be my servant
> to raise up the tribes of Jacob
> and to restore the survivors of Israel;
> I will give you as a light to the nations,
> that my salvation may reach to the end of the earth. (Isa 49:6)[3]

A concern for the "tribes" of Israel can again be seen in a plea to God to act for his people:

> Turn back for the sake of your servants,
> for the sake of the tribes that are your heritage. (Isa 63:17b)

Closely related to this concern for the twelve tribes of Israel is a second expectation that relates to the hope of the reunification of Israel. In the new era of salvation, the two "kingdoms" will become one. This constitutes an important element in the restoration program outlined in Isaiah 11, a remarkable passage especially since it originated in Jerusalem:

> The jealousy of Ephraim shall depart,

---

[2] Please refer to chapter three above.

[3] The reference to "the tribes of Jacob" can only be understood as referring to the twelve tribes of Israel (cf. Sir 36:13; 48:10). The verse that precedes this one highlights the concern that "Israel might be gathered" to Yahweh (Isa 49:5).

the hostility of Judah shall be cut off;
Ephraim shall not be jealous of Judah,
and Judah shall not be hostile towards Ephraim. (Isa 11:13)[4]

This anticipation of the reconstitution of Israel therefore affirms both the re-creation of the twelve-tribe Israel and the reunification of the divided kingdom. This anticipated act of reconstitution is considered an act of new creation, and the emphasis on Yahweh as the one responsible for this act can be found throughout the text of Isaiah 40–55 in the description of Yahweh as Israel's creator (ברא, 43:1, 15), potter (יצר, 43:1; 44:2, 24; 45:9, 11), and maker (עשׂה, 44:2; 51:13; 54:5).[5]

b. The Ingathering of the Exiles

In the rhetorical context of Isaiah, the reconstitution of Israel necessarily entails the ingathering of the exiles.[6] The prologue to Isaiah 40–55 expresses concern for the exiles:

He will feed his flock like a shepherd;
he will gather the lambs in his arms,
and carry them in his bosom,
and gently lead the mother sheep. (Isa 40:11)[7]

Explicit statements concerning the ingathering of the exiles can be found throughout Isaiah 40–55. In an address to Israel, Yahweh declares:

Do not fear, for I am with you;
I will bring your offspring from the east,
and from the west I will gather you;
I will say to the north, "Give them up,"
and to the south, "Do not withhold;
bring my sons from far away
and my daughters from the end of the earth —

---

[4] There is no question that Ephraim and Judah represent the two "divided" kingdoms. The phrase "Ephraim and the inhabitants of Samaria" in Isa 9:9 and other references in 7:1–9 show that the designation "Ephraim" refers to the entire Israel (as distinct from Judah). This usage probably originates from the fact that "Ephraim is the tribe which laid claim to a leadership position in Israel" (Hans Wildberger, *Isaiah 1–12: A Commentary* [trans. T. H. Trapp; Minneapolis: Fortress, 1991] 230). See also Isa 7:17 that explicitly mentions "the day that Ephraim departed from Judah."

[5] See Paul Del Brassey, "Metaphor and the Incomparable God in Isaiah 40–55" (Th.D. diss., Harvard University, 1997) 113, who notes that the creation of the heaven and earth is explicitly linked with the formation of the people of God in Isaiah (see 44:24 and 51:13).

[6] The ingathering of the exiles is already tied to the restoration program in Deut 30:3: "then the LORD your God will restore your fortunes and have compassion on you, gathering you again from all the peoples among whom the LORD your God has scattered you."

[7] The parallelism between 40:1–2 and vss 9–11, as discussed in chapter two above, points to the significance of the theme of the ingathering of exiles as defining the nature and content of the declaration of "Comfort" in vs 1.

everyone who is called by my name,
whom I created for my glory,
whom I formed and made." (Isa 43:5–7)[8]

The return of the exiles is closely tied with the imagery of "the Way" (דרך);[9] and this connection appears even beyond Isaiah 40–55 in a passage that betrays an apocalyptic tone:

A highway shall be there,
and it shall be called the Holy Way;
the unclean shall not travel on it,
but it shall be for God's people;
no traveler, not even fools, shall go astray.
No lion shall be there,
nor shall any ravenous beast come up on it;
they shall not be found there,
but the redeemed shall walk there.
And the ransomed of the LORD shall return,
and come to Zion with singing;
everlasting joy shall be upon their heads;
they shall obtain joy and gladness,
and sorrow and sighing shall flee away. (Isa 35:8–10)[10]

These passages form the central core of the Isaianic New Exodus in which the people of God are called to come out and return as the reconstituted nation of Israel. As in the Exodus story, the people will go out from the nations as "the LORD will go before you, and the God of Israel will be your rear guard" (52:12). God, the one who has "formed you [Israel] in the womb" (44:24), once again calls his people to come out as he creates the new community to be his "witnesses."

This emphasis on the ingathering of the exiles is naturally connected with the centrality of the concern for the Land. The reconstitution of the people cannot be discussed apart from the physical locality that provides substance

---

[8] See also 41:8; 49:18; 51:9–11; 52:11; and 54:7. The pre-exilic origin of the theme of the return of the exiles can be found in the name שאר ישוב (i.e., "a remnant shall return") in Isa 7:3 (cf. Isa 10:21; 11:12). For a discussion of the development of this theme from pre-exilic prophetic literature onwards, see Geo Widengren, "Yahweh's Gathering of the Dispersed," in W. B. Barrick and J. R. Spencer, eds., *In the Shelter of Elyon: Essays on Ancient Palestinian Life and Literature in Honor of G. W. Ahlström* (JSOTSup 31; Sheffield: Sheffield Academic Press, 1984) 227–30. Widengren further suggests that this theme has its origin in Mesopotamia (237–40).

[9] Please refer to chapter two above for the significance of this imagery in Isaiah and other Jewish writings that drew from it.

[10] See also Isa 60:4–7.

to the program.[11] The promise of salvation to the people of Israel is therefore intimately linked with an emphasis on the return to the Land:

> Thus says the LORD:
> In a time of favor I have answered you,
> on a day of salvation I have helped you;
> I have kept you and given you as a covenant to the people,
> to establish the land,
> to apportion the desolate heritages. (Isa 49:8)

In Isaiah, concern for the land is also symbolized by the expression of Yahweh's continuing love of Zion. To "possess the land" is therefore equated with an act to "inherit my [the LORD's] holy mountain" (Isa 57:13).[12] The numerous references to Zion and Jerusalem in Isaiah and the emphasis on Zion and Jerusalem as the locus of divine activity testify to the fact that these two names do not primarily function as geographical labels but icons that represent both the history and future of the people of God.

c. The Community of the Spirit

The reconstituted people of God is characterized by the work and power of the Holy Spirit. In Isa 44:1-4, the promise of the Spirit is made in connection with the reconstitution of Israel:

> But now hear, O Jacob my servant,
> Israel whom I have chosen!
> Thus says the LORD who made you,
> who formed you in the womb and will help you:
> Do not fear, O Jacob my servant,
> Jeshurun whom I have chosen.
> For I will pour water on the thirsty land,
> and streams on the dry ground;
> I will pour my spirit upon your descendants,
> and my blessing on your offspring.
> They shall spring up like a green tamarisk,
> like willows by flowing streams.[13]

---

[11] The relationship between the Jewish construction of community identity and the question of geographical locality is one of the central concerns that resurface once and again in literature spanning from the Second Temple period into the Rabbinic period. For a recent discussion of the continuing transformation of the understanding of the Land in Jewish traditions, see Isaiah M. Gafni, *Land, Centre, and Diaspora: Jewish Constructs in Late Antiquity* (JSPSup 21; Sheffield: Sheffield Academic Press, 1997).

[12] See also Isa 1:27-2:4. The significance of Zion and Jerusalem in the Isaianic vision has already been established in the discussion of Isa 40:1-11 in chapter two above.

[13] The emphasis on the Spirit in connection with the program of restoration is appropriate here as the note concerning the Spirit is situated within the metaphor of growth in the midst of an adverse situation (i.e. desert). Claus Westermann (*Isaiah 40-66: A Commentary* [trans. David M. G. Stalker; OTL; Philadelphia: Westminster, 1969] 136) has pointed out that this understanding of spirit as power is confirmed by the parallel term

Similarly, in 42:1, the Spirit is promised to the servant, one who will carry out the will of God:

> Here is my servant, whom I uphold,
> my chosen, in whom my soul delights;
> I have put my spirit upon him;
> he will bring forth justice to the nations.[14]

A direct connection between the arrival of the eschatological Spirit and the beginning of the age of restoration is clearly made in Isa 32:14–17, a passage depicting the outpouring of the Spirit upon the eschatological people of Israel:

> For the palace will be forsaken, the populous city deserted;
> the hill and the watchtower will become dens forever,
> the joy of wild asses, a pasture for flocks;
> until a spirit from on high is poured out on us,
> and the wilderness becomes a fruitful field,
> and the fruitful field is deemed a forest.
> Then justice will dwell in the wilderness,
> and righteousness abide in the fruitful field.
> The effect of righteousness will be peace,
> and the result of righteousness, quietness and trust forever.

In this passage, the Spirit that is usually expected to rest upon particular individuals who are to carry out specific tasks of Yahweh (cf. Isa 11:1–3) is now promised to be bestowed upon the entire eschatological community of the new era.[15] Such a shift can best be understood as the process of democratization of the Spirit. Moreover, the connection between the Spirit and the community in the days of restoration recalls the emphasis on the creative role of the Spirit in ancient Israelite traditions.[16] In the hope surrounding the eschatological age, one again finds the creative acts of the Spirit in the reconstitution of the people of God.

"blessing," one "which is used in its original sense of vitality or power which bestows fertility."

[14] The significance of Isa 61:1–2 and its relationship with the servant songs in Isaiah 40–55 have already been noted in the previous chapter. The connection between the Spirit and the call for the return of the "captives" is made clear: "The spirit of the Lord God is upon me, because the LORD has anointed me; he has sent me to bring good news to the oppressed, to bind up the brokenhearted, to proclaim liberty to the captives, and release to the prisoners" (61:1). Cf. Isa 11:2.

[15] Cf. Isa 59:21 and 63:14.

[16] Cf. Gen 2:7; Ps 104:30. Walther Eichrodt (*Theology of the Old Testament* [trans. J. A. Baker; Philadelphia: Westminster, 1967] 2.29) rightly emphasizes the work of the spirit as "the central miracle of the new age," and "the spirit as the living power of the new creation finds its proper place in eschatology." His understanding of the spirit primarily as a moral power (57–60) should, however, be questioned.

d. The Rebuilding of the Davidic Kingdom

The memory of the glorious past of the kingdom of David also plays an important role in the formation of the vision of the restored Israel. In the epilogue of Isaiah 40–55, the promise to David is evoked:

> Incline your ear, and come to me;
> listen, so that you may live.
> I will make you an everlasting covenant,
> my steadfast, sure love for David. (Isa 55:3)[17]

The expectation of a Davidic figure is explicitly mentioned in several passages in Isaiah 1–39.[18] For instance, the enthronement hymn in Isaiah 9 speaks of the anticipated ruler of the eschatological kingdom:

> For a child has been born for us, a son given to us;
> authority rests upon his shoulders;
> and he is named Wonderful Counselor, Mighty God,
> Everlasting Father, Prince of Peace.
> His authority shall grow continually,
> and there shall be endless peace
> for the throne of David and his kingdom.

---

[17] The exact relationship between the Davidic figure and the new Moses is not further explicated in Isaiah. It appears that the New Moses is tied with the process of the deliverance of the people of God in the New Exodus. The anticipation of the Davidic kingdom focuses, however, on the glorious reign of the restored kingdom. The same tension that exists in the emphases on these two figures as well as the same focus on the different roles attached to these paradigmatic models can also be found in Acts in which Jesus is understood as both the Davidic Son of God as well as the New Moses. Furthermore, in an examination of Isa 55:1–5 in connection with Psalm 89, Otto Eissfeldt ("The Promises of Grace to David in Isaiah 55:1–5," in Bernhard W. Anderson and Walter Harrelson, eds., *Israel's Prophetic Heritage: Essays in Honor of James Muilenburg* [New York: Harper & Brothers, 1962] 201–2) has noted that, unlike Psalm 89, the Davidic language in Isaiah 55 is "metaphorical"; and that the expectation is not directed towards the coming of the Davidic figure but to the glorious past now applied to the entire people of Israel. Kenneth E. Pomykala (*The Davidic Dynasty Tradition in Early Judaism: Its History and Significance for Messianism* [Atlanta, GA: Scholars Press, 1995] 41) has further concluded that in Isaiah 40–55, "hope for an individual davidic king or messiah has been abandoned." Nevertheless, one must note that the radical dichotomy between the Davidic ruler and the people cannot be maintained in the strictest sense. See Walter C. Kaiser, Jr., "The Unfailing Kindness Promised to David: Isaiah 55.3," *JSOT* 45 (1989) 91–98. The expectation of an individual Davidic ruler in Isaiah 1–39 is more explicit. In Isaiah 1–39, there is evidence for both the hope for the restored kingdom without the Davidic figure (12:4–6; 14:25; 17:12–14; 29:5–8) and one in which the Davidic figure plays a significant role (9:2–7; 11:1–9). See Norman K. Gottwald, *All the Kingdoms of the Earth: Israelite Prophecy and International Relations in the Ancient Near East* (New York: Harper & Row, 1964) 197.

[18] For a detailed discussion of the various passages, see Paul D. Wegner, *An Examination of Kingship and Messianic Expectation in Isaiah 1–35* (Lewiston, NY: Mellen, 1992).

> He will establish and uphold it with justice and
> with righteousness from this time onward and forevermore.
> The zeal of the LORD of hosts will do this. (Isa 9:6–7)[19]

The reign of the Davidic figure is a signal of the end of suffering and a sign of the eschatological rule of the God of Israel:

> When the oppressor is no more, and destruction has ceased,
> and marauders have vanished from the land,
> then a throne shall be established in steadfast love in the tent of David,
> and on it shall sit in faithfulness a ruler
> who seeks justice and is swift to do what is right. (Isa 16:4b–5)

The explicit reference to the symbol "David" points to the construction of a future that will witness the return of the glory of Israel.[20] It is this "glorious" state that forms the basis of the hope of restoration. The entire vision of restoration can best be summarized by the statement: "In the LORD all the offspring of Israel shall triumph and glory" (45:25);[21] and it is in this age that "the glory of the LORD shall be revealed" (40:5).[22]

e. Repentance and the Turn to the Lord

The discussion of restoration presupposes an exilic situation in which the people of Israel are scattered throughout neighboring lands. In Isaiah, the suffering of the people is understood as God's punishment for their sins. This is a recurring theme of Isaiah 1–39, and is clearly stated in Isa 50:1: "because

---

[19] Similarly, in Isaiah 11, a passage that lays out the program of restoration, one reads: "A shoot shall come out from the stump of Jesse, and a branch shall grow out of his roots" (vs 1), and "On that day the root of Jesse shall stand as a signal to the peoples; the nations shall inquire of him, and his dwelling shall be glorious" (vs 10).

[20] Cf. Isa 55:5.

[21] The application of the verb הלל to the offspring of Israel has led some (e.g., John D. W. Watts, *Isaiah 34–66* [WBC 25; Waco, TX: Word, 1987] 160, 163) to interpret this verse as referring to the offspring praising God. This rendering of the intransitive hithpael form is unnatural and should not be adopted especially in light of the contrast with the previous verse in which it is stated that "all who were incensed against him shall ... be ashamed" (45:24). As in Jer 4:2 (cf. Isa 41:16), the sense of "being exulted" is found in connection with the (hithpael) verb הלל. Moreover, the understanding of Isa 45:25 as referring to the exaltation of Israel is further supported by the LXX in which the verb is translated by the passive verb ἐνδοξασθήσεται.

[22] The reference to "the glory of the LORD" (כבוד יהוה) here recalls the glory of the temple of Jerusalem. Carroll Stuhlmueller ("The Painful Cost of Great Hopes: The Witness of Isaiah 40–55," in Daniel Durken, ed., *Sin, Salvation, and the Spirit: Commemorating the Fiftieth Year of The Liturgical Press* [Collegeville, MN: Liturgical Press, 1979] 151) has pointed out that in Isaiah 40–55 the glory of the temple has been transferred to the people as the people of God becomes the locus of divine acts. This, she argues, points to the process of "democratizing" sacred traditions.

of your sins you were sold, and for your transgressions your mother was put away."[23]

In Isaiah 40–55, the coming of the era of salvation is attributed primarily to an act of God in spite of the rebellious nature of his people:

> You have not bought me sweet cane with money,
> or satisfied me with the fat of your sacrifices.
> But you have burdened me with your sins;
> you have wearied me with your iniquities.
> I, I am He who blots out your transgressions for my own sake,
> and I will not remember your sins. (Isa 43:24–25)

It is in response to this salvific act of God that the call to turn back to the Lord is issued:

> I formed you, you are my servant;
> O Israel, you will not be forgotten by me.
> I have swept away your transgressions like a cloud,
> and your sins like mist;
> return to me, for I have redeemed you. (Isa 44:21b–22)[24]

While Isaiah 40–55 maintains the logical (and theological) priority of the act of God is maintained in Isaiah 40–55, one finds a greater emphasis on repentance as the condition for God's action in the final chapters of Isaiah (56–66).[25] In 59:1–21, for example, one finds a sustained appeal to the people of God to repent so that they will be able to witness the mighty acts of Yahweh. The first two verses of this chapter are sufficient to illustrate this point:

> See, the LORD's hand is not too short to save,
> nor his ear too dull to hear.
> Rather, your iniquities have been barriers
> between you and your God,
> and your sins have hidden his face from you
> so that he does not hear. (Isa 59:1–2)[26]

Finally, the communal psalm of lament in Isa 63:7–64:12 should also be highlighted especially considering the connection of this genre with the continuing expression of the hope of restoration in the Second Temple Jewish

---

[23] Cf. Isa 42:22–43:1.

[24] The Hebrew word שׁוּב literally points to an act to turn back. It is used in the sense of "repentance" here. This act of turning back is a theme that finds it natural place in the promise of "restoration."

[25] It must be noted, however, that an understanding of repentance as the basis of the acts of God can also be detected in Isaiah 40–55 although not in such an explicit form. For example, in Isa 55:6–7, one reads: "Seek the LORD while he may be found, call upon him while he is near; let the wicked forsake their way, and the unrighteous their thoughts; let them return to the LORD, that he may have mercy on them, and to our God, for he will abundantly pardon."

[26] See also the lengthy discussion in Isa 58:1–14 and 66:1–5.

literature.[27] This psalm recalls the sins of the people and concedes that the people "have all become like one who is unclean" (64:6). It concludes, however, with an appeal to God to restrain his anger and act on behalf of his people:

> Our holy and beautiful house,
> where our ancestors praised you, has been burned by fire,
> and all our pleasant places have become ruins.
> After all this, will you restrain yourself, O LORD?
> Will you keep silent, and punish us so severely? (Isa 64:11–12)

The theme of repentance functions here as a response to the salvific acts of God as well as the basis of the call to Yahweh to act again on behalf of the people whom he has chosen as in the days of old. Repentance therefore becomes a significant theme in the vision of the restoration of Israel.[28]

f. The Inclusion of the Outcasts

The focus on the nations in the Isaianic New Exodus has already been discussed in the previous chapters and will remain as one of the primary concerns of the following chapters.[29] However, Isaiah's focus on the "outcasts" of Israel requires further demonstration. This focus appears in Isaiah 1–39 and 56–66.

Isaiah 11 states that Yahweh "will raise a signal for the nations, and will assemble the outcasts of Israel" (vs 12).[30] More significantly, Isa 56:1–8, a

---

[27] For a list of relevant texts, see James M. Scott, "Philo and the Restoration of Israel," *SBLSP* 34 (1995) 565, who states: "the Jewish penitential prayers review the history of the people, confess their breach of covenant culminating in the destruction of the First temple and exile, acknowledge God's judgment as just in accordance with his word through Moses, and then appeal to the mercy of God to restore the nation from dispersion, which is emphasized as Israel's present plight."

[28] The issue of repentance should also be discussed along with the theme of remnant in Isaiah (see Isa 4:2–6; 10:20–23; 11:10–16; 46:3–4). Gerhard F. Hasel (*The Remnant: The History and Theology of the Remnant Idea from Genesis to Isaiah* [Berrien Springs, MI: Andrews University Press, 1974] 402) has credited Isaiah for being the one who eschatologized the remnant motif. One should question, however, if the remnant motif should be understood as being the center of Isaiah's restoration program. In later Jewish traditions, the emphasis on the restoration of (the entire) Israel appears to be the dominant theme. See the discussion in E. P. Sanders, *Jesus and Judaism* (Philadelphia: Fortress, 1985) 95–98; and James W. Watts, "The Remnant Theme: A Survey of New Testament Research, 1921–1987," *PRSt* 15 (1988) 109–29.

[29] See chapters five to seven below.

[30] The word נדח (literally: "dispersed, banished") can be understood simply as referring to the "exiles," but it can also be taken as referring to those who are separated from the people of Israel (i.e., "outcasts"). This understanding is supported by Isa 56:8 where the context points to an emphasis on the outcasts of Israel.

passage "in the tradition of Deutero-Isaiah,"[31] emphasizes Yahweh's concern for the outcasts when it concludes:

> Thus says the Lord God,
> who gathers the outcasts of Israel,
> I will gather others to them
> besides those already gathered. (Isa 56:8)

It is within this context that the example of the eunuch is presented:

> For thus says the LORD:
> To the eunuchs who keep my sabbaths,
> who choose the things that please me
> and hold fast my covenant,
> I will give, in my house and within my walls,
> a monument and a name better than sons and daughters;
> I will give them an everlasting name
> that shall not be cut off. (Isa 56:4–5)

Such pronounced emphasis on the condition of the eunuch[32] highlights the concern for the outcasts in the era of the reconstitution of the people of God.[33] The reconstituted Israel will not be merely a community that is restored to the previous state of its historic past; this community will be transformed into one in which every member will witness the mighty acts of God.[34]

The preceding discussion highlights six significant themes in Isaiah's program of restoration. All six themes play a critical role in the first half of the narrative of Acts.

---

[31] Westermann, *Isaiah 40–66*, 316.

[32] The exact identity of the eunuchs in Isaiah 56 cannot be determined with any certainty. It is probable that they are not to be identified as "foreigners" but exist as a group alongside the foreigners that are not reckoned to be part of the community of Israel. One can speculate on the relationship between this passage and Isa 39:7 in which it is said that some of the sons of the people of God will become "eunuchs in the palace of the king of Babylon."

[33] Both foreigners and eunuchs are, of course, considered "outcasts" since they are the ones who are not permitted to worship Yahweh (cf. Deut 23:1–9).

[34] The theme of the transformation of nature should also be mentioned here. The anticipation of an Eden-like situation in Isa 43:19–21 and the vision concerning the new heavens and the new earth in Isa 65:17–25 prepare the way for the development of an apocalyptic hope of restoration. See, in particular, Paul D. Hanson, *The Dawn of the Apocalyptic* (rev. ed.; Philadelphia: Fortress, 1979) 32–208.

4.3 Acts and the Restoration of Israel

In the narrative of Acts, Israel's restoration forms the foundation of the Lukan New Exodus program. The hope for this restoration has already been laid out in the Lukan prologue of the gospel. In Luke 1:54–55, the deliverance of Israel is announced:

ἀντελάβετο Ἰσραὴλ παιδὸς αὐτοῦ, μνησθῆναι ἐλέους,
καθὼς ἐλάλησεν πρὸς τοὺς πατέρας ἡμῶν,
τῷ Ἀβραὰμ καὶ τῷ σπέρματι αὐτοῦ εἰς τὸν αἰῶνα.

He has helped his servant Israel, in remembrance of his mercy,
according to the promise he made to our ancestors,
to Abraham and to his descendants forever.[35]

This passage provides the entry point for understanding the Lukan story. Moreover, Luke employs the language of Isaiah to alert the readers to the salvific event occurring in Israel.[36]

Throughout the Lukan narrative, this promise is expressed in terms of the "hope of Israel." The "incompletion" of the program laid out in the Lukan prologue is explicitly noted in the Emmaus story in the final chapter of Luke where two disappointed disciples stated that the "hope" remains unfulfilled: "But we had hoped that he was the one to redeem Israel" (ἡμεῖς δὲ ἠλπίζομεν ὅτι αὐτός ἐστιν ὁ μέλλων λυτροῦσθαι τὸν Ἰσραήλ, Luke 24:21a). Luke has made it clear, however, that this is not the final statement concerning the "hope of Israel." In Luke 24:44–49, the final saying of Jesus points forward to the narrative of Acts as the fulfillment of this hope. The promise to Israel is explicitly noted in vs 49, a statement that again alludes to Isaiah:[37]

καὶ [ἰδοὺ] ἐγὼ ἀποστέλλω τὴν ἐπαγγελίαν τοῦ πατρός μου ἐφ᾽ ὑμᾶς· ὑμεῖς δὲ καθίσατε ἐν τῇ πόλει ἕως οὗ ἐνδύσησθε ἐξ ὕψους δύναμιν.

And see, I am sending upon you what my Father promised; so stay here in the city until you have been clothed with power from on high.

---

[35] See also Luke 1:68–79; 2:29–32.

[36] See especially Isa 41:8–9: "But you, Israel, my servant, Jacob, whom I have chosen, the offspring of Abraham, my friend; you whom I took from the ends of the earth, and called from its farthest corners, saying to you, 'You are my servant, I have chosen you and not cast you off'" (Σὺ δέ, Ἰσραὴλ, παῖς μου Ἰακὼβ, ὃν ἐξελεξάμην, σπέρμα Ἀβραάμ, ὃν ἠγάπησα, οὗ ἀντελαβόμην ἀπ᾽ ἄκρων τῆς γῆς καὶ ἐκ τῶν σκοπιῶν αὐτῆς ἐκάλεσά σε καὶ εἶπά σοι Παῖς μου εἶ, ἐξελεξάμην σε καὶ οὐκ ἐγκατέλιπόν σε).

[37] See Isa 32:15 in which "a spirit from on high" (πνεῦμα ἀφ᾽ ὑψηλοῦ) is promised during the restoration of Israel. For a detailed discussion of Luke 24:44–49, please refer to chapter three above.

The fact that the "hope of Israel" lies at the center of the Lukan program in Acts is supported by the statement of Paul in Acts 26:6–7 concerning the reason for his own imprisonment:

καὶ νῦν ἐπ᾽ ἐλπίδι τῆς εἰς τοὺς πατέρας ἡμῶν ἐπαγγελίας γενομένης ὑπὸ τοῦ θεοῦ ἕστηκα κρινόμενος, εἰς ἣν τὸ δωδεκάφυλον ἡμῶν ἐν ἐκτενείᾳ νύκτα καὶ ἡμέραν λατρεῦον ἐλπίζει καταντῆσαι·

And now I stand here on trial on account of my hope in the promise made by God to our ancestors, a promise that our twelve tribes hope to attain, as they earnestly worship day and night.

In the final chapter of Acts, the "hope of Israel" is explicitly mentioned:

διὰ ταύτην οὖν τὴν αἰτίαν παρεκάλεσα ὑμᾶς ἰδεῖν καὶ προσλαλῆσαι, ἕνεκεν γὰρ τῆς ἐλπίδος τοῦ Ἰσραὴλ τὴν ἄλυσιν ταύτην περίκειμαι.

For this reason therefore I have asked to see you and speak with you, since it is for the sake of the hope of Israel that I am bound with this chain. (Acts 28:20)

From these passages, one can see that the promise to Israel lies at the very center of the Lukan program. While the hope of Israel remains unfulfilled in Luke's gospel, it becomes the focus of the narrative in Acts. In this section, I will provide a thematic analysis of the restoration program in Acts in light of the discussion offered above concerning Isaiah.[38]

a. The Reconstitution of Israel

The reconstitution of Israel is related to a concern for the twelve tribes of Israel as well as the reunification of the divided kingdom. Both concerns can also be found in Acts.

First, a concern for the twelve tribes of Israel can be found in the pericope of the election of Matthias in Acts 1:12–26. In this passage, the account of the death of Judas is followed by a description of the election of one to substitute him. The two accounts are linked with the particle οὖν (vs 21); and the death of Judas provides the need to elect one to replace him.[39] The significance of this pericope is highlighted by the fact that Matthias does not reappear in the rest of the Lukan narrative. The focus of this episode rests not so much on Matthias as an individual as on the need to establish the number of the apostles as "twelve."

The concern for the number "twelve" first appears in the description of Judas as the one who "was numbered among us" (κατηριθμημένος ἦν ἐν

---

[38] While previous studies on the restoration program in Acts have concentrated only on one or two aspects of the narrative, a systematic analysis of Acts in light of the various themes present in Jewish traditions (and especially in Isaiah) is still lacking. Cf. Jacob Jervell, *Luke and the People of God* (Minneapolis, MN: Augsburg, 1972).

[39] The Lukan hand can be felt behind this connection as it occurs only in Acts among the New Testament writings.

ἡμῖν, Acts 1:17). The verb καταριθμέω, one that occurs only here in the New Testament, highlights the importance of the act of numbering. In addition, at the end of the story, it is said that Matthias "was added to the eleven apostles" (συγκατεψηφίσθη μετὰ τῶν ἕνδεκα ἀποστόλων, vs 26).[40] This phrase points to the fact that it is the completion of the number "twelve" that is the focus of this passage.

The Lukan emphasis on the Twelve is further strengthened by the connection between this passage and Luke 22. As in Acts 1:17, the description of Judas as one of the twelve is stressed. In Luke 22:3, Judas is named as one "who was one of the twelve" (ὄντα ἐκ τοῦ ἀριθμοῦ τῶν δώδεκα). Furthermore, as in the case of καταριθμέω, the noun ἀριθμός used in connection with the Twelve points to the significance of the number itself, especially since the only appearance of this noun in Luke is in this context.[41]

Furthermore, the discussion of the role of the Twelve in Luke 22:28–30 should be noted. In this passage, it is promised that those among the Twelve who remain faithful to Jesus "will sit on thrones judging the twelve tribes of Israel" (καθήσεσθε ἐπὶ θρόνων τὰς δώδεκα φυλὰς κρίνοντες τοῦ Ισραήλ, vs 30b). Here, the twelve apostles are explicitly linked with the twelve tribes of Israel.[42] A comparison with the Matthean parallel (Matt 19:28) further underlines the Lukan emphases. In Matt 19:28, this saying is located within a futuristic framework ("at the renewal of all things," ἐν τῇ παλιγγενεσίᾳ).[43] In Luke, however, the bestowal of authority[44] takes places

---

[40] The verb συγκαταψηφίζομαι could have numerical significance. As Jervell (*Luke and the People of God*, 184–85) has pointed out, the related verb συμψηφίζω is clearly used in a numerical sense.

[41] In this context, both Matthew (26:14) and Mark (14:10) simply have ὁ εἷς τῶν δώδεκα.

[42] In an examination of this Lukan passage, Christian Grappe ("Le logion des douze trônes: Eclairages intertestamentaires," in Marc Philonenko, ed., *Le Trône de Dieu* [Tübingen: Mohr Siebeck, 1993] 204–12) has highlighted the significance of *Testament of Judah* 25.1 in which the sons of Jacob will become the judges of the twelve tribes. He concludes that the twelve apostles are now understood as substitutes to the sons of Jacob in their role as judges (210).

[43] The word παλιγγενεσία occurs only here in the synoptic gospels. In extra-biblical literature, it carries a range of meaning that includes regeneration and restoration. In the Matthean context, it probably refers to the age to come. See Friedrich Büchsel, "παλιγγενεσία," *TDNT* 1 (1964) 688.

[44] The meaning of the word κρίνοντες should not be limited to a narrow sense of judgment that leads to condemnation. It should be understood in the sense of the Hebrew טֹפֵשׁ that includes the exercising of authority, as suggested by W. D. Davies and Dale C. Allison, Jr., *The Gospel According to Saint Matthew* (ICC; Edinburgh: T & T Clark, 1997) 3.55–56.

during the very speech of Jesus.[45] Furthermore, while the Matthean saying mentions the enthronement of the Son of Man, this note is missing in Luke since authority is now transferred to the Twelve. These Lukan variations pave the way for understanding the significance of the Twelve in Acts.

The significance of the number "twelve" as a reference to the twelve tribes of Israel is further supported by an explicit reference in Acts 26:7 to the hope related to the promise made to the "twelve tribes" (τὸ δωδεκάφυλον), a word that is apparently coined by Luke. Luke's conscious use of the connotations of the number twelve is therefore undeniable,[46] and this should serve as the key for unlocking the significance of the episode concerning the election of Matthias in Acts 1:12–26.

Thus the relationship between the symbol "twelve" and the twelve tribes of Israel in the Lukan writings has been established. This use of the symbol is consistent with one frequently found in Second Temple Jewish traditions;[47] and the organization of the Qumran community according to the principle of "twelve" confirms the power of such a symbol.[48] This preoccupation with the number "twelve" testifies to the fact that "the expectation of the restoration of the twelve tribes is frequent and widespread."[49] In Acts 1:12–26, therefore, the election of Matthias to complete the circle of the twelve should be understood as signaling the beginning of the restoration of Israel, for the twelve apostles become representatives of the twelve tribes of Israel.[50] Situated at the very beginning of the narrative of Acts, this passage

---

[45] The statement ("and I confer on you ... a kingdom," κἀγὼ διατίθεμαι ὑμῖν ... βασιλείαν, vs 29) is located in the present situation even when the temporal reference to "my kingdom" (μου βασιλείαν) is debatable.

[46] See also the parallels between Jesus' selection of the Twelve in Luke 6:12–16 and Acts 1:15–26. As Gert Jacobus Steyn (*Septuagint Quotations in the Context of the Petrine and Pauline Speeches of the Acta Apostolorum* [CBET 12; Kampen: Pharos, 1995] 39) has pointed out, both begin with the phrase ἐν ταῖς ἡμέραις ταύταις and with a prayer. These two elements are unique to the Lukan accounts. Furthermore, in both, the twelve are called apostles with Peter taking a prominent position. Jesus' action should also be interpreted as pointing toward the restoration of Israel. See also E. P. Sanders, "Jesus and the Kingdom: The Restoration of Israel and the New People of God," in E. P. Sanders, ed., *Jesus, the Gospels, and the Church: Essays in Honor of William R. Farmer* (Macon, GA: Mercer University Press, 1987) 225–39.

[47] For a survey of the emphasis on the Twelve in Second Temple Jewish literature, see Sanders, *Jesus and Judaism*, 96–97; and William Horbury, "The Twelve and the Phylarchs," *NTS* 32 (1986) 505–9.

[48] See, for example, Joseph M. Baumgarten, "The Duodecimal Courts of Qumran, the Apocalypse, and the Sanhedrin," *JBL* 95 (1976) 59–78.

[49] Sanders, *Jesus and Judaism*, 96.

[50] Karl H. Rengstorf ("The Election of Matthias," in W. Klassen and G. F. Snyder, eds., *Current Issues in New Testament Interpretation: Essays in Honor of Otto A. Piper* [New York: Harper, 1962] 184), who argues that the restoration of Israel lies at the center of this passage, has rightly concluded that "the narrative is not interested in the organization of

forms both the foundation and the starting point of the New Exodus in Acts by emphasizing the arrival of the new era in which the hope of Israel is beginning to be fulfilled.

Before leaving this passage, the nature of the reconstituted Israel demands further discussion. While some have argued that the Twelve should be identified with physical Israel,[51] others have argued that the Twelve symbolizes the formation of the "new Israel"[52] or the "true Israel."[53] First, an examination of the use of the term "Israel" in the Lukan writings shows that when the term is used, it refers to the Jews.[54] Nevertheless, this does not necessarily lead one to the conclusion that the title "Israel" is to be identified with the entire Jewish people. The fact that the twelve apostles themselves are not physically related to the twelve different tribes should prevent one from denying a certain symbolic value of the term "Israel." More significantly, the presentation of the qualification of the one to complete the circle of the Twelve[55] shows that "Israel" is now to be defined restrictively in terms of a

---

the early church." See also Charles Masson, "La reconstitution du collège des douze d'après Actes 1:15–26," *RThPh* 5 (1955) 198; Jervell, *Luke and the People of God*, 81; and Philippe H. Menoud, "The Additions to the Twelve Apostles According to the Book of Acts," in *Jesus Christ and the Faith: A Collection of Studies by Philippe H. Menoud* (trans. Eunice M. Paul; Pittsburgh, PA: Pickwick, 1978) 142. The connection with Luke 22:28–30 also forces one to question the view that Acts 1:12–26 is primarily concerned with the transmission of traditions and the bridge between Jesus and the apostles. Cf. Alfons Weiser, "Die Nachwahl des Mattias (Apg 1,15–26). Zur Rezeption und Deutung urchristlicher Geschichte durch Lukas," in G. Dautzenberg, Helmut Merklein, and Karlheinz Müller, eds., *Zur Geschichte des Urchristentums* (QD 87; Freiburg: Herder, 1979) 109–110.

[51] See, for example, Jervell, *Luke and the People of God*, 81; Menoud, "The Additions to the Twelve Apostles According to the Book of Acts," 142.

[52] Among others, see Heinz O. Guenther, *The Footprints of Jesus' Twelve in Early Christian Traditions: A Study in the Meaning of Religious Symbolism* (New York/Frankfurt am Main: Peter Lang, 1985) 93.

[53] Franz Mußner, "Die Idee der Apokatastasis in der Apostelgeschichte," in Heinrich Groß and Franz Mußner, eds., *Lex tua veritas: Festschrift für Hubert Junker zur Vollendung des siebzigsten Lebensjahres am 8. August 1961* (Trier: Paulinus-Verlag, 1961) 305. Mention should also be made to the position of Masson ("La reconstitution du collège des douze d'après Actes 1:15–26," 193–201) who suggests that the historical intent of the passage points to the mission to the Jews. In the hands of Luke, however, this passage focuses on the theme of witness. My discussion above has, however, shown that "the Twelve" does play a significant role in the Lukan program.

[54] In his detailed study, Graham Harvey (*The True Israel: Uses of the Names Jew, Hebrew and Israel in Ancient Jewish and Early Christian Literature* [Leiden: Brill, 1996]) argues that the hypothetical category "true Israel" does not exist in ancient Jewish and Early Christian literature. Furthermore, the term "Israel" is consistently used in various groups of writings to refer to both pious ones (according to whatever criteria used by the communities behind the writings) as well as fallen ones.

[55] Acts 1:21–22: "So one of the men who have accompanied us during all the time that the Lord Jesus went in and out among us, beginning from the baptism of John until the day

certain kind of relationship to Jesus. This is consistent with the rest of the narrative of Acts when a call to submit to the name of Jesus is issued. Furthermore, the absence of the use of the designation "new Israel" in the Lukan writings is to be expected since the ancient Israelite tradition is claimed by the Lukan community. This claim of continuity with the sacred past may have prevented the early Christian communities from utilizing any form of "hyphenated-Israel." While the exact relationship between the Lukan community and the "physical" Israel is still in the process of being negotiated, one can at least conclude that a distinction between the early Christian community and that of the "mainline" Jewish community is already present. With the occurrence of competing claims to legitimacy, certain criteria are present for determining how the "true" destiny of the ancient Israelite tradition can be achieved. It is in this sense that an implicit claim to the title "true Israel" can be said to exist in the narrative of Acts.[56]

With this understanding of the nature of Israel in Acts, the second aspect of the program of restoration can now be discussed. In Isaiah, the reconstitution of Israel entails the reunification of the divided kingdom. The same concern also plays an important role in Acts through the Lukan emphasis on Samaria. Samaria is already mentioned in the programmatic statement in Acts 1:8:

ἀλλὰ λήμψεσθε δύναμιν ἐπελθόντος τοῦ ἁγίου πνεύματος ἐφ᾽ ὑμᾶς, καὶ ἔσεσθέ μου μάρτυρες ἔν τε ᾽Ιερουσαλὴμ καὶ [ἐν] πάσῃ τῇ ᾽Ιουδαίᾳ καὶ Σαμαρείᾳ καὶ ἕως ἐσχάτου τῆς γῆς.

But you will receive power when the Holy Spirit has come upon you; and you will be my witnesses in Jerusalem, in all Judea and Samaria, and to the ends of the earth.

As suggested above,[57] this statement does not simply lay out the various geographical regions related to the spreading of the gospel. This statement phrased with Isaianic wordings consists of three categories that include one city, two regions, and a reference to the Gentiles. These three categories should be understood in theopolitical terms since they outline the three stages of the Isaianic New Exodus program. Therefore the reference to "all Judea and

---

when he was taken up from us — one of these must become a witness with us to his resurrection."

[56] My use of the term "true Israel" here and throughout this study is therefore different from the one constructed to be destroyed by Harvey (*True Israel*, 272–73). While Harvey notes that the term "Israel" is used in an inclusive sense in many Jewish writings, he also recognizes that certain communities (e.g., Qumran) present arguments for certain forms of observance at variance with the majority culture. The fact that such rules can lead to a purer form of worship in anticipation of the eschatological event encourages one to rethink the possibility of the existence of the category "true Israel" at least in an ideological sense.

[57] See chapter three above.

Samaria" most likely points to the reunification of the two kingdoms during
the new era that witnesses the restoration and reconstitution of Israel.[58]

The occurrence of both "Judea" and "Samaria" together is a unique Lukan
feature that appears in the New Testament only in Acts.[59] Significantly, the
two terms reappear in Acts 8:1,[60] a statement placed right before the episode
of Philip's ministry in Samaria. The significance of the Samaria episode in the
New Exodus program in Acts needs to be noted.

Acts 8:5 explicitly notes that "Philip went down to the city of Samaria"
(Φίλιππος δὲ κατελθὼν εἰς [τὴν] πόλιν τῆς Σαμαρείας). The fact that
the city of Samaria no longer exists can probably serve to explain the omission
of the article τὴν in some manuscripts.[61] Nevertheless, the external support
for the inclusion of the article is strong,[62] and the article should be retained.
The reference should therefore be understood as one that points either to
Sebaste or the ancient Shechem.[63] In any case, it is apparent that Luke aims at
highlighting the importance of the symbol "Samaria" in this episode.[64] The
same emphasis on the name "Samaria" is present in Acts 8:14 when it is said
that "Samaria had accepted the word of God" (δέδεκται ἡ Σαμάρεια τὸν
λόγον τοῦ θεοῦ). This blanket statement concerning the conversion of an
entire city or region appears only here in the narrative of Acts; and this
peculiar fact can only be understood when the symbolic value of the name
"Samaria" is recognized.

The relationship between the conversion of Samaria and the reconstitution
of the people of God is further highlighted by the reference to the "apostles at

---

[58] Jervell (*Luke and the People of God*, 117–20) has provided a detailed argument and
rightly concludes that the Samaritans are not considered Gentiles in Acts. The fact that the
term ἀλλογενής is applied to the Samaritan leper in Luke 17:18 should, however, prevent
one from identifying the Samaritans entirely with the Jews.

[59] Acts 1:8; 8:1. See also 9:31.

[60] Acts 8:1bc: "That day a severe persecution began against the church in Jerusalem,
and all except the apostles were scattered throughout the countryside of Judea and Samaria."

[61] E.g., C D E Ψ 𝔐.

[62] E.g., 𝔓74 ℵ A B 69 181 460* 1175 1898. See the discussion in Bruce Metzger, *A
Textual Commentary on the Greek New Testament* (2nd ed.; New York: United Bible
Societies, 1994) 311.

[63] Franklin Scott Spencer (*The Portrait of Philip in Acts: A Study of Role and
Relations* (Sheffield: Sheffield Academic Press, 1992] 85) has argued that this verse recalls
Shechem, a city that has already been mentioned in the speech of Stephen (Acts 7:16).

[64] Charles K. Barrett (*A Critical and Exegetical Commentary on the Acts of the
Apostles* [ICC. Edinburgh: T & T Clark, 1994] 1.402) has suggested that this reference
"means *either* that Luke supposed that the district of Samaria possessed only one city, *or*
that he was referring to the capital city, the Samaria of the OT." In both cases, the evocative
power of the symbol of Samaria is maintained. See also Martin Hengel, *Between Jesus and
Paul: Studies in the Earliest History of Christianity* (Philadelphia: Fortress, 1983) 123–26,
who provides substantial support for the reading, "He went down into the (capital) city of
Samaria."

Jerusalem"[65] in Acts 8:14: "Now when the apostles at Jerusalem heard that Samaria had accepted the word of God, they sent Peter and John to them" (ἀκούσαντες δὲ οἱ ἐν Ἱεροσολύμοις ἀπόστολοι ὅτι δέδεκται ἡ Σαμάρεια τὸν λόγον τοῦ θεοῦ ἀπέστειλαν πρὸς αὐτοὺς Πέτρον καὶ Ἰωάννην). The observation by Ernst Haenchen that this verse shows that "the mission to the Samaritans was not completed by any subordinate outsider, but was carried out in due form by the legal heads of the Church in person"[66] is correct but inadequate. As the apostles in Jerusalem are the representatives of the people of God (cf. Luke 22:29–30; Acts 1:12–26), the acceptance extended by the formal delegation of the Jerusalem apostles signifies the acceptance of the Samaritans into the restored people of Israel.[67] The symbolism of "the Twelve" finds its climactic manifestation in this reunification of the people of Judea and Samaria; and the outpouring of the Holy Spirit that follows further confirms the significance of this passage that witnesses the accomplishment of a major step in the New Exodus program in Acts. With David Ravens,[68] one wonders if the statement in 9:31a that "the church throughout Judea, Galilee, and Samaria had peace" ('Η μὲν οὖν ἐκκλησία καθ' ὅλης τῆς Ἰουδαίας καὶ Γαλιλαίας καὶ Σαμαρείας εἶχεν εἰρήνην)[69] is intended to signify the healing of the divided kingdom in this new era of salvation.

b. The Ingathering of the Exiles

Related to the reconstitution of Israel is the theme of the ingathering of the exiles.[70] This theme is dramatically expressed in the Pentecost event of Acts 2

---

[65] In Luke-Acts, the Jerusalem apostles are generally identified with "the Twelve." See Gerhard Schneider, *Die Apostelgeschichte* (Freiburg: Herder, 1980) 1.223–25.

[66] Ernst Haenchen, *The Acts of the Apostles: A Commentary* (trans. R. McL. Wilson; Oxford: Basil Blackwell, 1971) 306.

[67] Jervell, *Luke and the People of God*, 127: "It should be evident that the apostles by their visit have sanctioned Samaria as belonging to the restored Israel."

[68] David Ravens, *Luke and the Restoration of Israel* (Sheffield: Sheffield Academic Press, 1995) 92 n.89. This work is particularly helpful in discussing the role of the Samaritans in the gospel of Luke and the implications for the restoration of Israel. Surprisingly several important themes related to the restoration of Israel (e.g., the ingathering of the exiles, the concern with "the Twelve," the role of the Holy Spirit) are ignored in a treatment that bears such a title.

[69] In Isaiah, the term "peace" is theologically significant as it signals the end of judgment and the beginning of the new era in which the restoration of Israel is just one of the characteristic features.

[70] E. P. Sanders (*Judaism: Practice and Belief, 63 BCE–66 CE* [Philadelphia: Trinity Press International, 1992] 290) states that the hope for the ingathering of the exiles is among the "common Jewish hopes for the future."

where the ingathering of the Jews from all over the world is emphasized.[71] In Acts 2:5, one reads:

Ἦσαν δὲ εἰς Ἱερουσαλὴμ κατοικοῦντες Ἰουδαῖοι, ἄνδρες εὐλαβεῖς ἀπὸ παντὸς ἔθνους τῶν ὑπὸ τὸν οὐρανόν.

Now there were devout Jews from every nation under heaven living in Jerusalem.

In this statement, both the universality of the regions represented and the particularity of the ethnic identity of the audience are emphasized.[72] The possibility that the crowd that witnesses the Pentecost event is made up of Gentiles is immediately ruled out by both the emphasis on the Jewish identity of the audience and the fact that the conversion of the Gentiles is not narrated before the conversion story of Cornelius in Acts 10–11.[73] While the universal mission may be implicit here,[74] the focus upon the Jews who are present cannot be denied. The same dual emphases on the identity of the Jews and the universality of the people present can also be found in the list of nations in 2:9–11. The list of nations is balanced again by a reference to "both Jews and proselytes" (Ἰουδαῖοί τε καὶ προσήλυτοι) in vs 11(10). While the origin of the list of nations is still one that cannot be determined with any certainty, Charles Barrett has rightly concluded that the "nearest analogy to Luke's list appears to be the accounts of the distribution of the Jews throughout the world."[75]

The best way to account for both the universal and particular aspects is to take Acts 2 as describing the ingathering of the exiles from the Jewish Diaspora. This reading is further supported by the curious fact that special mention is made concerning the residence of some Jews (from every nation) living in Jerusalem. Understanding the list of nations as pointing to the

---

[71] This has already been suggested by Antonin Causse, "Le pèlerinage à Jérusalem et la première Pentecôte," *RHPhR* 20 (1940) 120–41; followed by J. Schmitt, "L'Église de Jérusalem ou la 'restauration' d'Israel d'aprés les cinq premiers chapitres des Actes," *RevScRel* 27 (1953) 211.

[72] These dual emphases may have led to the various textual traditions that attempt to eliminate such apparent tension. For a discussion of the disappearance of the word Ἰουδαῖοι in some manuscripts, see Metzger, *A Textual Commentary on the Greek New Testament*, 251, who concludes that "it is easier to understand that, being present in the original text and witnessed by the overwhelming mass of manuscripts, Ἰουδαῖοι was either dropped as seemingly contradictory to ἀπὸ παντὸς ἔθνους, or moved to a position considered less objectionable from a stylistic point of view."

[73] Acts 2:22, 36 also show that the audience addressed by Peter was Jewish.

[74] For a discussion of the implications of Acts 2 for the mission to the Gentiles, please refer to chapter seven below.

[75] Barrett, *Acts of the Apostles*, 1.122. Cf. idem, "The Gentile Mission as an Eschatological Phenomenon," in W. Hulitt Gloer, ed., *Eschatology and the New Testament: Essays in Honor of George Raymond Beasley-Murray* (Peabody, MA: Hendrickson, 1988) 65–75.

"distribution of the Jews throughout the world" also fits well with this reading. As Rebecca Denova has suggested,[76] a similar list that serves the same purpose can be found in Isa 11:11:

> On that day the Lord will extend his hand yet a second time to recover the remnant that is left of his people, from Assyria, from Egypt, from Pathros, from Ethiopia, from Elam, from Shinar, from Hamath, and from the coastlands of the sea.[77]

Acts 2 should therefore be read within the context of the theme of the ingathering of the exiles. With the return of the Jewish people in the eschatological era, the hope of the restoration of Israel is beginning to find its fulfillment.[78]

c. The Community of the Spirit

The portrayal of the early Christian community in Acts as an eschatological community of the Spirit needs no elaborate demonstration. The connection between the outpouring of the Spirit in Acts 2 and the arrival of the eschatological age is signaled by the insertion of the phrase "in the last days" (ἐν ταῖς ἐσχάταις ἡμέραις) from Isa 2:1 at the beginning of the quotation from Joel (Acts 2:17). The possible connections between Pentecost and the Sinai tradition of the giving of the Law further highlight the importance of this event at the dawn of a new era with the reconstitution of the people of God.[79]

---

[76] Rebecca I. Denova, *The Things Accomplished Among Us: Prophetic Tradition in the Structural Pattern of Luke-Acts* (JSNTSup 141; Sheffield: Sheffield Academic Press, 1997) 173.

[77] *Contra* Leo O'Reilly, *Word and Sign in the Acts of the Apostles: A Study in Lucan Theology* (AnGr 82; Rome: Editrice Pontifica Universita Gregorians, 1987) 24, Isa 11:11 is a more relevant passage for understanding Acts 2 than Isa 2:1–3, a passage that points to the gathering of the Gentiles/nations in Jerusalem.

[78] One must admit that the development of the narrative of Acts shows that the ingathering of the exiles cannot be the central theme of the New Exodus program in Acts. The transformation of the Isaianic New Exodus program can be seen from the extraordinary emphasis placed on two Isaianic themes: (1) the replacement of the focus on the centripetal movement of the people of God to Jerusalem with the centrifugal movement of the word of God from Jerusalem (Isa 2:3); and (2) the emphasis on the mission to the Gentiles as the central concern of the narrative. The lack of emphasis on "the Land" is therefore understandable especially when the concept of "inheritance" is now transformed in Acts (see Acts 20:32 and the discussion in chapter five below). Nevertheless, the appearance of the theme at the very beginning of the narrative in Acts does signify the importance of the restoration of Israel as the foundation of the Lukan New Exodus program.

[79] The connection between the Pentecost event in Acts 2 and the Sinai tradition can be established through internal parallels between Acts 2 and the Law-giving event as well as external evidence concerning the presence of this connection within first century Jewish traditions especially as evident in the *targumim*. For a further discussion of such connections, see François Bovon, *Luke the Theologian: Thirty-Three Years of Research (1950–1983)* (trans. K. McKinney; PTMS 12; Allison Park, PA: Pickwick, 1987) 227, 340; William H. Shepherd, Jr., *The Narrative Function of the Holy Spirit as a Character in Luke-Acts*

More significant for this discussion of the Holy Spirit and the restoration of Israel is the difficult passage in Acts 3:19–21:

μετανοήσατε οὖν καὶ ἐπιστρέψατε εἰς τὸ ἐξαλειφθῆναι ὑμῶν τὰς ἁμαρτίας, ὅπως ἂν ἔλθωσιν καιροὶ ἀναψύξεως ἀπὸ προσώπου τοῦ κυρίου καὶ ἀποστείλῃ τὸν προκεχειρισμένον ὑμῖν Χριστόν, Ἰησοῦν, ὃν δεῖ οὐρανὸν μὲν δέξασθαι ἄχρι χρόνων ἀποκαταστάσεως πάντων ὧν ἐλάλησεν ὁ θεὸς διὰ στόματος τῶν ἁγίων ἀπ' αἰῶνος αὐτοῦ προφητῶν.

Repent therefore, and turn to God so that your sins may be wiped out, so that times of refreshing may come from the presence of the Lord, and that he may send the Messiah appointed for you, that is, Jesus, who must remain in heaven until the time of universal restoration that God announced long ago through his holy prophets.

The primary question surrounding this passage is the temporal reference of the "times of refreshing" (καιροὶ ἀναψύξεως) and the "time of universal restoration" (χρόνων ἀποκαταστάσεως). This is closely related to the question concerning the meaning of the two phrases.

Concerning the temporal reference of the first phrase, the dissertation by William Lane[80] should first be noted. While the word ἀνάψυξις only occurs once in the LXX (Exod 8:11) in a context that bears no resemblance with Acts 3:19–21, Lane points out that the word does appear in Symmachus' translation of Isa 32:15, a passage that makes reference to the outpouring of the Spirit. In Symmachus' translation, the outpouring of the Spirit is understood as the arrival of ἀνάψυξις:[81]

LXX Isa 32:15a

ἕως ἂν ἐπέλθῃ ἐφ' ὑμᾶς
πνεῦμα ἀφ' ὑψηλοῦ.

Symmachus Isa 32:15a

ἕως ἂν ἐπέλθῃ ἐφ' ὑμᾶς
ἀνάψυξις ἐξ ὕψους.

The relevance of Isa 32:15 to Acts 3:20 is clear, as both make reference to the coming of an eschatological age. The relationship between Acts 3:20 and Symmachus' translation of Isa 32:15 is even clearer in the Western text of Acts:[82]

(SBLDS 43; Atlanta, GA: Scholars Press, 1994) 160; and Max M. Turner, *Power from on High. The Spirit in Israel's Restoration and Witness in Luke-Acts* (Sheffield: Sheffield Academic Press, 1996) 280–82. See also Robert F. O'Toole, "Acts 2:30 and the Davidic Covenant of Pentecost," *JBL* 102 (1983) 245–58, who argues against the presence of such a connection by emphasizing instead that Acts 2 should be read in light of the promise to David. Such radical dichotomizing of the Davidic and Mosaic traditions is unacceptable especially in Acts 2 when both are evoked in the portrayal of the development of the restored kingdom within the broader New Exodus program.

[80] William L. Lane, "Times of Refreshment: A Study of Eschatological Periodization in Judaism and Christianity" (Th.D. diss., Harvard Divinity School, 1962).
[81] Ibid., 163.
[82] Ibid., 167.

Acts 3.20 Alexandrian	Isa 32.15 Symmachus	Acts 3.20 Western
ὅπως ἄν ἔλθωσιν	ἕως ἄν ἐπέλθη	ὅπως ἄν ἐπέλθωσιν
	ἐφ' ὑμᾶς	ὑμῖν
καιροὶ ἀναψύξεως	ἀνάψυξις	καιροὶ ἀναψύξεως
ἀπὸ προσώπου τ. κ.	ἐξ ὕψους	ἀπὸ προσώπου τ. κ.

The significance of Isa 32:15 for the Lukan writings has already been established,[83] as the phrase from the LXX, "until a spirit from on high is poured out on us" (ἕως ἄν ἐπέλθη ἐφ' ὑμᾶς πνεῦμα ἀφ' ὑψηλοῦ), is apparently behind Luke 24:49: "so stay here in the city until you have been clothed with power from on high" (ὑμεῖς δὲ καθίσατε ἐν τῇ πόλει ἕως οὗ ἐνδύσησθε ἐξ ὕψους δύναμιν). Understanding Acts 3:20 in terms of the outpouring of the Spirit is further strengthened by Lane's illustration of the parallel between Acts 2:38 and 3:19–20:[84]

Acts 2:38	Acts 3:19–20a
μετανοήσατε, [φησίν,] καὶ βαπτισθήτω	μετανοήσατε οὖν καὶ ἐπιστρέψατε
... εἰς ἄφεσιν τῶν ἁμαρτιῶν ὑμῶν,	εἰς τὸ ἐξαλειφθῆναι ὑμῶν τὰς
καὶ λήμψεσθε	ἁμαρτίας, ὅπως ἄν ἔλθωσιν
τὴν δωρεὰν τοῦ ἁγίου πνεύματος	καιροὶ ἀναψύξεως

This parallel further establishes the identity of the "times of refreshing" as the outpouring of the Spirit in Acts 2. The implications of this conclusion need to be highlighted. First, the outpouring of the Spirit in Acts 2 is tied to the program of restoration when that outpouring is equated with the "times of refreshing." This is not a surprising fact in light of the Isaianic program of the restoration of Israel depicted in Isaiah 32. Moreover, the connection of the Spirit with the program of restoration can already be found in the quotation of Joel 2:28–32, a passage that depicts the hope of restoration, in Acts 2:17–21.

Second, this connection establishes the temporal framework for the phrase "times of refreshing." The "times of refreshing" begin when the community has experienced the outpouring of the Spirit in Acts 2. This is consistent with a statement that occurs later in the same speech: "And all the prophets, as many as have spoken, from Samuel and those after him, also predicted these days" (καὶ πάντες δὲ οἱ προφῆται ἀπὸ Σαμουὴλ καὶ τῶν καθεξῆς ὅσοι ἐλάλησαν καὶ κατήγγειλαν τὰς ἡμέρας ταύτας, 3:24). The phrase "these days" (τὰς ἡμέρας ταύτας) clearly refers to a time contemporaneous with the early Christian community. The "times of refreshing" and "these

---

[83] See chapter three above.

[84] Lane, "Times of Refreshment," 171: "Repentance, conversion (baptism), the forgiveness of sins and the reception of the gift of God inform both passages. The parallelism supports the contention that the coming and presence of the Holy Spirit is what is meant by 'times of refreshment.'"

days" are times that the people of God had long anticipated and are now becoming a reality.

Those who insist that the phrase "times of refreshing" can only point to the future event of Jesus' return[85] fail to take note of the plural form of the word "times" (καιροί), one that commonly refers to a period of time.[86] This duration of time should not simply be conflated with the return of Jesus as referred to in the second part of the verse (3:20b). This period of time should rather be interpreted together with the previous phrase in which repentance becomes the way to participate in the community of the Spirit (vs 19).

Finally, the phrase "time of universal restoration" (χρόνων ἀποκαταστάσεως πάντων) also needs to be discussed. The word ἀποκατάστασις is a *hapax legomenon* but the verbal form ἀποκαθίστημι appears frequently in the LXX where this term "becomes a technical one for the restoration of Israel to its own land by Yahweh."[87] The verbal form appears in Acts 1:6 precisely where the restoration of Israel is at issue.

Again, the temporal reference of the phrase "time of universal restoration" has to be examined. In this case, the particle ἄχρι is the key for interpretation. If ἄχρι is to mean "until," then the "time of universal restoration" may refer to the final point in time. Nevertheless, the restoration of Israel can also be understood as a process that will reach its completion at the end of times, as the plural form of the noun χρόνος suggests.[88] If ἄχρι is to be translated as "after,"[89] however, the end of history is placed after the process of restoration; and the understanding of restoration as taking place in the present cannot be avoided. In both cases, therefore, one should understand the reference of the phrase as the restoration program that has already begun at the beginning of the narrative of Acts. This is consistent with the

---

[85] See, for example, Arthur W. Wainwright, "Luke and the Restoration of the Kingdom to Israel," *ExpTim* 89 (1977) 77; James Parker, III, *The Concept of Apokatastasis in Acts: A Study in Primitive Christian Theology* (Austin, TX: Schola Press, 1978) 30–31; and Larry R. Helyer, "Luke and the Restoration of Israel," *JETS* 36 (1993) 328.

[86] So Barrett, *Acts of the Apostles*, 1.205. Barrett also points out that ἀναψύξεως itself "suggests temporary relief rather than finality." Similarly, John T. Carroll (*Response to the End of History: Eschatology and Situation in Luke-Acts* [SBLDS 92; Atlanta, GA: Scholars Press, 1988] 143) has argued that the "analogous uses of καιροί in Luke 21:24, Acts 14:17 and 17:26 support the view that the expression 'seasons of refreshment' refers not to the end-time blessings of the kingdom, but rather to a span of time leading up to the sending (parousia) of Jesus (3:20b)."

[87] Albrecht Oepke, "ἀποκαθίστημι," *TDNT* 1 (1964) 388.

[88] Curiously, NRSV translates the plural καιροί with a plural noun ("times") but χρόνων with a singular ("time").

[89] Carroll, *Responses to the End of History*, 145, has pointed out that "Luke employs this preposition with a plural object only in Acts 3:21 and 20:6." In 20:6, ἄχρι certainly means "after." This raises the question of the meaning of the word in 3:21. See also Schneider, *Apostelgeschichte*, 1.327 n.109.

understanding of "times of refreshing" as referring to the outpouring of the Spirit in Acts 2; and one is justified in concluding that both the "times of refreshing" and the "time of universal restoration" refer to the same period of time. The relationship between the outpouring of the Spirit and the Lukan program of restoration is now established. Significantly, this relationship is established by Isa 32:15, a passage that plays an important role in the restoration programs of both Isaiah and Acts.

d. The Rebuilding of the Davidic Kingdom

Scholarly interests are not lacking in the investigation of the Lukan understanding of Jesus as a royal figure in the line of David.[90] The focus on the Davidic son of God at the right hand of God in Acts is especially evident after the ascension of Jesus.[91] In this section, several passages that highlight the Davidic kingdom in the restoration program in Acts will be discussed.

The first passage that needs to be mentioned contains a statement that is taken from the epilogue of Isaiah 40–55. After the use of Ps 2:7 in describing the sonship of the risen Jesus, Isa 55:3 is cited in Acts 13:34: "I will give you the holy promises made to David" (δώσω ὑμῖν τὰ ὅσια Δαυὶδ τὰ πιστά).[92] This quotation is followed by another verse from the Psalms (15[16]:10). The cluster of these three quotations,[93] together with the explicit mention of David in vs 36, point to the significance of the David tradition for understanding the status of the exalted Christ.[94] The explicit quotation of

---

[90] For a recent treatment, see Mark L. Strauss, *The Davidic Messiah in Luke-Acts: The Promise and Its Fulfillment in Lukan Christology* (JSNTSup 110; Sheffield: Sheffield Academic Press, 1995).

[91] Bovon (*Luke the Theologian*, 184) has noted that the "access to the right hand of God, thus to the Messianic power of the Son of David, takes place at the Ascension and not at Easter."

[92] Isa 55:3b: "I will make with you an everlasting covenant, the holy and sure blessings promised to David" (lit.; καὶ διαθήσομαι ὑμῖν διαθήκην αἰώνιον, τὰ ὅσια Δαυὶδ τὰ πιστά).

[93] The presence of such clusters in the New Testament has led some to posit the existence of Davidic *testimonia* in the early Church. See, for example, C. H. Dodd, *According to the Scriptures: The Sub-Structure of New Testament Theology* (London: Nisbet, 1952) 104–6; and F. F. Bruce, "The Davidic Messiah in Luke-Acts," in Gary A. Tuttle, ed., *Biblical and Near Eastern Studies: Essays in Honor of William Sanford LaSor* (Grand Rapids, MI: Eerdmans, 1978) 7–17.

[94] Concerning the adaptation of Isa 55:3 (LXX) in Acts 13:34, Steyn (*Septuagint Quotations in the Context of the Petrine and Pauline Speeches of the Acta Apostolorum*, 182) has suggested that the "emphasis on the David-tradition is complemented by the omission of διαθήσομαι ... διαθήκην αἰώνιον, which helps to move the focus to the promises made to David, rather than to the 'eternal covenant'."

Isaiah also suggests a reference to the Davidic promise in the restoration
program in Isaiah.

Earlier in the same chapter in Acts, the connection between Jesus and
David is established by a statement that makes reference to the descendant of
David: "Of this man's posterity God has brought to Israel a Savior, Jesus, as
he promised" (τούτου ὁ θεὸς ἀπὸ τοῦ σπέρματος κατ᾽ ἐπαγγελίαν
ἤγαγεν τῷ Ἰσραὴλ σωτῆρα Ἰησοῦν, 13:23). This is consistent with the
picture one obtains from the beginning of the narrative in Acts where it is
stated that David "was a prophet, he knew that God had sworn an oath to
him that he would put one of his descendants on his throne" (προφήτης οὖν
ὑπάρχων, καὶ εἰδὼς ὅτι ὅρκῳ ὤμοσεν αὐτῷ ὁ θεὸς ἐκ καρποῦ τῆς
ὀσφύος αὐτοῦ καθίσαι ἐπὶ τὸν θρόνον αὐτοῦ, Acts 2:30). The reference
to Jesus being on the "throne of David"[95] also points further back to Luke
1:32: "He will be great, and will be called the Son of the Most High, and the
Lord God will give to him the throne of his ancestor David" (οὗτος ἔσται
μέγας καὶ υἱὸς ὑψίστου κληθήσεται, καὶ δώσει αὐτῷ κύριος ὁ θεὸς
τὸν θρόνον Δαυὶδ τοῦ πατρὸς αὐτοῦ). These references to David's
throne recall the statement in Isaiah 9 in which the imagery of the "throne of
David" is used to describe the reign of the eschatological figure during the
restoration of Israel: "His authority shall grow continually, and there shall be
endless peace for the throne of David and his kingdom" (μεγάλη ἡ ἀρχὴ
αὐτοῦ, καὶ τῆς εἰρήνης αὐτοῦ οὐκ ἔστιν ὅριον ἐπὶ τὸν θρόνον Δαυὶδ
καὶ τὴν βασιλείαν αὐτοῦ, Isa 9:6[7]).[96]

In yet another passage in Acts, the relationship between the Davidic
kingdom and the restoration of Israel is made explicit through the quotation
from Amos 9:11–12:

Μετὰ ταῦτα ἀναστρέψω
καὶ ἀνοικοδομήσω τὴν σκηνὴν Δαυὶδ τὴν πεπτωκυῖαν,
καὶ τὰ κατεσκαμμένα αὐτῆς ἀνοικοδομήσω
καὶ ἀνορθώσω αὐτήν,
ὅπως ἂν ἐκζητήσωσιν οἱ κατάλοιποι τῶν ἀνθρώπων τὸν κύριον,
καὶ πάντα τὰ ἔθνη ἐφ᾽ οὓς ἐπικέκληται τὸ ὄνομά μου ἐπ᾽ αὐτούς,
λέγει κύριος ποιῶν ταῦτα γνωστὰ ἀπ᾽ αἰῶνος.

After this I will return,
and I will rebuild the dwelling of David, which has fallen;
from its ruins I will rebuild it,
and I will set it up,
so that all other peoples may seek the Lord —
even all the Gentiles over whom my name has been called.

---

[95] The statement that follows in Acts 2:31–33 shows that the exaltation of Jesus should
be understood within the framework provided by the Davidic promise.
[96] Cf. 2 Sam 7:16.

Thus says the Lord, who has been making these things
known from long ago. (Acts 15:16–18)[97]

First, the meaning of the phrase "the dwelling of David" (τὴν σκηνὴν
Δαυὶδ)[98] has to be determined. Ernst Haenchen insists on a strict
christological reading in which the phrase would have to refer solely to the
resurrection of Jesus.[99] Others such as Jacob Jervell argue that the quotation
is concerned with the restoration of the people of God and that this is
supported by the focus on the hope of restoration in the Amos quotation.[100]
Furthermore, Jervell argues that the connection between Acts 15:16 and vs 17
can only be understood when the restoration of Israel is considered as the
focus of the passage.[101] While the connection between the Davidic tradition
and the exaltation of Jesus cannot be denied, an ecclesiological emphasis is
clearly present in the use of the Amos quotation in Acts 15, a chapter that
deals with the boundary of the people of God. Furthermore, as Max Turner
has noted, "one can hardly imagine any Jew speaking of God's re-
establishment of the royal 'house of David' in glory without implying the
Davidid's saving and restoring rule in Israel (cf. Luke 1.68–71)."[102] One
should therefore understand the quotation primarily as one that is concerned
with the restoration of Israel[103] without denying the foundational event of the

---

[97] The final phrase ("known from long ago") is not part of the Amos quotation. This is
probably added as an editorial comment. The confusion surrounding the exact meaning and
function of this phrase may have given rise to the various textual variants. See the discussion
in Haenchen, *Acts of the Apostles*, 448 n.5; and Metzger, *A Textual Commentary on the
Greek New Testament*, 379.

[98] It is unlikely that the use of the word σκηνή/חכס instead of οἶκος/תיב expresses
"the present humble state and fragility of the dynasty," as suggested by Strauss (*Davidic
Messiah in Luke-Acts*, 187). Noticing the connection with Isa 4:5, John Mauchline
("Implicit Signs of a Persistent Belief in the Davidic Empire," *VT* 20 [1970] 290–291) has
argued instead that the word חכס points to the presence of the glory of the Lord as in the
days of the wilderness.

[99] Haenchen, *Acts of the Apostles*, 448: "When he speaks of the re-erection of the ruined
tabernacle of David, he does not see this as the restoration of the Davidic kingdom, nor does
he even see in it an image of the true Israel. He conceives it as adumbrating the story of
Jesus, culminating in the Resurrection, in which the promise made to David has been
fulfilled."

[100] Jervell, *Luke and the People of God*, 51–54. See also Mußner, "Die Idee der
Apokatastasis in der Apostelgeschichte," 299–301; Stephen G. Wilson, *The Gentiles and the
Gentile Mission in Luke-Acts* (SNTSMS 23; Cambridge: Cambridge University Press, 1973)
224; and Royce Dickinson, Jr., "The Theology of the Jerusalem Conference: Acts 15:1–35,"
ResQ 32 (1990) 65–83.

[101] Jervell, *Luke and the People of God*, 52–53.

[102] Turner, *Power from on High*, 314.

[103] The reference to Edom in Amos 9:12 shows that the tent of David does not simply
refer to the Southern Kingdom. Instead, it points to the twelve tribes of the reconstituted
Israel.

exaltation of Jesus.[104] The promise to rebuild (ἀνοικοδομήσω) and restore (ἀνορθώσω) the Davidic kingdom is explicitly made at the point in the narrative of Acts that focuses on defining the people of God.[105]

The Amos quotation in Acts 15 shows that not only is the risen Lord recognized as the Son of David, the development of the early Christian community is also understood within the paradigm of the anticipation of the Davidic kingdom. The christological focus of the David tradition should be supplemented by an ecclesiological one. As in the restoration program in Isaiah, Luke's emphasis on the Davidic dynasty plays an important role in the restoration program of Acts.

e. Repentance and the Turn to the Lord

In his survey of Jewish restoration theology, E. P. Sanders notes the curious absence of emphasis on the collective repentance of the people of Israel in the message of Jesus:

> The great themes of national repentance and God's forgiveness, shown in restoring his repentant people, are prominent in all the literature which looks towards Jewish restoration. Jesus fits *somehow* into that view of God, the world and his people; but his message curiously lacks emphasis on one of the most important themes in the overall scheme.[106]

The same cannot be said about the restoration program of Acts, however.[107] Emphasis on the call to repentance is already present in Luke 24:47, a

---

[104] Turner (*Power from on High*, 312–15) and Strauss (*Davidic Messiah in Luke-Acts*, 187–90) argue for a similar position although Strauss goes on to say that "it is not the church or the nation Israel but the Davidic dynasty (or 'kingly reign') that is here said to be rebuilt" (190). This distinction may not be one that Luke would understand. The connection between the restoration of the people of God and the ethnic Israel cannot be denied although the understanding of the "people of God" is in the process of being reformulated. Moreover, the distinction between the Davidic dynasty and the people of Israel demands further demonstration.

[105] Here, the restoration of Israel is connected with the question of the Gentiles. Unlike Jervell (*Luke and the People of God*, 190) who argues that the Gentiles are to remain a separate entity, I will argue that the Gentiles are now accepted into the people of God. This is supported by the statement that precedes the Amos quotation, one that applies the term λαός to the Gentiles (vs 14). For a further discussion of the Lukan conception of the people of God, see chapter seven below.

[106] Sanders, *Jesus and Judaism*, 113.

[107] See, however, the telling critique of Sanders' broad and general statement in Bruce D. Chilton, "Jesus and the Repentance of E. P. Sanders," *TynBul* 39 (1988) 1–18. For a discussion of the Lukan emphasis on repentance, see also Bovon, *Luke the Theologian*, 271–89.

programmatic statement that sets the stage for the narrative in Acts.[108] In the early chapters of Acts, the call to repentance is the focus of the apostles' message. Significantly, twice the call to repent is immediately followed by an account of mass conversion of the Jews. The first passage can be found at the Peter's instruction to the crowd after giving the Pentecost speech:

Μετανοήσατε, [φησίν,] καὶ βαπτισθήτω ἕκαστος ὑμῶν ἐπὶ τῷ ὀνόματι Ἰησοῦ Χριστοῦ εἰς ἄφεσιν τῶν ἁμαρτιῶν ὑμῶν, καὶ λήμψεσθε τὴν δωρεὰν τοῦ ἁγίου πνεύματος·

Repent, and be baptized every one of you in the name of Jesus Christ so that your sins may be forgiven; and you will receive the gift of the Holy Spirit. (Acts 2:38)

The bestowal of the eschatological gift of the Spirit is promised to those of the people of God who are willing to turn away from their sins. In response to the call of Peter, many were baptized and "that day about three thousand persons were added" (προσετέθησαν ἐν τῇ ἡμέρᾳ ἐκείνῃ ψυχαὶ ὡσεὶ τρισχίλιαι, Acts 2:41).

Similarly, in Acts 3:19, a passage that has already been examined above,[109] a call to repentance is issued in connection with the program of restoration:

μετανοήσατε οὖν καὶ ἐπιστρέψατε εἰς τὸ ἐξαλειφθῆναι ὑμῶν τὰς ἁμαρτίας, ὅπως ἂν ἔλθωσιν καιροὶ ἀναψύξεως ἀπὸ προσώπου τοῦ κυρίου.

Repent therefore, and turn to God so that your sins may be wiped out, so that times of refreshing may come from the presence of the Lord. (Acts 3:19–20a)

Again, a mass conversion of the Jews is recorded in response to this call and those who believed "numbered about five thousand" (ἐγενήθη [ὁ] ἀριθμὸς τῶν ἀνδρῶν [ὡς] χιλιάδες πέντε, Acts 4:4). Such mass conversion of the Jews symbolizes the process of restoration as the people of God return to their God.

The reason Luke's emphasis on the call to repentance, and the response it elicits, occurs only in the second volume of the Lukan writings is given in a statement concerning the exalted status of the risen Lord:

τοῦτον ὁ θεὸς ἀρχηγὸν καὶ σωτῆρα ὕψωσεν τῇ δεξιᾷ αὐτοῦ, [τοῦ] δοῦναι μετάνοιαν τῷ Ἰσραὴλ καὶ ἄφεσιν ἁμαρτιῶν.

God exalted him at his right hand as Leader and Savior that he might give repentance to Israel and forgiveness of sins. (Acts 5:31)

Here, it is stated that repentance is given "to Israel" (τῷ Ἰσραὴλ) as the collective people of God "after" the exaltation of Jesus. This emphasis on the

---

[108] The Lukan emphasis on the call to repentance becomes even clearer when one notes that this call is not present in the Matthean parallel in 28:18–20. For a further discussion of Luke 24:44–47, please refer to chapter three above.
[109] The parallel between Acts 2:38 and 3:19 has already been established in the discussion in section 4.3c above.

repentance of Israel can only be understood within the wider program of the restoration of Israel.[110]

f. The Inclusion of the Outcasts

While the Lukan concern for the outcasts is frequently noted,[111] few have recognized the significance of this concern in the development of the narrative of Acts. In this section, I will focus on Acts 8:26–40, a passage whose significance for the Lukan program is rarely highlighted.[112]

The presence of the episode of the Ethiopian eunuch in the development of the narrative in Acts (8:26–40) has always puzzled commentators. Most are preoccupied with the precise ethnic identity of the eunuch. Some argue that the eunuch is to be understood as a proselyte[113] but many suggest that this episode should be read as a prelude or a foreshadowing of the conversion of Cornelius in Acts 10.[114] Hans Conzelmann argues that Luke included a competing account of the conversion of a Gentile here even though he modified it in a way that retains the paradigmatic significance of the Cornelius account.[115] After concluding that the identity of the eunuch cannot be determined with any certainty, Haenchen concludes that the ethnic identification of the Ethiopian eunuch is to be located somewhere between a Samaritan and a Gentile.[116]

---

[110] As the narrative develops, it will become clear that "God has given even to the Gentiles the repentance that leads to life" (καὶ τοῖς ἔθνεσιν ὁ θεὸς τὴν μετάνοιαν εἰς ζωὴν ἔδωκεν, Acts 11:18). See also Acts 17:30; 20:21; and 26:20.

[111] Many such studies have concentrated on the motif of the poor in the gospel. E.g., John O. York, *The Last Shall Be First: The Rhetoric of Reversal in Luke* (JSNTSup 46; Sheffield: JSOT Press, 1991).

[112] For the discussion of the Lukan emphasis on the Gentiles, see chapter seven below.

[113] For example, Wilson (*Gentiles and the Gentile Mission in Luke-Acts*, 171) argues that for the author of Acts, "the man was a proselyte rather than a God-fearer, a Jew rather than a Gentile, for Acts 10–11 make it clear that he saw Cornelius as the first Gentile convert."

[114] See Schneider, *Apostelgeschichte*, 1.498, who sees the passage as "Präludium" and "Vorspiel" to the Cornelius episode. For a recent discussion, see also Spencer, *Portrait of Philip in Acts*, 187, who concludes that "Philip functions as Peter's forerunner," and the "outreach to the Ethiopian eunuch sets the stage for (or serves as a 'prelude' to) Peter's climactic mission to the Gentiles, represented by Cornelius and family."

[115] Hans Conzelmann (*Acts of the Apostles: A Commentary on the Acts of the Apostles* [trans. James Limburg, A. Thomas Kraabel, and Donald H. Juel; Philadelphia: Fortress, 1987] 67) suggests that this passage "was apparently told in Hellenistic circles as the first conversion of a Gentile" and "thus rivals the account of Cornelius's conversion in chapters 10–11." Cf. Schneider, *Apostelgeschichte*, 1.498.

[116] Haenchen (*Acts of the Apostles*, 314) states that "it remains uncertain what the eunuch really is; but it is precisely this screen of secrecy about his person which is best suited to the stage now reached in the history of the mission .... Luke here leaves the reader

Such disagreement concerning the identity of the Ethiopian eunuch shows that the ethnic identity of this individual should not be constructed as the central issue in an examination of the function of this passage in the narrative of Acts. Instead, I will argue that this passage should be read as completing the account of the restoration of Israel in Acts as the outcasts are now included in the restored people of God.[117] Only in light of the completion of this program of restoration can the story of Gentile conversion be developed. This reading also fits well within the context of Isaiah in which the inclusion of the outcasts is an important element in the anticipated restored kingdom of Israel.

First of all, while the convert is designated once as an "Ethiopian" (Αἰθίοψ, Acts 8:27) and a "court official" (δυνάστης, vs 27), it is his status as a "eunuch" (εὐνοῦχος) that is emphasized throughout the passage. In this brief passage, the designation "eunuch" floods the text (8:27, 34, 36, 38, 39);[118] and it is his status as a eunuch that is the focus of the narrative. Moreover, the fact that he is an Ethiopian does not settle the question of ethnic identity;[119] and the existence of the term δυνάστης to qualify further the socio-political status of the eunuch suggests that the term εὐνοῦχος should be understood primarily in a physical/biological sense.

The inclusion of the conversion story of a "eunuch" within the restoration program of Luke is best understood as a sign that points to the place of the outcasts in the reconstituted people of God. Luke's reference to the eunuch recalls Isa 56:3–5, a passage thematically tied with the Isaianic New Exodus program of Isaiah 40–55:[120]

μὴ λεγέτω ὁ ἀλλογενὴς ὁ προσκείμενος πρὸς κύριον
'Αφοριεῖ με ἄρα κύριος ἀπὸ τοῦ λαοῦ αὐτοῦ·
καὶ μὴ λεγέτω ὁ εὐνοῦχος ὅτι 'Εγώ εἰμι ξύλον ξηρόν.
τάδε λέγει κύριος Τοῖς εὐνούχοις,
ὅσοι ἂν φυλάξωνται τὰ σάββατά μου καὶ ἐκλέξωνται
ἃ ἐγὼ θέλω καὶ ἀντέχωνται τῆς διαθήκης μου,
δώσω αὐτοῖς ἐν τῷ οἴκῳ μου καὶ ἐν τῷ τείχει μου
τόπον ὀνομαστὸν κρείττω υἱῶν καὶ θυγατέρων,
ὄνομα αἰώνιον δώσω αὐτοῖς καὶ οὐκ ἐκλείψει.

---

with the feeling that with this new convert the mission has taken a step beyond the conversion of Jews and Samaritans."

[117] An awareness of the Deuteronomic legislation (Deut 23:1–7) is assumed here.

[118] Five of the six New Testament occurrences of the noun εὐνοῦχος appear within these fifteen verses (Acts 8:26–40).

[119] This designation may simply be referring to "Ethiopian Jew," as similar designations in the list of nations in Acts 2 show.

[120] See, in particular, W. A. M. Beuken, "An Example of the Isaianic Legacy of Trito-Isaiah," in J. W. van Henton et al., eds., *Tradition and Re-Interpretation in Jewish and Early Christian Literature: Essays in Honour of Jurgen C. H. Lebram* (Leiden: Brill, 1986) 48–64, who argues for the use of Isaiah 55 in 56:1–8.

> Do not let the foreigners joined to the LORD say,
> "The LORD will surely separate me from his people";
> and do not let the eunuch say, "I am just a dry tree."
> For thus says the LORD:
> To the eunuchs who keep my sabbaths,
> who choose the things that please me and hold fast my covenant,
> I will give, in my house and within my walls,
> a monument and a name better than sons and daughters;
> I will give them an everlasting name that shall not be cut off.

This passage concludes with a statement that explicitly makes reference to the reconstitution of Israel (Isa 56:8).[121] The probability that Luke has the Isaianic program in mind is strengthened by the explicit reference to Isaiah 53 in Acts 8:32–33. The Lukan emphasis on this Isaianic passage can be seen both by the fact that the quotation forms the center of the narrative[122] and by the observation that this is the only scriptural quotation in Acts that comes from the voice of the narrator. In view of this emphasis on the Isaianic text, understanding Isaiah 56 as the hermeneutical key to this passage cannot be doubted.[123]

One can conclude that Acts 8:26–40 is not primarily concerned with the ethnic identity of the main character. Luke's repeated emphases on the character as a eunuch is understandable only against the context of Isa 56:1–8, a passage that points to the inclusion of the outcasts in the restoration program.[124] Acts 8:26–40 is, therefore, not simply inserted because of its presence in the Lukan source. It plays a part in the restoration program in Acts.

---

[121] See the discussion of this verse in section 4.2f above.

[122] See the structural analysis of Acts 8:25–40 in Spencer, *Portrait of Philip in Acts*, 132.

[123] The Isaianic reference has frequently been noted by commentators but the significance of the connections between the restoration programs of Isaiah and Acts has seldom been noticed. The failure to recognize the Isaianic pattern explains the fact that most simply dismiss the relevance of this Isaianic passage. See, for example, Barrett, *Acts of the Apostles*, 1.421, who dismisses the significance of Isaiah 56 simply because the passage is not explicitly quoted in Acts 8. This conclusion fails to appreciate the way the Isaianic program is evoked throughout the narrative of Acts.

[124] Mikeal C. Parsons ("Isaiah 53 in Acts 8: A Reply to Professor Morna Hooker," in William H. Bellinger, Jr., and William R. Farmer, eds., *Jesus and the Suffering Servant: Isaiah 53 and Christian Origins* [Harrisburg, PA: Trinity Press International, 1998] 104–119) further argues that in this episode one finds a "thinly veiled antitemple polemic" (113) when an individual rejected by the temple cult is now included into the Christian community. Nevertheless, the fulfillment of the Isaianic program of restoration seems to overshadow concerns for "replacement" at this point of the narrative.

4.4 Conclusion

In this chapter, I have argued that various passages in Acts should be examined in light of the Isaianic program of restoration. This program of restoration is the foundation upon which other motifs of the Isaianic New Exodus are developed in the narrative of Acts. The suggestion that the fulfillment of the hope of restoration has begun to take place within the early Christian community establishes a claim to the treasured hope of Israel. Against the other competing communities, this Lukan community claims to be the true extension of the people of God. The many explicit and implicit references to the Isaianic program therefore provide the hermeneutical framework in which the development of this early Christian movement is to be understood.

Excursus: The Continuing State of Exile

My discussion of the restoration of Israel presupposes that the Jews of the first century continued to consider themselves to be in a state of exile. This assumption is best stated by N. T. Wright:

> Most Jews of this period, it seems, would have answered the question "where are we?" in language which, reduced to its simplest form, meant: we are still in exile. They believed that, in all the senses which mattered, Israel's exile was still in progress. Although she had come back from Babylon, the glorious message of the prophets remained unfulfilled. Israel still remained in thrall to foreigners; worse, Israel's god had not returned to Zion.[125]

Wright himself bases his conclusion on Second Temple Jewish texts that reflect the understanding of their exilic condition as well as an expectation for God to reverse their predicament.[126] For example, Tobit, a work written when the Babylonian exile was a distant memory, notes:

> But God will again have mercy on them, and God will bring them back into the land of Israel; and they will rebuild the temple of God, but not like the first one until the period when the times of fulfillment shall come. After this they all will return from their exile and will rebuild Jerusalem in splendor; and in it the temple of God will be rebuilt, just as the prophets of Israel have said concerning it. (14.5)

The historical Babylonian return is ignored and the hope of deliverance remains unfulfilled. Similarly, in Baruch, a similar understanding can be found: "See, we are today in our exile where you have scattered us, to be reproached

---

[125] N. T. Wright, *The New Testament and the People of God* (London: SPCK, 1992) 268–69. See also the earlier work of Michael A. Knibb, "The Exile in the Literature of the Intertestamental Period," *HeyJ* 17 (1976) 253–72. Knibb demonstrates how the prophecy in Jeremiah 25 and 29 that the exile would end in seventy years is transformed in later Jewish texts. A similar transformation of Ezekiel 4 generates other traditions.

[126] Wright, *New Testament and the People of God*, 269–70.

and cursed and punished for all the iniquities of our ancestors, who forsook the Lord our God" (3.8).

While questions have been raised concerning Wright's position,[127] recent studies have confirmed Wright's conclusion. Craig A. Evans, for example, shows that the understanding of the continuation of the exilic state was widespread in the Second Temple period.[128] An examination of texts from different groups also affirms this reading.[129] The refusal to see the return of the Babylonian exiles as the fulfillment of prophecy of deliverance can be already found within the canonical text. Nehemiah presents a striking example where the account of post-exilic events stands together with a belief in the continuing exilic status of God's people as noted in Ezra's speech of Nehemiah 9:

> Here we are, slaves to this day—slaves in the land that you gave to our ancestors to enjoy its fruit and its good gifts. Its rich yield goes to the kings whom you have set over us because of our sins; they have power also over our bodies and over our livestock at their pleasure, and we are in great distress. (Neh 9:36–37)

The exilic status did not cease with the return of the exiles. A greater deliverance is yet to come.

Moving beyond Second Temple texts, the hope for restoration can be found even after the fall of the Jerusalem Temple in 70 CE. In *Fourth Ezra*, for example, the post-exilic condition is not even mentioned and Ezra the scribe is depicted as belonging to the end of the fifth century. In *Second Baruch*, the rebuilding of Zion is yet to take place. More importantly, the choice of Baruch and Ezra as pseudonyms reflects the self-understanding of the authors that they remain in the state of exile.[130] Moreover, this is not limited to apocalyptic texts. Josephus also sees Israel as a nation in exile although an expectation of return does not play a prominent role in his writings.[131]

---

[127] See, for example, Maurice Casey, "Where Wright is Wrong: A Critical Review of N. T. Wright's *Jesus and the Victory of God*," *JSNT* 69 (1998) 95–103.

[128] Craig A. Evans, "Jesus and the Continuing Exile of Israel," in Carey C. Newman, *Jesus and the Restoration of Israel: A Critical Assessment of N. T. Wright's Jesus and the Victory of God* (Downers Grove, IL: InterVarsity Press, 1999) 77–100. Evans lists additional texts in support of Wright's position, e.g., Sir 36; Bar 2.7–10; Tob 13.5, 2 Macc 2.5–7, 18, *1 En.* 89, *T. Mos.* 4.8–9, 13, *Pss. Sol.* 8.28.

[129] See the essays in James M. Scott, ed., *Exile: Old Testament, Jewish, and Christian Conceptions* (JSJSup 56; Leiden: Brill, 1997).

[130] See Knibb, "Exile in the Literature of the Intertestamental Period," 270–71.

[131] See Louis H. Feldman, "The Concept of Exile in Josephus," James M. Scott, ed., *Exile: Old Testament, Jewish, and Christian Conceptions* (JSJSup 56; Leiden: Brill, 1997)145–72. This understanding of the status of Israel extends to the rabbinic period. See Chaim Milikowsky, "Notions of Exile, Subjugation and Return in Rabbinic Literature," in Scott, ed., *Exile*, 265–96.

Outside of the vision embedded in these texts, certain prophetic movements during the Second Temple period also presuppose the exilic condition of Israel. The continue evocation of the ancient paradigm of deliverance in these movements points to an expectation of God to act to restore his people.[132] Most striking is the case of the Qumran community. As in other Second Temple texts, this community ignores the post-exilic history of Israel. However, the self-understanding of this community goes beyond this assumption in their affirmation that in them is found the fulfillment of Yahweh's promise of restoration. The community's "self-integration into biblical Israel culminates in their claim as 'the first returners of the Land' after the deportation which came in the wake of the destruction of Jerusalem."[133] This provides the context in which to situate the early Christian movement.[134]

I will conclude by noting the role of Isaiah in the development of later conceptions of exile and restoration. The cosmic transformation depicted in the vision of Isaiah 40–55 encourages one to look beyond the bleak outlook of the post-exilic period for the restoration of God's people. Here, the cosmic struggle between Yahweh and the evil forces continues until a time when chaotic powers are contained.[135] When the return of the Babylonian exiles failed to fulfill such hopes, the exact definition of "exile" underwent a transformation. The physical sense was substituted by a moral if not a cosmic sense. Moreover, since exile was understood as the punishment for sins, one may agree with Wright that "return from exile simply *is* the forgiveness of sins,"[136] although a concern for the Land continues to exist.[137]

The task of interpreting the Isaianic texts naturally provided a setting for the development of this exile theology. In the *Isaiah Targum*, whose

[132] See Richard A. Horsley and John S. Hanson, *Bandits, Prophets, and Messiahs: Popular Movements at the Time of Jesus* (San Francisco: Harper & Row, 1985) 135–89.

[133] Shemaryahu Talmon, "Between the Bible and the Mishna," *The World of Qumran from Within: Collected Studies* (Leiden: Brill, 1989) 48.

[134] In early Christian literature, this understanding of exile and restoration is not limited to Acts. For a discussion of Jesus in light of the restoration theology of the Second Temple period, see also Sanders, *Jesus and Judaism*, 77–119. For Paul, see Scott J. Hafemann, "Paul and the Exile of Israel in Galatians 3–4," in James M. Scott, ed., *Exile: Old Testament, Jewish, and Christian Conceptions* (JSJSup 56; Leiden: Brill, 1997) 329–71.

[135] See, in particular, Theodore M. Ludwig, "The Traditions of the Establishing of the Earth in Deutero-Isaiah," *JBL* 92 (1973) 345–57.

[136] N. T. Wright, "The Servant and Jesus: The Relevance of the Colloquy for the Current Quest for Jesus," in William H. Bellinger, Jr., and William R. Farmer, *Jesus and the Suffering Servant: Isaiah 53 and Christian Origins* (Harrisburg, PA: Trinity Press International, 1998) 290.

[137] See Isaiah M. Gafni, *Land, Center and Diaspora: Jewish Constructs in Late Antiquity* (JSPSup 21; Sheffield: Sheffield Academic Press, 1997) 19–40 for the conceptions of Diaspora existence that go beyond the "punishment for sins" paradigm.

traditions can be dated to the first century CE,[138] references to exile appear throughout the text.[139] The exile remains an unfulfilled promise. In *Tg. Isa.* 66.9, for example, one reads: "I, God, created the world from the beginning, says the LORD. I created all men; I scattered them among the nations. I am also about to gather your exiles ...."[140] More importantly, the absence of God is connected to the condition of the exiles: "I took up my Shekinah from them and cast them away, I scattered their exiles" (*Tg. Isa.* 57:17b).[141] The exile is no longer simply understood in physical terms. The absence of God denotes an exilic condition. Although the people of God may live in "the Land", they expect God to return to their community. Therefore, corresponding to the development of exile theology in moral terms, the exile is also understood in terms of the absence of God. The early Christian announcement of the presence of God among His people is therefore an announcement of the end of the exile.

[138] See Bruce D. Chilton, *The Glory of Israel: The Theology and Provenience of the Isaiah Targum* (JSOTSup 23; Sheffield: JSOT Press, 1983) 12; and idem, *The Isaiah Targum: Introduction, Translation, Apparatus and Notes* (ArBib 11; Wilmington, DE: Michael Glazier, 1987) xx–xxvii.

[139] See Chilton, *The Glory of Israel*, 28–33.

[140] Ibid., 29. Similarly, the epilogue in *Tg. Isa.* 55 contains the statement: "For you shall go out in joy from among the Gentiles, and be led in peace to your land; the mountains and the hills before you shall shout in singing, and all the trees of the field shall clap with their branches." This text is taken from Chilton, *Isaiah Targum.*

[141] Chilton, *Glory of Israel*, 29, suggests that references to Shekinah may point to a date shortly before and after 70 CE.

Chapter 5

The Agent of the New Exodus: The Word of God

5.1 Introduction

In chapter two, the importance of the word of God in the New Exodus of Isaiah was noted. In this chapter, I will focus on the role of the word of God in Acts and show that this emphasis should be discussed within the context of Isaiah and the Exodus traditions. The focus again is on the function of the term both in the organization of the material in Acts as well as its connection with the concerns of the Lukan community.

The frequency of the appearance of the term λόγος in Acts is itself noteworthy. In Acts, the phrase ὁ λόγος τοῦ θεοῦ appears eleven times while the phrase ὁ λόγος τοῦ κυρίου[1] appears ten times. Other phrases that should be considered include ὁ λόγος τῆς σωτηρίας (Acts 13:26), τῷ λόγῳ τῆς χάριτος αὐτοῦ (14:3; 20:32), and τὸν λόγον τοῦ εὐαγγελίου (15:7). In addition, the absolute use of the term λόγος can be found throughout the first twenty chapters of Acts.[2]

In Luke, however, the phrase ὁ λόγος τοῦ θεοῦ appears only four times while ὁ λόγος τοῦ κύριου appears only once.[3] These appearances are significant especially when compared to the parallel synoptic accounts, and they will be discussed later in this chapter. They define the nature and significance of the phrase for the narrative of Acts. Nevertheless, it seems clear that the term λόγος does not play as central a role in the development of the narrative of Luke as it does in Acts.

---

[1] In certain cases the manuscript evidence does not help in deciding between the variants "the word of God" and "the word of the Lord" (cf. Acts 13:44, 48; 19:20). These variants seems to point to the fact that the two phrases are interchangeable. For a further discussion of the textual problems, see Jacques Dupont, "Notes sur les Actes des Apôtres," *RB* 62 (1955) 47–9; and Gerhard Schneider, *Die Apostelgeschichte* (Freiburg: Herder, 1980) 1.410. In this study, I will consider the two phrases as essentially identical in meaning.

[2] The absence of the λόγος-terminology in the final chapters of Acts will be discussed in section 5.2a below.

[3] The word λόγος itself is a significant term in Luke and its importance will be discussed in section 5.3a below.

The significance of the term λόγος in Acts can be further discussed by comparing its usage with the usage of the term ῥῆμα. In the narrative of Acts ῥῆμα almost always appears in the plural form.[4] Although it can be used in reference to the Christian message (Acts 5:20; 10:37, 44; 13:42), the term is most often used to refer to the specific words spoken by the various characters. Unlike λόγος, it is not qualified by the phrase τοῦ θεοῦ/κυρίου.[5] Furthermore, the verbs related to the two terms in Acts should also be considered. The term λόγος can be found connected with particular verbs denoting the preaching and teaching of the Christian message such as εὐαγγελίζω (Acts 8:4; 15:35), διαμαρτύρομαι (8:25), διδάσκω (15:35; 18:11), and παρρησιάζομαι (14:3). In contrast, none of these verbs are used in connection with the term ῥῆμα, a word that is almost always the object of the verb λαλέω in Acts.[6] Most significant of all is that unlike λόγος, ῥῆμα is not used as the subject of a verb.[7] These observations suggest that in Acts the use of ῥῆμα cannot be equated with that of λόγος;[8] and λόγος is used in a special sense as a reference to the word of God.[9]

The recognition of the importance of the word of God in Acts leads François Bovon to conclude that the episodes in Acts "narrate the diffusion of the Word."[10] Previous studies have focused on particular theological themes related to this term. In an attempt to respond to the salvation-historical

---

[4] The exceptions are Acts 10:37 (in reference to that which took place [τὸ γενόμενον ῥῆμα] in Judea); 11:16 (in reference to a saying of Jesus); and 28:25 (in reference to the final word of Paul).

[5] In Acts, the only exception is in 11:16 that refers to the memory of one specific saying of Jesus. The only other exception in the Lukan writings can be found in the prophetic formula in Luke 3:2 that uses ῥῆμα θεοῦ (cf. Jer 1:1).

[6] See 5:20; 6:11, 13; 10:44; 11:14; 13:42. Cf. 16:38; 26:15.

[7] See 6:7; 12:24; 18:5; 19:20; cf. 20:32. This unique use of the term λόγος will be discussed more than once in this chapter.

[8] Moreover, while λόγος appears twice as frequently in Acts (64 times) as it does in Luke (32 times), the frequency of the appearances of ῥῆμα is almost the same in Luke (19 times) as in Acts (14 times). This is consistent with my hypothesis that λόγος plays an especially important role in Acts and that it cannot be understood simply as equivalent to ῥῆμα.

[9] In Luke, one can find one instance of the phrase ῥῆμα θεοῦ (without the definite article) in the prophetic formula in 3:2. Curiously, this usage does not reappear throughout the Lukan writings. For a further discussion of the particular Lukan usage of the term ῥῆμα, see Christoph Burchard, "A note on 'PHMA in JosAs 17:1f.; Luke 2:15, 17; Acts 10:37," *NovT* 27 (1985) 281–95.

[10] François Bovon, *Luke the Theologian: Thirty-Three Years of Research (1950–1983)* (trans. K. McKinney; PTMS 12; Allison Park, PA: Pickwick, 1987) 238. This is followed by, among others, Leo O'Reilly, *Word and Sign in the Acts of the Apostles: A Study in Lucan Theology* (AnGr 82; Rome: Editrice Pontifica Universita Gregorians, 1987) 11.

framework offered by Hans Conzelmann, Claus-Peter März[11] provides a thematic study on the theology of preaching/kerygma in the Lukan writings. The selective examination of certain verses and the failure to examine this theme within the development of the theological program of the Lukan writings prevent this study from offering a coherent picture of the theology of the word in the Lukan writings. In an insightful study, Jerome Kodell[12] highlights the ecclesiological aspects of the three summary statements concerning the growth of the word. Unfortunately he does not go on to show how these statements relate to other statements on the spread of the word of God in Acts. Juan S. Hazelton,[13] on the other hand, limits his examination of the term λόγος to its christological use in Luke. This study fails to highlight the wider ecclesiological emphasis and function of the term. In his monograph, Leo O'Reilly concentrates on the examination of the relationship between preaching and signs in Acts. His study focuses on the early chapters of Acts and so does not deal extensively with the particular terminology of λόγος.[14]

The most recent attempt at a systematic study of the word of God in Luke-Acts is carried out by Yun Lak Chung.[15] The primary focus of this study is "on the dynamic meaning of the word of God within the narrative."[16] The major weakness of this study lies in its insistence on a purely synchronic reading that ignores the possible source(s) of the Lukan usage. Furthermore, the author does not examine the particular nuances of the Lukan conception of the term λόγος, for he simply states at the very beginning of his study that "the phrase 'the word of God' is used to define the Christian message."[17] Finally, the particular narrative movement of "the word" is missed in this narratological study; and this study fails to note why the absolute use of the term can be found in the first twenty chapters of Acts but not in its remaining parts.

In this chapter, I will insist that the word of God should not be examined apart from the other theological emphases of Acts. I will argue that both the appearance of the word of God throughout the travel narratives in Acts and the summary statements concerning the growth of the word need to be

---

[11] Claus P. März, *Das Wort Gottes bei Lukas: Die lukanische Worttheologie als Frage an die neuere Lukasforschung* (EThSt 11; Leipzig: St. Benno-Verlag, 1974).

[12] Jerome Kodell, "'The Word of God Grew': The Ecclesial Tendency of Λόγος in Acts 6,7; 12,24; 19,20," *Bib* 55 (1974) 505–19.

[13] Juan S. Hazelton, "Aspectos de la cristología de Lucas revelados por su uso del término 'Logos'," *Cuadernos de Teología* 2 (1972) 124–38.

[14] O'Reilly, *Word and Sign in the Acts of the Apostles*.

[15] Yun Lak Chung, "'The Word of God' in Luke-Acts: A Study in Lukan Theology" (Ph.D. diss., Emory University, 1995).

[16] Ibid., 20.

[17] Ibid., 11.

understood within the paradigm of the Isaianic New Exodus.[18] With the development of the narrative, the word becomes the powerful force that is able to conquer the world. These summary statements declare the result of such a conquest: the creation and growth of the people of God. While the power and the spread of the word follow the scheme set out by the Isaianic program, Luke's summary statements utilize the language of the growth of the covenant people. Above all, the function of these thematic emphases is to portray the early Christian community as the continuation of the covenant people of the ancient Israelite traditions; and it is in them alone that the word of God is now deposited.

5.2 The Process of the New Exodus: The Conquest of the Word

In discussing the role of the word of God in Acts, I will first examine the travel of the word of God within the Isaianic context. Then, the hypostatization and power of the word will be discussed. Both together suggest that the word should be considered the central character of Acts. It is the powerful agent that accomplishes the program of the New Exodus.

a. The Itinerary of the Word of God

First of all, the "itinerary" of the journey of the word needs to be traced. Previous studies have been so preoccupied by the content of the preaching (i.e., word) of the early Christians that the pattern of the journey of the word in Acts has entirely escaped the notice of scholars. I will examine all the instances in which the phrase ὁ λόγος τοῦ θεοῦ/τοῦ κυρίου appears in the narrative of Acts. Included within this examination will be the absolute usage of the term ὁ λόγος, when this term is clearly used to refer to the word of God, and related phrases including ὁ λόγος τῆς σωτηρίας, ὁ λόγος τῆς χάριτος αὐτοῦ, and ὁ λόγος τοῦ εὐαγγελίου. I will show that the word conquers in the midst of opposition and that the word never visits a geographical location twice during its journey even when the various Lukan characters in Acts may have visited a city more than once. These will provide a foundation for the discussion of the conquest of the word. The function of this emphasis on the prevailing of the "Christian" word will also become clear.

Naturally, the first appearance of "the word" is in Jerusalem. In Acts 4:4, there is a statement concerning the massive growth of the community; and members of this group are those who believed the word: πολλοὶ δὲ τῶν ἀκουσάντων τὸν λόγον ἐπίστευσαν, καὶ ἐγενήθη [ὁ] ἀριθμὸς τῶν

---

[18] The meaning of the term cannot be reduced to either "the preaching" or "the Church." The dynamic complex embodied in this term will be explicated throughout this chapter.

ἀνδρῶν [ὧς] χιλιάδες πέντε ("But many of those who heard the word believed; and they numbered about five thousand"). Significantly, this statement appears in the midst of persecution from the leaders of the Jews as they "arrested them in custody until the next day, for it was already evening" (4:3). The theme of the conquest of the word is intimately related to Jewish opposition. Furthermore, the report of the number that constitute the community is important in that in Israelite traditions numbering "men" (that amounts to thousands) most often appears in military contexts[19] where thousands of "men" were involved.[20] In Acts 4, therefore, the formation of the community as well as the victory (with its militaristic overtones) over the opposing force are important themes related to the term λόγος.[21]

In 4:29, in the prayer of the early Christians, the word again appears in the context of threats from the Jewish authorities: καὶ τὰ νῦν, κύριε, ἔπιδε ἐπὶ τὰς ἀπειλὰς αὐτῶν, καὶ δὸς τοῖς δούλοις σου μετὰ παρρησίας πάσης λαλεῖν τὸν λόγον σου ("And now, Lord, look at their threats, and grant to your servants to speak your word with all boldness"). The prayer was answered when the believers, being filled with the Holy Spirit, "spoke the word of God with boldness" (ἐλάλουν τὸν λόγον τοῦ θεοῦ μετὰ παρρησίας, 4:31).[22] The victory of the word under threats from opposition is again made clear.

In 6:2–4, in response to the conflict between the Hebrews and the Hellenists, the twelve affirmed their responsibility as they committed to devote themselves "to serving the word" (τῇ διακονίᾳ τοῦ λόγου, 6:4). The result of this commitment to the word is summarized in the final statement concerning the word in the area of Jerusalem where the locality is

---

[19] See, for example, Judg 1:4; 3:28–30; 4:6–14; 20:1–48; 1 Sam 4:1–11; 2 Sam 9:1–19; 1 Chr 12:20–37. For the use of the combination of the three words (ἀνήρ, ἀριθμός, and χιλίας) in the LXX in military contexts, see 2 Sam 24:9; 1 Chr 7:40; 21:5 (the other two occurrences can be found in the context of the building of the temple: 1 Chr 23:3; 2 Chr 2:16). Note also the military organization of the Qumran community that involves thousands of men (1QS 2:21–2; CD 13:1–2) and the discussion in Yigael Yadin, *The Scroll of the War of the Sons of Light Against the Sons of Darkness* (trans. B. Rabin and C. Rabin; London: Oxford University Press, 1962) 49–53. Within the Lukan writings, see Luke 14:31 where the word "thousand" (χιλιάς) appears in the context of military campaigns. See also the "four-thousand" (τετρακισχιλίους) who are involved in the revolt of the Egyptian in Acts 21:38.

[20] Even in the accounts of the census (e.g., Num 1:20–53), the militaristic context is explicitly stated as the counting involves only "male from twenty years old and upward, everyone able to go to war" (Num 1:20).

[21] The appearance of statements concerned with the growth of the community in relation to the use of the word λόγος will be discussed in detail in the next section of this chapter.

[22] For the frequent use of the words παρρησία and παρρησιάζομαι in Acts to signify the victory of the early Christian movement over the opposing forces, see Willem C. van Unnik, "The Christian's Freedom of Speech in the New Testament," *Sparsa Collecta: The Collected Essays of W. C. van Unnik* (NovTSup 30; Leiden: Brill, 1980) 2.269–89.

explicitly mentioned: ὁ λόγος τοῦ θεοῦ ηὔξανεν, καὶ ἐπληθύνετο ὁ ἀριθμὸς τῶν μαθητῶν ἐν Ἰερουσαλὴμ σφόδρα (lit.: "The word of God grew and the number of the disciples increased greatly in Jerusalem," 6:7). The "conquest" of Jerusalem is now complete; and, significantly, in the remaining part of Acts ὁ λόγος does not return to Jerusalem.

In Acts 8, one finds the travel of the word of God beyond the Jerusalem area. Immediately following the death of Stephen and the account of the persecution of the church in Jerusalem (8:1–3) is a note concerning the word: Οἱ μὲν οὖν διασπαρέντες διῆλθον εὐαγγελιζόμενοι τὸν λόγον ("Now those who were scattered went from place to place, proclaiming the word," 8:4). Without being overcome by the opposing forces, the word embarked on a journey beyond the confines of Judea. The word came to Samaria and it is reported that "Samaria had accepted the word of God" (δέδεκται ἡ Σαμάρεια τὸν λόγον τοῦ θεοῦ, 8:14; cf. vs 25).[23]

After Samaria, the word of God came to Cornelius. This is the word that God sent "to the people of Israel" (10:36) and with the story of the God-fearer Cornelius Luke can declare that καὶ τὰ ἔθνη ἐδέξαντο τὸν λόγον τοῦ θεοῦ ("the Gentiles had also accepted the word of God," 11:1). Nevertheless, the activity of the word is for the most part still confined within the boundaries of the Jewish world (11:19). In the second summary statement concerning the growth of the word, one again finds reference to persecution. Despite the efforts of Herod who, attempting to please the Jews (12:3), persecuted the believers of the word, "the word of God grew and multiplied" (lit.; ὁ δὲ λόγος τοῦ θεοῦ ηὔξανεν καὶ ἐπληθύνετο, 12:24).

With the beginning of the Pauline mission, the word traveled to Salamis of Cyprus where Paul and Barnabas "proclaimed the word of God in the synagogues of the Jews" (κατήγγελλον τὸν λόγον τοῦ θεοῦ ἐν ταῖς συναγωγαῖς τῶν Ἰουδαίων, 13:5). Despite opposition (vss 7–8), the word prevailed and was accepted even by the proconsul (vs 12).

Moving to Pisidian Antioch, the word of God plays an important role in the narrative relating the activity of Paul and Barnabas. In 13:26, speaking to the Jews (υἱοὶ γένους Ἀβραὰμ) and the God-fearers (οἱ ἐν ὑμῖν φοβούμενοι τὸν θεόν), Paul announced that it was for them that "the word of this salvation" (lit.; ὁ λόγος τῆς σωτηρίας ταύτης) had been sent.[24] Their initial interest motivated the audience to invite Paul and Barnabas back

---

[23] Here, it is noteworthy that while not necessarily everyone in Samaria had accepted the message of Philip, it is said that "Samaria had accepted." With this victory, the word is able to move forward. For a discussion of this verse in light of the restoration program, see section 4.3a above.

[24] While the reference here refers primarily to the vertical sending of the word from God to the descendants of Abraham, the horizontal mediation carried out by the ministers of the word cannot be ruled out.

so that they could hear the word of God (13:42–44). However, the resurfacing of Jewish opposition provided the context in which Paul declared that the word of God would turn to the Gentiles (vs 46) and "when the Gentiles heard this, they were glad and praised the word of the Lord" (ἀκούοντα δὲ τὰ ἔθνη ἔχαιρον καὶ ἐδόξαζον τὸν λόγον τοῦ κυρίου, vs 48). Similarly, in Lystra, Paul and Barnabas spoke in the Jewish synagogue and the unbelieving Jews rose up against them. The failure of this opposition is noted when Paul and Barnabas continued to speak and the Lord himself confirmed his own word: ἱκανὸν μὲν οὖν χρόνον διέτριψαν παρρησιαζόμενοι ἐπὶ τῷ κυρίῳ τῷ μαρτυροῦντι [ἐπὶ] τῷ λόγῳ τῆς χάριτος αὐτοῦ, διδόντι σημεῖα καὶ τέρατα γίνεσθαι διὰ τῶν χειρῶν αὐτῶν ("they remained for a long time, speaking boldly for the Lord, who testified to the word of his grace by granting signs and wonders to be done through them," 14:3).

The next appearance of the word in Perga should be noted. While Paul and Barnabas had already been to Perga (13:13), the word of God did not appear in that context. In a brief summary statement in 14:25, however, Luke notes that the word was now deposited in Perga: καὶ λαλήσαντες ἐν Πέργῃ τὸν λόγον κατέβησαν εἰς Ἀττάλειαν ("When they had spoken the word in Perga, they went down to Attalia").

In 15:35, the word finally reached Antioch:[25] Παῦλος δὲ καὶ Βαρναβᾶς διέτριβον ἐν Ἀντιοχείᾳ διδάσκοντες καὶ εὐαγγελιζόμενοι μετὰ καὶ ἑτέρων πολλῶν τὸν λόγον τοῦ κυρίου ("But Paul and Barnabas remained in Antioch, and there, with many others, they taught and proclaimed the word of the Lord"). In the next verse (15:36), Paul summarized his previous mission as one characterized by the action of announcing the word of the Lord (cf. 15:7). Then, Paul decided to visit the cities where he had previously been. Significantly, mention of the word of God does not reappear during this second tour when he returned to these cities (16:1–5).

In 16:6, one finds the statement on the prohibition of the spread of the word: Διῆλθον δὲ τὴν Φρυγίαν καὶ Γαλατικὴν χώραν, κωλυθέντες ὑπὸ τοῦ ἁγίου πνεύματος λαλῆσαι τὸν λόγον ἐν τῇ Ἀσίᾳ ("They went through the region of Phrygia and Galatia, having been forbidden by the Holy Spirit to speak the word in Asia"). This signifies the redirection of the journey of the word; and it is here that the word began its journey to Macedonia.

The next appearance of the word can be found in Philippi when Paul and Silas spoke to their jailer: καὶ ἐλάλησαν αὐτῷ τὸν λόγον τοῦ κυρίου

---

[25] In Acts 11:19, one finds a statement concerning the limitation of the spreading of the word to the Jewish circles in Antioch. Acts 15:35 should therefore be considered as the point where the word has "captured" Antioch.

154 Chapter 5

σὺν πᾶσιν τοῖς ἐν τῇ οἰκίᾳ αὐτοῦ ("They spoke the word of the Lord to
him and to all who were in his house," 16:32).

From Philippi the word traveled to Beroea where the people "received the
word with great eagerness" (lit.; ἐδέξαντο τὸν λόγον μετὰ πάσης
προθυμίας, 17:11). Opposition resurfaced when the Jews heard "that the
word of God had been proclaimed by Paul in Beroea as well" (ὅτι καὶ ἐν τῇ
Βεροίᾳ κατηγγέλη ὑπὸ τοῦ Παύλου ὁ λόγος τοῦ θεοῦ, vs 13).
Ironically, this opposition served as the force that pushed the word forward.

In Corinth, the active role of the word is confirmed. In 18:5, one reads:
συνείχετο τῷ λόγῳ ὁ Παῦλος διαμαρτυρόμενος τοῖς Ἰουδαίοις εἶναι
τὸν Χριστόν Ἰησοῦν (lit.: "Paul was pressed by the word, testifying to the
Jews that the Messiah was Jesus," 18:5).[26] This again is followed by the
opposition from the Jews. Again, the Jews failed to succeed in their action;
and the activity of Paul in Corinth is characterized by the teaching of the
"word of God" (18:11).

After Corinth, Paul visited Ephesus, and then returned to Caesarea and
Antioch. The word of God does not appear in the narrative related to these
places. While the word appeared earlier in Caesarea and Antioch, its absence
in Ephesus is especially significant since Paul "himself went into the
synagogue and had a discussion with the Jews" (αὐτὸς δὲ εἰσελθὼν εἰς τὴν
συναγωγὴν διελέξατο τοῖς Ἰουδαίοις, 18:19). From the pattern
previously observed, one expects the word of God to appear in this setting.
Its absence can only be explained by the presence of the word during Paul's
second trip to Ephesus in Acts 19. Moreover, this confirms the principle
established in the previous chapters of Acts—the word does not appear in a
city twice. The conquest of the word is reserved for Paul's lengthy stay
during his final visit to Ephesus.

When Paul returned from Antioch, the word appeared in the Ephesus area.
While the Holy Spirit forbade the word to be spread in the province of Asia in
16:6, the situation is completely reversed in 19:10 as a result of Paul's lecture
in the hall of Tyrannus: ὥστε πάντας τοὺς κατοικοῦντας τὴν Ἀσίαν
ἀκοῦσαι τὸν λόγον τοῦ κυρίου, Ἰουδαίους τε καὶ Ἕλληνας ("so that
all the residents in Asia, both Jews and Greeks, heard the word of the Lord").
Thus, another stage of the conquest of the word is now complete, as signaled
by the third of the three parallel summary statements. Just as 6:7 summarizes
the first stage of the conquest of the word in Jerusalem and 12:24 summarizes
the conquest of the word in Judea and Samaria, 19:20 summarizes the third

---

[26] I am taking συνείχετο as a passive and the following dative as a dative of agent.
Moreover, the variant πνεύματι implies that some took the word as a dative of agent.
Commentators who translate this phrase as "occupied with proclaiming the word" are
probably motivated by a refusal to acknowledge the active role of the word in Acts, the same
reason the textual variant was introduced.

stage of the conquest of the word throughout the Gentile world:[27] Οὕτως κατὰ κράτος τοῦ κυρίου ὁ λόγος ηὔξανεν καὶ ἴσχυεν (lit.: "Thus with power the word of the Lord grew and became strong"). With the phrase κατὰ κράτος, this final summary statement confirms the nature of the journey of the word as one of conquest. The military connotation of this phrase cannot be missed for it defines the character of the entire journey of the word of God.[28]

When Paul returned to Macedonia and Greece in 20:1–12, the word of God did not reappear since the conquest had already been accomplished during his previous journey. Paul then went to Miletus where he sent for the elders in Ephesus. Here, in Paul's speech to the elders, one finds the final statement concerning the word in the narrative of Acts: καὶ τὰ νῦν παρατίθεμαι ὑμᾶς τῷ θεῷ καὶ τῷ λόγῳ τῆς χάριτος αὐτοῦ τῷ δυναμένῳ οἰκοδομῆσαι καὶ δοῦναι τὴν κληρονομίαν ἐν τοῖς ἡγιασμένοις πᾶσιν (lit.: "And now I commend you to God and to the word of his grace, the one that is able to build you up and to give you the inheritance among all who are sanctified," 20:32). While a detailed discussion of this verse will be provided later in this chapter, it is sufficient to note that the word is again recognized as an active agent. It is ultimately the word, as an agent of God, who will be responsible for those who have accepted him.

The most striking fact in favor of understanding the word of God as an agent of conquest is its absolute absence from the remaining eight chapters of Acts.[29] The word of God does not return to Jerusalem and Caesarea, places it had already conquered. The contrast between the numerous references to the word of God in the first twenty chapters of Acts and its total disappearance in the final chapters highlights the role of the word as the main actor of the conquest and its goal in the construction of the community of the word.

One remaining fact needs to be discussed, the absence of the word of God in Rome. One possible explanation is that the goal of the journey of the word is indeed Ephesus, a representative city of the Gentile world. A more likely explanation, however, sees Rome as the ultimate end of the word's journey although the precise description of the activity of the word is absent. This latter understanding is supported by Paul's statement to the Ephesians elders.

---

[27] This corresponds to the three stages of the Isaianic New Exodus as noted in Acts 1:8. See my discussion in section 3.4b above.

[28] Again, a discussion of these three summary statements is presented in section 5.3a below.

[29] The word λόγος appears three more times in Acts but is not used to refer to the word of God. In 20:35, the plural form appears in reference to the sayings of Jesus. In 20:38, λόγος is used in reference to a particular statement Paul had made. Finally, in 22:22, λόγος is used to refer to the final statement of Paul's speech. In none of these instances, therefore, is the term used in an absolute sense to refer to the word of God; and in none does the qualifier τοῦ θεοῦ or τοῦ κυρίου appear.

In summing up his entire ministry (as well as the journey of the word) in 20:25, the Lukan Paul used the phrase κηρύσσων τὴν βασιλείαν ("proclaiming the kingdom"). The exact same phrase reappears in the very last verse of the narrative of Acts (28:31) but nowhere else in the book.[30] The ministry of the word left in Ephesus is now picked up eight chapters later in Rome. The uni-directional journey of the word is thus maintained as it travels all the way from Jerusalem to Rome. One can conclude, therefore, that the same act of the word reappears in Rome although its activities are summarized in one concise statement.

In the preceding paragraphs, I have shown that (1) the central character of the travel narrative is the word of God; (2) the nature of the travel of the word of God is one of conquest as the word prevails in the midst of opposing forces; and (3) the word's journey is a linear one. Although the ministers of the word may travel in circular journeys, the word itself travels from Jerusalem to the ends of the earth (i.e., the Gentile world) without returning to the same city twice.

I will now show how this discussion should be understood in light of the Isaianic New Exodus program as outlined in the previous chapters of this study. I will also show that this depiction of the journey of the word identifies the Christian community as one that truly belongs to the ancient prophetic traditions. Moreover, Luke's portrayal of the word suggests that the opposition from the competing communities will not be able to resist the power of the word (or the community that possesses the word).

The journey of the word from Jerusalem naturally recalls Isa 2:2–4, a passage that explicitly states that "the word of the LORD [will go forth] from Jerusalem" (λόγος κυρίου ἐξ ᾽Ιερουσαλήμ, 2:3):

> In days to come
> the mountain of the LORD's house shall be established
> as the highest of the mountains,
> and shall be raised above the hills;
> all the nations shall stream to it.
> Many peoples shall come and say,
> "Come, let us go up to the mountain of the LORD,
> to the house of the God of Jacob;
> that he may teach us his ways and that we may walk in his paths."
> For out of Zion shall go forth instruction,
> and the word of the LORD from Jerusalem.
> He shall judge between the nations,
> and shall arbitrate for many peoples;
> they shall beat their swords into plowshares,
> and their spears into pruning hooks;

---

[30] The two other occurrences of this phrase in the New Testament are in Luke 8:1 and 9:2.

nation shall not lift up sword against nation,
neither shall they learn war any more.

The exact relationship between this passage and the related passage in Mic
4:1–4 needs only a brief mention.[31] The verbal correspondence between these
two passages has generated numerous proposals concerning the origin of this
passage. Some attempt to show an Isaianic origin[32] while others argue for a
post-exilic origin where the passage was inserted into both Isaiah 2 and Micah
4 at a later time.[33] For the discussion of the Isaianic New Exodus in Acts,
however, the issue of the source of Isa 2:2–4 does not need to be resolved
here.[34] On the other hand, the thematic connections between Isa 2:2–4 and
40–55 should be discussed in greater detail, especially in relation to the
narrative of Acts.[35]

First, the phrase ἐν ταῖς ἐσχάταις ἡμέραις (lit.: "in the last days," 2:2)
points to the eschatological orientation of the text. This precise understanding
is not required by the Hebrew phrase באחרית הימים (lit.: "in the backward
side of days")[36] although the broader context of 2:2–4 does have an

---

[31] However, the difference in the ending of the passage in Micah (4:5) should be noted.

[32] For example, Gerhard von Rad ("The City on the Hill," *The Problem of the
Hexateuch and Other Essays* [trans. E. W. Trueman Dicken; New York: McGraw-Hill, 1966]
233) argues that "it cannot well be doubted that the text is Isaianic in origin" because "it fits
perfectly into the overall pattern of Isaianic thought, but one cannot say the same of the
occurrence in Micah." See also the more recent defense of this position in Hans Wildberger,
Isaiah 1–12: A Commentary (trans. T. H. Trapp; Minneapolis: Fortress, 1991) 85–87.

[33] This is first developed in B. Stade, "Deuterozacharja: Eine kritische Studie, II," *ZAW*
1 (1881) 165–67; and idem, "Bemerkungen zu vorstehendem Aufsatze," *ZAW* 4 (1884) 292.
A useful summary of the arguments for this position can be found in E. Cannawurf, "The
Authenticity of Micah IV 1–4," *VT* 13 (1963) 26–33. John T. Willis ("Isaiah 2:2–5 and the
Psalms of Zion," in Craig C. Broyles and Craig A. Evans, eds., *Writing and Reading the
Scroll of Isaiah: Studies of an Interpretive Tradition, vol. 1* [Leiden: Brill, 1997] 295–316),
on the other hand, argues that both Isaiah and Micah "borrowed an earlier poem (or prophetic
oracle [which borrowed heavily from such a poem]) extolling Zion" (311–12). The view that
the passage originated in Micah has faded out as a real possibility. See also the discussion in
Bernard Renaud, *La formation du livre de Michée* (Paris: Gabalda, 1977) 160–63.

[34] Recent studies on the complexity of the relationship between Isaiah 1–39 and 40–55
have, however, shifted the focus of the discussion concerning the source of Isa 2:2–4. The
abandonment of a strictly linear relationship between 1–39 and 40–55 has rekindled the
debate concerning the thematic relationship between 2:2–4 and 40–55. See, for example,
Anthony J. Tomasino, "Isaiah 1:1–2:4 and 63–66, and the Composition of the Isaianic
Corpus," *JSOT* 57 (1993) 81–98; and Hugh G. M. Williamson, *The Book Called Isaiah:
Deutero-Isaiah's Role in Composition and Redaction* (Oxford: Clarendon, 1994) 149–53.

[35] It is apparent, however, that Luke has the assumption of a single Isaiah in his
appropriation of material from the book.

[36] The Hebrew phrase can be found in passages such as Gen 49:1; Num 24:14; Deut
31:29; and Jer 23:20; and these passages point to the fact that the phrase can denote any
future point in history. See Otto Kaiser, *Isaiah 1–12: A Commentary* (trans. John Bowden;
2nd ed.; OTL; Philadelphia: Westminster, 1983) 53.

eschatological sense.[37] This eschatological orientation connects these verses with the promise of the New Exodus in Isaiah 40–55. Significantly, in the Pentecost speech of Peter, the exact same phrase (ἐν ταῖς ἐσχάταις ἡμέραις, Acts 2:17) is used at the beginning of the quotation from Joel. That this is an allusion to Isa 2:2 is confirmed by the fact that the phrase appears nowhere else in the Septuagint, or in the rest of the New Testament writings.[38] The appearance of this phrase in Acts 2 evokes the Isaianic framework in which the rest of the narrative is to be understood.

Second, the centrality of Zion-Jerusalem as the locus of God's revelation in 2:2–4 also stands out from its immediate context. As von Rad notes, "this is the first and also the earliest expression of a belief in the eschatological glorification of the holy mountain ʒnd of its significance for the redemption of the entire world."[39] The parallel of the terms "Zion" and "Jerusalem" reappears in Isaiah 40–55 as seen in its prologue:

> Get you up to a high mountain,
> O Zion, herald of good tidings,
> lift up your voice with strength,
> O Jerusalem, herald of good tidings;
> lift it up, do not fear;
> say to the cities of Judah,
> "Here is your God!" (Isa 40:9)[40]

In Isaiah 2 as well as 40–55, Jerusalem becomes the place where the salvific event will be announced. The role of Jerusalem in the Isaianic New Exodus can be further delineated through the connections between Sinai and Zion. Just as the Law of Moses came from Sinai, so now the תורה will go out from Zion. Within this New Exodus, one can argue that Zion has become "the heir to Sinai."[41] The dependence of Isaiah 40–55 upon Isa 2:3 can also be seen in 51:4: "a teaching will go out from me, and my justice for a light to the peoples."[42] Jerusalem also plays a significant role in Luke's appropriation of the Isaianic New Exodus. As early as Luke 2:38, the anticipated salvation event is described as "the redemption of Jerusalem." In Acts, Jerusalem is the

---

[37] Cf. Wildberger, *Isaiah 1–12*, 88.

[38] The closest parallels are in 2 Tim 3:1 and Jas 5:3 where the phrase ἐν ἐσχάταις ἡμέραις appears.

[39] Von Rad, "The City on the Hill," 233.

[40] For the centrality of Jerusalem/Zion, see also Isa 40:1–2; 49:13–18; and 51:3.

[41] For a discussion of the relationship between Sinai and Zion within the biblical traditions, see Jon D. Levenson, *Sinai and Zion* (Minneapolis, MN: Winston, 1985) 187, from which I have borrowed this phrase.

[42] The context assumes that Yahweh the speaker is already present in Zion.

starting point of the journey of the word but its significance is not limited to these early chapters.[43]

Third, the universalistic emphasis of Isa 2:2–4 also anticipates the emphasis one finds in Isaiah 40–55. The sending off of the word of the Lord from Jerusalem and the coming of all the nations to the mountain of the Lord (2:2; cf. 45:14–23) signify a period when Yahweh will be worshipped by all. In the New Exodus of Isaiah 40–55, "the glory of the LORD shall be revealed, all people shall see it together" (40:5). Again, the proclamation of salvation from Jerusalem to the end of the earth is central to the narrative of Acts. A further discussion of the universalism of the Isaianic New Exodus and Acts is provided in chapter seven. However, the preceding discussion confirms the view that Isa 2:2–4 belongs to the Isaianic New Exodus as expressed in Isaiah 40–55.[44]

I will now return to the focus of this section: the journey of the word of God. The phrase λόγος κυρίου ἐξ ᾽Ιερουσαλήμ (Isa 2:3) becomes a one sentence summary statement of the journey of the word in Acts. As in Isaiah 2, the word of God in Acts travels from Jerusalem, the center of the Lukan writings, into the world of the nations. The discussion of the itinerary of the word's journey in Acts shows that the word should be considered the main character of the narrative. This character is understandable only within the Isaianic New Exodus framework that places a consistent emphasis on the role of the word in the proclamation of the salvific event "in the last days." By reworking the traditions concerning the early Christian movement in terms of the journey of the word of God, Luke is able to claim that the Christian message embodies the ancient Israelite traditions and that the Christian community is the only legitimate recipient of the word.[45]

---

[43] In the Lukan writings, Jerusalem is not simply a place of rejection by the Jews. See J. Bradley Chance, *Jerusalem, the Temple, and the New Age in Luke-Acts* (Macon, GA: Mercer University Press, 1988) who, in reacting against the view of Hans Conzelmann (*The Theology of St. Luke* [trans. Geoffrey Buswell; New York: Harper & Row, 1960] 209–13), offers a more balanced treatment of the role of Jerusalem in the Lukan writings. This work fails, however, to articulate the significance of this emphasis in light of ancient Israelite traditions.

[44] Williamson (*The Book Called Isaiah*, 146) has concluded that "2:2–4 was known to Deutero-Isaiah" and that "it was a passage that influenced him in his own composition." Similarly, Richard J. Clifford (*Fair Spoken and Persuading: An Interpretation of Second Isaiah* [New York: Paulist, 1984] 46 n.8) notes that 2:1–5 is "a text mined more than once by Second Isaiah."

[45] Robert L. Wilken ("*In novissimis diebus*: Biblical Promises, Jewish Hopes and Early Christian Exegesis," *JECS* 1 [1993] 1–19) has provided further evidence for the competitive uses of Isa 2:2–4 among Christian and Jewish circles as reflected in early Christian commentaries on Isaiah.

b. The Hypostatization and the Power of the Word

Earlier I have hinted that Luke understands the word as an independent reality that possesses an active will. In this section, I will focus on the hypostatization[46] of the word of God in Acts and the power attributed to this being. The most obvious starting point for understanding the word as an individual being is the existence of three summary statements in Acts that point to the "growth" of the word:

Καὶ ὁ λόγος τοῦ θεοῦ ηὔξανεν. (lit.: "And the word of God grew," 6:7.)

Ὁ δὲ λόγος τοῦ θεοῦ ηὔξανεν καὶ ἐπληθύνετο. (lit.: "And the word of God grew and multiplied," 12:24.)

Οὕτως κατὰ κράτος τοῦ κυρίου ὁ λόγος ηὔξανεν καὶ ἴσχυεν. (lit.: "So with the power of the Lord the word grew and became strong," 19:20.)

In these verses, the imperfect form of the verb αὐξάνω appears in all three instances in connection with ὁ λόγος.[47] In the Lukan writings, this verb is only used in relation to living matters.[48] Significantly, the same form of the verb is used twice in Luke with the "growth" of John the Baptist and Jesus:

Τὸ δὲ παιδίον ηὔξανεν καὶ ἐκραταιοῦτο πνεύματι. ("The child grew and became strong in spirit," 1:80.)

Τὸ δὲ παιδίον ηὔξανεν καὶ ἐκραταιοῦτο πληρούμενον σοφία. ("The child grew and became strong, filled with wisdom," 2:40.)

The parallels between John the Baptist, Jesus, and the word are apparent, and the inference that the word is an individual being cannot be overlooked.[49]

This is the word that God sent to the sons of Israel (Acts 10:36);[50] and the mission is phrased in the language of Isaianic New Exodus: εὐαγγελιζόμενος εἰρήνην (cf. Isa 52:7). The mission of the word is affirmed in Acts 13:26 when Paul declared that ἡμῖν ὁ λόγος τῆς σωτηρίας

---

[46] I am using the word "hypostatization" to refer to the attainment of an actual reality. *Contra* Chung, "'The Word of God' in Luke-Acts," 215, it is not simply a metaphorical usage of the term since the action carried out by the λόγος in Acts goes beyond the category that is traditionally related to "speech." For a history of the usage of the term ὑπόστασις, see Helmut Koester, "ὑπόστασις," *TDNT* 8 (1972) 572–89.

[47] The use of the word λόγος as the subject of a verb has probably caused the substitution of ἡ πίστις for ὁ λόγος in some textual witnesses (e.g., D).

[48] See Luke 12:27 (the lilies); 13:19 (mustard seed); and Acts 7:17 (the people). This last instance will be discussed further in section 5.3a below.

[49] Both the power of the word and the understanding of the word as a community in connection with these three verses will be discussed in section 5.3a below.

[50] For a discussion of the textual and grammatical difficulties surrounding this verse, see Leo O'Reilly, *Word and Sign in the Acts of the Apostles: A Study in Lucan Theology* (AnGr 82; Rome: Editrice Pontifica Universita Gregorians, 1987) 74–75.

ταύτης ἐξαπεστάλη (lit.: "to us that this word of salvation has been sent").
The relationship between the identity of the word and that of Jesus can be
seen in 6:5 where it is said that the apostles will be devoted "to the service of
the word" (τῇ διακονίᾳ τοῦ λόγου). This phrase has close parallels with
the description of the Christians as ὑπηρέται τοῦ λόγου ("servants of the
word") in Luke 1:2. The Lord whom they serve is of course the risen Jesus
who called his followers to be his servants (cf. Acts 26:16).

The clearest indication that Luke presents the word as an independent
being can be found in Acts 13:48 when the Gentiles who heard the message
ἐδόξαζον τὸν λόγον τοῦ κυρίου ("praised the word of the Lord"). To
claim that this "can hardly mean anything other than that they gave glory to
the Lord for the word that they had heard"[51] simply fails to recognize the
unique use of this phrase; and this understanding can only be supported upon
the assumption that the word cannot be the object of δοξάζω.[52] Here, the
word as the object of glorification is to be highlighted. In the Lukan writings,
the object of the verb δοξάζω is always either God[53] or Jesus.[54] The only
exception is here in Acts 13:48 where the word of the Lord is the object. The
word that deserves to be glorified is the agent of God who accomplishes the
divine will in the narrative of Acts.

Finally, Acts 20:32 should also be mentioned. In the first part of the verse,
Paul commends the Ephesian elders to "the Lord and to the word of his grace"
(lit.; τῷ θεῷ καὶ τῷ λόγῳ τῆς χάριτος αὐτοῦ). This same word is able "to
build up and to give the inheritance among all who are sanctified" (lit.;
οἰκοδομῆσαι καὶ δοῦναι τὴν κληρονομίαν ἐν τοῖς ἡγιασμένοις
πᾶσιν). Again, one finds a parallel between the Lord and his word; and the
word becomes the active agent that carries out certain tasks when Paul is
absent. This identification of the Lord with his word affirms the thesis that
the Lukan word is a being that represents the divine will. Paul's comment that
the word will be carrying out tasks when he is not with the Ephesians shows
that the word is an active agent that is not necessarily contingent upon the one
who utters it.[55]

---

[51] Charles K. Barrett, *A Critical and Exegetical Commentary on the Acts of the
Apostles* (ICC; Edinburgh: T & T Clark, 1994) 1.658.

[52] This unusual construction has probably given rise to alternate readings that either
substitute ἐδέξαντο for ἐδόξαζον (D gig mae) or replace the object of the verb: ἐδόξαζον
τὸν θεὸν καὶ ἐπίστευσαν τῷ λόγῳ τοῦ κυρίου (614 876 1799 2412 syr^h). See Bruce M.
Metzger, *A Textual Commentary on the Greek New Testament* (2nd ed.; New York: United
Bible Societies, 1994) 369–70.

[53] Luke 2:20; 5:25, 26; 7:16; 13:13; 17:15; 18:43; 23:47; Acts 4:21; 11:18; 21:20.

[54] Luke 4:15; Acts 3:13.

[55] I will return to this verse in section 5.3b below.

One can therefore reasonably speak of the hypostatization of the word in the Lukan writings, especially in the travel narrative in Acts.[56] The word is an agent of God but it almost acquires its own existence during its journey in Acts. In his portrayal of the conquest of the word, however, Luke goes one step further in emphasizing the power of the word. The word is able to overcome opposing forces to accomplish the divine will from Jerusalem to the end of the earth. This power of the word is highlighted in a number of passages in Acts.

First, the summary statement in Acts 19:20 that was discussed above, will first be mentioned. The phrase κατὰ κράτος that qualifies the word should be discussed in greater detail. There is no doubt that the word κράτος itself sufficiently highlights the power of the word.[57] The word is used only once more in the Lukan writings in a context where war imagery cannot be missed: ἐποίησεν κράτος ἐν βραχίονι αὐτοῦ, διεσκόρπισεν ὑπερηφάνους διανοίᾳ καρδίας αὐτῶν ("He [the Lord] has shown strength with his arm; he has scattered the proud in the thoughts of their hearts," Luke 1:51). Here, the word κράτος is connected with the imagery of the arm. This imagery is prominent in both the Exodus traditions[58] and the Isaianic New Exodus.[59]

More importantly, though, is the combination of the two words in 19:20: κατὰ κράτος. This phrase appears nowhere else in the New Testament. In Hellenistic literature, the phrase is most often employed in military contexts;[60] and its only occurrence in the LXX (Judg 4:13) also confirms this militaristic emphasis. This raises the possibility of understanding this phrase

---

[56] Hubert Cancik, "The History of Culture, Religion, and Institutions in Ancient Historiography: Philological Observations Concerning Luke's History," *JBL* 116 (1997) 674, argues from Acts 9:31 that the church is hypostatized in the Lukan narrative and that it is a "proper 'historical subject' in Luke's history." Cancik rightly points to the ecclesiological focus of Acts, but his case would be strengthened if the connection between the word and the church were made. Furthermore, the historical subject should not be narrowly defined as the church in the Lukan narrative. It is the power of the word that is emphasized in the Lukan text.

[57] Wilhelm Michaelis ("κράτος," *TDNT* 3 [1965] 906) has noted that in the LXX, "in the overwhelming majority of instances" the word κράτος is used in reference to God. He also notes that "in the NT there is no place in which it is said of man that he either has or can gain κράτος" (907).

[58] See, for example, Exod 6:1, 6; Deut 3:24; 7:19.

[59] See, Isa 51:5, 9; 53:1; cf. 30:30. For a further discussion of this imagery, see David Rolph Seely, "The Image of the Hand of God in the Exodus Traditions" (Ph.D. diss., University of Michigan, 1990).

[60] See Michaelis, "κράτος," 905. The adverbial force of this phrase had also become prominent in the Hellenistic period.

in a militaristic sense. The conquest of the word is therefore one that is carried out "mightily."⁶¹

In the portrayal of the power of the word, the qualifier τῆς χάριτος that is connected with ὁ λόγος in Acts 14:3 and 20:32 is also an important term that contributes to the Lukan characterization of the word. As I have discussed earlier,⁶² χάρις can be understood as denoting the power (δύναμις) of God.⁶³ This is reflected in Acts 4:33 where the phrase "with greater power" (δυνάμει μεγάλῃ) stands in parallel with "great grace" (χάρις μεγάλη) in a context where proclamation is the central concern: καὶ δυνάμει μεγάλῃ ἀπεδίδουν τὸ μαρτύριον οἱ ἀπόστολοι τῆς ἀναστάσεως τοῦ κυρίου Ἰησοῦ, χάρις τε μεγάλη ἦν ἐπὶ πάντας αὐτούς ("with great power the apostles gave their testimony to the resurrection of the Lord Jesus, and great grace was upon them all"). The parallel between χάρις and δύναμις reappears in 6:8: Στέφανος δὲ πλήρης χάριτος καὶ δυνάμεως ἐποίει τέρατα καὶ σημεῖα μεγάλα ἐν τῷ λαῷ ("Stephen, full of grace and power, did great wonders and signs among the people"). In these verses, the connection between "grace" and "power" is established. Therefore, the phrase ὁ λόγος τῆς χάριτος should be understood as referring to "the word of power."

The importance of Acts 6:8 also lies in the fact that in this verse χάρις is connected with the phrase ἐποίει τέρατα καὶ σημεῖα. This connection can also be found in 14:3 where ὁ λόγος τῆς χάριτος is associated with the related phrase σημεῖα καὶ τέρατα.⁶⁴ In the LXX, the phrase σημεῖα καὶ τέρατα is a formulaic expression most often used to refer to the work of God the warrior in the Exodus traditions.⁶⁵ Through "signs and wonders" God fights for his people and delivers them out of the hands of the enemy. The use of this phrase to evoke the Exodus traditions is made explicit in Acts 7:36 where the phrase is used in reference to the national story of God's act of deliverance: οὗτος ἐξήγαγεν αὐτοὺς ποιήσας τέρατα καὶ σημεῖα ἐν γῇ Αἰγύπτῳ καὶ ἐν Ἐρυθρᾷ Θαλάσσῃ καὶ ἐν τῇ ἐρήμῳ ἔτη τεσσεράκοντα ("He led them out, having performed wonders and signs in

---

⁶¹ The word ἴσχυεν will be discussed in section 5.3a below within the context of Exod 1:7 and 20.

⁶² Please refer to chapter three above.

⁶³ Hans Conzelmann ("χάρις," *TDNT* 9 [1974] 376) has pointed out that, in the Hellenistic period, "χάρις becomes power in a substantial sense." This sense appears in the θεῖος ἀνήρ tradition. See Ludwig Bieler, *ΘΕΙΟΣ ΑΝΗΡ: Das Bild des "göttlichen Menschen" in Spätantike und Frühchristentum* (Darmstadt: Wissenschaftliche Buchgesellschaft, 1976) 1.49–56.

⁶⁴ The two phrases with different word order are interchangeable in Acts.

⁶⁵ Cf. Exod 7:3, 9; 11:9; 11:10; Deut 4:34; 6:22; 7:19; 13:2, 3; 26:8; 28:46; 29:3; 34:11. See the discussion in Selby Vernon McCasland, "Signs and Wonders," *JBL* 76 (1957) 150; and O'Reilly, *Word and Sign in the Acts of the Apostles*, 173–74.

164   *Chapter 5*

Egypt, at the Red Sea, and in the wilderness for forty years"). Both "the word" and "signs and wonders" are manifestations of the power of God in his fight for his own people.[66] In Acts, the word becomes the powerful agent that parallels the figure of Jesus who is described as "mighty in deed and in word before God and all the people" (δυνατὸς ἐν ἔργῳ καὶ λόγῳ ἐναντίον τοῦ θεοῦ καὶ παντὸς τοῦ λαοῦ, Luke 24:19).[67]

The portrayal of the word as a powerful entity is already hinted at in Luke. In the Nazareth synagogue scene of Luke 4:16–30, it is the "word of grace" that left an impression among those present: Καὶ πάντες ἐμαρτύρουν αὐτῷ καὶ ἐθαύμαζον ἐπὶ τοῖς λόγοις τῆς χάριτος τοῖς ἐκπορευομένοις ἐκ τοῦ στόματος αὐτοῦ ("All spoke well of him and were amazed at the gracious words that came from his mouth," 4:22).[68] The power of the word is again affirmed in 4:32 where the people are astounded at Jesus "because his word was with authority/power" (lit.; ὅτι ἐν ἐξουσίᾳ ἦν ὁ λόγος αὐτοῦ).[69] In 4:36, the power of the word that came out of Jesus' mouth gave rise to the question from the people: Τίς ὁ λόγος οὗτος; (lit.: "What is this word?").[70] The word as the medium of power in Luke foreshadows the role of the word as the powerful agent of conquest in the New Exodus program of Acts.[71]

In chapter two above, I established the importance of the word in the New Exodus of Isaiah. Here, the hypostatization and power of the word will be further discussed. Unique in the Isaianic conception of the word is the idea that the creative word works in history to accomplish the divine will. Already in Isa 9:7(8), the word is being sent as an instrument of the judgment of God. Interestingly, while the Hebrew text notes that "the Lord sent a word (דבר) against Jacob, and it fell on Israel," in the LXX it is "death" (θάνατον) that

---

[66] The unique Lukan usage of the phrase τέρατα καὶ σημεῖα/σημεῖα καὶ τέρατα in Acts is highlighted by the fact that in the New Testament eight out of eleven appearances of this phrase occur in Acts. More significant is the fact that the phrase does not appear in Luke at all.

[67] The connections with the Exodus traditions can again be seen in Acts 7:22 where Moses is portrayed as "powerful in his words and works" (δυνατὸς ἐν λόγοις καὶ ἔργοις αὐτοῦ).

[68] See, in particular, the discussion in John Nolland, "Words of Grace (Luke 4:22)," *Bib* 84 (1984) 44–60.

[69] Compare the Markan parallel in 1:22 in which the people were astounded with Jesus' authority but his "word" is not highlighted as the focus.

[70] Again, compare the Markan version that simply states: τί ἐστιν τοῦτο; ("What is this?" Mark 1:27).

[71] Against the position of Conzelmann (*Theology of St. Luke*, 190–93), one cannot affirm that miracles are considered as the primary medium of authority in Luke. See the discussion in Schürmann, *Das Lukasevangelium* (HKNT 3; Freiburg: Herder, 1969) 1.221–57.

the Lord sent against Jacob.[72] In this passage, the focus is on the power and not the content of the word. The word "is a reality in and of itself, not as a word that is to be conveyed as a message to someone else; it is not something that is to be heard but is an actual event about which one becomes aware."[73] This paved the way for understanding the word as a powerful agent in Isaiah 40–55.

In the prologue to Isaiah 40–55, it is declared that "the word (דבר)[74] of our God will stand forever" (40:8).[75] In this passage, the focus is again upon the power of the word as developed through the contrasts highlighted in 40:7–8. The "breath of the LORD" and the "word of our God" become identical phrases that point to God's superior power in relation to humanity who are represented by grass and flowers. Furthermore, the identification between the word and God himself is brought out by the fact that while in vs 8 the word of God is present, vs 10 explicitly states that "the Lord God comes with might." The power of the word is identified with the power of God; and this theme resurfaces throughout Isaiah 40–55.[76]

The emphasis upon the powerful word and its relationship to the Lord is best illustrated in 45:22–24, a passage that highlights the universal sovereignty of Israel's God:

Turn to me and be saved,
all the ends of the earth!
For I am God, and there is no other.
By myself I have sworn,
from my mouth has gone forth in righteousness

---

[72] As Wildberger (Isaiah 1–12, 220) has suggested, it seems that the translator of the LXX read דבר as דֶּבֶר ("pestilence").

[73] Ibid., 229. Oskar Grether (*Name und Wort Gottes im Alten Testament* [BZAW 64; Giessen: Töpelmann, 1934] 104) has already noted that this is the first appearance of the "word" as a powerful force that points to no specific content. Of course, Isa 2:2–4, a passage that has been discussed in the previous section, should also be noted here.

[74] In the Greek translation of Isaiah, both λόγος and ῥῆμα were used to translate the term דבר; and in this case, ῥῆμα was used. Unlike the more formulaic use of λόγος in Acts, the difference between the two is not a significant one in Isaiah. Here, I follow the conclusion of Otto Procksch ("λέγω," *TDNT* 4 [1967] 92) who concludes that "the LXX uses them as full synonyms." This difference does not affect my analysis of the thematic connections between Isaiah and Acts.

[75] Carroll Stuhlmueller (*Creative Redemption in Deutero-Isaiah* [Rome: Pontifical Biblical Institute, 1970] 181–82) has correctly noted that the verb "stand" fails to express fully the dynamic character of the Hebrew word קום. Stuhlmueller argues that Yahweh or his word does not "stand" forever but is "continually 'rising' to energize his full promises and desires for Israel" (182).

[76] The active force of "the word" can be seen when the term is connected with active verbs. For example, in Isa 50:4, the word is able "to sustain the weary." The prominence of this powerful word is not, however, limited to verses where the term דבר appears. The creative speech-acts of God can be seen in passages such as Isa 41:17–20 and 43:1–7.

a word (דבר) that shall not return:
"To me every knee shall bow, every tongue shall swear."
Only in the LORD, it shall be said of me,
are righteousness and strength;
all who were incensed against him
shall come to him and be ashamed.

This passage also points to the conception of the mission of the word as it is sent to accomplish the divine will. In 46:10, the Lord declares that "My purpose shall stand and I will fulfill my intention." The identification of the Lord with his word is seen in 55:10–11 where the word is going to carry out his will:

For as the rain and the snow come down from heaven,
and do not return there until they have watered the earth,
making it bring forth and sprout,
giving seed to the sower and bread to the eater,
so shall my word be that goes out from my mouth;
it shall not return to me empty,
but it shall accomplish that which I purpose,
and succeed in the thing for which I sent it.

It is not only the "hearers" who will be affected by the word. The cosmic effect of the powerful word is highlighted as the word is able to accomplish whatever the Lord wills. Therefore, the word cannot simply be identified by the message it conveys to those who receive it. The word is an entity the operations of which extend beyond the individual words uttered.

In Isa 55:10–11, the word that will accomplish the will of the Lord is also connected with the word that God utters in the ancient Exodus traditions. In Deut 32:47, Moses declared that one should not consider the word of the Lord as "empty" (ריק). In 55:11, the fact that the word will not return "empty" (ריק) is reaffirmed.[77]

The word of the Isaianic New Exodus is portrayed as a powerful agent of the sovereign Lord. As in the narrative of Acts, it has been sent forth to accomplish the divine will. It is both the creative word and also the one that works within history.[78] Nevertheless, it is still related to the one who utters it and who acts through such utterances. Thus, one can speak of the

---

[77] For a discussion of the relationship between the Deuteronomistic and Isaianic conceptions of the word, see Gerhard von Rad, *Old Testament Theology, vol. II: The Theology of Israel's Prophetic Traditions* (trans. D. M. G. Stalker; New York: Harper & Row, 1965) 82–83; Stuhlmueller, *Creative Redemption in Deutero-Isaiah*, 174; and Klaus Koch, "The Language of Prophecy: Thoughts on the Macrosyntax of the *debar* YHWH and Its Semantic Implications in the Deuteronomistic History," in H. T. C. Sun, K. L. Eades, J. M. Robinson, and G. I. Moller, eds., *Problems in Biblical Theology: Essays in Honor of Rolf Knierim* (Grand Rapids, MI: Eerdmans, 1997) 210–221.

[78] The affinity of the Isaianic word and that of the Psalms is established by Walther Zimmerli, "Jahwes Wort bei Deuterojesaja," *VT* 32 (1982) 104–24.

hypostatization of the prophetic word[79] without having the full-blown portrayal of the independent λόγος of the later wisdom traditions.[80] It is precisely this understanding of the word that one finds in the narrative of Acts. In both Isaiah and Acts, the word is related to the speaker and yet attains its own existence as an active entity.[81] In both, the goal is to create a new community as the people of God. In this sense, the word is also a tool with which the true identity of the people of God can be identified. It is to this ecclesiological aspect of the word that I must now turn.

5.3 The Goal of the New Exodus: The Creation of the Community of the People of God

In the remaining part of this chapter, I will discuss the ecclesiological aspects of Luke's λόγος-terminology. First, I will argue that the description of the growth of the word-community alludes to the formation of the people of God in the Exodus traditions. Second, the identity of the word-community as the true people of God will be discussed.

a. The Growth of the Word and the New Community of the Exodus Traditions

The ecclesiological focus of the use of λόγος-terminology is most clearly reflected in the three summary statements mentioned above concerning the growth of the early Christian movement (Acts 6:7; 12:24; 19:20). The position of these three verses and the unique vocabulary chosen to describe the growth of the community demand further discussion. Here, these three verses should again be noted with the three different verbs they use highlighted:

Καὶ ὁ λόγος τοῦ θεοῦ <u>ηὔξανεν</u>. (6:7)

Ὁ δὲ λόγος τοῦ θεοῦ <u>ηὔξανεν</u> καὶ ἐπληθύνετο. (12:24)

Οὕτως κατὰ κράτος τοῦ κυρίου ὁ λόγος <u>ηὔξανεν</u> καὶ <u>ἴσχυεν</u>. (19:20)

---

[79] Ibid., 106.

[80] It seems likely that the Lukan conception of the word is developed from the prophetic tradition of Isaiah and not directly from wisdom material such as the Wisdom of Solomon. Interestingly, both Isaiah and the Wisdom of Solomon use λόγος terminology in their reworkings of the Exodus traditions. See the discussion in the excursus at the end of this chapter.

[81] Bruce D. Chilton (*The Glory of Israel: The Theology and Provenience of the Isaiah Targum* [Sheffield: JSOT Press, 1983] 59–68) suggests that the Isaiah Targum attests to the use of מימרא as a theologumenon in a period roughly contemporary with the Lukan writings.

168 Chapter 5

While Jerome Kodell has noted the uses of αὐξάνω and πληθύνω in the fourteen passages in the LXX to describe the growth of the people of God,[82] he fails to notice the significance of the use of a different verb (ἰσχύω) in the third summary statement of 19:20.[83] This failure to notice the additional verb and the peculiar fact that a different combination of verbs is used in the three statements in Acts results in the failure to appreciate the more specific context in which the three statements should be located. I will argue that the uses of these three verbs allude to a particular situation in the first chapter of Exodus at the earliest stage of rebuilding the community of God. This allusion to the complex of Exodus events to describe the early Christian community in Acts suggests that this language functions as a hermeneutic key for understanding the Christian community as the people of God as described in the paradigmatic event of the national story of Israel. Here, one should go beyond the analysis of the two verbs (αὐξάνω and πληθύνω) and notice the appearance of the combination of these three verbs in the first chapter of Exodus:

οἱ δὲ υἱοὶ Ἰσραὴλ <u>ηὐξήθησαν</u> καὶ ἐπληθύνθησαν καὶ χυδαῖοι ἐγένοντο καὶ <u>κατίσχυον</u> σφόδρα σφόδρα, ἐπλήθυνεν δὲ ἡ γῆ αὐτούς (lit. "And the children of Israel grew and multiplied, and became numerous and grew exceedingly strong, and the land is filled with them," Exod 1:7).

εὖ δὲ ἐποίει ὁ θεὸς ταῖς μαίαις, καὶ ἐπλήθυνεν ὁ λαὸς καὶ <u>ἴσχυεν</u> σφόδρα (lit. "And God did well to the midwives, and the people multiplied, and grew exceedingly strong," Exod 1:20).

These two verses provide the context for the three summary statements in Acts. First, the presence of ἰσχύω (and the related form κατaισχύω) in Exod 1:7 and 20 explains the presence of the same verb in the summary statement of Acts 19:20. With the presence of the same three verbs in Exodus

---

[82] Jerome Kodell, "'The Word of God Grew': The Ecclesial Tendency of Λόγος in Acts 6,7; 12,24; 19,20," Bib 55 (1974) 510–11: Gen 1:22, 28; 8:17; 9:1, 7; 17:20; 28:3; 35:11; 47:27; 48:4; Exod 1:7; Lev 26:9; Jer 3:16; 23:3. See also Paul Zingg, Das Wachsen der Kirche. Beiträge zur Frage der lukanischen Redaktion und Theologie (Göttingen: Vandenhoeck & Ruprecht, 1974) 23–29.

[83] The same criticism applies to the study of O'Reilly, Word and Sign in the Acts of the Apostles, 82–83, one that follows Kodell in his analysis of the summary statements. See also the recent work of Wolfgang Reinhardt, Das Wachstum des Gottesvolkes: Untersuchungen zum Gemeindewachstum im lukanischen Doppelwerk auf dem Hintergrund des Alten Testaments: Mit zwei Schaubildern und vier Tabellen (Göttingen: Vandenhoeck & Ruprecht, 1995) 59–64, who highlights the LXX background of the words of various growth statements but also fails to notice the importance of the set of verbs in Exod 1:7, 20 and its significance for the New Exodus community of Acts. Another study that should be mentioned is Meinert H. Grumm, "Another Look at Acts," ExpTim 96 (1985) 333–37. Surprisingly, this study that focuses on the growth statements in Acts is unaware of Kodell's article. Grumm did not discuss the LXX context of these statements and only examined the verb αὐξάνω, and then only in light of the Pauline usage.

1 in a context concerning the growth of the people of God in the midst of opposition, the connections between Exodus 1 and the three summary statements in Acts cannot be doubted. Second, in Exod 1:20, only the verbs πληθύνω and ἰσχύω are used. This shows that the combination of the two verbs αὐξάνω and πληθύνω is not as important as the presence of the complex of the three verbs in both Exodus 1 (and nowhere else in the LXX) and the three summary statements in Acts. In other words, the fourteen texts that Kodell has highlighted that contain the two verbs αὐξάνω and πληθύνω are not as important as the two specific texts in Exodus 1:7 and 20, especially when the combination of the two verbs is absent in two of the three summary statements (Acts 6:7 and 19:20). The connection with Exod 1:7 is especially clear since it is alluded to in Acts 7:17: ηὔξησεν ὁ λαὸς καὶ ἐπληθύνθη ἐν Αἰγύπτῳ (lit.: "the people increased and multiplied in Egypt"). Finally, the presence of the two verses in Exodus 1 in the same context while different verbs are used also explains the shift in the usage of verbs in the three summary statements in Acts, a fact that is otherwise inexplicable. In short, the use of αὐξάνω in 6:7; αὐξάνω and πληθύνω in 12:24; and αὐξάνω and ἰσχύω in 19:20 can only be explained in light of Exodus 1.

In the context of Exodus, Exod 1:7 "forms the background for the events which initiate the exodus."[84] Together with 1:20, these statements point to the growth of the people of God in spite of opposing forces. Their position at the beginning of the story of Exodus shows that these should also be understood as an introduction to the creation of a new people by an act of God. It is this context that is evoked in the three summary statements in Acts. The powerful word of God is now identified with the community as God once again "creates" a new people for himself.[85] The early Christian community is therefore presented as the continuation of the "ancient" people of God. The community in which the "word" can be found is the true heir to the ancient Israelite traditions. The ecclesiological significance of the terminology is therefore made explicit. The powerful word that conquers and the word that is identified with the community are one and the same in terms of the function of λόγος in the narrative of Acts. The emphases that the word is the powerful word of the Isaianic New Exodus and that it is contained in a community parallel those which one finds in the ancient Exodus traditions.

---

[84] Brevard S. Childs, *The Book of Exodus* (OTL; Louisville, KY: Westminster, 1974) 3.

[85] This does not mean that the community of the word is the "new" people of God in an absolute sense. Creation language is adopted here in light of the influence of this language in the depiction of the Isaianic New Exodus.

These emphases are able to create a claim concerning the identity of the early Christian movement against other rival claims.[86]

While the growth of the community should be understood against the background of the first chapter of Exodus, the issue concerning the identification of the community with the word still needs to be discussed. The link between the word and the community is provided by the theme of witness in both Isaiah and Acts. In Isaiah 40–55, a particular understanding of the community as witnesses is developed. Here, the word of God becomes embodied in the community, and the people of God become the mouthpiece of their God.[87] In Isa 43:10, the people of God are called to be witnesses of God:

You are my witnesses (עֵדַי; LXX: μοι μάρτυρες), says the LORD,
and my servant whom I have chosen,
so that you may know and believe me and understand that I am he.
Before me no god was formed, nor shall there by any after me.

Similarly in Acts, the witness-theme plays an important role in the narrative. One can see this in the command of Jesus in Acts 1:8 where the apostles are called to be "my witnesses" (μου μάρτυρες).[88] As witnesses, they serve as mouthpieces of God who testify to the message of salvation.[89] It is this characterization of the community as witnesses that leads to the identification of the word with the community in Acts. The community is the word as it testifies to the power and salvation of the God of Israel.

Before leaving these summary statements on the growth of the word, the Lukan parable of the sower (Luke 8:4–15) should also be mentioned. The Markan interpretation of the parable begins with the sentence: "The sower sows the word" (ὁ σπείρων τὸν λόγον σπείρει, Mark 4:14). In the Lukan version, the identification of the word of God with the seed is emphasized: "The seed is the word of God" (σπόρος ἐστὶν ὁ λόγος τοῦ θεοῦ, Luke

---

[86] A discussion of the precise placement of these statements can be found within the discussion of the itinerary of the word in section 5.2a above.

[87] See the discussion in Zimmerli, "Jahwes Wort bei Deuterojesaja," 121. Richard J. Clifford ("The Function of Idol Passages in Second Isaiah," *CBQ* 42 [1980] 450–64) has also highlighted the contrast between the Lord of Israel and the deities of the nations as Yahweh has Israel as his witnesses but the idols who represent the gods of the nations are not able to speak.

[88] The word μάρτυς appears thirteen times in Acts, more than twice the amount than the text with the next highest frequency (five times in Revelation). Other related terms include μαρτυρεῖν, διαμαρτύρεσθαι, μαρτύρεσθαι, μαρτύριον, and μαρτυρία. For a further discussion of the theme of witness in Acts, see Richard J. Dillon, *From Eye-Witnesses to Ministers of the Word: Tradition and Composition in Luke 24* (AnBib 82; Rome: Pontifical Biblical Institute, 1978); and Marion L. Soards, *The Speeches in Acts: Their Content, Context, and Concerns* (Louisville, KY: Westminster/John Knox, 1994) 194–200.

[89] See, especially, Acts 10:39–43 in which the theme of "witness" saturates the passage.

8:11).[90] This understanding of the word as a seed that grows prepares the way for the summary statements in Acts concerning the growth of the word. Furthermore, this parable should also be understood in light of Isa 55:10–11.[91] As discussed above, this passage is critical for understanding the role of the word in the Isaianic New Exodus. In both the parable of the sower and this Isaianic passage, one finds the metaphor of the seed; and in both the importance of the word is highlighted. Therefore, one can reasonably conclude that the parable of the sower provides the context in which further discussion of the growth of the word can be developed. More importantly, the parable also provides a link between the role of the word in the Isaianic New Exodus and the understanding of the word in the narrative of Acts where the Isaianic word is identified as the word that God has sent through the mission of Jesus.[92]

b. The Early Christian Community as the Sole Possessor of the Word

First of all, the growth of the word in the midst of opposition should again be noted. The development of such a theme in Acts serves to identify the early Christian community as the true people of God and the sole possessor of the word of God.

Luke's allusion to the first chapter of Exodus allows him to evoke the Exodus tradition to interpret of the existence of opposition to the early Christian movement. The two verses (Exod 1:7, 20) that are alluded to in the summary statements of Acts frame the narrative concerning the oppression of God's people by the king of Egypt. The statement on the growth of the people of God in Exod 1:7 is immediately followed by the description of the plan to eliminate the people of God:

> Now a new king arose over Egypt, who did not know Joseph. He said to his people, "Look, the Israelite people are more numerous and more powerful than we. Come, let us deal shrewdly with them, or they will increase and, in the event of war, join our enemies and fight against us and escape from the land." (Exod 1:8–10)

The decision to eliminate the people of Israel is carried out via the attempt of the king of Egypt to eliminate the children of Israel through their midwives. Immediately after the report of this plan, however, one reads that the midwives refused because they feared God; thus, "God dealt well with the midwives; and the people multiplied and became very strong" (Exod 1:20). The two growth statements, therefore, frame the narrative depicting Pharaoh's

---

[90] The equivalence of Mark 4:14 is not present in the Matthean version.

[91] See, in particular, Craig A. Evans, "On the Isaianic Background of the Sower Parable," *CBQ* 47 (1985) 464–68, who argues that "the parable and its interpretation reflect the same metaphor and theology that we have in Isa 55:10–11" (466).

[92] This includes both the understanding of Jesus as the word and the message he proclaims. In Acts, apparently this word is also the message "about" Jesus.

attempt to destroy the people of God. In the midst of opposition, however, the people grew even stronger.

In the New Exodus of Isaiah 40–55, it is the word of God that continues to stand strong in the midst of opposition. The power of the word of God is contrasted with that of idols who are not able to witness to the powerful acts of the deities they represent.[93] More importantly, however, these idols become representatives of the power of the foreign nations arrayed against the people of God.[94] The two statements (Isa 40:8; 55:11) that frame the narrative affirm the power of the word to accomplish the purpose of the divine will. In the context of Isaiah 40–55, this power of the word is contrasted with the power (or powerlessness) of the Babylonian rulers in their oppressive acts against the people of God.[95] The discussion of the power of the word reflects the emphasis of the power of Yahweh to deliver his people from the hands of Babylon:

> I have spoken, and I will bring it to pass;
> I have planned, and I will do it.
> Listen to me, you stubborn of heart,
> you who are far from deliverance:
> I will bring near by deliverance, it is not far off,
> and my salvation will not tarry;
> I will put salvation in Zion, for Israel my glory. (Isa 46:11b–13)

The word of the God who has spoken becomes a symbol of the power of Yahweh in his battle against the power of the Babylonians. In Isaiah, the Babylonians take the place of the Egyptians as the enemy of God. The power

---

[93] Cf. Isa 41:21–24; 44:6–8; 45:20–25; 46:7. See also the discussion in Horst Dietrich Preuss, *Verspottung fremder Religionen im Alten Testament* (BWANT 92; Stuttgart: Kohlhammer, 1971) 192–237; and Clifford, "The Function of Idol Passages in Second Isaiah," 450–64.

[94] In Isaiah 40–55, four groups are interrelated in the description of the oppressive powers: deities, idols, nations, and human rulers. See the contrast of the power of Yahweh with all four interchangeable entities in 40:12–31 and the discussion in chapter six below.

[95] See Zimmerli, "Jahwes Wort bei Deuterojesaja," 115–117, who discusses the emphasis on the power of the word in the *Disputationswortes*. The contrast between the power of Yahweh and the Babylonian deity becomes the focus of the disputation discourse; and the power of the word promises deliverance from the hands of the Babylonians. See also Alexander Rofé ("How is the Word Fulfilled? Isaiah 55:6–11 within the Theological Debate of its Time," in Gene M. Tucker, David L. Petersen, and Robert R. Wilson, eds., *Canon, Theology, and Old Testament Interpretation: Essays in Honor of Brevard S. Childs* [Philadelphia: Fortress, 1988] 250) who suggests that "Second Isaiah develops here a dialectical attitude toward the hymns directed to the Babylonian gods, hymns that exalted them for the power of their word."

of the word ensures the deliverance of the community from the hands of the enemy that threatens the survival of the people of God.[96]

This leads one to the function of the description of the growth of the word in the narrative of Acts. The growth of the community is described in the language of Exodus 1. Through the Isaianic emphasis on the power of the word, the growth of the community is identified as the growth of the word in Acts. Moreover, as in Exodus and Isaiah, the community becomes strong in the midst of opposition.[97]

Ironically, whereas the enemies of the people of God were the Egyptians and the Babylonians in Exodus and Isaiah, the Jews are among the enemies of the word, and therefore also of God, in Acts. The growth of the early Christian movement shows that the word resides in them and that the they are the people of God. This is most clearly noted in a statement made by Gamaliel that provides a model for the interpretation of the growth of the word:

> καὶ τὰ νῦν λέγω ὑμῖν, ἀπόστητε ἀπὸ τῶν ἀνθρώπων τούτων καὶ ἄφετε αὐτούς· ὅτι ἐὰν ᾖ ἐξ ἀνθρώπων ἡ βουλὴ αὕτη ἢ τὸ ἔργον τοῦτο, καταλυθήσεται· εἰ δὲ ἐκ θεοῦ ἐστιν, οὐ δυνήσεσθε καταλῦσαι αὐτούς· μήποτε καὶ θεομάχοι εὑρεθῆτε.

> So in the present case, I tell you, keep away from these men and let them alone; because if this plan or this undertaking is of human origin, it will fail; but if it is of God, you will not be able to overthrow them — in that case you may even be found fighting against God! (Acts 5:38–39)

This passage provides the criterion by which the early Christian movement can be judged. According to Luke, the fact that the opposing force is not able to overthrow the early Christian community shows that it is from God. This community of the word therefore claims to be the people of God. On the other hand, the term that is used in describing the opposing force of the movement should also be noted. Those who oppose the word are θεομάχοι (lit.: "fighters against God").[98] The military imagery used here is appropriate when one considers the conquest of the word within the paradigm of the New Exodus. Within this context, those who resist naturally become those who are fighting against God. Here, the development of the identity of the early Christian community as the people of God against the competitive claim of the unbelieving Jews is apparent.[99] As the three summary statements (Acts

---

[96] For the polemical function of the discourse on the power of the word, see also von Rad, *Old Testament Theology*, 92–94.

[97] See the discussion of the conquest journey of the word through opposing forces in section 5.2a above.

[98] For a discussion of the background of this term, see Barrett, *Acts of the Apostles*, 1.297–98.

[99] The claim that "the Lord" is on the side of the early Christian movement is also noted in the statement addressed to Paul in Acts 18:9–10: "Do not be afraid (μὴ φοβοῦ), but

6:7; 12:24; 19:20) affirm the continuing growth of the word, the narrative ends
with the statement that Paul is "proclaiming the kingdom of God and teaching
about the Lord Jesus Christ with all boldness and without hindrance"
(κηρύσσων τὴν βασιλείαν τοῦ θεοῦ καὶ διδάσκων τὰ περὶ τοῦ
κυρίου Ἰησοῦ Χριστοῦ μετὰ πάσης παρρησίας ἀκωλύτως, Acts
28:31).[100] This final statement together with the three summary statements
provide the appropriate response to Gamaliel's statement in Acts 5:38–39.

Finally, I must return to the final statement in which the word appears in
Acts. In his farewell speech to the Ephesian elders, Paul commended his
audience to the word, one "that is able to build you up and to give you the
inheritance among all who are sanctified" (αὐτοῦ τῷ δυναμένῳ
οἰκοδομῆσαι καὶ δοῦναι τὴν κληρονομίαν ἐν τοῖς ἡγιασμένοις
πᾶσιν, Acts 20:32). Several aspects of this verse have already been noted.
Here, I will concentrate on the concept of "inheritance" and its connection
with the journey of the word.

The usage of the term κληρονομία ("inheritance") in Acts and in the
LXX recalls the Exodus-Conquest traditions when God delivered his people
from Egypt and gave them the promised land as an inheritance. The only other
occurrence of this noun in Acts appears in the speech of Stephen where
Israel's anticipated entrance into the promised land is alluded to in connection
with the ancient promise to Abraham:

> καὶ οὐκ ἔδωκεν αὐτῷ κληρονομίαν ἐν αὐτῇ οὐδὲ βῆμα ποδός, καὶ ἐπηγγείλατο
> δοῦναι αὐτῷ εἰς κατάσχεσιν αὐτὴν καὶ τῷ σπέρματι αὐτοῦ μετ' αὐτόν, οὐκ ὄντος
> αὐτῷ τέκνου.
>
> He did not give him any of it as an inheritance, not even a foot's length, but promised to
> give it to him as his possession and to his descendants after him, even though he had no
> child. (Acts 7:5)

---

speak and do not be silent; for I am with you, and no one will lay a hand on you to harm
you, for there are many in this city who are my people." Here, the employment of the "fear-
not formula" recalls the ancient Israelite traditions of holy war in which God fights for his
people. In such a context, those who are on the side of God have no need to fear while the
enemies of God will be destroyed by fear. For the use of the fear-not formula in the Isaianic
New Exodus and the wider Israelite holy war tradition, see Paul-Eugène Dion, "The 'Fear
Not' Formula and Holy War," *CBQ* 32 (1970) 565–70; Edgar W. Conrad, "The Fear Not
Oracles in Second Isaiah," *VT* 34 (1984) 126–52; and idem, *Fear Not Warrior* (BJS 75;
Chico, CA: Scholars Press, 1985).

[100] Note that the entire narrative ends with the word ἀκωλύτως, a word that defines the
movement of the word as well as opens the future for the continuing growth of the word. See
Reinhardt (*Das Wachstum des Gottesvolkes*, 307) who rightly concludes that Rome is not the
end of the earth but is yet another center from which the gospel will continue to spread freely
despite the existence of all tensions and oppositions.

In the LXX, the word κληρονομία and its related forms are often used in reference to the Exodus-Conquest traditions.[101] The classic statement can be found in Gen 15:7 in which the verbal form is used:

εἶπεν δὲ πρὸς αὐτόν Ἐγὼ ὁ θεὸς ὁ ἐξαγαγών σε ἐκ χώρας Χαλδαίων ὥστε δοῦναί σοι τὴν γῆν ταύτην κληρονομῆσαι.

Then he said to him, "I am the LORD who brought you from Ur of the Chaldeans, to give you this land to possess."

The promise is not immediately fulfilled, however, and it looks forward to the Exodus-Conquest period. This connection is made in Exod 6:8 (cf. Deut 1:8) where the related word κλῆρος is used:

καὶ εἰσάξω ὑμᾶς εἰς τὴν γῆν, εἰς ἣν ἐξέτεινα τὴν χεῖρά μου δοῦναι αὐτὴν τῷ Ἀβραὰμ καὶ Ἰσαὰκ καὶ Ἰακὼβ, καὶ δώσω ὑμῖν αὐτὴν ἐν κλήρῳ· ἐγὼ κύριος.

I will bring you into the land that I swore to give to Abraham, Isaac, and Jacob; I will give it to you for a possession. I am the LORD.

The word κληρονομία itself is used in the Song of Moses (Exod 15:17) in the context of the conquest:

εἰσαγαγὼν καταφύτευσον αὐτοὺς εἰς ὄρος κληρονομίας σου,
εἰς ἕτοιμον κατοικητήριόν σου, ὃ κατειργάσω, κύριε,
ἁγίασμα, κύριε, ὃ ἡτοίμασαν αἱ χεῖρές σου.

You brought them in and planted them
on the mountain of your own possession,
the place, O LORD, that you made your abode,
the sanctuary, O LORD, that your hands have established.

The conquest of the land is completed when Israel receives her inheritance as promised to Moses:

καὶ ἔλαβεν Ἰησοῦς πᾶσαν τὴν γῆν, καθότι ἐνετείλατο κύριος τῷ Μωυσῇ, καὶ ἔδωκεν αὐτοὺς Ἰησοῦς ἐν κληρονομίᾳ Ἰσραὴλ ἐν μερισμῷ κατὰ φυλὰς αὐτῶν. καὶ ἡ γῆ κατέπαυσεν πολεμουμένη.

So Joshua took the whole land, according to all that the LORD had spoken to Moses; and Joshua gave it for an inheritance to Israel according to their tribal allotments. And the land had rest from war. (Josh 11:23)

In these passages, the word κληρονομία (and its related forms) is used in reference to the promise given to Abraham and fulfilled during the Exodus-Conquest period. The same word is used in the description of the New Exodus of Isaiah 40–55 where the Lord will again give the land to Israel as her inheritance:

---

[101] For the use of κληρονομία in the LXX, see Werner Foerster, "κλῆρος," *TDNT* 3 (1965) 759–61.

οὕτως λέγει κύριος Καιρῷ δεκτῷ ἐπήκουσά σου καὶ ἐν ἡμέρᾳ σωτηρίας ἐβοήθησά σοι καὶ ἔδωκά σε εἰς διαθήκην ἐθνῶν τοῦ καταστῆσαι τὴν γῆν καὶ κληρονομῆσαι κληρονομίαν ἐρήμου.

Thus says the LORD:
In a time of favor I have answered you, on a day of salvation I have helped you;
I have kept you and given you as a covenant to the people, to establish the land,
to inherit the inheritance of the wilderness. (lit.; Isa 49:8)

In light of these passages that show the connections between the promise of inheritance and the Exodus paradigm both in Exodus and in Isaiah, the promise that the word will give the believers an "inheritance" (κληρονομία) becomes a fitting climax to the conquest of the word in Acts. As in the ancient Exodus traditions and the Isaianic New Exodus, the language of inheritance becomes significant at the end of the journey. Although the nature of the inheritance cannot be identified as the land of Israel,[102] the use of the term evokes the Exodus tradition. Therefore, once again one finds allusions that support the understanding of the journey of the word as a New Exodus journey. In identifying the word with the community and in limiting the word of God to that community, however, the identity of the community is established against those who also claim to have obtained the inheritance promised to their fathers. The travel of the word is a new journey that produces a new community with the promise of a new inheritance.

5.4 Conclusion

In this chapter, I have shown that the word of God in the narrative of Acts is an active agent that travels to the end of the earth. The goal of this journey is to conquer the world and to create a community as the true people of God. Even when the suffering of the ministers of the word is mentioned throughout the narrative, the word itself is portrayed as undefeated. Themes such as the journey of the word, the nature of the word, the growth of the word-community, and the identity of the word-community as the people of God can be properly understood only against the context of the Exodus traditions as transformed in Isaiah 40–55. The function of such evocation of traditions is to establish and justify the identity claim of the early Christian community as the true heirs of the ancient Israelite traditions.

---

[102] On the transformation of the concept of inheritance in the New Testament, see the detailed discussion in Jacques Dupont, *Le discours de Milet: Testament pastoral de Paul Actes 20, 18–36* (Paris: Cerf, 1962) 261–83.

Excursus: The Word of God in Context

It is a well established fact that the use of λόγος-terminology to depict an active and powerful agent of God is not limited to either Isaiah nor Luke.[103] As in Isaiah, the word of God is connected with the creative work of God elsewhere in Scripture (Gen 1:3ff). In Ps 146(147):15–18, for example, the term points to the powerful act of God:

> He sends out his command to the earth; his word (λόγος) runs swiftly.
> He gives snow like wool; he scatters frost like ashes.
> He hurls down hail like crumbs—who can stand before his cold?
> He sends out his word (λόγον), and melts them;
> he makes his wind blow, and the waters flow.

Similarly, in Ps 32(33):6, ones reads: "By the word (λόγῳ) of the LORD the heavens were made, and all their host by the breath of his mouth." Creation language is here used to highlight the power of Yahweh who is able to deliver his people as in ancient times. This understanding reappears in Second Temple Jewish literature.[104]

The word as the powerful agent of God who acts beyond the point of creation is reflected in Hellenistic circles. In Hab 3:5, for example, the Hebrew text reads: "Before him went pestilence, and plague followed close behind." When the text is translated into Greek, however, one finds the role of the word being emphasized: "Before him the word (λόγος) will go, and it shall go into the plains" (Hab 3:5 LXX).

For a fully developed form of λόγος theology, one has wait for the voluminous work of Philo. In Philo, wisdom theology is combined with conceptions of the word as the agent of creation.[105] In this construction, Stoic philosophical influence cannot be denied, yet the role of Torah can also be

---

[103] In this section, I am not attempting to trace the origin of λόγος-terminology. My goal is to show that the (1) contemporary usage of this terminology shows that Luke's usage would have been understood by his audience; and (2) the influence of Isaiah on λόγος-terminology can be detected beyond the Lukan writings. For a survey of the problem of origin, see the discussion and extensive bibliography in H. Haarbeck et al, "Word," *NIDNTT* 3 (1986) 1078–117, 1143–145.

[104] See, for example, Sir 42.15; *Jub.* 1.4; and *Sib. Or.* 3.20. Cf. Jdt 16.14.

[105] Cf. *Leg.* 1.65; *Her.* 191; *Somn* 2.242–45; *Cher.* 127. For a discussion of wisdom traditions from Sirach to Wisdom of Solomon, see John J. Collins, "Cosmos and Salvation: Jewish Wisdom and Apocalyptic in the Hellenistic Age," *HR* 17 (1977) 121–142; Robert L. Duncan, "The Logos: From Sophocles to the Gospel of John," *Christian Scholar's Review* 9 (1979) 121–30; and Ben Witherington, III, *Jesus the Sage: The Pilgrimage of Wisdom* (Minneapolis: Fortress, 1994) 75–116. The parallelism between the word and wisdom in Wis 9.1–2 paves the way for the identification of the two in Philo. See also Aristobulus' comments on wisdom and the word as reported in Eusebius, *Prae. Evang.* 13.12.3–4.

178

observed.[106] While the Lukan conception of the word shows no trace of Philo's λόγος theology, Philo's work shows how the earlier understanding of λόγος as the powerful agent of God could be developed.

The understanding of λόγος as an active and powerful agent can also be found in texts within the New Testament outside of the Lukan corpus. The word is connected with creation in Heb 11:3: "By faith we understand that the worlds were prepared by the word of God." Similarly in 2 Pet 3:5, one reads that "by the word of God heavens existed long ago." In this context, however, the theme of judgment is also introduced: "by the same word the present heavens and earth have been reserved for fire, being kept until the day of judgment and destruction of the godless." Not only is the creative word one of destruction, the λόγος is naturally connected with the salvific act of God. In Col 1:6, for example, the λόγος is "bearing fruit and growing in the whole world."[107] Finally, the significance of the λόγος in the Johannine prologue requires no detailed comment. Here one finds the culmination of λόγος conceptions in the New Testament.[108] These appearances of the λόγος do not reflect a linear development of λόγος theology from either Jewish or Hellenistic traditions. What they show is that the understanding of λόγος as an agent of God is current in early Christian circles.

Equally important for my discussion of the Lukan use of Isaiah is the evidence of possible influence of the Isaianic word-concept upon other texts. While literary relationship is difficult to ascertain in many cases, examples can be provided where Isaianic influence is probable. As in the case of Isaiah 40–55, λόγος terminology appears in the reworkings of Exodus traditions. Λόγος appears as a divine warrior in two texts where both the Exodus traditions and Isaiah play a critical role. In the Wisdom of Solomon, within a description of the killing of the first-born in Egypt, one reads:

For while gentle silence enveloped all things,
and night in its swift course was now half gone,
your all-powerful word (λόγος) leaped from heaven, from the royal throne,
into the midst of the land that was doomed,
a stern warrior carrying the sharp sword of your authentic command,
and stood and filled all things with death,
and touched heaven while standing on earth. (Wis 18:14–16)

This text is among the earliest ones where the hypostatization of the word can be clearly identified. In light of the wider relationship between Wisdom of

---

[106] See H. A. Wolfson, *Philo* (Cambridge, MA: Harvard University Press, 1947) 177–246; and David Winston, *Logos and Mystical Theology in Philo of Alexandria* (Cincinnati: Hebrew Union College, 1985).

[107] See also the depiction of the "word of God" (ὁ λόγος τοῦ θεοῦ) as "sharper than any two-edged sword" in Heb 4:12.

[108] Dupont (*Le discours de Milet*, 244) suggests that the Lukan conception of the word is only one step behind the developed doctrine of the logos in the Gospel of John.

Solomon and Isaiah, the influence of the Isaianic traditions concerning the word is likely.[109]

A clearer case of Isaianic influence appears in Revelation, a work that is heavily dependent on the Exodus traditions in portraying the coming judgment. In a passage (Rev 19:13–15) that alludes to Isaiah, a description of word as the divine warrior is provided:

> He is clothed in a robe dipped in blood, and his name is called The Word of God (ὁ λόγος τοῦ θεοῦ). And the armies of heaven, wearing fine linen, white and pure, were following him on white horses. From his mouth comes a sharp sword with which to strike down the nations, and he will rule them with a rod of iron; he will tread the winepress of the fury of the wrath of God the Almighty.

Jan Fekkes has shown that Rev 19:13, 15 allude to Isa 63:2–3, a passage that portrays Yahweh as a warrior returning from battle, covered with the blood of his enemies.[110] It may now be added that the christological title word of God in Rev 19:13, a title that Fekkes admits not being able to find a "clear OT source" for,[111] is also dependent upon the Isaianic conception of the word as the powerful agent of God.

Both the existence of λόγος as an active agent of God in texts contemporary to Luke and the appearance of λόγος-terminology within

---

[109] As Pancratius C. Beentjes ("Wisdom of Solomon 3,1–4,19 and the Book of Isaiah," in J. van Ruiten and M. Vervenne, eds., *Studies in the Book of Isaiah: Festschrift Willem A. M. Beuken* [BETL 132; Leuven: Leuven University Press, 1997] 421) has observed, "scholars do fully agree that the Book of Isaiah is rather fully used by the author of the Book of Wisdom." See also Patrickt W. Skehan, *Studies in Israelite Poetry and Wisdom* (CBQMS 1; Washington, DC: Catholic Biblical Association of America, 1971) 149–236, who notes that "there is no chapter of Wis which has not some expression that is closely paralleled in the LXX of Isaiah" (165). For a further discussion of the origin of λόγος-terminology in Wisdom of Solomon, see Bogdan Ponizy, "Logos in the Book of Wisdom 18:14–16," in M. Augustin and K.-D. Schunck, eds., *"Dort ziehen Schiffe dahin ...": Collected Communications to the XIVth Congress of the International Organization for the Study of the Old Testament, Paris 1992* (Frankfurt am Main: Peter Lang, 1996) 169–77.

[110] Jan Fekkes, III, *Isaiah and Prophetic Traditions in the Book of Revelation: Visionary Antecedents and their Development* (JSNTSup 93; Sheffield: JSOT Press, 1994) 196–98.

[111] Ibid., 75 n.31.

context where Isaianic influence is evident provides support for my reconstruction of the use of the Isaianic word in Acts.[112]

---

[112] Some have pointed to the functions of *memra* in the targumim for a parallel development of the conceptions of the word as divine agent. Bruce Chilton (*The Glory of Israel: The Theology and Provenience of the Isaiah Targum* [JSOTSup 23; Sheffield: JSOT Press, 1983] 56) notes that *memra* "is perhaps the best known targumic paraphrase for God, and it predominates over all others in the Isaiah Targum." While not developed from the text of Isaiah, it represents another tradition where the utterances of God took on a new significance. The relationship between *memra* and New Testament usage of λόγος is uncertain, but its frequent appearances in the targumim provide yet another context in which λόγος-terminology can be understood. For the possibility of a literary relationship between New Testament λόγος theology and *memra*, see G. Reim, "Targum und Johannesevangelium," *BZ* 27 (1983) 1–13; Bruce Chilton, "Recent and Prospective Discussion of *Memra*," in J. Neusner, E. S. Frerichs and N. M. Sarna, eds., *From Ancient Israel to Modern Judaism, vol. 2* (BJS 173; Atlanta, GA: Scholars Press, 1989) 119–37; idem, "Typologies of *memra* and the fourth Gospel," in Paul V. M. Flesher, ed., *Targum Studies, Vol. One: Textual and Contextual Studies in the Pentateuchal Targums* (Atlanta, GA: Scholars, 1992) 89–100; and Craig A. Evans, *Word and Glory: On the Exegetical and Theological Background of John's Prologue* (Sheffield: JSOT Press, 1993) 124–30.

Chapter 6

The Lord of the Nations:
The Anti-Idol Polemic

6.1 Introduction

In the context of the New Exodus in Isaiah, the power of Yahweh and his word is contrasted with the impotence of idols. In this chapter, I will discuss the anti-idol polemic in Acts against the context provided by the Isaianic model. First, the anti-idol polemic in Isaiah will be examined. Both the way idols were depicted and the function of such anti-idol polemic will be discussed. Then, in discussing the anti-idol polemic in Acts, I will examine the Areopagus speech in Acts 17 where an explicit attack on idols can be found. Other passages in Acts in which anti-idol language can be detected will also be examined and the function of these passages will be discussed. In both sections, I will argue that the sovereignty of the Lord[1] over the nations should be considered the focus of these passages. On the one hand, this emphasis stands out from other ancient Israelite as well as early Christian traditions that emphasize the purity of the people of God through the condemnation of the idol-worshipping. On the other hand, the anti-idol polemic in Isaiah and particularly in Acts should not be entirely identified in either form or function with the exorcism stories in the early Christian gospel literature.[2]

Isolating the anti-idol passages provides a window into the Lukan presentation of the supremacy of the Lord behind the Christian movement. In the Isaianic New Exodus, the supremacy of Yahweh is established through the contrast of the power of Yahweh with the futile efforts of the nations, their rulers, their deities, and their idols (and idol-makers). These four categories should not be viewed as four separate groups since they were understood as referring to the same entity. Idols are, however, frequently singled out as the

---

[1] In Acts, the identification of the Lord is naturally made in reference to the risen Jesus.

[2] Or at least various "kinds" of exorcism stories should be noted. In the gospel stories, the struggle centers on the kingdom of God and the power of Satan. In Acts, the anti-idol polemic should also be understood in light of the struggle of the early Christian communities with the other competing communities in their claims to divine power. The failure to clarify such distinctions scars the otherwise helpful work of Susan R. Garrett, *The Demise of the Devil: Magic and the Demonic in Luke's Writings* (Minneapolis: Fortress, 1989).

visual manifestation of the powers that oppose Yahweh. Similarly, in Acts, idols are identified as the symbol of those who oppose the Lord of the early Christian movement. Opposition from the rulers of the nations should therefore also be understood within the same context. It is with this understanding that one can also appreciate the power of the anti-idol passages as one form of anti-imperialistic propaganda in that the divine power of the reigning political authority is called into question.

In establishing the supremacy of the Lord of the early Christian movement, the author of Acts strips away the power of the nations and declares the early Christian community the sole possessor of divine truth. As in the ancient Exodus traditions, power becomes the focus of the New Exodus in Acts[3] for the establishment of the new community is intricately tied with a denial of the authority and legitimacy of other competing communities and sovereign bodies.

6.2 Anti-Idol Polemic and the Isaianic New Exodus

Although anti-idol polemic can be found throughout the Hebrew Bible, "idol parodies clustered in one literary context are found only in Isaiah 40–55"[4] and they also become a critical element in the program of the Isaianic New Exodus.[5] In the context of Isaiah 40–55, the universal sovereignty of Yahweh becomes a message that needs to be reaffirmed. The anti-idol passages should

---

[3] In discussing the focus on power in the Exodus traditions, Thomas B. Dozeman (*God at War: Power in the Exodus Tradition* [New York: Oxford University Press, 1996] 3) notes: "The destruction of the Egyptian army is the primary story of salvation for Israel, and central to it is the portrait of God in combat. So important is this image of divine power that the annihilation of the enemy by Yahweh marks the moment of salvation for Israel and prompts its victory hymn of celebration in Exod 15:3, 'Yahweh is a warrior!' The war cry underscores how salvation is an event of divine warfare, in which the destruction of the enemy is victory for God and liberation for Israel."

[4] Wolfgang M. W. Roth, "For Life, He Appeals to Death (Wis 13:18): A Study of Old Testament Idol Parodies," *CBQ* 37 (1975) 32. See Hab 2:18–19; Jer 10:1–16; Pss 115 and 135.

[5] Gerhard von Rad (*Wisdom in Israel* [trans. James D. Marton; Nashville: Abingdon, 1972] 179) notes that unlike Habakkuk and Jeremiah in which anti-idol passages can be considered as "wisdom" interpolations, "the case of Deutero-Isaiah is different, for here the polemic can be regarded to some extent as part of the total message of the prophet." For a discussion of the integrity of the anti-idol passages, see especially Hendrik C. Spykerboer, *The Structure and Composition of Deutero-Isaiah: With Special Reference to the Polemics against Idolatry* (Franeker, Netherlands: T. Wever, 1976) 116–18; and Richard J. Clifford, "The Function of Idol Passages in Second Isaiah," *CBQ* 42 (1980) 450–64.

be understood as a way to reestablish the claim that Yahweh is the one who is able to rebuild the people of God.

a. The Powerlessness of the Idols and the Nations in Isaiah 40–55

In Isaiah 40–55, four anti-idol passages in particular should be discussed: Isa 40:12–31; 41:1–10; 44:9–20; and 46:1–13.[6] I will argue that the power of Yahweh over all the nations is the focus of these passages. Furthermore, the power of Yahweh is manifested through his salvific acts on behalf of his own people, a power that cannot be found among the idols of the nations. The survival and deliverance of the community are therefore at the center of such discourse.[7]

In the passage immediately following the prologue of Isa 40:1–11, there is a lengthy discussion of the supremacy of Yahweh that contrasts Yahweh with four related categories: nations (vss 15–17), idols (vss 18–20), rulers (vss 21–24), and deities (vss 25–26). These four categories cannot be examined as independent entities since criticisms directed against one apply also to the others. For the purpose of this study, the section related to idols will be cited together with the section related to the rulers:

> To whom then will you liken God, or what likeness compare with him?
> An idol? — A workman casts it, and a goldsmith overlays it with gold,
> and casts for it silver chains.
> As a gift one chooses mulberry wood — wood that will not rot —
> then seeks out a skilled artisan to set up an image that will not topple.
> Have you not known? Have you not heard?
> Has it not been told you from the beginning?
> Have you not understood from the foundations of the earth?
> It is he who sits above the circle of the earth,
> and its inhabitants are like grasshoppers;
> who stretches out the heavens like a curtain,
> and spreads them like a tent to live in;
> who brings princes to naught,
> and makes the rulers of the earth as nothing.
> Scarcely are they planted, scarcely sown,
> scarcely has their stem taken root in the earth,
> when he blows upon them, and they wither,
> and the tempest carries them off like stubble. (Isa 40:18–24)

In this passage, the procedure for manufacturing idols is described in great detail to set up a contrast with Yahweh the creator.[8] The idols that have to be

---

[6] Other passages in Isaiah 40–44 that contain anti-idol polemic include: Isa 42:17; 45:16, 20–21; 48:5–8.

[7] I will argue that religious purity should not be understood as the primary focus of the anti-idol polemic in Isaiah 40–55.

[8] For a detailed discussion of such contrasts, see Rémi Lack, *La Symbolique du Livre d'Isaïe* (AnBib 59; Rome: Biblical Institute Press, 1973) 95–99.

created cannot be compared to Yahweh who is the creator of all. It is also because of the creative act of Yahweh that the rulers of the nations are reduced to nothing. More importantly, while the passage begins by mentioning idols, the shift of attention to the acts of the one creating the idols repudiates any attempt to compare them with Yahweh. This strategy becomes apparent when one recognizes that the act of creation defines the power relationship between the two groups of beings.[9] In labeling the idols as beings created by human hands (vss 19–20),[10] and then in emphasizing that human beings are like grasshoppers (vss 22) who are living on the earth created by Yahweh, the idols' utter lack of power and authority becomes evident.[11]

Furthermore, the relationship between rulers and idols as established in this passage shows that neither can be compared with Yahweh who is the creator of all. The attack on idols is therefore not primarily religious but political, although the two cannot be strictly distinguished, for Yahweh is proclaimed as Lord of all. The one behind the people of Israel is the one whose work the nations cannot resist.

The second passage appears in a trial scene, a genre utilized in Isaiah 40–55 to express the message of Yahweh for the nations:[12]

Who has performed and done this, calling the generations from the beginning?

---

[9] For a discussion of creation as the overcoming of the power of chaos, see Bernhard W. Anderson, *Creation Versus Chaos: The Reinterpretation of Mythical Symbolism in the Bible* (New York: Association Press, 1967); and Jon D. Levenson, *Creation and the Persistence of Evil* (New York: Harper & Row, 1988). On the understanding of creation-terminology primarily as one that belongs to the semantic realm of mastery and authority, see also Stephen Lee, "Power not Novelty: The Connotations of ברא in the Hebrew Bible," in A. Graeme Auld, ed., *Understanding Poets and Prophets: Essays in Honour of George Wishart Anderson* (Sheffield: JSOT Press, 1993) 199–212.

[10] The difficulties surrounding the phrase המסכך תרומה do not affect my interpretation of this passage. See the discussion in Hugh G. M. Williamson, "Isaiah 40,20 — A Case of Not Seeing the Wood for the Trees," *Bib* 67 (1986) 1–19.

[11] Significantly, four of the verbs used in 40:19–20 (רקע, צרף, בחד, and כון) to describe the creative acts of the idol-manufacturers are also used in Isaiah 40–55 to describe the creative acts of Yahweh. Based on this observation, Knut Holter (*Second Isaiah's Idol-Fabrication Passages* [Frankfurt am Main/New York: Peter Lang, 1995] 54–58) argues that idol-fabricators and not idols are the subject of Isa 40:19–20 (and other passages [see 122–26]) and the contrast is between idol-fabricators and Yahweh. This conclusion is unjustifiable in light of vs 19 that introduces idols as the subject. Furthermore, this approach fails to appreciate the use of creation language to strip power away from the idols. The hierarchy established here among Yahweh, idol-fabricators, and idols should not be missed. Finally, the silencing of the idols seems to be intentional and the focus on the idol-fabricators should be understood as a rhetorical strategy that denies the existence of the power and status of idols.

[12] Roy F. Melugin (*The Formation of Isaiah 40–55* [BZAW 141; Berlin/New York: Walter de Gruyter, 1976] 53) has rightly emphasized that the trial speeches in Isaiah 40–55 are primarily concerned with the rival claims of power.

I, the LORD, am first, and will be with the last.
The coastlands have seen and are afraid, the ends of the earth tremble;
they have drawn near and come.
Each one helps the other, saying to one another, "Take courage!"
The artisan encourages the goldsmith, and the one who smooths with the hammer
encourages the one who strikes the anvil, saying of the soldering, "It is good";
and they fasten it with nails so that it cannot be moved. (Isa 41:4–7)

This passage shows the incomparability of Yahweh and is followed by a discussion of Israel/Jacob as the people that God had chosen. The ironic description of mutual encouragement among the idol-fabricators depicts the idols' impotence since they are not able to give their makers any comfort when confronted by the judgment acts of Yahweh. The virtual denial of the power of the idols is further accomplished through the absence of any actual mention of the idols themselves.[13]

Unlike the impotent idols, Yahweh is in possession of power and authority. This is highlighted in vs 4 by the use of verbs associated with creation language: פעל ועשׂה (lit.: "to do and to make"). Furthermore, מראשׁ קרא הדרות ("calling the generations from the beginning") points to the assertion of Yahweh as the Lord of history; and this affirmation is accompanied by the declaration: "I, the LORD, am first, and will be with the last" (אני יהוה ראשׁון ואת־אחרנים אני־הוא).[14]

The failure of the idols to offer any comfort is contrasted with the relationship between Yahweh and his chosen people described in the verses that immediately follow (41:8–10). While the idols are silent, Yahweh is able to comfort his own people:

Do not fear, for I am with you, do not be afraid, for I am your God;
I will strengthen you, I will help you,
I will uphold you with my victorious right hand. (Isa 41:10)

In this verse, the contrast between Yahweh/Israel and the idols/nations is established. Yahweh is the sovereign one who is in control, and only the people that belong to him will survive. Again, the attack on the idols is an attack on the nations. The survival of the Israelite community is ensured by the power of Yahweh. It is only within this context that the Isaianic anti-idol polemic can be understood.

---

[13] Although "idols" are not mentioned, the understanding that this passage deals primarily with "idol-fabrication" cannot be denied. This is best supported by the fact that the two terms חרשׁ (artisan) and צרף (goldsmith) are used in Isaiah 40–55 only in reference to manufacturing idols.

[14] The polarity of "the first and the last" is used in Isaiah 40–55 to emphasize the sovereignty of Yahweh. See, in particular, Isa 44:6: "Thus says the LORD, the King of Israel, and his Redeemer, the LORD of hosts: I am the first and I am the last; besides me there is no god."

The next anti-idol passage appears in 44:9–20. This passage, a satiric song that is situated within another trial speech of the nation (44:6–8, 21–23),[15] is the longest and most detailed one in Isaiah 40–55 concerning the powerlessness of idols. This long passage begins with a direct attack on idols and idol-fabricators:

> All who make idols are nothing, and the things they delight in do not profit; their witnesses neither see nor know. And so they will be put to shame. Who would fashion a god or cast an image that can do no good? Look, all its devotees shall be put to shame; the artisans too are merely human. Let them all assemble, let them stand up; they shall be terrified, they shall all be put to shame. (Isa 44:9–11)

Again, idols are reduced to created beings with no power of their own. The same contrasts with the relationship between Yahweh and Israel can again be detected. In the preceding verse, Israel is called the "witnesses" of Yahweh (44:8). In 44:9, the idols in turn are "witnesses" of their makers but they are not able to see nor know. Therefore, as Yahweh is being declared as the sovereign one (44:6), the idol-fabricators are put to shame because of the impotence of the idols.[16] As a result, while the nations that rely on their idols are "terrified" (44:11), Israel is comforted by "his Redeemer" (44:6) with these words: "Do not fear, or be afraid" (44:8). These contrasts show that this attack on idols and idol-fabricators aims at highlighting the sovereignty of Yahweh and therefore also the status of the Israelite community as the sole locus of divine presence.

The verses that follow (44:12–17) provide a description of the work of the idol-fabricators. The attack on idols and idol-fabricators resumes in vs 18:[17]

> They do not know, nor do they comprehend; for their eyes are shut, so that they cannot see, and their minds as well, so that they cannot understand. No one considers, nor is there knowledge or discernment to say, "Half of it I burned in the fire; I also baked bread on its coals, I roasted meat and have eaten. Now shall I make the rest of it an abomination? Shall I fall down before a block of wood?" He feeds on ashes; a deluded mind has led them astray, and he cannot save himself or say, "Is not this thing in my right hand a fraud?" (Isa 44:18–20)

---

[15] Claus Westermann (*Isaiah 40–66: A Commentary* [trans. David M. G. Stalker; OTL; Philadelphia: Westminster, 1969] 139) suggests that vss 6–8 and 21–22 contain "a complete trial speech and a complete assurance of salvation combined to form a single oracle." Concerning vss 9–20, Westermann argues that these verses are inserted later into the oracles of Isaiah 40–55 (147). Recent critics have, however, argued for the authenticity of this passage. See, for example, Antoon Schoors, *I am God Your Saviour* (VTSup 24; Leiden: Brill, 1973) 252–3; and Andrew Wilson, *The Nations in Deutero-Isaiah* (Lewiston, NY: Edwin Mellen, 1986) 181.

[16] Cf. Isa 45:16–17.

[17] The appearances of plural verbal forms in vss 9–11, 18 and singular in vss 12–17, 19–20 have led to various proposals from source-critical and literary perspectives. See Spykerboer, *Structure and Composition of Deutero-Isaiah*, 117.

In the conclusion of this anti-idol passage, the attack on idols for their impotence is extended to the ignorance of those who worship them. The contrast between Yahweh/Israel and the idols/nations is again made. While the author concludes that idols cannot save themselves since they are made by human hands, the verses that follow assert that Yahweh is able to save Israel because he has created his own people:

> Remember these things, O Jacob, and Israel, for you are my servant;
> I formed you, you are my servant; O Israel, you will not be forgotten by me.
> I have swept away your transgressions like a cloud, and your sins like mist;
> return to me, for I have redeemed you.
> Sing, O heavens, for the LORD has done it; shout, O depths of the earth;
> break forth into singing, O mountains, O forest, and every tree in it!
> For the LORD has redeemed Jacob, and will be glorified in Israel. (Isa 44:21–23)

This confirms the understanding that the condemnation of idols and idol-fabricators is directly related to the theme of Yahweh's sovereignty and power to deliver his own chosen people. The emphasis on the lordship of Yahweh over Israel (vss 21–22) is extended to the entire creation (vs 23).[18] Yahweh's sovereignty over all nations is again the focus of this passage.

The final passage that will be considered is Isa 46:1–13, another text constructed with two contrasts between Yahweh/Israel and idols/nations.[19] The first contrast can be found in 46:1–4:

> Bel bows down, Nebo stoops, their idols are on beasts and cattle;
> these things you carry are loaded as burdens on weary animals.
> They stoop, they bow down together; they cannot save the burden,
> but themselves go into captivity.
> Listen to me, O house of Jacob, all the remnant of the house of Israel,
> who have been borne by me from your birth, carried from the womb;
> even to your old age I am he, even when you turn gray I will carry you.
> I have made, and I will bear; I will carry and will save.

Since idols[20] are merely manufactured objects, they have to be carried (נשא, vs 1) and they will not be able to save (מלט, vs 2). On the other hand,

---

[18] The unity of Isa 44:21–23 is established through the repetition of the structure: imperatives with כי-sentences. See the discussion in Holter, *Second Isaiah's Idol-Fabrication Passages*, 192.

[19] A consensus cannot be found among form-critics as to the genre and literary structure of Isaiah 46. While some have understood the first part (46:1–7) as a disputation speech with the remaining verses (46:8–13) being the exhortation, others have noted that the theme of carrying and salvation is extended beyond vs 7. I will argue that Isaiah 46 consists of two parts (vss 1–5, 6–13) and both are constructed with a contrast between Yahweh/Israel and idols/nations. For a further discussion, see Melugin, *The Formation of Isaiah 40–55*, 133; and Richard J. Clifford, *Fair Spoken and Persuading: An Interpretation of Second Isaiah* (New York: Paulist, 1984) 130–32.

Yahweh is not the created one but the one from whom Israel came into being
(vs 3). Therefore, Yahweh is able both to carry (נשׂא, vs 4) and to save (מלט,
vs 4).

In the second part of the passage, a similar contrast can be found. First a
description of idols and idol-fabricators is presented in language similar to vss
1–4:

> Those who lavish gold from the purse,
> and weigh out silver in the scales —
> they hire a goldsmith, who makes it into a god;
> then they fall down and worship!
> They lift it to their shoulders, they carry it,
> they set it in its place, and it stands there;
> it cannot move from its place.
> If one cries out to it, it does not answer
> or save anyone from trouble. (Isa 46:6–7)

While the inability of idols to save and the fact that they have to be carried
recall the contrast in vss 1–4, this passage extends the former contrast by
noting that when those who worship idols cry out to them, they will not
answer (vs 7). It is in contrast to this failure to respond to people that the
power and willingness of Yahweh to answer the cries of his people is
highlighted:

> I am God, and there is no one like me,
> declaring the end from the beginning
> and from ancient times things not yet done,
> saying, "My purpose shall stand,
> and I will fulfill my intention,"
> calling a bird of prey from the east,
> the man for my purpose from a far country.
> I have spoken, and I will bring it to pass;
> I have planned, and I will do it. (Isa 46:9c–11)

Furthermore, as Richard Clifford[21] has suggested, the final verse of Isaiah 46
should be understood in light of the beginning of the chapter where the failure
of the idols to save is noted with the result that they will "go into captivity"
(46:2):

> I bring near my deliverance, it is not far off,
> and my salvation will not tarry;
> I will put salvation in Zion,
> for Israel my glory. (Isa 46:13)

---

[20] This is the only place in Isaiah 40–55 where the names of the gods are given
(Bel=Marduk and Nebo=the son of Marduk, Nabu). Here, the gods are identified with the
idols.

[21] Clifford, "The Function of Idol Passages in Second Isaiah," 456.

This promise to deliver the people of Israel from exile again forms a contrast with the impotent idols who are not able to act on behalf of their people. This final verse also confirms the conclusion that the attack on idols is also an attack on the nations; and the affirmation of the power of Yahweh is at the same time a declaration of the promise of deliverance for the Israelite community. The proper context in which the anti-idol polemic should be understood is therefore the political situation of the Israelite community; and the focus is the power relationship between the people of God and the other nations that surround them.

b. The Sovereignty of Yahweh in Isaiah 40–55

The importance of the anti-idol passages for the claim of lordship has already been alluded to. In this section, I will further discuss the peculiarity of the anti-idol polemic in Isaiah 40–55. A more precise understanding and definition of the function of this anti-idol polemic will pave the way for the analysis of the anti-idol polemic in Acts.

I have already suggested that the sovereignty of Yahweh should be understood as the primary focus of the anti-idol polemic in Isaiah 40–55. In these anti-idol passages, the frequent appearances of the theme of creation serve to highlight the power and authority of Yahweh against idols that have to be manufactured by those who will eventually worship them. As the creator of all, Yahweh is the only one who is able to save and deliver his people. Those who oppose the reign of Yahweh will thus be destroyed. Therefore, the anti-idol polemic should be understood together with (1) the repeated emphasis on the power of Yahweh as well as (2) the impotence of the nations in opposing his plan and his people.

The depiction of the power of Yahweh is one of the central themes of Isaiah 40–55, and the unique authority of Yahweh is a distinctive feature of these chapters.[22] First, the term אנכי יהוה should be noted. Sheldon Blank[23] has established that in the prophetic writings, this designation has become the characteristic designation of the universal God. The term should therefore be translated not merely as "Yahweh" but as "the One God." The repeated uses of this designation in Isaiah constitute the central claim of the New Exodus program. This designation is also connected with the claim of Yahweh's sovereignty. For example, in Isa 43:11, Yahweh declares: "I, I am the LORD (אנכי אנכי יהוה), and besides me there is no savior." Similarly,

---

[22] Among others, C. J. Labuschagne (*The Incomparability of Yahweh in the Old Testament* [Leiden: Brill, 1966] 122–23) has noted: "In Deutero-Isaiah, as nowhere else in the Old Testament, God's uniqueness is repeatedly emphasized."

[23] Sheldon Blank, "Studies in Deutero-Isaiah," *HUCA* 15 (1940) 1–46. This is further developed in Julian Morgenstern, "Deutero-Isaiah's Terminology for Universal God," *JBL* 62 (1943) 269–80.

"I am the Lord (אנכי יהוה), who made all things, who alone stretched out the heavens, who by myself spread out the earth" (44:24); and again: "I am the Lord (אני יהוה), and there is no other; besides me there is no god" (45:5). The assertion of Yahweh as the one and only true God finds its climactic expression in 45:21–22:

> Declare and present your case; let them take counsel together!
> Who told this long ago? Who declared it of old?
> Was it not I, the Lord (אני יהוה)? There is no other god besides me,
> a righteous God and a Savior; there is no one besides me.
> Turn to me and be saved, all the ends of the earth!
> For I am God, and there is no other.

In Isaiah 40–55, not only does one find explicit assertions of the uniqueness of Yahweh, the use of rhetorical questions to emphasize the status of Yahweh as the incomparable one also plays an important role.[24] Many of these rhetorical questions appear precisely within the anti-idol passages. For example, it is noted in 40:18: "To whom then will you liken God, or what likeness compare with him?" Again, in 40:25, Yahweh declares: "To whom then will you compare me, or who is my equal?" In yet another anti-idol passage, Yahweh again declares: "Who is like me? Let them proclaim it, let them declare and set it forth before me. Who has announced from of old the things to come? Let them tell us what is yet to be" (44:7). Furthermore, in 46:5, one finds the question: "To whom will you liken me and make me equal, and compare me, as though we were alike?" These questions that appear in the anti-idol polemic of Isaiah emphasize the supremacy of the God of Israel.[25]

The second theme that should be examined in relation to the anti-idol polemic in Isaiah is the emphasis on the impotence of the nations. The contrast between Yahweh and idols is also one between Israel and the nations. The theme of the powerlessness of the nations is therefore intimately related to the depiction of Yahweh as the incomparable one. In all four major anti-idol passages in Isaiah 40–55, the incompetence of the nations is highlighted. This is best illustrated in the first anti-idol passage in 40:12–31:

> Even the nations are like a drop from a bucket,
> and are accounted as dust on the scales;

---

[24] The use of rhetorical questions in establishing the incomparability of Yahweh can be found already in Exodus 15 (vs 11).

[25] See Paul Del Brassey, "Metaphor and the Incomparable God in Isaiah 40–55" (Th.D. diss., Harvard University, 1997), a study that examines the depiction of the power and authority of Yahweh with the metaphors of creator, sovereign, and kin. For the importance of the master-servant relationship in the theological language of Isaiah 40–55, see also Klaus Baltzer, "Liberation from Debt Slavery After the Exile in Second Isaiah and Nehemiah," in Patrick D. Miller, Jr., Paul D. Hanson, and S. Dean McBride, eds., *Ancient Israelite Religion: Essays in Honor of Frank Moore Cross* (Philadelphia: Fortress, 1987) 477–84.

see, he takes up the isles like fine dust.
Lebanon would not provide fuel enough,
nor are its animals enough for a burnt offering.
All the nations are as nothing before him;
they are accounted by him as less than nothing and emptiness. (Isa 40:15–17)

The connections between the impotence of the nations and the power of Yahweh are emphasized throughout Isaiah 40–55. For example, in 41:21–42:9, one finds the combination of these two themes: first the nations are to be defeated, then the sovereignty of Yahweh is announced. Concerning the nations, it is proclaimed that "their works are nothing" (41:29); and then Yahweh declares, "I am the LORD, that is my name; my glory I give to no other, nor my praise to idols" (42:8).[26] While a further discussion of the submission of the nations will be provided in the next chapter, it is sufficient to note that the attack upon idols should be understood within the discussion of the power of Yahweh and the impotence of the nations.

The emphasis upon the power of Yahweh over against the challenge of the nations alerts us to the peculiar context and function of the anti-idol polemic in Isaiah. First, in the anti-idol passages of Isaiah 40–55, the primary concern is not the religious purity of the people of Israel, and the threat of religious assimilation should not be considered as the primary focus of the use of anti-idol language.[27] The focus is rather upon the predicament of the people of God and the promise of Yahweh to deliver his people out of their oppressed condition. The use of anti-idol polemic is, therefore, a way to express the power of Yahweh over against the power of the nations. The political condition of the people of Israel becomes the context in which this anti-idol polemic should be understood. Only in this context can one appreciate the peculiar identification of the idols with both the nations and their leaders. This conclusion is further supported by the observations made by Andrew Wilson who points out two distinctive features of the anti-idol polemic in Isaiah 40–55 where the author "separates his polemics against idolatry from the

---

[26] Wilson (*Nations in Deutero-Isaiah*, 59) notes that the same dual emphases can be detected in Psalm 2 where Yahweh first defeats the nations (vss 1–5) and then is declared king (vss 6–9). He also notes that both Psalm 2 and the Isaianic emphasis on the two themes drew from a tradition where "the autumn festival reenactment of Yahweh's battle with his enemies preceded his enthronement as king along with confirmation of his Davidic representative."

[27] This stands in contrast to the anti-idol polemic in other prophetic writings (e.g., Hosea, Jeremiah) where the cultic sanctity of the people of God is the primary concern. I am not suggesting, however, that concern for the religious devotion of the people of Israel is entirely missing in Isaiah 40–55 (cf. 48:5). The focus of this anti-idol polemic cannot be reduced to and understood primarily as a concern for the religious purity of the people of God. It is here that I differ from Brassey ("Metaphor and the Incomparable God in Isaiah 40–55," 61) who argues that "the extreme rhetoric with which DI attacks foreign gods implies that Israel's greatest threat was religious assimilation."

demands of covenant, and he then sets them in the context of a universal judgment of the nations."[28]

The emphasis upon the sovereignty of Yahweh over the nations also provides a link between Isaiah 40–55 and the Exodus traditions. The traditions concerning the plagues in Egypt contain the most explicit account of the manifestation of Yahweh's power in the midst of opposing forces.[29] The memories of overcoming the Egyptian army in the passage through the sea and the stories of the conquest lead to the declaration: "The LORD will reign forever and ever" (Exod 15:18). The fact that the affirmation of Yahweh's uniqueness forms the center of the Exodus program is expressed at the very beginning of the Decalogue:

> I am the LORD your God, who brought you out of the land of Egypt, out of the house of slavery; you shall have no other gods before me. You shall not make for yourself an idol, whether in the form of anything that is in heaven above, or that is on the earth beneath, or that is in the water under the earth. You shall not bow down to them or worship them; for I the LORD your God am a jealous God, punishing children for the iniquity of parents, to the third and fourth generation of those who reject me, but show steadfast love to the thousandth generation of those who love me and keep my commandments. (Exod 20:2–6)

It is not surprising, therefore, that as the promise of salvation in Isaiah 40–55 draws from the Exodus tradition, one also finds the declaration of the incomparability of Yahweh and the impotence of idols. In the context of the Isaianic New Exodus, the fate of the people of God will be reversed because their God, whose action cannot be resisted, will overcome the power of his enemies in delivering his own people from among the nations. The assertion of Yahweh's sovereignty and the anti-idol polemic are therefore political claims that are directly relevant to the Isaianic community.

This sets the stage for a discussion of the anti-idol polemic in the New Exodus program in Acts. As in the case of Isaiah 40–55, religious assimilation is not the primary concern of the anti-idol passages of Acts. Rather, anti-idol polemic in Acts functions as a rhetorical strategy to construct the claim of the lordship of the risen Christ. It is precisely because Jesus is Lord of all that no one can resist the advancement of the word and the early Christian movement.

---

[28] Wilson, *Nations in Deutero-Isaiah*, 188. It should also be pointed out that the contrast between the "word" and the idol can also be detected in Isaiah 40–55. The power of the word and Yahweh who speaks is contrasted with idols whose visual image is created by human craftsmen. For a further discussion of the Isaianic anti-idol polemic in light of this contrast, see Matitiahu Tsevat, "The Prohibition of Divine Images According to the Old Testament," in M. Augustin and K.-D. Schunck, eds., *Wünschet Jerusalem Frieden: Collected Communications to the XIIth Congress of the International Organization for the Study of the Old Testament, Jerusalem 1986* (Frankfurt am Main/New York: Peter Lang, 1988) 211–20.

[29] See Labuschagne, *Incomparability of Yahweh in the Old Testament*, 132–46.

Behind the anti-idol polemic is the claim that the early Christian community is the sole possessor of divine truth. It is to the development of this claim that I must now turn.

6.3 Anti-Idol Polemic and the New Exodus in Acts

First, I will examine the Areopagus speech in Acts 17 in which one finds the most explicit expression of the anti-idol polemic in Acts. This will be followed by a discussion of passages in which anti-idol language is used to refute any false claim of deity. In these passages in Acts, the anti-idol polemic is extended to other rulers/nations and the focus is upon the power of Yahweh and of his community. Therefore, in the second section, I will examine Luke's portrayal of the risen Jesus as Lord of all.

a. The Powerlessness of the Idols and the Nations in Acts

The Areopagus speech contained in the episode of Paul in Athens in Acts 17:16–34 should be the starting point of any discussion of the anti-idol polemic in Acts since the pattern found in the anti-idol polemic of Isaiah can also be identified here. This passage has often been considered a *sui generis* speech on natural theology. Martin Dibelius, for example, has argued that "what we have before us is a *hellenistic* speech about the true knowledge of God;" and "when we consider the Areopagus speech as a whole, we see that it has a rational character which is foreign to the New Testament."[30] I will argue, however, that this passage should also be considered in relation to the other anti-idol passages in both Isaiah and Acts.[31]

At the very beginning of the description of Paul's stay in Athens, it is stated that "he was deeply distressed to see that the city was full of idols" (παρωξύνετο τὸ πνεῦμα αὐτοῦ ἐν αὐτῷ θεωροῦντος κατείδωλον

---

[30] Martin Dibelius, *Studies in the Acts of the Apostles* (ed. Heinrich Greeven; trans. Mary Ling; New York: Charles Scribner's Sons, 1956) 57, 58. See also Dean Zweck, "The *Exordium* of the Areopagus Speech, Acts 17.22, 23," *NTS* 35 (1989) 94–103.

[31] I am not arguing that this speech should be understood as a "Jewish" instead of a "Hellenistic" speech. Hellenistic influence cannot be denied; and, moreover, a strict distinction between "Jewish" and "Hellenistic" cannot be made. I am arguing, however, that this speech is not a unique and isolated phenomenon within the text of Acts. The affinities of the Areopagus speech with the other anti-idol passages in Acts show that this speech should be considered within the wider context in which it is situated. Cf. Bertil E. Gärtner, *The Areopagus Speech and Natural Revelation* (Uppsala: C. W. K. Gleerup, 1955); and Heinz Külling, *Geoffenbartes Geheimnis: Eine Auslegung von Apostelgeschichte 17, 16–34* (Zürich: Theologischer Verlag, 1993).

οὖσαν τὴν πόλιν, Acts 17:16).³² This programmatic statement defines the focus of the narrative that follows. In introducing the risen Jesus as Lord of all, Paul is at the same time attacking idol worship and the validity of other claims of deity. These emphases are reflected in that part of the Areopagus speech in which Paul introduces the one true God:

ὁ θεὸς ὁ ποιήσας τὸν κόσμον καὶ πάντα τὰ ἐν αὐτῷ, οὗτος οὐρανοῦ καὶ γῆς ὑπάρχων κύριος οὐκ ἐν χειροποιήτοις ναοῖς κατοικεῖ οὐδὲ ὑπὸ χειρῶν ἀνθρωπίνων θεραπεύεται προσδεόμενός τινος, αὐτὸς διδοὺς πᾶσι ζωὴν καὶ πνοὴν καὶ τὰ πάντα· ἐποίησέν τε ἐξ ἑνὸς πᾶν ἔθνος ἀνθρώπων κατοικεῖν ἐπὶ παντὸς προσώπου τῆς γῆς, ὁρίσας προστεταγμένους καιροὺς καὶ τὰς ὁροθεσίας τῆς κατοικίας αὐτῶν, ζητεῖν τὸν θεὸν εἰ ἄρα γε ψηλαφήσειαν αὐτὸν καὶ εὕροιεν, καί γε οὐ μακρὰν ἀπὸ ἑνὸς ἑκάστου ἡμῶν ὑπάρχοντα. Ἐν αὐτῷ γὰρ ζῶμεν καὶ κινούμεθα καὶ ἐσμέν, ὡς καί τινες τῶν καθ᾽ ὑμᾶς ποιητῶν εἰρήκασιν, Τοῦ γὰρ καὶ γένος ἐσμέν. γένος οὖν ὑπάρχοντες τοῦ θεοῦ οὐκ ὀφείλομεν νομίζειν χρυσῷ ἢ ἀργύρῳ ἢ λίθῳ, χαράγματι τέχνης καὶ ἐνθυμήσεως ἀνθρώπου, τὸ θεῖον εἶναι ὅμοιον. τοὺς μὲν οὖν χρόνους τῆς ἀγνοίας ὑπεριδὼν ὁ θεὸς τὰ νῦν παραγγέλλει τοῖς ἀνθρώποις πάντας πανταχοῦ μετανοεῖν, καθότι ἔστησεν ἡμέραν ἐν ᾗ μέλλει κρίνειν τὴν οἰκουμένην ἐν δικαιοσύνῃ ἐν ἀνδρὶ ᾧ ὥρισεν, πίστιν παρασχὼν πᾶσιν ἀναστήσας αὐτὸν ἐκ νεκρῶν.

The God who made the world and everything in it, he who is Lord of heaven and earth, does not live in shrines made by human hands, nor is he served by human hands, as though he needed anything, since he himself gives to all mortals life and breath and all things. From one ancestor he made all nations to inhabit the whole earth, and he allotted the times of their existence and the boundaries of the places where they would live, so that they would search for God and perhaps grope for him and find him — though indeed he is not far from each one of us. For "In him we live and move and have our being"; as even some of your own poets have said, "For we too are his offspring." Since we are God's offspring, we ought not to think that the deity is like gold, or silver, or stone, an image formed by the art and imagination of mortals. While God has overlooked the times of human ignorance, now he commands all people everywhere to repent, because he has fixed a day on which he will have the world judged in righteousness by a man whom he has appointed, and of this he has given assurance to all by raising him from the dead. (Acts 17:24–31)

This lengthy passage is constructed with many of the prominent themes of the anti-idol program in Isaiah 40–55. First, God is the one creator and the source of all living beings. The description of God as one "who made the world and everything in it, he who is Lord of heaven and earth" (ὁ ποιήσας τὸν κόσμον καὶ πάντα τὰ ἐν αὐτῷ, οὗτος οὐρανοῦ καὶ γῆς ὑπάρχων κύριος, vs 24) and as one who "gives to all mortals life and breath and all things" (αὐτὸς διδοὺς πᾶσι ζωὴν καὶ πνοὴν καὶ τὰ πάντα, vs

---

³² R. E. Wycherley ("St. Paul at Athens," *JTS* 19 [1968] 619) suggests that κατείδωλον should be translated as "a forest of idols" based on the observation that most compound words with κατά refer to luxuriant vegetation. In the use of this word, therefore, "the association with trees and plants is predominant" and it is likely that the author "deliberately used κατείδωλος with a touch of humorous exaggeration."

25) alludes to Isa 42:5: "Thus says God, the LORD, who created the heavens and stretched them out, who spread out the earth and what comes from it, who gives breath to the people upon it and spirit to those who walk in it" (οὕτως λέγει κύριος ὁ θεὸς ὁ ποιήσας τὸν οὐρανὸν καὶ πήξας αὐτόν, ὁ στερεώσας τὴν γῆν καὶ τὰ ἐν αὐτῇ καὶ διδοὺς πνοὴν τῷ λαῷ τῷ ἐπ' αὐτῆς καὶ πνεῦμα τοῖς πατοῦσιν αὐτήν).

Since God is the creator of all, he does not live in "shrines made by human hands" (χειροποιήτοις ναοῖς, Acts 17:24).[33] Seven out of the nine appearances of the word χειροποίητος in the canonical text of the LXX appear in Isaiah,[34] and in all nine passages the term is used in reference to idols. For example, in Isa 46:6, it is said that "they hire a goldsmith, who makes it into an idol; then they fall down and worship!" (μισθωσάμενοι χρυσοχόον ἐποίησαν χειροποίητα καὶ κύψαντες προσκυνοῦσιν αὐτοῖς).[35] In the description of God as the creator of all, human work cannot be understood as in any way contributing to the existence and well-being of God.[36] A concern to distinguish the one true God from idols is again apparent.

The attack on idols continues in Acts 17:29: "we ought not to think that the deity is like gold, or silver, or stone, an image formed by the art and imagination of mortals" (οὐκ ὀφείλομεν νομίζειν χρυσῷ ἢ ἀργύρῳ ἢ λίθῳ, χαράγματι τέχνης καὶ ἐνθυμήσεως ἀνθρώπου, τὸ θεῖον εἶναι ὅμοιον). Materials like gold, silver, and stone are used in the construction of idols; and an allusion to the passage in Deut 29:15(16)–16(17) concerning God's deliverance of his people from the land of Egypt that is filled with idols can be identified:

> You know how we lived in the land of Egypt, and how we came through the midst of the nations through which you passed. You have seen their detestable things, the filthy idols of wood and stone, of silver and gold, that were among them.

---

[33] This phrase echoes Acts 7:48: "Yet the Most High does not dwell in houses made with human hands" (ἀλλ' οὐχ ὁ ὕψιστος ἐν χειροποιήτοις κατοικεῖ). The parallels between Stephen's speech in Acts and the Areopagus speech go beyond this phrase. See Gärtner, *Areopagus Speech and Natural Revelation*, 208.

[34] Isa 10:11; 16:12; 19:1; 21:9; 31:7; 46:6; cf. Lev 26:1, 30.

[35] Instead of "idol," NRSV translated the word χειροποίητος as "god." The translation "idol" should be adopted especially in light of the Isaianic strategy of the rhetorical annihilation of false deities. Furthermore, the description of artisans working on the object of worship justifies the translation "idol." Nevertheless, either translation will lead to an understanding of this text as a piece of anti-idol polemic.

[36] The focus on the self-sufficient god and the rejection of things produced through "human hands" is again highlighted by the second phrase: "nor is he served by human hands" (οὐδὲ ὑπὸ χειρῶν ἀνθρωπίνων θεραπεύεται, vs 25).

More importantly, the phrase τὸ θεῖον εἶναι ὅμοιον (vs 29) together with mention of the material used to construct idols points one to the first anti-idol passage in Isaiah 40–55:[37]

> To whom then will you liken God,
> or what likeness compare with him?
> An idol? — A workman casts it,
> and a goldsmith overlays it with gold,
> and casts for it silver chains.
> As a gift one chooses mulberry wood
> — wood that will not rot —
> then seeks out a skilled artisan
> to set up an image that will not topple. (Isa 40:18–20)[38]

In Acts 17:29, one therefore finds the climax of this piece of anti-idol polemic that should be understood within the wider framework of the anti-idol polemic in Isaiah.

Finally, as in Isaiah in which the anti-idol polemic serves to unveil the sovereignty of God over all the nations, the anti-idol sentiments in the Areopagus speech are accompanied by an affirmation of the authority and power of God over all the nations. In Acts 17:26–27, the focus is on the fate of the nations. The God who "made the world" (ὁ ποιήσας τὸν κόσμον, vs 24) is now described as the creator of the nations who "from one ancestor ... made all nations to inhabit the whole earth" (ἐποίησέν τε ἐξ ἑνὸς πᾶν ἔθνος ἀνθρώπων κατοικεῖν ἐπὶ παντὸς προσώπου τῆς γῆς, vs 26). The center of the Areopagus speech[39] that issues a call to the nations to "search for God" (ζητεῖν τὸν θεὸν) as "he is not far from each one of us" (οὐ μακρὰν ἀπὸ ἑνὸς ἑκάστου ἡμῶν ὑπάρχοντα, vs 27) recalls the passage immediately following the call to the nations to turn to God in Isa 55:6: "Seek the LORD while he may be found, call upon him while he is near" (Ζητήσατε τὸν θεὸν καὶ ἐν τῷ εὑρίσκειν αὐτὸν ἐπικαλέσασθε· ἡνίκα δ' ἂν ἐγγίζῃ ὑμῖν). This God of all nations "commands all people everywhere to repent" (παραγγέλλει τοῖς ἀνθρώποις πάντας πανταχοῦ μετανοεῖν, vs 30) because he will be the judge of all (cf. vs 31).[40] The attack on idols is

---

[37] It is possible that this passage is dependent upon, among others, Deut 29:15–16.

[38] See also the detailed description of and satire on the process of idol-manufacturing in Isa 44:9–20.

[39] For the discussion of the structure of the Areopagus speech, see Édouard des Places, "Actes 17,27," *Bib* 48 (1967) 1.

[40] An ironic reversal can be detected here. While the people aimed at judging the new deity introduced by Paul, Paul declares that his God will be the judge of all. For a discussion of the legal language used in Acts 17:17–19, see Bruce W. Winter ("On Introducing Gods to Athens: An Alternative Reading of Acts 17:18–20," *TynBul* 47 [1996] 71–90) who argues that 17:19 should be understood as: "We therefore wish to make a judgment (γνῶναι) on what it is being claimed (or decreed) these things are" (82).

therefore ultimately a rhetorical strategy that highlights the impotence of the false deities and the nations. The universal call to submit to the Lord of the early Christian community is thus accomplished. All these allusions to Isaiah confirm the understanding of Acts 17:16–34 as a piece of anti-idol polemic constructed within the tradition of anti-idol polemic in the New Exodus program in Isaiah 40–55.[41]

Moving beyond the Areopagus speech, one can also identify passages in Acts in which the sovereignty of the risen Jesus is established through a depiction of the impotence of both the idols and the false gods. Although these passages do not contain the explicit pattern of Isaianic anti-idol polemic found in Acts 17, the language used should be understood in light of Paul's sustained discussion of idols in the Areopagus speech.

The first passage that needs to be discussed is Philip's encounter with Simon Magus in Acts 8:4–24. The first part of the story introduces Simon and should be cited in full:

Ἀνὴρ δέ τις ὀνόματι Σίμων προϋπῆρχεν ἐν τῇ πόλει μαγεύων καὶ ἐξιστάνων τὸ ἔθνος τῆς Σαμαρείας, λέγων εἶναί τινα ἑαυτὸν μέγαν, ᾧ προσεῖχον πάντες ἀπὸ μικροῦ ἕως μεγάλου λέγοντες, Οὗτός ἐστιν ἡ δύναμις τοῦ θεοῦ ἡ καλουμένη Μεγάλη. προσεῖχον δὲ αὐτῷ διὰ τὸ ἱκανῷ χρόνῳ ταῖς μαγείαις ἐξεστακέναι αὐτούς. ὅτε δὲ ἐπίστευσαν τῷ Φιλίππῳ εὐαγγελιζομένῳ περὶ τῆς βασιλείας τοῦ θεοῦ καὶ τοῦ ὀνόματος Ἰησοῦ Χριστοῦ, ἐβαπτίζοντο ἄνδρες τε καὶ γυναῖκες. ὁ δὲ Σίμων καὶ αὐτὸς ἐπίστευσεν, καὶ βαπτισθεὶς ἦν προσκαρτερῶν τῷ Φιλίππῳ, θεωρῶν τε σημεῖα καὶ δυνάμεις μεγάλας γινομένας ἐξίστατο.

Now a certain man named Simon had previously practiced magic in the city and amazed the people of Samaria, saying that he was someone great. All of them, from the least to the greatest, listened to him eagerly, saying, "This man is the power of God that is called Great." And they listened eagerly to him because for a long time he had amazed them with his magic. But when they believed Philip, who was proclaiming the good news about the kingdom of God and the name of Jesus Christ, they were baptized, both men and women. Even Simon himself believed. After being baptized, he stayed

[41] This is not to deny the importance of allusions to Greco-Roman literature such as those of Epimenides and especially the quotation of Aratus. Nevertheless, the Lukan reinterpretation and use of such material should be noted. It may be possible to argue that these allusions are incorporated into the framework of anti-idol polemic in the tradition of Isaiah 40–55. In his discussion of the quotation of Aratus in Acts 17:28, Hans Conzelmann (*Acts of the Apostles: A Commentary on the Acts of the Apostles* [trans. James Limburg, A. Thomas Kraabel, and Donald H. Juel; Philadelphia: Fortress, 1987] 145) rightly concludes that "the intention of the statement as Luke uses it is not ontological — as if to say something about the essence of humanity as superior to nature. Rather it is intended as a criticism, aimed at the restoration of the proper kind of worship of God." Moreover, the presence of various linguistic parallels between the Areopagus speech and Isaiah 40–55 together with the thematic connections to the Isaianic themes of creation and the one God, the anti-idol polemics, and the call to the nations suggest that Isaiah provides both the structure and content for the material in Acts 17:22–31.

constantly with Philip and was amazed when he saw the signs and great miracles that took place. (Acts 8:9–13)

This introduction of Simon is presented immediately after Luke's description of the activity of Philip in Samaria. In this passage, it is said that Simon himself claimed to be "someone great" (τινα μέγαν, vs 9).[42] The contrast between the message of Philip and that of Simon cannot be missed. While Philip proclaimed τὸν Χριστόν, Simon himself claimed to be a divine figure.[43] Furthermore, among the Samaritans he was declared to be "the power of God that is called Great" (ἡ δύναμις τοῦ θεοῦ ἡ καλουμένη Μεγάλη, vs 10). Both "power" and "greatness" are common epithets of deities.[44] This description points to an understanding of Simon Magus as a "god" himself; and the act of honoring Simon becomes an act of idolatry. The eventual acceptance of the word of God by the Samaritans (vs 12) and also by Simon (vs 13) shows the overcoming of the power of Simon and the triumph of the "name of Jesus" (vs 12).

The second part of the story (8:4–24) describes the attempt of Simon to gain possession of the divine power (i.e., Holy Spirit) by offering money to the apostles. Such an attempt was rebuked by the apostles who urged Simon to repent. In this context, Simon is described as being in "the gall of bitterness and the chains of wickedness" (χολὴν πικρίας καὶ σύνδεσμον ἀδικίας, vs 23). The expression "gall of bitterness" suggests the passage should be viewed as an example of anti-idol polemic for it alludes to Deut 29:17(18) that holds a warning for those who practice idolatry.[45]

The second phrase "chains of wickedness" alludes to Isa 58:6, a verse that has already appeared in the Lukan writings in reference to the ministry of Jesus.[46] When used in the context of Acts 8:23, this phrase is of course the reversal of Isa 58:6 that calls for the loosening of the chains of wickedness. The contrast between the power of Jesus whose ministry releases the chains

---

[42] Cf. Acts 5:36 in which a similar phrase is used in describing the claim of Theudas.

[43] Hans Conzelmann (*History of Primitive Christianity* [trans. John E. Steely; Nashville: Abingdon, 1973] 126) argues that Simon himself is here claiming to be "the Most High God himself or the revelation of God, and thus the Son."

[44] See Jarl E. Fossum, *The Name of God and the Angel of the Lord: Samaritan and Jewish Concepts of Intermediation and the Origin of Gnosticism* (WUNT 36; Tübingen: Mohr Siebeck, 1985) 162–91, who argues that the name "Great Power" is a Samaritan name for Yahweh.

[45] See Deut 29:16(17)–17(18): "You have seen their detestable things, the filthy idols of wood and stone, of silver and gold, that were among them. It may be that there is among you a man or woman, or a family or tribe, whose heart is already turning away from the LORD our God to serve the gods of those nations. It may be that there is among you a root sprouting poisonous and bitter growth (LXX: ἄνω φύουσα ἐν χολῇ καὶ πικρίᾳ)."

[46] Cf. Luke 4:18 and Acts 10:38.

of wickedness and Simon who is condemned to the chains of wickedness cannot be missed.

Acts 8:14–24 should therefore be understood as an example of anti-idol polemic since the false claim to deity is rebuked and the power of the message of the kingdom of God is manifested. This passage also sets the tone for the rest of the narrative in Acts by showing that no one (and nothing) is able to resist the power of the word in this New Exodus program.[47]

The second passage that needs to be examined is the pericope relating the death of Herod:

Ἦν δὲ θυμομαχῶν Τυρίοις καὶ Σιδωνίοις· ὁμοθυμαδὸν δὲ παρῆσαν πρὸς αὐτόν, καὶ πείσαντες Βλάστον τὸν ἐπὶ τοῦ κοιτῶνος τοῦ βασιλέως ἠτοῦντο εἰρήνην, διὰ τὸ τρέφεσθαι αὐτῶν τὴν χώραν ἀπὸ τῆς βασιλικῆς. τακτῇ δὲ ἡμέρᾳ ὁ Ἡρῴδης ἐνδυσάμενος ἐσθῆτα βασιλικὴν [καὶ] καθίσας ἐπὶ τοῦ βήματος ἐδημηγόρει πρὸς αὐτούς· ὁ δὲ δῆμος ἐπεφώνει, Θεοῦ φωνὴ καὶ οὐκ ἀνθρώπου. παραχρῆμα δὲ ἐπάταξεν αὐτὸν ἄγγελος κυρίου ἀνθ᾽ ὧν οὐκ ἔδωκεν τὴν δόξαν τῷ θεῷ, καὶ γενόμενος σκωληκόβρωτος ἐξέψυξεν.

Now Herod was angry with the people of Tyre and Sidon. So they came to him in a body; and after winning over Blastus, the king's chamberlain, they asked for a reconciliation, because their country depended on the king's country for food. On an appointed day Herod put on his royal robes, took his seat on the platform, and delivered a public address to them. The people kept shouting, "The voice of a god, and not of a mortal!" And immediately, because he had not given the glory to God, an angel of the Lord struck him down, and he was eaten by worms and died. (Acts 12:20–23)

This passage has not been traditionally understood as one that involves a struggle between spiritual forces and is therefore frequently neglected in treatments dealing with the struggle for divine authority.[48] I will argue, however, that this passage should be considered as an example of anti-idol polemic in Acts together with other similar passages in which one finds attempts to construct false claims of deity being overcome.

The beginning of the chapter portrays Herod as an enemy of the church: "About that time King Herod laid violent hands upon some who belonged to the church" (Κατ᾽ ἐκεῖνον δὲ τὸν καιρὸν ἐπέβαλεν Ἡρῴδης ὁ βασιλεὺς τὰς χεῖρας κακῶσαί τινας τῶν ἀπὸ τῆς ἐκκλησίας, 12:1). The narrative concerning Herod's death at the end of the chapter depicts how another instance of opposition to the early Christian movement had failed.

---

[47] For a discussion of the portrayal of Philip as the "prophet like Moses" in Acts 8:4–24, and the parallel between Simon and Pharaoh, see Franklin Scott Spencer, *The Portrait of Philip in Acts: A Study of Role and Relations* (Sheffield: Sheffield Academic Press, 1992) 106–8.

[48] In the work of Garrett (*Demise of the Devil*, 20), the passage is discussed in passing in the discussion of the wilderness temptation of Jesus in Luke 4:1–13. In this work, the Simon Magus episode and other related stories are understood together with the gospel exorcism stories, an approach that needs to be questioned.

The statement immediately following the description of Herod's death affirms the power of the word of God in the face of opposition: "But the word of God grew and multiplied" (lit.; Ὁ δὲ λόγος τοῦ θεοῦ ηὔξανεν καὶ ἐπληθύνετο, 12:24).

Significantly, the cause of the death of Herod is explicitly linked to his refusal to give glory to God (vs 23) when the people declared: "The voice of a god, and not of a mortal (vs 22)!"[49] Again, a false claim to be divine is met with violent punishment. The act of honoring Herod is thus interpreted as an act of idolatry that cannot be accepted. Furthermore, Luke's contrast between the claims of Peter earlier in the chapter and that of Herod should be noted. In 12:11, after escaping from prison, Peter honored God for this salvific act: "Now I am sure that the Lord has sent his angel and rescued me from the hands of Herod and from all that the Jewish people were expecting" (Νῦν οἶδα ἀληθῶς ὅτι ἐξαπέστειλεν [ὁ] κύριος τὸν ἄγγελον αὐτοῦ καὶ ἐξείλατό με ἐκ χειρὸς Ἡρῴδου καὶ πάσης τῆς προσδοκίας τοῦ λαοῦ τῶν Ἰουδαίων). The risen Jesus is Lord of all, and Herod's failure to recognize this led to his destruction by an "angel of the Lord" (ἄγγελος κυρίου, vs 23), the same being acknowledged to be the agent of salvation for Peter in vs 11.

Precedents for the fall of evil rulers can be found in both Exodus and Isaiah. For instance, Isa 14:4–20 announces the downfall of the King of Babylon:

> How you are fallen from heaven,
> O Day Star, son of Dawn!
> How you are cut down to the ground,
> you who laid the nations low! (Isa 14:12)[50]

The basis for this condemnation is a false claim of deity:

> You said in your heart, "I will ascend to heaven;
> I will raise my throne above the stars of God;
> I will sit on the mount of assembly on the heights of Zaphon;
> I will ascend to the tops of the clouds,
> I will make myself like the Most High." (Isa 14:13–14)[51]

In an examination of the wider context of Acts 12:20–23, Wesley Allen[52] argues that the entire narrative in Acts 12 should be viewed as a single unit

---

[49] Cf. Josephus, *Ant* 19.343–52. See especially 19.345 that contains a similar claim to divinity understood as the cause of Herod's demise.

[50] The downfall of the King of Babylon has been interpreted as describing the downfall of Satan in Jewish interpretive traditions. See the discussion in Garrett, *Demise of the Devil*, 40, 130 n.20.

[51] Cf. Ezekiel 28 and the discussion in Mark R. Strom, "An Old Testament Background to Acts 12.20–23," *NTS* 32 (1986) 289–92.

and that this extended narrative should be understood against the background of the Exodus narrative. The summary statement concerning Herod's activity in Acts 12:1 recalls the description of the evil action of Pharaoh in Exodus 3. Acts 12:3–4 explicitly evokes the Passover traditions. Peter's escape from prison and the recollection of events recall the departure of the Israelites from Egypt in Exodus 12–14, 18. The death of Herod in 12:20–23 therefore can also be understood as the destruction of Pharaoh. This connection is further evinced by a description of the glorification of God in connection with Pharaoh's destruction.[53]

In the context of Acts, Herod's death can therefore be understood as an attack on the unjustifiable worship of one other than the risen Lord. The power of the word and the universal sovereignty of the Lord is again established through the destruction of those who made competitive claims to power and authority.

The third passage appears at the very beginning of the Pauline mission in Acts 13. In Cyrus, the apostles confronted Bar-Jesus/Elymas who is described as "a certain magician, a Jewish false prophet" (τινὰ μάγον ψευδοπροφήτην Ἰουδαῖον, vs 6; cf. vs 8). When Bar-Jesus opposed Barnabas and Saul, Paul said:

Ὦ πλήρης παντὸς δόλου καὶ πάσης ῥᾳδιουργίας, υἱὲ διαβόλου, ἐχθρὲ πάσης δικαιοσύνης, οὐ παύσῃ διαστρέφων τὰς ὁδοὺς [τοῦ] κυρίου τὰς εὐθείας; καὶ νῦν ἰδοὺ χεὶρ κυρίου ἐπὶ σέ, καὶ ἔσῃ τυφλὸς μὴ βλέπων τὸν ἥλιον ἄχρι καιροῦ.

You son of the devil, you enemy of all righteousness, full of all deceit and villainy, will you not stop making crooked the straight paths of the Lord? And now listen — the hand of the Lord is against you, and you will be blind for a while, unable to see the sun. (Acts 13:10–11a)

Paul's speech reveals the true nature of Elymas not only as a false prophet and a magician but also the "son of the devil" and the "enemy of all righteousness" (vs 10). The description "son of the devil" (υἱὲ διαβόλου)[54] points to the portrayal of Elymas as the representative of the evil force, whereas Paul and Barnabas, being called by the Holy Spirit (vs 2), are representatives of the risen Lord.[55] The portrayal of Elymas as the enemy of

---

[52] O. Wesley Allen, Jr., *The Death of Herod: The Narrative and Theological Function of Retribution in Luke-Acts* (Atlanta, GA: Scholars Press, 1997) 98–101. Cf. Susan R. Garrett, "Exodus from Bondage: Luke 9:31 and Acts 12:1–24," *CBQ* 52 (1990) 656–80.

[53] Allen, *Death of Herod*, 101. See Exod 14:4, 17, 18; 15:1, 2, 6.

[54] In Acts 10:38, the ministry of Jesus is summarized as "doing good and healing all who were oppressed by the devil" (εὐεργετῶν καὶ ἰώμενος πάντας τοὺς καταδυναστευομένους ὑπὸ τοῦ διαβόλου).

[55] Charles K. Barrett (*A Critical and Exegetical Commentary on the Acts of the Apostles* [ICC; Edinburgh: T & T Clark, 1994] 1.617) suggests that the son of the devil "was probably understood at some stage in the tradition as the opposite of Bar-Jesus. 'Son of Jesus, do you call yourself? I say you are a son of the devil.'"

the risen Lord who is called "the Righteous One" (τὸν δίκαιον, 22:14; cf. 3:14; 7:52) is also evident in the use of the epithet: "enemy of all righteousness" (ἐχθρὲ πάσης δικαιοσύνης). Furthermore, the description of Elymas' work as "making crooked the straight paths of the Lord" (διαστρέφων τὰς ὁδοὺς [τοῦ] κυρίου τὰς εὐθείας, vs 10) is the exact reversal of the definitive statement of the Isaianic New Exodus (Isa 40:3) as cited in Luke 3:4: "Prepare the way of the Lord, make his paths straight" (ἑτοιμάσατε τὴν ὁδὸν κυρίου, εὐθείας ποιεῖτε τὰς τρίβους αὐτοῦ).

The attempt of Elymas "to turn the proconsul away from the faith" (διαστρέψαι τὸν ἀνθύπατον ἀπὸ τῆς πίστεως, vs 8) is therefore an attempt to turn the proconsul from the true god to worship the false deity and the enemy of the Lord that Elymas represents. The act of idolatry is further highlighted by the mentioning of Elymas as a Jew. The triumph of the word is made apparent when Paul's warning is realized as "mist and darkness came over him" (ἔπεσεν ἐπ᾽ αὐτὸν ἀχλὺς καὶ σκότος, vs 11).[56] This symbolism is significant in both Isaiah and the Lukan writings as the polarity of sight/light and blindness/darkness points to the contrast between salvation and condemnation;[57] and the Pauline mission is described in Isaianic terms as Paul was sent "to open their eyes so that they may turn from darkness to light and from the power of Satan to God" (ἀνοῖξαι ὀφθαλμοὺς αὐτῶν, τοῦ ἐπιστρέψαι ἀπὸ σκότους εἰς φῶς καὶ τῆς ἐξουσίας τοῦ Σατανᾶ ἐπὶ τὸν θεόν, 26:18).[58]

The confrontation scene in Acts 13 therefore defines the nature of the Pauline mission as one that defeats the power of evil and challenges false claims of deity. In overcoming the works of false prophets and magicians, the lordship-claim of the risen Jesus over all can be maintained. Furthermore, this confrontation identifies the early Christian community as the sole mediator of divine power.

---

[56] The word ἀχλύς is used as a medical term for blindness due to ulceration. In this context, however, this term is probably not used in a technical sense. See Barrett, *Acts of the Apostles*, 1.618.

[57] Cf. Luke 2:32; Acts 13:47 (Isa 49:6); Luke 3:4–6 (Isa 40:3–5); and Luke 4:18–19 (Isa 61:1–2). See the discussion in Dennis Hamm, "Sight to the Blind: Vision as Metaphor in Luke," *Bib* 67 (1986) 457–77; and Ronald E. Clements, "Patterns in the Prophetic Canon: Healing the Blind and the Lame," in Gene M. Tucker, David L. Petersen, and Robert R. Wilson, eds., *Canon, Theology, and Old Testament Interpretation: Essays in Honor of Brevard S. Childs* (Philadelphia: Fortress, 1988) 189–200.

[58] Cf. Isa 42:16: "I will turn the darkness before them into light, the rough places into level ground" (ποιήσω αὐτοῖς τὸ σκότος εἰς φῶς καὶ τὰ σκολιὰ εἰς εὐθεῖαν).

The next passage where anti-idol polemic can again be identified appears in the speech delivered in Lystra.[59] When Paul healed a crippled man in Lystra, the people shouted: "The gods have come down to us in human form!" (Οἱ θεοὶ ὁμοιωθέντες ἀνθρώποις κατέβησαν πρὸς ἡμᾶς, Acts 14:11b). Then, they called Barnabas Zeus and Paul Hermes (vs 12); and the priest of Zeus and the crowd wanted to offer sacrifice to them (vs 13). Refusing to be worshipped, Paul and Barnabas shouted:

Ἄνδρες, τί ταῦτα ποιεῖτε; καὶ ἡμεῖς ὁμοιοπαθεῖς ἐσμεν ὑμῖν ἄνθρωποι, εὐαγγελιζόμενοι ὑμᾶς ἀπὸ τούτων τῶν ματαίων ἐπιστρέφειν ἐπὶ θεὸν ζῶντα ὃς ἐποίησεν τὸν οὐρανὸν καὶ τὴν γῆν καὶ τὴν θάλασσαν καὶ πάντα τὰ ἐν αὐτοῖς· ὃς ἐν ταῖς παρῳχημέναις γενεαῖς εἴασεν πάντα τὰ ἔθνη πορεύεσθαι ταῖς ὁδοῖς αὐτῶν· καίτοι οὐκ ἀμάρτυρον αὐτὸν ἀφῆκεν ἀγαθουργῶν, οὐρανόθεν ὑμῖν ὑετοὺς διδοὺς καὶ καιροὺς καρποφόρους, ἐμπιπλῶν τροφῆς καὶ εὐφροσύνης τὰς καρδίας ὑμῶν.

Friends, why are you doing this? We are mortals just like you, and we bring you good news, that you should turn from these worthless things to the living God, who made the heaven and the earth and the sea and all that is in them. In past generations he allowed all the nations to follow their own ways; yet he has not left himself without a witness in doing good — giving you rains from heaven and fruitful seasons, and filling you with food and your hearts with joy. (Acts 14:15–17)

Unlike Simon Magus and Herod, Paul and Barnabas refused to be honored as divine beings since they recognized they were mere "mortals" having the same nature as their audience (vs 15: ὁμοιοπαθεῖς ἐσμεν ὑμῖν ἄνθρωποι). They urged the audience to turn away "from these worthless things" (ἀπὸ τούτων τῶν ματαίων, vs 15). The word μάταιος is frequently used in the LXX in reference to idols[60] and should be understood as such here in Acts 14:15. The speech therefore centers on the call to turn from idols to worship the one true God.

The one true God is "the living God" (θεὸς ζῶν, vs 15). This peculiar designation appears most often in contexts affirming the sovereignty of Yahweh over against idols (and other powers) that are not able to see and know, and to save and deliver those who worship them.[61] Furthermore, as in the anti-idol passages in Isaiah, the affirmation is made in reference to God the creator as the one who "made the heaven and the earth and the sea and all that

---

[59] The connection between this passage and the passages examined above (and those mentioned below) is often missed since the common theme of anti-idol polemic is not recognized as a critical component in the New Exodus program of Acts.

[60] E.g., Lev 17:7; Isa 2:20; 30:15; cf. Isa 44:9. O. Bauernfeind ("μάταιος," *TDNT* 4 [1967] 521–22) states that "the distinctiveness of μάταιος in the LXX is — purely lexically — that it is constantly used for the other world. The gods of the ἔθνη are primarily μάταια, i.e., the very gods who in the Greek world are supposed in some way to be the guarantors of that which escapes the μάταιον. Only the one God is the living God."

[61] Cf. Deut 5:26; Josh 3:10; 1 Sam 17:26, 36; Ps 41(42):3; 83(84):3; Jer 10:10; 23:36; Dan 6:20, 26; Hos 1:10.

is in them" (ἐποίησεν τὸν οὐρανὸν καὶ τὴν γῆν καὶ τὴν θάλασσαν καὶ πάντα τὰ ἐν αὐτοῖς, vs 15).[62]

The call to turn to this one God is also the call to affirm the power of the risen Lord who is in control of all, including the nations and their rulers.[63] This explains the transition from the affirmation of the sovereignty of the Lord in Acts 14:15 to the concern with "all the nations" (πάντα τὰ ἔθνη) in vs 16. A suggestive parallel that has often been neglected can be found in the prayer of Hezekiah in Isa 37:14–20 in which similar designations are used to assert the sovereignty of Yahweh over the nations:[64]

> O LORD of hosts, God of Israel, who are enthroned above the cherubim, you are God, you alone, of all the kingdoms of the earth; you have made heaven and earth (σὺ ἐποίησας τὸν οὐρανὸν καὶ τὴν γῆν). Incline your ear, O LORD, and hear; open your eyes, O LORD, and see; hear all the words of Sennacherib, which he has sent to mock the living God (θεὸν ζῶντα).... So now, O LORD our God, save us from his hand, so that all the kingdoms of the earth may know that you alone are the LORD. (Isa 37:16–17, 20)

Therefore, as in the anti-idol passages in Isaiah, the response of Paul and Barnabas in Acts 14:15–17 is also a call to turn away from idols and an affirmation of the sovereignty of the creator Lord over all the nations. No false claims of deity can be accepted and no nations can resist the power of the Lord.

Finally, the events surrounding Paul's stay in Ephesus need to be discussed. Acts 19:11–20 highlights the power of the name of Jesus over against the power of other authorities. In vss 11–12, God worked through Paul in healing the sick and casting out demons. Such acts of power attracted the attention of the seven sons of the Jewish high priest Sceva who were trying to use the name of Jesus but failed to produce any results (vss 13–15).[65] Instead, they were overcome by the demons. The power of the

---

[62] This is the language often used in affirming the power of Yahweh who is the creator of all. See especially Exod 20:11 where creation is described as an act in which "the LORD made heaven and earth, the sea, and all that is in them" (ἐποίησεν κύριος τὸν οὐρανὸν καὶ τὴν γῆν καὶ τὴν θάλασσαν καὶ πάντα τὰ ἐν αὐτοῖς; cf. Ps 145[146]:6).

[63] As I have discussed above, a strict distinction cannot be made between idols/deities and nations/rulers.

[64] I will also argue (in section 6.3b below) that Luke's particular interest in this prayer can also be detected in the prayer of the believers in Acts 4:23–31.

[65] The sudden introduction of the "Jewish" high priest has led to numerous suggestions concerning the integrity of the text. Ernst Haenchen (*The Acts of the Apostles: A Commentary* [trans. R. McL. Wilson; Oxford: Basil Blackwell, 1971] 564) argues that the Western text omits Ἰουδαίου to ease the difficulty of the text. The absence of Ἰουδαίου signals, however, a reading with the understanding of the presence of two groups of exorcists: the Jewish ones in vs 13 and the Gentile ones in vs 14. For a further discussion of the textual problem surrounding this text, see W. A. Strange, "The Sons of Sceva and the Text of Acts 19:14," *JTS* 38 (1987) 97–106, who argues for the authenticity of the reading of the Western textual tradition.

name of Jesus and those who had access to this power is contrasted with those who did not belong to the early Christian community. This contrast led to the glorification of the name of the Lord Jesus (vs 17) and the conversion of many (vs 18). The public act of burning magical books (vs 19) highlights the triumph of the power of God over other claims to power and authority; and this emphasis is summarized in the statement that follows this episode: "So the word of the Lord grew mightily and prevailed" (Οὕτως κατὰ κράτος τοῦ κυρίου ὁ λόγος ηὔξανεν καὶ ἴσχυεν, vs 20).[66] From this brief survey, one can see that not only is this a story about the contest between God and Satan,[67] it is also one that is concerned with the restriction of access to the divine power to a certain community.

In the second half of the account of Paul's stay in Ephesus, there is a disturbance concerning "the Way."[68] In this context, the speech of Demetrius, a silversmith who produced silver shrines of Artemis, should be quoted:

Ἄνδρες, ἐπίστασθε ὅτι ἐκ ταύτης τῆς ἐργασίας ἡ εὐπορία ἡμῖν ἐστιν, καὶ θεωρεῖτε καὶ ἀκούετε ὅτι οὐ μόνον Ἐφέσου ἀλλὰ σχεδὸν πάσης τῆς Ἀσίας ὁ Παῦλος οὗτος πείσας μετέστησεν ἱκανὸν ὄχλον, λέγων ὅτι οὐκ εἰσὶν θεοὶ οἱ διὰ χειρῶν γινόμενοι. οὐ μόνον δὲ τοῦτο κινδυνεύει ἡμῖν τὸ μέρος εἰς ἀπελεγμὸν ἐλθεῖν, ἀλλὰ καὶ τὸ τῆς μεγάλης θεᾶς Ἀρτέμιδος ἱερὸν εἰς οὐθὲν λογισθῆναι, μέλλειν τε καὶ καθαιρεῖσθαι τῆς μεγαλειότητος αὐτῆς, ἣν ὅλη ἡ Ἀσία καὶ ἡ οἰκουμένη σέβεται.

Men, you know that we get our wealth from this business. You also see and hear that not only in Ephesus but in almost the whole of Asia this Paul has persuaded and drawn away a considerable number of people by saying that gods made with hands are not gods. And there is danger not only that this trade of ours may come into disrepute but also that the temple of the great goddess Artemis will be scorned, and she will be deprived of her majesty that brought all Asia and the world to worship her. (Acts 19:25b–27)

Through the mouth of Demetrius, the ministry of Paul in Ephesus and throughout Asia is described as one that is focused on the attack of idols and foreign gods. The phrase, "gods made with hands are not gods" (οὐκ εἰσὶν θεοὶ οἱ διὰ χειρῶν γινόμενοι, vs 26), provides a succinct summary statement of the arguments against idols in Isaiah 40–55 and throughout the

---

[66] For a discussion of the significance of this verse, please refer to chapter five above.

[67] Garrett (*Demise of the Devil*, 90) argues that "Luke uses the story of the seven sons of Sceva, whatever its origin and whether or not told in a humorous vein, to advance the theme of the ongoing Christian triumph over Satan, and, consequently, over magic." One can hardly question this statement; but I will emphasize that access to the power of the one true god by those who belong to the early Christian movement should be understood as the focus of the passage. To reduce all tensions into one that solely concerns God and Satan is not adequate in the examination of Acts 19 and other similar texts in the narrative of Acts.

[68] I will limit myself to the discussion of anti-idol polemic in this pericope. For a discussion of the riot act and the role of Alexander the Jew, please refer to chapter two above.

LXX.[69] Furthermore, in vs 27, the threat upon the Artemis cult can be felt for the phrase εἰς οὐθὲν λογισθῆναι (lit.: "reckoned into nothing") alludes again to the first anti-idol passage in Isaiah 40–55 in which all the nations "were counted as nothing" (εἰς οὐθὲν ἐλογίσθησαν, Isa 40:17). The fluidity of the distinction between nations and idols can again be seen as the attack against Artemis becomes an attack against the people who worshipped her.

Although the rest of the narrative in Acts 19 does not portray the collapse of the cult of Artemis, the assertion that through Paul's ministry the great goddess Artemis "will be deprived of her majesty that brought all Asia and the world to worship her" (μέλλειν τε καὶ καθαιρεῖσθαι τῆς μεγαλειότητος αὐτῆς, ἣν ὅλη ἡ Ἀσία καὶ ἡ οἰκουμένη σέβεται, vs 27) does highlight the threat of the power of the word of God upon competing claims of deity. The assertion that the Lord of the early Christian movement is the God of all nations can thus be maintained.[70]

Before leaving this section, the significant transformation and development of the Isaianic anti-idol polemic in Acts also needs to be considered. In the speech of Stephen in Acts 7, one can detect the charge of idolatry against the ancestors of the Jews. While the anti-idol polemic is directed primarily against the nations in Isaiah 40–55, the same polemic in Acts is directed against all who oppose the early Christian movement, which apparently includes the Jews. Acts 7:39–41 records the rejection of Moses by Israel and their turn to idols:

ᾧ οὐκ ἠθέλησαν ὑπήκοοι γενέσθαι οἱ πατέρες ἡμῶν ἀλλὰ ἀπώσαντο καὶ ἐστράφησαν ἐν ταῖς καρδίαις αὐτῶν εἰς Αἴγυπτον, εἰπόντες τῷ Ἀαρών, Ποίησον ἡμῖν θεοὺς οἳ προπορεύσονται ἡμῶν· ὁ γὰρ Μωϋσῆς οὗτος, ὃς ἐξήγαγεν ἡμᾶς ἐκ γῆς Αἰγύπτου, οὐκ οἴδαμεν τί ἐγένετο αὐτῷ. καὶ ἐμοσχοποίησαν ἐν ταῖς ἡμέραις ἐκείναις καὶ ἀνήγαγον θυσίαν τῷ εἰδώλῳ, καὶ εὐφραίνοντο ἐν τοῖς ἔργοις τῶν χειρῶν αὐτῶν.

Our ancestors were unwilling to obey him; instead, they pushed him aside, and in their hearts they turned back to Egypt, saying to Aaron, "Make gods for us who will lead the way for us; as for this Moses who led us out from the land of Egypt, we do not know what has happened to him." At that time they made a calf, offered a sacrifice to the idol, and reveled in the works of their hands.

This description of idolatry asserts that even the Jews had forsaken the one true God and turned their back on the one who had delivered them from their

---

[69] This is also essentially the same argument as that which appears in the aforementioned Areopagus speech of Acts 17.

[70] In arguing against the common consensus, Rick Strelan (*Paul, Artemis, and the Jews in Ephesus* [Berlin/New York: Walter de Gruyter, 1996] 130) is correct to insist that there is no evidence that Paul brought down the cult of the Ephesian Artemis. Nevertheless, he has certainly overstated his case when he concludes that "the cult of Artemis remained virtually unchallenged in the face of Paul's proclamation in Ephesus" (163). The Lukan emphasis on the effects of the Pauline ministry in Ephesus should not be neglected (cf. Acts 19:27).

enemies.[71] Instead of worshipping God, they "reveled in the works of their hands" (εὐφραίνοντο ἐν τοῖς ἔργοις τῶν χειρῶν αὐτῶν, vs 42).[72] The theme of idolatry continues and appears surprisingly in a description of the center of the Jewish cult. Concerning the temple built by Solomon, it is said:

ἀλλ' οὐχ ὁ ὕψιστος ἐν χειροποιήτοις κατοικεῖ· καθὼς ὁ προφήτης λέγει,
'Ο οὐρανός μοι θρόνος, ἡ δὲ γῆ ὑποπόδιον τῶν ποδῶν μου·
ποῖον οἶκον οἰκοδομήσετέ μοι, λέγει κύριος,
ἢ τίς τόπος τῆς καταπαύσεώς μου;
οὐχὶ ἡ χείρ μου ἐποίησεν ταῦτα πάντα;

Yet the Most High does not dwell in houses made with human hands;
as the prophet says,
"Heaven is my throne, and the earth is my footstool.
What kind of house will you build for me, says the Lord,
or what is the place of my rest?
Did not my hand make all these things." (Acts 7:48–50)

In a most striking fashion, the temple is described as "made with human hands" (χειροποιήτοις, vs 48). As I have pointed out in connection with Acts 17:24, in the LXX the word χειροποίητος is always used in connection with acts of idolatry.[73] The misuse of the temple is therefore considered an act of idolatry.[74] Furthermore, the quotation from Isa 66:1–2 in vss 49–50 reiterates themes from the anti-idol polemic in Isaiah 40–55 as it claims that Yahweh is the creator of all and he is therefore Lord of all. The contrast

---

[71] This is supported by a quotation from Amos 5:25–27 in Acts 7:42–43. Instead of "Damascus," the text in Acts has "Babylon" in the Amos quotation: "so I will remove you beyond Babylon" (Acts 7:43). This change cannot be fully explained. Perhaps the wider context of the (Isaianic) New Exodus is presupposed here as the Jewish people are also in exile and in need of the deliverance of God. Furthermore, the comparison between the "old" Exodus and the new one is also made. As in the old Exodus, the Jews rebelled and turned away from the God who delivered them. In the same way, in the New Exodus of Acts, the Jews are also turning away from the God who has provided them with a salvific message. The connection between those who rebelled in the old Exodus event and the Jewish audience in Acts is made clear by the use of the word σκληροτράχηλοι ("stiff-necked") in Acts 7:51, a word that alludes to the rebellious people of Israel in Exod 33:3.
[72] Cf. Isa 40:19–20; 44:12–17.
[73] See also the similar description of the creation of idols within the Stephen speech as discussed above (7:39–41) where the people "reveled in the works of their hands" (εὐφραίνοντο ἐν τοῖς ἔργοις τῶν χειρῶν αὐτῶν, vs 41) after making and worshipping idol.
[74] Acts 7:51 shows that it is not the temple but the people against whom this criticism is leveled. This is confirmed by 6:13 where the claim that Stephen spoke against the Temple is presented as a false accusation made by "false witnesses." For a discussion of the issue of anti-temple rhetoric in Acts 7, see, for example, Graham Stanton, "Stephen in Lucan Perspective," *StudBib* 3 (1978) 345–60; and Gerhard Schneider, *Die Apostelgeschichte* (Freiburg: Herder, 1980) 1.467–68. Cf. John J. Kilgallen, *The Stephen Speech* (AnBib 67; Rome: Biblical Institute Press, 1976) 91–3, 115–18; and Rudolf Pesch, *Die Apostelgeschichte* (EKK 5; Zürich: Benziger Verlag, 1986) 1.256–60.

between the creator and the created beings is again used in an attack on idolatry.

This attack on the idolatrous acts of the Jewish people is succinctly captured in the verse that immediately follows the quotation from Isa 66:1–2:

Σκληροτράχηλοι καὶ ἀπερίτμητοι καρδίαις καὶ τοῖς ὠσίν, ὑμεῖς ἀεὶ τῷ πνεύματι τῷ ἁγίῳ ἀντιπίπτετε, ὡς οἱ πατέρες ὑμῶν καὶ ὑμεῖς.

You stiff-necked people, uncircumcised in heart and ears, you are forever opposing the Holy Spirit, just as your ancestors used to do. (Acts 7:51)

This statement identifies the Jewish audience as the enemy of the Holy Spirit.[75] Stephen is therefore able to claim that while the early Christians worship the one God manifested in the risen Jesus, the Jews are turning away from this one true God. As in the past, they have once again forsaken the sovereign Lord and committed idolatrous acts. Moreover, this statement establishes the boundary between the Jews and the early Christian community. The shift from "our ancestors" (οἱ πατέρες ἡμῶν), a phrase that is used ten times in the speech of Stephen,[76] to "your ancestors" (οἱ πατέρες ὑμῶν) in 7:51[77] highlights the division between the two communities and the refusal of the early Christian community to be identified completely with the Jewish community despite the fact that they share the same roots.

In the anti-idol polemic in Acts, both the non-believing Jews and the nations are accused of committing idolatrous acts.[78] This anti-idol rhetoric identifies the true people of God. The language of idolatry becomes the boundary-marker that separates those who are within and those who are outside of the early Christian community. As in the anti-idol polemic in Isaiah, the primary focus of the anti-idol polemic in Acts is not the possible temptation of Christians to commit idolatrous acts. The aim is, rather, to underscore the power and sovereignty of the risen Jesus over all the opposing forces.

---

[75] It is likely that this verse alludes to Isa 63:10: "But they rebelled and grieved his holy spirit; therefore he became their enemy; he himself fought against them" (αὐτοὶ δὲ ἠπείθησαν καὶ παρώξυναν τὸ πνεῦμα τὸ ἅγιον αὐτοῦ· καὶ ἐστράφη αὐτοῖς εἰς ἔχθραν, καὶ αὐτὸς ἐπολέμησεν αὐτούς).

[76] Cf. Acts 7:2, 11, 12, 15, 19, 38, 39, 44, 45 (twice).

[77] The phrase "your ancestors" is repeated in the next verse (7:52).

[78] See also Acts 26:17–18 where the risen Lord spoke to Paul. Here, the Jews and the Gentiles are understood as a group from whom deliverance is needed: "I will rescue you from your people and from the Gentiles — to whom I am sending you to open their eyes so that they may turn from darkness to light and from the power of Satan to God, so that they may receive forgiveness of sins and a place among those who are sanctified by faith in me."

b. The Sovereignty of the Risen Jesus in Acts

In the preceding section, I suggested that the lordship of the risen Jesus and the impotence of the nations and their idols should be understood as the focus of the anti-idol polemic of Acts. In this section, I will highlight several passages in which the Lordship of Jesus over all is explicitly articulated.[79]

The power of Jesus over the forces of evil is already established in Luke. When the messengers of Jesus returned from their mission and told Jesus that the demons submitted to them when the name of Jesus was evoked, he answered with a statement unique to Luke: "I watched Satan fall from heaven like a flash of lightning" (Ἐθεώρουν τὸν Σατανᾶν ὡς ἀστραπὴν ἐκ τοῦ οὐρανοῦ πεσόντα, Luke 10:18). This statement alludes to Isa 14:12 that notes the relationship between the evil power and the nations: "How you are fallen from heaven, O Day Star, son of Dawn! How you are cut down to the ground, you who laid the nations low!" (πῶς ἐξέπεσεν ἐκ τοῦ οὐρανοῦ ὁ ἑωσφόρος ὁ πρωὶ ἀνατέλλων; συνετρίβη εἰς τὴν γῆν ὁ ἀποστέλλων πρὸς πάντα τὰ ἔθνη).[80]

The second passage in Luke that needs to be mentioned is Luke 11:14–23 in which the act of Jesus is compared to that of a strong man who is able to plunder the domain the evil one (vss 21–22).[81] This passage recalls Isa 49:24–25 in which the deliverance from the mighty one by the Lord is announced.[82] Although the authority of Jesus over Satan is highlighted in the gospel, the power of Jesus as the risen Lord over all the nations is made

---

[79] In this brief section, I do not intend to examine the wider issues concerning the Christology of Luke-Acts. For a discussion of the related issues and a survey of scholarship, see François Bovon, *Luke the Theologian: Thirty-Three Years of Research (1950–1983)* (trans. K. McKinney; PTMS 12; Allison Park, PA: Pickwick, 1987) 109–97; and H. Douglas Buckwalter, *The Character and Purpose of Luke's Christology* (SNTSMS 89; Cambridge: Cambridge University Press, 1996) 3–24.

[80] In this passage, the tyrant is overcome by his own pride. Note the LXX translation of הֵילֵל as ἑωσφόρος ὁ πρωὶ ἀνατέλλων ("Morning Star who rises in the morning"). For the significance of the identification of the king of Babylon with the cosmic rebel, see Neil Forsyth, *The Old Enemy: Satan and the Combat Myth* (Princeton: Princeton University Press, 1987) 134–39, who, among others, suggests that in Isa 14:10–15, one finds "a blending of the Ugaritic traditions with a story very much like the Phaethon myth" (134). It should also be noted that this passage is situated within the collection of pronouncements against the nations in Isaiah 13–23.

[81] Cf. Mark 3:22–27 and Matt 12:22–30. Joseph A. Fitzmyer (*The Gospel According to Luke X–XXIV* [AB 28A; Garden City, NJ: Doubleday, 1985] 917) notes that the Lukan version has most likely drawn from Q with no significant influence from Mark.

[82] Isaiah 49:24–25: "Can the prey be taken from the mighty, or the captives of a tyrant be rescued? But thus says the LORD: Even the captives of the mighty shall be taken, and the prey of the tyrant be rescued; for I will contend with those who contend with you, and I will save your children." See Heinz Schürmann, *Das Lukasevangelium* (HKNT 3; Freiburg: Herder, 1994) 2.1.243–44.

explicit only in the narrative of Acts where one also finds the numerous anti-idol passages.

At the end of Peter's Pentecost Speech in Acts 2, the assertion that the risen Jesus is Lord of all is made with the quotation from Ps 109(110):1:

τῇ δεξιᾷ οὖν τοῦ θεοῦ ὑψωθεὶς τήν τε ἐπαγγελίαν τοῦ πνεύματος τοῦ ἁγίου λαβὼν παρὰ τοῦ πατρὸς ἐξέχεεν τοῦτο ὃ ὑμεῖς [καὶ] βλέπετε καὶ ἀκούετε. οὐ γὰρ Δαυὶδ ἀνέβη εἰς τοὺς οὐρανούς, λέγει δὲ αὐτός,
Εἶπεν [ὁ] κύριος τῷ κυρίῳ μου,
Κάθου ἐκ δεξιῶν μου ἕως ἂν θῶ τοὺς ἐχθρούς σου ὑποπόδιον τῶν ποδῶν σου.
ἀσφαλῶς οὖν γινωσκέτω πᾶς οἶκος Ἰσραὴλ ὅτι καὶ κύριον αὐτὸν καὶ Χριστὸν ἐποίησεν ὁ θεός, τοῦτον τὸν Ἰησοῦν ὃν ὑμεῖς ἐσταυρώσατε.

Being therefore exalted at the right hand of God, and having received from the Father the promise of the Holy Spirit, he has poured out this that you both see and hear. For David did not ascend into the heavens, but he himself says,
"The Lord said to my Lord,
'Sit at my right hand, until I make your enemies your footstool.'"
Therefore let the entire house of Israel know with certainty that God has made him both Lord and Messiah, this Jesus whom you crucified. (Acts 2:33–36)

Here, the resurrection and exaltation of Jesus are understood as his enthronement as Lord of all.[83] This becomes the foundation for the rest of the narrative in which the power and authority of Jesus are manifested. Through his powerful word, the risen Jesus is able to maintain his sovereignty as Lord of all.[84]

As in Isaiah 40–55, the affirmation of the universal sovereignty of the Lord entails the claim that only he is the one who should be worshipped. In Acts 4:12, it is stated:

καὶ οὐκ ἔστιν ἐν ἄλλῳ οὐδενὶ ἡ σωτηρία, οὐδὲ γὰρ ὄνομά ἐστιν ἕτερον ὑπὸ τὸν οὐρανὸν τὸ δεδομένον ἐν ἀνθρώποις ἐν ᾧ δεῖ σωθῆναι ἡμᾶς.

There is salvation in no one else, for there is no other name under heaven given among mortals by which we must be saved.

The phrase "under heaven" (ὑπὸ τὸν οὐρανὸν) only underlines this exclusive and universal claim. The same idea is repeated in the description of the ministry of Jesus in Acts 10:36–38 in which one finds the affirmation concerning Jesus: "He is Lord of all" (οὗτός ἐστιν πάντων κύριος,

---

[83] The term "Lord" (κύριος) may refer to the name of God in the LXX. For this discussion, it is sufficient to note that Jesus becomes "Lord" of all in the sense that everything is now under his control. For a further discussion of the title "Lord," see Eric Franklin, *Christ the Lord: A Study in the Purpose and Theology of Luke-Acts* (London: SPCK, 1975); and James D. G. Dunn, "ΚΥΡΙΟΣ in Acts," in *The Christ and the Spirit: Vol. 1 Christology* (Grand Rapids, MI: Eerdmans, 1998) 241–53.

[84] See chapter five for the discussion of the power of the word of God/the Lord as the agent of divine will in the narrative of Acts.

10:36).[85] This claim follows the statement that people from all nations will be able to turn to this Lord (vs 35). Jesus' lordship over all the nations is affirmed. Statements such as these provide the hermeneutical key for the interpretation of the anti-idol passages. The overcoming of the power of the nations and their gods/idols serves to illustrate the claim that the risen Jesus is Lord of all.

The final passage that needs to be mentioned is the believers' prayer recorded in Acts 4:24b–30:

Δέσποτα, σὺ ὁ ποιήσας τὸν οὐρανὸν καὶ τὴν γῆν καὶ τὴν θάλασσαν καὶ πάντα τὰ ἐν αὐτοῖς, ὁ τοῦ πατρὸς ἡμῶν διὰ πνεύματος ἁγίου στόματος Δαυὶδ παιδός σου εἰπών,
    'Ινατί ἐφρύαξαν ἔθνη καὶ λαοὶ ἐμελέτησαν κενά;
    παρέστησαν οἱ βασιλεῖς τῆς γῆς
    καὶ οἱ ἄρχοντες συνήχθησαν ἐπὶ τὸ αὐτὸ κατὰ τοῦ κυρίου
    καὶ κατὰ τοῦ Χριστοῦ αὐτοῦ.
συνήχθησαν γὰρ ἐπ' ἀληθείας ἐν τῇ πόλει ταύτῃ ἐπὶ τὸν ἅγιον παῖδά σου 'Ιησοῦν, ὃν ἔχρισας, 'Ηρῴδης τε καὶ Πόντιος Πιλᾶτος σὺν ἔθνεσιν καὶ λαοῖς 'Ισραήλ, ποιῆσαι ὅσα ἡ χείρ σου καὶ ἡ βουλή [σου] προώρισεν γενέσθαι. καὶ τὰ νῦν, κύριε, ἔπιδε ἐπὶ τὰς ἀπειλὰς αὐτῶν, καὶ δὸς τοῖς δούλοις σου μετὰ παρρησίας πάσης λαλεῖν τὸν λόγον σου, ἐν τῷ τὴν χεῖρά [σου] ἐκτείνειν σε εἰς ἴασιν καὶ σημεῖα καὶ τέρατα γίνεσθαι διὰ τοῦ ὀνόματος τοῦ ἁγίου παιδός σου 'Ιησοῦ.

Sovereign Lord, who made the heaven and the earth, the sea, and everything in them, it is you who said by the Holy Spirit through our ancestor David, your servant:
"Why did the Gentiles rage,
and the peoples imagine vain things?
The kings of the earth took their stand,
and the rulers have gathered together
against the Lord and against his Messiah."
For in this city, in fact, both Herod and Pontius Pilate, with the Gentiles and the peoples of Israel, gathered together against your holy servant Jesus, whom you anointed, to do whatever your hand and your plan had predestined to take place. And now, Lord, look at their threats, and grant to your servants to speak your word with all boldness, while you stretch out your hand to heal, and signs and wonders are performed through the name of your holy servant Jesus.

This passage ties together the various themes that are highlighted above: the appeal to God as the sovereign Lord (δέσποτα), the understanding of God as creator and therefore the powerful one, the peoples/nations as enemies of the Lord, and the appeal for the Lord to "stretch out your hand" (τὴν χεῖρά [σου] ἐκτείνειν). The parallels with the prayer of Hezekiah in Isa 37:15–20

---

85 Jacques Dupont ("'Le Seigneur de tous' [Ac 10:36; Rm 10:12]: Arrière-fond scripturaire d'une formule christologique," in Gerald F. Hawthorne and Otto Betz, eds., *Tradition and Interpretation in the New Testament: Essays in Honor of E. Earle Ellis for His 60th Birthday* [Grand Rapids, MI: Eerdmans, 1987] 229–36) suggests that this christological affirmation finds its roots in Joel 2:28(3:5) in the context where the entrance of the Gentiles into the Christian community becomes an issue.

have already been suggested.[86] In both, God is addressed as the creator; and both contain the phrases ἐπ' ἀληθείας (Isa 37:18/Acts 4:27) and καὶ νῦν, κύριε (Acts 4:29; cf. Isa 37:20: νῦν δὲ κύριε). Moreover, both prayers are made under the threat of the enemies.[87] Significantly, the prayer of Hezekiah explicitly mentions the impotence of idols to protect their people (Isa 37:19).

The narrative that follows this prayer shows that the prayer has been answered. The sovereignty of the Lord is manifested, and neither nations nor their gods/idols are able to resist the power of the risen Jesus and his messengers. This emphases upon the lordship of the risen Jesus and the impotence of the idols should therefore be understood as interrelated themes that are developed throughout the New Exodus program in Acts.

6.4 Conclusion

In this chapter I have shown that in both Isaiah and Acts, the anti-idol polemic appears primarily in contexts that affirm the sovereignty of the Lord over against the challenges of the other peoples and their idols/deities. The Isaianic and Lukan communities are therefore portrayed as the sole bearer of the divine truth. The rhetorical annihilation of the idols serves to strip away the power of those who oppose the (renewed) people of God of the New Exodus. The delineation of the true people of God is therefore accomplished through such language.

This reading of the text should replace the view that anti-idol polemic is either merely an attempt to prevent the people of God from falling away from their religious community or an illustration of the power of God over that of Satan in the realm of spiritual realities. God's victory over the idols symbolizes the power of the true people of God over against other competitive claims to legitimacy and power. This understanding paves the way for a further examination of the relationship between the people of God and the nations in both Isaiah and Acts.

---

[86] Linda M. Maloney, *"All that God had Done with Them": The Narration of the Works of God in the Early Christianity as Described in the Acts of the Apostles* (Frankfurt am Main/New York: Peter Lang, 1991) 48. Cf. 2 Kgs 19:14–19.

[87] Haenchen (*Acts of the Apostles*, 227) notes that grammatically the pronoun "their" (αὐτῶν) in vs 29 refers to Herod and Pilate but in the present context points to the present enemy of the church. He concludes that "the seam between verses 28 and 29 is obvious." This observation misses the identification of Jesus with the apostles and the early Christian movement. The attack on the apostles is therefore an attack on Jesus himself. Furthermore, the enemy of the church is now widened to include all those who oppose the word.

Excursus: Isaianic Influence on Second Temple Jewish Idol Parodies

Anti-idol polemic naturally plays a role in Second Temple Jewish works especially when the survival of the people of God among the nations is one of the central issues.[88] In the Hebrew Bible outside of the Isaianic material, examples of idol parodies can be found in Hab 2:18–19; Jer 10:1–16; Pss 115:4–8; and 135:15–18. Jeremiah 10 comes closest to the Isaianic material although the contrast between Yahweh and idol-fabricators is not in consistent focus there.[89] Moreover, Jeremiah's anti-idol polemic does not play as essential a role as Isaiah's does in their respective theological programs.[90] The relationship between Isaiah 40–55 and Jeremiah 10 continues to be a contested issue.[91] The brief passage in Hab 2:18–19 describes the material from which idols were made. Psalms 115 and 135 provide a description of idol-fabrication similar to the Isaianic material and the dependence of the lifeless objects on their worshippers is also noted. The relationship between these passages and Isaiah remain unclear. In all of them, anti-idol polemic functions to highlight the impotence of the nations, but the extensive correspondence between God's salvific act and the impotence of the idols and their makers only appears in Isaiah.

Outside of the Hebrew canon, idol parodies can be found in different types of material. In discourse, it can be found in the Epistle of Jeremiah (Baruch 6). The idols of the foreigners are portrayed as the ones who need to be carried: "Now in Babylon you will see gods made of silver and gold and wood, which people carry on their shoulders, and which cause the heathen to fear" (Bar 6.3–4). Influence from Isaianic passages such as 46:7 is likely: "They lift it to their shoulders, they carry it, they set it in its place, and it stands there." The author goes on to describe how the idols were created and their inability to perform various tasks is outlined in detail. Dependence upon canonical Scripture is clear, and the letter shows an awareness of other

---

[88] See the survey of texts in Horst Dietrich Preuss, *Verspottung fremder Religionen im Alten Testament* (BWANT 92; Stuttgart: W. Kohlhammer, 1971); and Wolfgang M. W. Roth, "For Life, He Appeals to Death (Wis 13:18)," *CBQ* 37 (1975) 21–47.

[89] In Acts, Isaianic influence is undeniable although the Isaianic contrast between Yahweh and idol-fabricator does not frequently surface.

[90] Robert P. Carroll (*Jeremiah: A Commentary* [OTL; Philadelphia: Westminster, 1986] 254) further questions the authenticity of this passage: "The ethos of the poem is so very different from that of the rest of the book that it is difficult to see how Jeremiah could have uttered it." For a different evaluation, see William L. Holladay, *Jeremiah 1: A Commentary on the Book of the Prophet Jeremiah Chapters 1–25* (Hermeneia; Philadelphia: Fortress, 1986) 326.

[91] See T. W. Overholt, "The Falsehood of Idolatry: An Interpretation of Jeremiah x.1–16," *JTS* 16 (1965) 1–16; and Umberto Cassuto, "On the Formal and Stylistic Relationship between Deutero-Isaiah and Other Biblical Writers," *Biblical and Oriental Studies, I, Bible* (Jerusalem: Magnees, 1973) 149–60.

material besides Isaiah. In terms of arguments, however, one does not find any
development beyond that which already exists in the canonical material.

In the *Sibylline Oracles*, one finds numerous instances of attacks on the
idols. In Book 3, for example, the God of Israel is contrasted with idols:

> There is one God, sole ruler, ineffable, who lives in the sky,
> self-begotten, invisible, who himself sees all things.
> No sculptor's hand made him, nor does a cast
> of gold or ivory reveal him, by the crafts of man,
> but he himself, eternal, revealed himself
> as existing now, and formerly and again in the future. (*Sib. Or.* 3.11–16)

Dependence upon Isaiah, especially Isa 40:18–26, can be felt although an
explicit example of idol parody is absent. The sovereignty of God the creator
is established with the depiction of the impotence of the idols.

Fully developed forms of idol parodies in discourse material can be found
in Wis 13.1–15.19. This extended excursus follows the comment that the
Egyptians worshipped "creatures that they had thought to be gods" (12.27).
Various topics are treated in this long section. 13.1–9 discusses the worship
of nature; 13.10–19 describes idol-fabrication; 14.1–31 contains discussion on
the origin and consequences of idol-worship; 15.1–13 concludes with the a
further description of idol-fabrication and a statement on the worship of
animals. This discussion represents a new stage in the development of idol
parodies.[92] The first section that describes idol-fabrication (13.10–19)
"closely resembles the polemic of Second Isaiah."[93] It proceeds, however, to a
discussion of theories concerning the beginning of idolatry, the origin of which
cannot be located within the canonical texts.[94] Close parallels to Wis 13–15
can be found in the extensive work of Philo that contains polemic material
against idols and Egyptian animal worship.[95]

---

[92] See the extensive discussion in Maurice Gilbert, *La Critique des dieux dans le Livre
de la Sagesse* (AnBib 53; Rome: Biblical Institute Press, 1973).

[93] John J. Collins, *Jewish Wisdom in the Hellenistic Age* (OTL; Louisville, KY:
Westminster/John Knox, 1997) 210. See also Patrick W. Skehan, *Studies in Israelite Poetry
and Wisdom* (CBQMS 1; Washington, DC: Catholic Biblical Association of America, 1971)
165 n.7, who identifies Isaianic references behind Wis 13–15.

[94] Wis 14.21–31 lists two theories: (1) the father of a dead child set up a statue in honor
of him; (2) the well-decorated statues of rulers later became objects of adoration. See David
Winston, *The Wisdom of Solomon* (AB 43; Garden City, NY: Doubleday, 1979) 270–71 for
a discussion of the relationship between Wisdom of Solomon and Euhemerus' theory of the
origins of the gods. Winston also note the similar discussion in the *Epistle of Aristeas*
134–37.

[95] See, for example, *Decal.* 52–81; *Contempl.* 3–9; *Spec.* 1.13–29; and the discussion in
Collins, *Jewish Wisdom in the Hellenistic Age,* 209. In his extensive use of Greek
philosophical thoughts, Philo's treatment of idolatry move beyond Wisdom's treatment of
idolatry. See Maren R. Niehoff, "Philo's Views on Paganism," in Graham N. Stanton and

Moving beyond discourse material, Isaianic influence can also be felt in narrative material. In *Jub.* 12.1–15, the call of Abraham is depicted as a turn from the idols; and Isa 46:7 is alluded to in 12.5: "Because they are works of the hands, and you are carrying them upon your shoulders, and there is no help from them for you.".[96] Similarly, in *Joseph and Aseneth*, the conversion account focuses on the turn from pagan idols (10.12–23; 11.4–5; 12.12; 13.11; 19.5). Most striking of all is the story in Bel and the Dragon, a story that centers around the impotence of the idols. The inability of Bel to eat the offerings and the failure of the Dragon to protect himself best illustrates the idol parodies in narrative form. Various theories of origins have been proposed,[97] and Isaianic influence cannot be ruled out. George W. E. Nickelsburg, in particular, suggests that a "number of remarkable parallels to Isaiah 45–46 suggest that the double narrative in Bel and the Dragon may have developed as an exegesis on these chapters of Isaiah."[98] Even if one questions Nickelsburg theory of the origin of the tales, the influence of Isaiah remains likely.[99]

These examples show that Isaianic anti-idol polemic continued to exert influence on a number of Second Temple Jewish texts. The use of Isaianic phrases without adopting the full blown idol parody in Acts can be explained by the fact that Luke was constrained by the traditions at his disposal.[100]

Guy S. Stroumsa, eds., *Tolerance and Intolerance in Early Judaism and Christianity* (Cambridge: Cambridge University Press, 1998) 135–58.

[96] In *Jub.* 11.4–6, however, a departure from Isaiah is clear since the author sees evil spirits working behind the idols. The same depiction of Abraham's call as a turn from the idols can be found in the *Apocalypse of Abraham* 1–8.

[97] See Carey A. Moore, *Daniel, Esther and Jeremiah: The Additions* (AB 44; Garden City: NY: Doubleday, 1977) 121–22.

[98] George W. E. Nickelsburg, "Stories of Biblical and Early Post-Biblical Times," in Michael E. Stone, ed., *Jewish Writings of the Second Temple Period* (CRINT 2.2; Philadelphia: Fortress, 1984) 39, points to the following: "The Lord addresses Cyrus (45:1), who does not know him (45:4), but who will come to know him (45:3). He is the Lord; besides him there is no other God (45:5, 6 etc. See Bel 41). He has created the heavens and the earth (45:18; see Bel 5; cf. also Isa 45:23). Isaiah 46:1–7 is an anti-idol polemic, which begins, 'Bel has fallen'."

[99] For a further example of idol parody in narrative form, see the story concerning the Jewish archer Mosollamus in *C. Ap.* 1.22.201–4; and the discussion in Lawrence M. Wills, *The Jew in the Court of the Foreign King* (HDR 26; Minneapolis: Fortress, 1990) 132.

[100] In other texts, it is not the idol parody but the anti-nation rhetoric (from the Isaianic anti-polemic passages) that is alluded to. See, for example, *4 Ezra* 5.56: "As for the other nations which have descended from Adam, you have said that they are nothing, and that they are like spittle, and you have compared their abundance to a drop from a bucket." The allusion to the anti-idol polemic in Isa 40:12–31 is clear: "Even the nations are like a drop from a bucket .... All the nations are as nothing before him; they are accounted by him as less than nothing and emptiness" (40:15, 17). Cf. Sir 26.22. This can be compared to the use of anti-idol polemic in Acts.

22

Isaiah left its mark, however, particularly on the framework in which Luke develops his story of the overcoming of opposing powers.

Chapter 7

The Transformation of the Isaianic Vision:
The Status of the Nations/Gentiles

7.1 Introduction

In the previous chapters, the importance of the concern for the Gentiles in
both Isaiah and Acts has been shown. In the programmatic statements for the
narrative of Acts, the appearance of specific quotations of and allusions to
Isaiah highlights the importance of Gentiles in the program of Acts.[1] In my
discussion of the restoration program in Acts, I noted Luke's emphasis on the
inclusion of the outcasts and the Gentiles.[2] In my depiction of the journey of
the word of God, I examined the power and authority of the word over the
Gentile regions in light of the Isaianic program presented in Isa 2:1–4.[3] The
corresponding polemic against the idols also depicts the Lord of the early
Christian movement as the sovereign Lord of all nations.[4] Therefore, the
universalistic emphasis of the New Exodus in Acts does not require further
demonstration.

In this final chapter, therefore, I will focus on the one aspect that best
illustrates the transformation of the Isaianic program in Acts. I will first
provide a further discussion of Isaiah's particular understanding of the
nations. I will then show that the Lukan understanding of the Gentiles as an
important element in the redefinition of the people of God has transformed
the New Exodus in Acts into one that goes beyond that which is anticipated
by the Exodus program in Isaiah. Instead of providing a comprehensive
discussion of the issue of Jews and Gentiles in Acts, I will therefore focus on
ways in which the narrative of Acts goes beyond the Isaianic program.

---

[1] See chapter three above.
[2] See chapter four above.
[3] See chapter five above.
[4] See chapter six above.

7.2 The Nations/Gentiles in the Isaianic New Exodus

In this section, a listing of the passages that reflect a universalistic concern
will be followed by a listing of those that betray a particularistic concern for
the elevated status of Israel. I will suggest that the relationship between the
two emphases should be construed in such a way that the significance of
neither is downplayed. However, I will also show that the peculiar conception
of universalism in Isaiah still needs to be qualified.

a. The Universalistic Concern for the Nations in Isaiah

In Isaiah, texts that reflect a universalistic outlook are not difficult to locate. In
42:10–12, one finds an anticipation of the glorification of Yahweh by all the
nations as they see the salvation that comes to the people of God:

> Sing to the LORD a new song,
> his praise from the end of the earth!
> Let the sea roar and all that fills it,
> the coastlands and their inhabitants.
> Let the desert and its towns lift up their voice,
> the villages that Kedar inhabits;
> let the inhabitants of Sela sing for joy,
> let them shout from the tops of the mountains.
> Let them give glory to the LORD,
> and declare his praise in the coastlands. (Isa 42:10–12)

In Isaiah 51, the promise that salvation will go forth is stated. Not only will
the people of God be able to experience Yahweh's deliverance, his salvific
message will also reach beyond the confines of Israel:

> Listen to me, my people,
> and give heed to me, my nation;
> for a teaching will go out from me,
> and my justice for a light to the peoples.
> I will bring near my deliverance swiftly,
> my salvation has gone out
> and my arms will rule the peoples;
> the coastlands wait for me,
> and for my arm they hope. (Isa 51:4–5)[5]

Isaiah's concern for those beyond the people of Israel is most clearly stated
when Israel is called to be "a light of the nations":

---

[5] Cf. Isa 40:5; 42:4. The understanding of קוה and יחל as "waiting in dread" as
suggested by Norman Snaith ("Isaiah 40–66: A Study of the Teaching of the Second Isaiah
and Its Consequences," in N. H. Snaith and H. M. Orlinsky, eds., *Studies on the Second
Part of the Book of Isaiah* [VTSup 14; Leiden: Brill, 1967] 164–65) has been successfully
refuted by D. W. van Winkle, "The Relationship of the Nations to Yahweh and to Israel in
Isaiah xl–lv," *VT* 35 (1985) 448–49.

It is too light a thing that you should be my servant
to raise up the tribes of Jacob
and to restore the survivors of Israel;
I will give you as a light to the nations,
that my salvation may reach to the end of the earth. (Isa 49:6)[6] *Mission*

Given that the message of the Lord's salvation will be delivered to the nations, their acceptance and willingness to join the people of God is also noted:

See, you shall call nations that you do not know,
and nations that do not know you shall run to you,
because of the LORD your God,
the Holy One of Israel,
for he has glorified you. (Isa 55:5)

Isaiah's emphases on the diffusion of the salvific message and on the ingathering of the nations to give homage to the Lord of Israel are combined in the paradigmatic passage in Isa 2:2–3:

In days to come the mountain of the LORD's house
shall be established as the highest of the mountains,
and shall be raised above the hills;
all the nations shall stream to it.
Many peoples shall come and say,
"Come, let us go up to the mountain of the LORD,
to the house of the God of Jacob;
that he may teach us his ways
and that we may walk in his paths."
For out of Zion shall go forth instruction,
and the word of the LORD from Jerusalem.

These two emphases reappear at the very end of Isaiah:

For I know their works and their thoughts, and I am coming to gather all nations and tongues; and they shall come and shall see my glory. (Isa 66:18)

---

[6] Cf. Isa 42:6; 51:4. The exact meaning of the phrase "a light to the nations" has been disputed by some who argue against a universalistic reading. For example, Snaith ("Isaiah 40–66: A Study of the Teaching of the Second Isaiah and Its Consequences," 155–56) argues that the phrase is directed to the exiled people of Israel among the nations. Others such as Pieter A. H. de Boer (*Second Isaiah's Message* [OTS 11; Leiden, 1956] 92–93) define the function of the "light" simply as invoking respect and awe but with no specific salvific intent. Most considered such readings forced in light of the immediate literary context in which this phrase appears. See, for example, the discussion in Anthony Gelston, "Universalism in Second Isaiah," *JTS* 43 (1992) 393–94. Furthermore, as Ronald E. Clements ("A Light to the Nations: A Central Theme of the Book of Isaiah," in James W. Watts and Paul R. House, eds., *Forming Prophetic Literature: Essays on Isaiah and the Twelve in Honor of John D. W. Watts* [Sheffield: Sheffield Academic Press, 1996] 57–69) has noted, the contrast between darkness and light as a metaphor for salvation throughout the Isaianic corpus should not be ignored.

From this brief survey, one can see that the presence of the concern for the nations in Isaiah cannot be denied.

b. *The Particularistic Emphasis on Israel in Isaiah*

Alongside the preceding passages, however, one also finds many that betray a distinctly particularistic outlook.[7] In these passages, the salvation of Israel is contrasted with the judgment of the nations. A concern for the well-being of the people of Israel over against that of the nations is highlighted in Isa 43:3–4. In this text the nations become a ransom for the deliverance of Israel:

> For I am the LORD your God,
> the Holy One of Israel, your Savior.
> I give Egypt as your ransom,
> Ethiopia and Seba in exchange for you.
> Because you are precious in my sight,
> and honored, and I love you,
> I give people in return for you,
> nations in exchange for your life.

More important is the repeated emphasis on the submission of the nations before Israel. For example, in Isa 45:14, the nations are described as bowing down before Israel:

> Thus says the LORD:
> The wealth of Egypt and the merchandise of Ethiopia,
> and the Sabeans, tall of stature,
> shall come over to you and be yours,
> they shall follow you;
> they shall come over in chains and bow down to you.

Similarly, in 49:23, one reads:

> Kings shall be your foster fathers,
> and their queens your nursing mothers.
> With their faces to the ground
> they shall bow down to you,
> and lick the dust of your feet.
> Then you will know that I am the LORD;
> those who wait for me shall not be put to shame.[8]

This description of the nations culminates in the attack of Babylon, the enemy of the people of Israel:

> But evil shall come upon you,
> which you cannot charm away;

---

[7] One should also note the attack on the gods of the nations as discussed in the previous chapter.

[8] The imageries employed in this verse also appear in Ps 72:9 and Mic 7:16–17; and these parallels affirm the negative connotations of such acts.

disaster shall fall upon you,
which you will not be able to ward off;
and ruin shall come on you suddenly,
of which you know nothing. (Isa 47:11)[9]

c. Universalism and Nationalism in Isaiah

These and other similar passages highlight the tension between universalism and nationalism in Isaiah. This tension also forces one to reevaluate the characterization of the Isaianic New Exodus program as universalistic. In light of the passages that reflect the particularistic concern for the deliverance of Israel, some have argued for an exclusively nationalistic understanding of the Isaianic program. Norman H. Snaith, for example, provides a succinct statement of this position when he argues that in Isaiah 40–55, "The whole prophecy is concerned with the restoration and exaltation of Jacob-Israel, the Servant of the Lord, the Righteous Remnant, and any place which the heathen have in the new order is entirely and debasingly subservient."[10] Furthermore, he suggests that even the term "nationalism" has to be qualified when applied to the vision of the author: "His nationalism has an exclusiveness which would deny those who are of the same blood. The nation, the People of God, is composed only of the exiles in Babylon."[11] Such an extreme position fails to acknowledge the presence of the numerous passages that display a universalistic outlook.[12] Moreover, a common thread through the studies that argue for an exclusively nationalistic reading is the assumption that a universalistic reading necessarily entails seeing an inherent equality between Israel and the nations. One can argue, however, that the lack of equality between Israel and the nations is not a sufficient condition to rule out a universalistic reading.

---

[9] The consistently negative portrayal of Babylon as Israel's enemy should be noted. Christopher T. Begg, "Babylon in the Book of Isaiah," in J. Vermeylen, ed., *The Book of Isaiah — Le Livre d'Isaïe. Les oracles et leurs relectures. Unité et complexité de l'ouvrage* (BETL 81; Leuven: Leuven University Press, 1989) 124, has pointed out that "Isaiah's stress on the finality of Babylon's doom contrasts with its own announcements of a future revival and 'conversion' for other traditional opponents to Israel."

[10] Norman H. Snaith, "The Servant of the Lord in Deutero-Isaiah," in H. H. Rowley, ed., *Studies in Old Testament Prophecy Presented to Professor Theodore H. Robinson by the Society for Old Testament Study on his Sixty-Fifth Birthday, August 9th, 1946* (Edinburgh: T. & T. Clark, 1950) 191.

[11] Snaith, "Isaiah 40–66: A Study of the Teaching of the Second Isaiah and Its Consequences," 174–75. See also de Boer, *Second Isaiah's Message*, 92–100. Cf. Joseph Blenkinsopp, "Second Isaiah — Prophet of Universalism," *JSOT* 41 (1988) 91.

[12] Moving beyond the linguistic arguments of Snaith and de Boer, D. E. Hollenberg ("Nationalism and 'The Nations' in Isaiah XL–LV," *VT* 19 [1969] 31) has proposed that "when Second Isaiah is challenging 'the nations', he is really challenging Israelites within the nations." Such reading has gained few supporters as most have considered it an implausible reading of terms such as "nations," "end of the earth," and "coastlands."

On the other end of the spectrum, there are those who argue for a universalistic reading at the expense of the passages that betray a distinctly nationalistic emphasis. This universalistic reading finds its roots in the early Christian usage of Isaiah where one finds "a distinctive emphasis in the selection of texts" as "the earliest Christian interpreters of Isaiah used him first and foremost to authorize their mission to the Gentiles."[13] This emphasis on the universalistic passages has influenced many to read Isaiah as a missionary tract. Roman Halas, for example, argues that Isaiah's "prophetic universalism, which includes even the Gentiles in the participation of the messianic blessings, supersedes the exclusive nationalism which Jewish theology wishes to advance."[14] This approach fails, however, to reckon with the numerous passage in which a more particularistic reading is required. Moreover, the understanding that the deliverance of and salvation for Israel forms the center of the Isaianic New Exodus program cannot be ruled out.[15]

While not denying either the nationalistic or universalistic aspects of the text of Isaiah, some have argued that this combination is incomprehensible[16] and should therefore be understood as a "paradox."[17] I will show, however, that a complementary view can be maintained when the issues of nationalism and universalism are examined within the wider context of the New Exodus program in Isaiah. While maintaining the compatibility of both positions, one may conclude that neither of the terms "nationalism" and "universalism" does justice to the Isaianic understanding of the role of the nations.

First, in Isaiah 40–55, the existence of various kinds of "nations" or "Gentiles" needs to be recognized. Some have been identified as the enemies of Israel to whom Yahweh's power will be manifested.[18] For example, in Isa 41:11–12, the enemies of Israel are explicitly condemned:

Yes, all who are incensed against you

---

[13] John F. A. Sawyer, *The Fifth Gospel: Isaiah in the History of Christianity* (Cambridge: Cambridge University Press, 1996) 32.

[14] Roman Halas, "The Universalism of Isaias," *CBQ* 12 (1950) 162. See also C. C. Torrey, *The Second Isaiah: A New Interpretation* (New York: Charles Scribner's Sons, 1928).

[15] This is reflected in both the prologue and epilogue to Isaiah 40–55. See the discussion in chapter two above.

[16] Johannes Lindblom, *The Servant Songs in Deutero-Isaiah: A New Attempt to Solve an Old Problem* (Lund: C. W. K. Gleerup, 1951) 73.

[17] For example, Robert Davidson ("Universalism in Second Isaiah," *SJT* 16 [1963] 166–85) argues that the view of Isaiah 40–55 reflects the unique message of the Hebrew Bible: "Particularism and universalism are not opposites, they are the tension points in the paradoxical Old Testament doctrine of mission."

[18] For a further distinction of the different kinds of nations in the presentation of Isaiah, see Graham I. Davies, "The Destiny of the Nations in the Book of Isaiah," in J. Vermeylen, ed., *The Book of Isaiah — Le Livre d'Isaïe. Les oracles et leurs relectures. Unité et complexité de l'ouvrage* (BETL 81; Leuven: Leuven University Press, 1989) 104.

shall be ashamed and disgraced;
those who strive against you
shall be as nothing and shall perish.
You shall seek those who contend with you,
but you shall not find them;
those who war against you shall be as nothing at all.

This attack on the enemies of the people of Israel should not be understood as an attack upon the nations in general, however. The preceding passage[19] sheds light on the particularly harsh statement in Isa 52:1–2, one that may otherwise be interpreted as a declaration of the denial of salvation to all the Gentiles:

Awake, awake, put on your strength, O Zion!
Put on your beautiful garments, O Jerusalem, the holy city;
for the uncircumcised and the unclean shall enter you no more.
Shake yourself from the dust, rise up, O captive Jerusalem;
loose the bonds from your neck, O captive daughter Zion!

These references to Jerusalem and Zion as "captive" highlight the fact that this passage refers to those who opposed Yahweh and his people. Therefore, the inference from passages such as this one that a blanket condemnation of the nations is issued cannot be justified. It is not surprising that in another group of passages the salvific message reaches those who are outside of the people of Israel.

Second, the presence of both an attack on the nations and an offer of the salvific message parallels the fate of the people of Israel. The accusations against Israel together with the promise of salvation appear in Isaiah 48. First, the sins of Israel are mentioned:

You have never heard, you have never known,
from of old your ear has not been opened.
For I knew that you would deal very treacherously,
and that from birth you were called a rebel. (Isa 48:8)[20]

Although Israel is stubborn, Yahweh does not withhold his salvific hand from his people. This is declared within the same pericope:

Go out from Babylon, flee from Chaldea,
declare this with a shout of joy, proclaim it,
send it forth to the end of the earth;
say, "The LORD has redeemed his servant Jacob!"
They did not thirst when he led them through the deserts;
he made water flow for them from the rock;
he split open the rock and the water gushed out. (Isa 48:20–21)

---

[19] See also Isa 49:25–26 and 51:22–23.

[20] The attacks on the nations and the exile of God's people as the punishment for their sins is the literary context within which the salvation oracles in Isaiah 40–55 should be read.

The punishment of Israel for her sins and her eventual deliverance is a theme that runs through Isaiah.[21] Considering these parallels, it is no longer improbable to understand both the punishment and salvation of the nations as prominent themes in the Isaianic New Exodus.[22]

Third, the relationship between nationalism and universalism should also be examined in light of the understanding of Israel as the elected people who are to serve as witnesses to the power and authority of Yahweh. Arguing that universalism and nationalism are complementary themes in Isaiah, Andrew Wilson has rightly concluded that: "the election of a particular people ... is understood in its best sense as election to service. The election of a particular people is inseparable from the universal mission to which it is called."[23] As has already been mentioned, the people of God are to become "a light to the nations."[24] The call to Israel to be Yahweh's witnesses is explicitly made in Isa 44:8: "Do not fear, or be afraid; have I not told you from of old and declared it? You are my witnesses!" Similarly, in Isa 43:10–12, one reads:

> You are my witnesses, says the LORD, and my servant whom I have chosen,
> so that you may know and believe me and understand that I am he.
> Before me no god was formed, nor shall there be any after me.
> I, I am the LORD, and besides me there is no savior.
> I declared and saved and proclaimed, when there was no strange god among you;
> and you are my witnesses, says the LORD.[25]

This designation of Israel as witnesses becomes a link between the particularistic concern for the people of Israel and the universalistic emphasis on the impact of Yahweh's salvific act beyond the confines of his own people.

While the preceding discussion provides perspectives from which the issue of nationalism and universalism in Isaiah can be approached, an

---

[21] See also Isa 43:23–44:8 where one also finds both an accusation against the rebellious people of Israel and the promise of salvation.

[22] In this context, the significance of the phrase "survivors of the nations" (הגוים פליטי, Isa 45:20) should also be noted. This concept of remnant points to those who survive the judgment of God, a concept that finds its closest parallel in the description of the remnant of Israel. For a further discussion of this phrase, see Gelston, "Universalism in Second Isaiah," 386–87.

[23] Andrew Wilson, *The Nations in Deutero-Isaiah* (Lewiston, NY: Edwin Mellen, 1986) 8. See also the discussion in Brevard S. Childs, *Old Testament Theology in a Canonical Context* (Philadelphia: Fortress, 1985) 103–4; van Winkle, "The Relationship of the Nations to Yahweh and to Israel in Isaiah xl–lv," 452–56; and Rikki E. Watts, *Isaiah's New Exodus and Mark* (WUNT 2.88; Tübingen: Mohr Siebeck, 1997) 320–21.

[24] Isa 42:6; 49:6. For a discussion of this phrase, see n. 6 above.

[25] In this passage (43:8–13), the call to the people of Israel to be witnesses to the mighty acts of Yahweh is contrasted with the failure of the nations to bring forth witnesses to testify to the acts of their false deities and idols. For a further discussion of the theme "witnesses" in both Isaiah and Acts, see chapter three above.

examination of the wider context of the Isaianic New Exodus shows that the central concern of the Isaianic program transcends the apparent tension between the emphases on Israel and the nations. As I have shown in the discussion of the anti-idol polemic in Isaiah,[26] the sovereignty of Yahweh provides the dominating framework for the various themes developed in Isaiah. This emphasis on the power and might of Yahweh is also the focus of passages that highlight the deliverance of Israel and of those that depict the lordship of Yahweh over all the nations.[27]

The connection between the universal aspect of the salvific message and the submission of the nations can be found in one passage that stresses the ultimate sovereignty of Yahweh:

> Turn to me and be saved, all the ends of the earth!
> For I am God, and there is no other.
> By myself I have sworn,
> from my mouth has gone forth in righteousness a word that shall not return:
> "To me every knee shall bow, every tongue shall swear."
> Only in the LORD, it shall be said of me, are righteousness and strength;
> all who were incensed against him
> shall come to him and be ashamed. (Isa 45:22–24)

At the beginning of this passage, Yahweh's concern for the salvation of the nations is declared. The subsequent affirmation of the existence of the one God and the power of his will that leads to the submission of all nations shows, however, that the ultimate concern is the establishment of the lordship-claim of the God of Israel. The reception of salvation among the nations and their submission is therefore joined together by the acclamation of the power and might of Yahweh.[28]

Similarly, in Isa 49:26, the submission of Israel's enemies is mentioned together with an affirmation of the lordship of Yahweh:

> I will make your oppressors eat their own flesh,
> and they shall be drunk with their own blood as with wine.
> Then all flesh shall know that I am the LORD your Savior,
> and your Redeemer, the Mighty One of Jacob.

---

[26] See chapter six above.

[27] In addition to the studies cited in the discussion of the sovereignty of Yahweh in Isaiah in the previous chapter, see especially Roy F. Melugin, "Israel and the Nations in Isaiah 40–55," in H. T. C. Sun, K. L. Eades, J. M. Robinson, and G. I. Moller, eds., *Problems in Biblical Theology: Essays in Honor of Rolf Knierim* (Grand Rapids, MI: Eerdmans, 1997) 249–64, who examines the various passages concerning Israel and the nations in light of the theme of Yahweh's glory.

[28] Wilson (*Nations in Deutero-Isaiah*, 194–95) has suggested that behind Isaiah's treatment of the nations is the Canaanite mythic pattern of the victory of the god over all and the universal acclamation by all. In an adaptation of this pattern, the nations in Isaiah also have two roles: (1) the enemies that are defeated by Yahweh; and (2) those who offer glory and praise to the one king of all.

The lordship-claim of Yahweh is made not only through the description of the fate of the nations (both concerning their submission and salvation) but also through the election of Israel that is understood as an act through which the glory of Yahweh is manifested. Concerning his own people, Yahweh said: "You are my servant, Israel, in whom I will be glorified" (Isa 49:3). Because of his acts of deliverance for the people of Israel, Yahweh is able to claim: "I am the LORD, your Holy One, the Creator of Israel, your King" (43:15). This repeated emphasis of the lordship of Yahweh in connection with the status of Israel as the people and witnesses of Israel can again be found in Isa 44:6–8:

> Thus says the LORD, the King of Israel, and his Redeemer, the LORD of hosts:
> I am the first and I am the last; besides me there is no god.
> Who is like me? Let them proclaim it, let them declare and set it forth before me.
> Who has announced from of old the things to come?
> Let them tell us what is yet to be.
> Do not fear, or be afraid; have I not told you from of old and declared it?
> You are my witnesses! Is there any god besides me?
> There is no other rock; I know not one.

Both the nationalistic passages that depict the deliverance of Israel at the expense of the nations and the universalistic ones that highlight the possibility of the nations to receive the salvific message of the God of Israel center around the depiction of Yahweh as Lord of all. The relationship between Israel and the nations in Isaiah therefore should not be construed simply in terms of such polarities as nationalism and universalism.

The recognition of the existence of passages that show a concern for the nations must not, however, lead to the conclusion that in Isaiah the nations acquire a status equal to that of Israel. The sovereignty of Yahweh is manifested in his mighty deeds for the people of Israel; and the salvific act that the nations will witness is first and foremost an act of deliverance for the people of God. The submission of the nations therefore remains a significant element in the Isaianic New Exodus. This understanding is best stated by D. van Winkle:

> The tension between universalism and nationalism may be resolved by recognizing that for Deutero-Isaiah the salvation of the nations does not preclude their submission to Israel. The prophet does not envisage the co-equality of Jews and gentiles. He expects that Israel will be exalted, and that she will become Yahweh's agent who will rule the nations in such a way that justice is established and mercy is shown. This rule is both that for which the nations wait expectantly and that to which they must submit.[29]

---

[29] Van Winkle, "The Relationship of the Nations to Yahweh and to Israel in Isaiah xl–lv," 457. This position has gained wide acceptance among Isaianic scholars. See Barnabas Lindars, "Good Tidings to Zion: Interpreting Deutero-Isaiah Today," *BJRL* 68 (1986) 494; Wilson, *Nations in Deutero-Isaiah*, 249; and Gelston, "Universalism in Second Isaiah," 380.

These emphases upon the sovereignty of the Lord of Israel and the anticipated submission of the nations force one to question the use of the term "universalism" in its modern sense in connection with the Isaianic New Exodus. While a universalistic concern for the salvation of the nations cannot be denied, an understanding of "universalism" that entails equality among the people of Israel and the nations with an emphasis on the active mission to the nations is still lacking in the text of Isaiah. It is only with this understanding that one can proceed in examining the role of the Gentiles in Acts as the New Exodus in Acts both draws from and goes beyond the vision of the Isaianic program.

7.3 The Gentiles in the New Exodus in Acts

Luke's quotations of and allusions to the various passages in Isaiah in the development of the universalistic message of the New Exodus in Acts have already been discussed in the previous chapters. In this section, I will focus on three aspects in which the New Exodus program in Acts transcends that which one finds in Isaiah. First, the unique focus on and the active portrayal of the mission to the Gentiles will be briefly discussed. Second, the move beyond a particularistic understanding of election towards one that approaches equality among Jews and Gentiles will be discussed in connection with the Cornelius episode in Acts 10–11 and the account of the Jerusalem Council in Acts 15. Third, the peculiar connection between the response of the Jews and the move to the Gentiles will also be considered. For Luke, these transformations signify the dawn of a new stage in the history of salvation.

a. The Focus on the Mission to the Gentiles in Acts

The focus on the mission to the Gentiles in Acts needs no elaborate demonstration.[30] It will be useful, however, to highlight several passages in which a concern for the Gentiles is explicitly noted in the Lukan narrative. This preoccupation with and concentration on the issue of the Gentiles as a critical element in the New Exodus in Acts goes beyond the Isaianic program although it can be understood as its logical extension. A concern for the

---

[30] For a survey of significant works on the mission to the Gentiles in Acts, see François Bovon, *Luke the Theologian: Thirty-Three Years of Research (1950–1983)* (trans. K. McKinney; PTMS 12; Allison Park, PA: Pickwick, 1987) 323–43; and idem, "Studies in Luke-Acts: Retrospect and Prospect," *HTR* 85 (1992) 186–90. See also Jacques Dupont, *The Salvation of the Gentiles: Studies in the Acts of the Apostles* (trans. J. R. Keating; New York: Paulist, 1979) 11–33, who argues that the *raison d'être* of Acts is to show that the Gentile mission is the continuation of the work of the Jesus of the gospel.

mission to the Gentiles can already be felt in the gospel.[31] In the Lukan prologue one reads:

Νῦν ἀπολύεις τὸν δοῦλόν σου, δέσποτα, κατὰ τὸ ῥῆμά σου ἐν εἰρήνῃ·
ὅτι εἶδον οἱ ὀφθαλμοί μου τὸ σωτήριόν σου
ὃ ἡτοίμασας κατὰ πρόσωπον πάντων τῶν λαῶν,
φῶς εἰς ἀποκάλυψιν ἐθνῶν καὶ δόξαν λαοῦ σου Ἰσραήλ.

Master, now you are dismissing your servant in peace,
according to your word; for my eyes have seen your salvation,
which you have prepared in the presence of all peoples,
a light for revelation to the Gentiles
and for glory to your people Israel. (Luke 2:29–32)

The phrases "in the presence of all peoples" (κατὰ πρόσωπον πάντων τῶν λαῶν)[32] and "a light for revelation to the Gentiles" (φῶς εἰς ἀποκάλυψιν ἐθνῶν)[33] point to an anticipation of the arrival of the salvific message to people among the nations.

At the very beginning of the description of the ministry of John the Baptist and Jesus, the extended quotation from Isa 40:3–5 is found only in Luke (3:4–6) among the synoptics. The significance of the final phrase, "and all flesh shall see the salvation of God" (καὶ ὄψεται πᾶσα σὰρξ τὸ σωτήριον τοῦ θεοῦ), has already been dealt with in detail.[34] The concern for the Gentiles resurfaces.

Not only is the concern for the Gentiles explicitly stated at the beginning of the gospel, Luke also ends with a statement by the risen Jesus which includes the evangelization of the nations in the christological program. In Luke 24:47, the proclamation of the name of Jesus "to all nations" (εἰς

---

[31] For a detailed discussion, see Thomas J. Lane, *Luke and the Gentile Mission: Gospel Anticipates Acts* (Frankfurt am Main/New York: Peter Lang, 1996) who concludes: "While there is a partial krypsis of the Gentile mission in the Gospel, it is only partial. There are numerous subtle hunts of the Gentile mission in the Gospel whose full meaning becomes clear by reading Acts" (210).

[32] Unlike the usual usage of the noun λαός, the plural λαῶν here refers to the Gentiles as the parallel in the following phrase shows. This usage of the plural noun may be indebted to the language of Isaiah (e.g., 55:5; 60:5; 61:9).

[33] This phrase is discussed in detail in chapter three above. The phrase is taken from Isa 49:6 (cf. 42:6) and reappears in Acts 13:47. The suggestion of George D. Kilpatrick ("ΛΑΟΙ at Luke II. 31 and Acts IV. 25, 27," *JTS* 16 [1965] 127) that the phrase should be understood simply as "a light for all the Gentiles to see" is inadequate especially when the phrase that follows in Isa 49:6 is taken into account: "I will give you as a light to the nations, that my salvation may reach to the end of the earth." Furthermore, the metaphor of sight used in both Isaiah and Luke-Acts in relation to the reception of salvation points to something that goes beyond the mere fact of detached observation (cf. Acts 26:23). See also n. 6 above.

[34] See the treatment of Isa 40:3–5 as it appears in both Isaiah and Acts in chapter two above.

πάντα τὰ ἔθνη) is announced. This emphasis on the nations provides the link between the two volumes of the Lukan writings.[35] Moving to the text of Acts,[36] the focus upon the Gentiles is developed in the early chapters of the narrative. First, the paradigmatic statement in Acts 1:8 introduces the progression of the narrative:

ἀλλὰ λήμψεσθε δύναμιν ἐπελθόντος τοῦ ἁγίου πνεύματος ἐφ᾽ ὑμᾶς, καὶ ἔσεσθέ μου μάρτυρες ἔν τε Ἰερουσαλὴμ καὶ [ἐν] πάσῃ τῇ Ἰουδαίᾳ καὶ Σαμαρείᾳ καὶ ἕως ἐσχάτου τῆς γῆς.

But you will receive power when the Holy Spirit has come upon you; and you will be my witnesses in Jerusalem, in all Judea and Samaria, and to the ends of the earth.

While the geographical sense of the phrase "ends of the earth" (ἕως ἐσχάτου τῆς γῆς) cannot be denied, this Isaianic phrase should be understood primarily in an ethnic sense as it refers to the Gentiles.[37] This phrase provides direction for the narrative and locates the mission to the Gentiles as the ultimate goal of the New Exodus program in Acts.

More importantly, the primary concern of the Isaianic New Exodus is expressed partly through the question raised in Acts 1:6: "Lord, is this the time when you will restore the kingdom to Israel?" (Κύριε, εἰ ἐν τῷ χρόνῳ τούτῳ ἀποκαθιστάνεις τὴν βασιλείαν τῷ Ἰσραήλ;). This Isaianic focus is transformed in the answer provided by the risen Jesus since the mighty act of God is now no longer focused on the return of the exiles but on the sending out of witnesses to the nations.[38] This response of Jesus not only affirms the Isaianic New Exodus but also highlights the important reformulation of this program in that the centripetal return of the exiles toward Zion is replaced by the centrifugal diffusion of the word to the world of the Gentiles.[39] The tension developed through the emphasis in Acts 1:6 and the qualification provided in 1:8 provides a hermeneutical lens for understanding the development of the issue of Gentiles in the presentation of the traditions concerning the development of the early Christian movement.

---

[35] See the discussion of Luke 24:46–47 in section 3.3b above.

[36] To the preceding statements that reflect the concern for the Gentiles in Luke, one may also add the story of the centurion in Luke 7:1–10 as well as the pericope of the healing of a demon-possessed man in the region of the Gerasenes in 8:26–39.

[37] See Isa 49:6 and the discussion in chapter three above. See also Rudolf Pesch, *Die Apostelgeschichte* (EKK 5; Zürich: Benziger Verlag, 1986) 1.79; and Gerhard Schneider, *Die Apostelgeschichte* (Freiburg: Herder, 1980) 1.225–27.

[38] See also David L. Tiede, "The Exaltation of Jesus and the Restoration of Israel in Acts 1," *HTR* 79 (1986) 278–86, who argues that the reply of Jesus in Acts 1:8 is not a refutation of the question of the disciples but a qualification and redefinition of the program of the restoration of Israel in which the mission to the Gentiles plays an important part.

[39] Both are of course present in Isaiah but the focus of the movement away from Jerusalem plays an especially prominent role in the structure of the New Exodus program in Acts.

In the Pentecostal account in Acts 2, the universalistic concern is again emphasized. The setting of the speech notes the presence of people from all nations (Acts 2:9–11). Although it seems probable that those who are present are Jews from among the nations,[40] the presence of this list may again point to a universalistic concern.[41] In addition, in the final statement of the speech of Peter, one finds a passage that expresses concern for the Gentiles:

Μετανοήσατε, [φησίν,] καὶ βαπτισθήτω ἕκαστος ὑμῶν ἐπὶ τῷ ὀνόματι Ἰησοῦ Χριστοῦ εἰς ἄφεσιν τῶν ἁμαρτιῶν ὑμῶν, καὶ λήμψεσθε τὴν δωρεὰν τοῦ ἁγίου πνεύματος· ὑμῖν γάρ ἐστιν ἡ ἐπαγγελία καὶ τοῖς τέκνοις ὑμῶν καὶ πᾶσιν τοῖς εἰς μακρὰν ὅσους ἂν προσκαλέσηται κύριος ὁ θεὸς ἡμῶν.

Repent, and be baptized every one of you in the name of Jesus Christ so that your sins may be forgiven; and you will receive the gift of the Holy Spirit. For the promise is for you, for your children, and for all who are far away, everyone whom the Lord our God calls to him. (Acts 2:38–39)

The phrase "for all who are far away" (πᾶσιν τοῖς εἰς μακρὰν, vs 39) alludes to Isa 57:19: εἰρήνην ἐπ᾽ εἰρήνην τοῖς μακρὰν καὶ τοῖς ἐγγὺς οὖσιν· καὶ εἶπεν κύριος Ἰάσομαι αὐτούς ("Peace, peace, to the far and the near, says the LORD; and I will heal them").[42] While the phrase may refer to the Diaspora Jews among the nations,[43] it is more likely in the context of Acts 2 that it already points to the mission to the Gentiles.[44] If the audience of the Pentecostal speech is portrayed as Jews from the nations (vss 9–11), this will be the group described in the first two parts of the three-part

---

[40] Cf. Acts 2:5. The phrase "both Jews and proselytes" (Ἰουδαῖοί τε καὶ προσήλυτοι, 2:11 [vs 10]) may technically be applied only to the preceding phrase: "visitors to Rome" (οἱ ἐπιδημοῦντες Ῥωμαῖοι, vs 10); and it raises the question of the identity of the others mentioned in this list that includes both races and nations. For a discussion of the various issues surrounding this list, see Charles K. Barrett, *A Critical and Exegetical Commentary on the Acts of the Apostles* (ICC; Edinburgh: T & T Clark, 1994) 1.121–25. See also the discussion in section 4.3b above.

[41] It is possible to argue that this universalistic concern explains partly the peculiar fact that even Judea is included in this list (vs 9). As Stephen G. Wilson (*The Gentiles and the Gentile Mission in Luke-Acts* [SNTSMS 23; Cambridge: Cambridge University Press, 1973] 122) has pointed out, this inclusion "is best explained ... as a loose way of saying that all nations are present." For a discussion of the list of nations in light of the list of conquered people in *Aeneid* 8.722–28, see Marianne Palmer Bonz, "The Best of Times, the Worst of Times: Luke-Acts and Epic Tradition" (Th.D. diss., Harvard Divinity School, 1996) 143–44. In any case, the theme of the return of the exiles should not be ignored even when a hint of a universalistic emphasis can be detected in Acts 2.

[42] See the discussion in Dupont, *Salvation of the Gentiles*, 22–23; Schneider, *Apostelgeschichte*, 1.278; and Barrett, *Acts of the Apostles*, 1.155–56.

[43] See Wilson, *Gentiles and the Gentile Mission*, 219; Jurgen Roloff, *Die Apostelgeschichte* (NTD 5; Göttingen: Vandenhoeck and Ruprecht, 1988) 63; and Rebecca I. Denova, *The Things Accomplished Among Us: Prophetic Tradition in the Structural Pattern of Luke-Acts* (JSNTSup 141; Sheffield: Sheffield Academic Press, 1997) 169–75.

[44] So, among others, Bovon, *Luke the Theologian*, 241.

sentence: "For this promise is for you, for your children" (ὑμῖν γάρ ἐστιν ἡ ἐπαγγελία καὶ τοῖς τέκνοις ὑμῶν).⁴⁵ The third part of the sentence ("for all who are far away," πᾶσιν τοῖς εἰς μακρὰν) should therefore be understood as referring to a group distinct from the Diaspora Jews. This is further supported by the phrase within the recounting of the call of Paul in Acts 22:21 in which those who are far away are identified with the Gentiles: Πορεύου, ὅτι ἐγὼ εἰς ἔθνη μακρὰν ἐξαποστελῶ σε ("Go, for I will send you far away to the Gentiles").

The final phrase in Acts 2:39 also needs to be examined: "everyone whom the Lord our God calls to him" (ὅσους ἂν προσκαλέσηται κύριος ὁ θεὸς ἡμῶν). This last phrase leads one to the discussion of Acts 2:38–39 in light of Joel 3:1–5 (2:28–32). While the bulk of the passage in Joel 3:1–5 is quoted in Acts 2:17–21, only the first part of Joel 3:5 is quoted and the final phrase reappears only in Acts 2:39. First, the passage in Joel 3:1–5 should be cited in full:

Καὶ ἔσται μετὰ ταῦτα καὶ ἐκχεῶ ἀπὸ τοῦ πνεύματός μου ἐπὶ πᾶσαν σάρκα,
καὶ προφητεύσουσιν οἱ υἱοὶ ὑμῶν καὶ αἱ θυγατέρες ὑμῶν,
καὶ οἱ πρεσβύτεροι ὑμῶν ἐνύπνια ἐνυπνιασθήσονται,
καὶ οἱ νεανίσκοι ὑμῶν ὁράσεις ὄψονται·
καὶ ἐπὶ τοὺς δούλους καὶ ἐπὶ τὰς δούλας
ἐν ταῖς ἡμέραις ἐκείναις ἐκχεῶ ἀπὸ τοῦ πνεύματός μου.
καὶ δώσω τέρατα ἐν τῷ οὐρανῷ καὶ ἐπὶ τῆς γῆς,
αἷμα καὶ πῦρ καὶ ἀτμίδα καπνοῦ·
ὁ ἥλιος μεταστραφήσεται εἰς σκότος καὶ ἡ σελήνη εἰς αἷμα
πρὶν ἐλθεῖν ἡμέραν κυρίου τὴν μεγάλην καὶ ἐπιφανῆ.
καὶ ἔσται πᾶς, ὃς ἂν ἐπικαλέσηται τὸ ὄνομα κυρίου, σωθήσεται·
ὅτι ἐν τῷ ὄρει Σιὼν καὶ ἐν Ἰερουσαλὴμ
ἔσται ἀνασῳζόμενος, καθότι εἶπεν κύριος,
καὶ εὐαγγελιζόμενοι, οὓς κύριος προσκέκληται.

Then afterward I will pour out my spirit on all flesh;
your sons and your daughters shall prophesy,
your old men shall dream dreams,
and your young men shall see visions.
Even on the male and female slaves,
in those days, I will pour out my spirit.
I will show portents in the heavens and on the earth,
blood and fire and columns of smoke.
The sun shall be turned to darkness, and the moon to blood,
before the great and terrible day of the LORD comes.
Then everyone who calls on the name of the LORD shall be saved;
for in Mount Zion and in Jerusalem

---

⁴⁵ That this group is understood as referring to the Jews present is supported by the use of first person pronouns (ἡμῖν, ἡμῶν) in some manuscript traditions (D [p] mae Aug) to identify the audience with the speaker himself.

there shall be those who escape, as the LORD has said,
and among the survivors shall be those whom the LORD calls.

In Acts 2:17–21, the citation of the passage in Joel stops at the phrase "then everyone who calls on the name of the LORD shall be saved" in Joel 3:5a. The final phrase in the passage from Joel is picked up at the final point of Peter's speech in Acts 2:39 as ὅσους ἂν προσκαλέσηται κύριος ὁ θεὸς ἡμῶν ("everyone whom the Lord our God calls") alludes to οὓς κύριος προσκέκληται (Joel 3:5d). Significantly, the phrase in Joel 3:5bc that is directed specifically to the concerns of Zion and Jerusalem is omitted: ὅτι ἐν τῷ ὄρει Σιὼν καὶ ἐν Ἰερουσαλὴμ ἔσται ἀνασῳζόμενος, καθότι εἶπεν κύριος ("for in Mount Zion and in Jerusalem there shall be those who escape, as the LORD has said"). Instead of this phrase, Isa 57:19 is alluded to in Acts 2:39 (πᾶσιν τοῖς εἰς μακρὰν, "for all who are far away"), and it stands in apposition to the phrase taken from Joel 3:5d. This Isaianic phrase, one that is understood in a universal sense in Acts,[46] therefore transforms the understanding of the Joel passage by replacing a phrase in Joel that centers on the fate of Zion and Jerusalem with one that emphasizes the universal concern for the Gentiles.[47]

This transformation also forces one to reexamine the meaning of the sentence "I will pour out my spirit on all flesh" (ἐκχεῶ ἀπὸ τοῦ πνεύματός μου ἐπὶ πᾶσαν σάρκα) as it appears at the very beginning of the quotation from Joel in Acts 2:17. While the phrase πᾶσαν σάρκα probably points to the Diaspora Jews in the context of Joel, one is justified in understanding this phrase as pointing to the universal mission in the context of Acts 2.[48] The same can probably be said regarding the phrase ὃς ἂν ἐπικαλέσηται τὸ ὄνομα κυρίου, σωθήσεται ("everyone who calls on the name of the Lord shall be saved") at the end of the quotation from Joel 3:5 (Acts 2:21).

Not only does the appearance of the phrase from Isaiah transform the Joel quotation from a particularistic statement to one expressing a concern for the nations, it also qualifies the meaning of the passage in its wider context in Joel. In Joel, the passage quoted is immediately followed by an extended discussion of the judgment and punishment that will fall upon the nations (4:1–21

---

[46] As mentioned above, Isa 57:19 is also alluded to in Acts 22:21 where reference to the Gentiles is explicitly made.

[47] Barrett (*Acts of the Apostles*, 1.156) has pointed out that in Acts, the relative pronoun is generalized (ὅσους ἄν for οὕς) and the verb is changed from the perfect (προσκέκληται) to the aorist subjunctive (προσκαλέσηται). These changes support a universalistic reading as the anticipated act of Gentiles calling upon God is now in view.

[48] For the use of this phrase in the Lukan writings, see especially the quotation of Isa 40:5 in Luke 3:6 in which a universal sense cannot be denied: καὶ ὄψεται πᾶσα σάρξ τὸ σωτήριον τοῦ θεοῦ ("and all flesh shall see the salvation of God").

[3:1–21]). The precise point where the quotation ends is significant[49] as the expected punishment of the nations is now transformed into the promise of salvation to those among the nations.[50] Here, the implicit criticism of the Isaianic New Exodus is made: the nations are no longer portrayed as the object of the judgment of God since the mission to the Gentiles is now considered the focus of the New Exodus program in Acts.

In yet another speech of Peter, the concern for the Gentiles resurfaces in connection with the mentioning of the covenant of Abraham:

ὑμεῖς ἐστε οἱ υἱοὶ τῶν προφητῶν καὶ τῆς διαθήκης ἧς διέθετο ὁ θεὸς πρὸς τοὺς πατέρας ὑμῶν, λέγων πρὸς Ἀβραάμ, Καὶ ἐν τῷ σπέρματί σου [ἐν]ευλογηθήσονται πᾶσαι αἱ πατριαὶ τῆς γῆς.

You are the descendants of the prophets and of the covenant that God gave to your ancestors, saying to Abraham, "And in your descendants all the families of the earth shall be blessed." (Acts 3:25)

While the Jewish audience is described as "the descendants of the prophets and of the covenant that God gave to your ancestors" (οἱ υἱοὶ τῶν προφητῶν καὶ τῆς διαθήκης ἧς διέθετο ὁ θεὸς πρὸς τοὺς πατέρας ὑμῶν), the Gentiles are most certainly included in the phrase "all the families of the earth" (πᾶσαι αἱ πατριαὶ τῆς γῆς).[51] This verse alludes to Gen 22:18: "and by your offspring shall all the nations of the earth gain blessing for themselves" (καὶ ἐνευλογηθήσονται ἐν τῷ σπέρματί σου πάντα τὰ ἔθνη τῆς γῆς). The use of πᾶσαι αἱ πατριαὶ τῆς γῆς instead of πάντα τὰ ἔθνη τῆς γῆς should not cast doubt on the meaning of this phrase as a reference to the Gentiles. Instead of πάντα τὰ ἔθνη τῆς γῆς as in Gen 18:18 and 22:18, the phrase πᾶσαι αἱ φυλαὶ τῆς γῆς appears in Gen 12:3.[52] This is sufficient to show that the variation in Acts 3:25 should be understood in

---

[49] For a discussion concerning the ending of the quotation, see, for example, Martin Rese, *Alttestamentliche Motive in der Christologie des Lukas* (StNT 1; Gütersloh: Gütersloher Verlagshaus, 1969) 50, who has already pointed out the possibility that the ending reflects a refusal to limit the offer of salvation to the Jews.

[50] For a discussion of the quotation of Joel in Acts 2, see Gert Jacobus Steyn, *Septuagint Quotations in the Context of the Petrine and Pauline Speeches of the Acta Apostolorum* (CBET 12; Kampen: Pharos, 1995) 89–95. See also the detailed argument presented in Hubertus van de Sandt, "The Fate of the Gentiles in Joel and Acts 2: An Intertextual Study," *EThL* 66 (1990) 56–77, who has also suggested that the two gatherings in Joel (the glorious return of the exiles and the gathering of the nations to be destroyed by Yahweh) now become one in Acts 2 where the ingathering of all (both Jews and Gentiles) takes place since salvation is no longer limited to the people of Israel.

[51] So Bovon, *Luke the Theologian*, 241. Cf. Jacques Schlosser, "Moïse, serviteur du kérygme apostolique d'après Ac 3,22–29," *RevScRel* 61 (1987) 26, who, while admitting that the focus is on Israel, concludes that the universalistic emphasis can still be felt in light of the use of πρῶτον in vs 26.

[52] Barrett (*Acts of the Apostles*, 1.212) points to the conflation of Gen 12:3; 18:18; and 22:18 behind Acts 3:25.

the same way as the ones that appear in Genesis.[53] Furthermore, the use of the Abrahamic covenant in reference to the mission to the Gentiles is found elsewhere in the early Christian traditions.[54] In Acts 3:25, therefore, one finds a clear reference to the concern for the Gentiles.

The programmatic statement in Acts 1:8 and the reformulation of the Isaianic New Exodus as manifested in the speeches of Peter in Acts 2 and 3 locate the concern for the Gentiles at the center of the program in Acts. Although the nations have played a significant role in Isaiah, the concern for the nations is subsumed under the promise of deliverance for the people of Israel. In Acts, however, the universalistic emphasis provides the main direction for the movement of the narrative. This is most clearly seen in the three accounts of the call of Paul.[55] The repetition of the account at three different points (Acts 9, 22, 26) of the narrative provides structure and meaning to the narrative. These three retellings of Paul's conversion provide a framework within which the story is to be read.[56]

In the first account of the call of Paul in Acts 9, his future mission is described as one that is "to bring my name before the Gentiles and kings and before the people of Israel" (βαστάσαι τὸ ὄνομά μου ἐνώπιον ἐθνῶν τε καὶ βασιλέων υἱῶν τε Ἰσραήλ, 9:15). The second account appears in Acts 22 where one again finds an account in which Paul is called to be a witness to all: "for you will be his witness to all the world of what you have seen and heard" (ἔση μάρτυς αὐτῷ πρὸς πάντας ἀνθρώπους ὧν ἑώρακας καὶ ἤκουσας, 22:15).[57] The meaning of this call is further

---

[53] The suggestion of Ernst Haenchen (*The Acts of the Apostles: A Commentary* [trans. R. McL. Wilson; Oxford: Basil Blackwell, 1971] 209) that the exact phrase πάντα τὰ ἔθνη τῆς γῆς is not used in Acts 3:25 and therefore the allusion to the Gentiles is avoided is without basis. Cf. Hans Conzelmann (*Acts of the Apostles: A Commentary on the Acts of the Apostles* [trans. James Limburg, A. Thomas Kraabel, and Donald H. Juel; Hermeneia; Philadelphia: Fortress, 1987] 30) who argues that the change is made "out of regard for his audience."

[54] See, for example, Richard Hays, *Echoes of Scripture in the Letters of Paul* (New Haven, CT: Yale University Press, 1989) 554–57; and Jeffrey S. Siker, *Disinheriting the Jews: Abraham in Early Christian Controversy* (Louisville, KY: Westminster/John Knox, 1991).

[55] For an understanding of the accounts in Acts 9, 22, and 26 as the call of Paul, see the representative statement in Krister Stendahl, *Paul among Jews and Gentiles* (Philadelphia: Fortress, 1976) 7–23. Cf. Johannes Munck, *Paul and the Salvation of Mankind* (trans. F. Clarke; Atlanta, GA: John Knox, 1977) 24–35.

[56] The discussion that follows emphasizes narratological development and the way the intervening narrative is framed. For a discussion of the differences between the three accounts and the literary device of redundancy, see Daniel Marguerat, "Saul's Conversion (Acts 9, 22, 26) and the Multiplication of Narrative in Acts," in Christopher M. Tuckett, ed., *Luke's Literary Achievement* (JSNTSup 116; Sheffield: Sheffield Academic Press, 1995) 127–55.

[57] The universalistic emphasis is particularly clear in the words πρὸς πάντας ἀνθρώπους ("to all the world").

clarified by the direct statement of the risen Lord in which the mission to the Gentiles becomes the primary intent of the call: "Go, for I will send you far away to the Gentiles" (Πορεύου, ὅτι ἐγὼ εἰς ἔθνη μακρὰν ἐξαποστελῶ σε, 22:21).[58] Finally 26:17–18 again highlights the mission to the Gentiles:

ἐξαιρούμενός σε ἐκ τοῦ λαοῦ καὶ ἐκ τῶν ἐθνῶν, εἰς οὓς ἐγὼ ἀποστέλλω σε ἀνοῖξαι ὀφθαλμοὺς αὐτῶν, τοῦ ἐπιστρέψαι ἀπὸ σκότους εἰς φῶς καὶ τῆς ἐξουσίας τοῦ Σατανᾶ ἐπὶ τὸν θεόν, τοῦ λαβεῖν αὐτοὺς ἄφεσιν ἁμαρτιῶν καὶ κλῆρον ἐν τοῖς ἡγιασμένοις πίστει τῇ εἰς ἐμέ.

I will rescue you from your people and from the Gentiles — to whom I am sending you to open their eyes so that they may turn from darkness to light and from the power of Satan to God, so that they may receive forgiveness of sins and a place among those who are sanctified by faith in me.

In this passage, Paul is promised deliverance from the hands of Jews and Gentiles, but he is explicitly sent to the Gentiles. As Ernst Haenchen rightly points out, the words εἰς οὓς probably refer specifically to the Gentiles as the following statement within vs 18 indicates.[59] Therefore, the call itself directed Paul to go to the Gentiles. In examining the three accounts of the call of Paul, one can see a progression from a call to both Jews and Gentiles in Acts 9, to a call directed solely to Gentiles in Acts 22 and 26. Although the priority of the Gentile mission is already present in 9:15, since it is placed first in the statement of the call, this progression should not be missed.[60] Its explanation lies in the intervening events of Acts 13:46–47 and 18:6 that explicitly mention Paul's turn from the Jews to the Gentiles. Paul's initial call to both Gentiles and Jews and the eventual narrowing of focus upon the Gentiles again shows how the narrative of Acts has moved beyond the paradigm provided by Isaiah. This also points to the issue of the equality between Jews and Gentiles in the New Exodus in Acts, an issue that is dealt with after the first account of the call of Paul.

---

[58] While the setting of this call is said to be in Jerusalem, in Acts 22 this vision is connected with and interprets the call of Paul. The exact nature of Paul's visit to Jerusalem remains unclear. See Edward P. Blair, "Paul's Call to the Gentiles Mission," *BR* 10 (1965) 19–32.

[59] Haenchen, *Acts of the Apostles*, 686. The word ἀποστέλλω also recalls 22:21 as mentioned above in which Paul is called to the Gentiles. Schneider (*Apostelgeschichte*, 2.374 n.60) further argues that this points to the concept of the "apostle to the Gentiles."

[60] Charles W. Hedrick ("Paul's Conversion/Call: A Comparative Analysis of the Three Reports in Acts," *JBL* 100 [1981] 420) argues that Acts 9:15–16 is modeled upon the programmatic statement of Acts 1:8: "Acts 9:15–16 is the only commissioning statement that specifically mentions both Gentile and Jewish missions and the commission has a structure and style similar to Acts 1:8."

b. The Impartiality of God and the Soteriological Equality of Jews and Gentiles

Luke's detailed account of the conversion of Cornelius situates the Gentiles within the economy of the Lukan salvific program.[61] The first part of the story (Acts 10:1–23) centers around the vision of Peter while the second part (10:24–48) provides an account of the preaching of Peter and the conversion of Cornelius and those with him. The story is retold in 11:1–18 in Peter's report to the Church at Jerusalem. Not only does this story provide a striking account of the inclusion of Gentiles within the early Christian community, it also illustrates the way Gentiles can become part of this new people of God without being circumcised.

First, the connection between the vision of Peter and the conversion of Cornelius has to be mentioned.[62] The vision involves the question of unclean food and reaches its climax with the following declaration by a voice: "What God has made clean, you must not call profane" (ἃ ὁ θεὸς ἐκαθάρισεν σὺ μὴ κοίνου, 10:15). The problem concerning the exact relationship between the vision and the conversion of Cornelius has long been noted. There is no question, however, that in the context of Acts the vision is applied to the Gentiles for they are now no longer considered unacceptable to God.[63] This reading is confirmed by Peter's statement in 10:28: "You yourselves know that it is unlawful for a Jew to associate with or to visit a Gentile; but God has shown me that I should not call anyone profane or unclean" (Ὑμεῖς ἐπίστασθε ὡς ἀθέμιτόν ἐστιν ἀνδρὶ Ἰουδαίῳ κολλᾶσθαι ἢ προσέρχεσθαι ἀλλοφύλῳ· κἀμοὶ ὁ θεὸς ἔδειξεν μηδένα κοινὸν ἢ ἀκάθαρτον λέγειν ἄνθρωπον).[64] The placement of the vision alongside the

---

[61] The Lukan characterization of the ethnic status of the Ethiopian eunuch is ambiguous. There is no question, however, that Cornelius is considered as the first Gentile convert in Acts. See, for example, Wilson, *Gentiles and the Gentile Mission,* 171–95. Haenchen (*Acts of the Apostles,* 315) argues that the story originates from Hellenistic Christian circles and "the story of the eunuch is the Hellenistic parallel to Luke's account of the first Gentile-conversion by Peter: its parallel — and rival." See also the discussion in section 4.3f above.

[62] See, for example, the succinct statement provided by Conzelmann (*Acts of the Apostles,* 80): "the original intention of the vision does not conform with Luke's use of it. Its original point did not have to do with human relationships (Jews and Gentiles), but with foods — that is, with the issue of clean and unclean." Cf. Schneider, *Apostelgeschichte,* 2.61–64; and Barrett, *Acts of the Apostles,* 1.493–94, 497.

[63] See, in particular, François Bovon, "Tradition et rédaction en Actes 10,1–11,18," *ThZ* 26 (1970) 22–45, who suggests that the vision is traditionally concerned with the question of purity while at the redactional level it is connected to the consideration of Gentiles as being acceptable to God. Cf. Martin Dibelius, *Studies in the Acts of the Apostles* (ed. Heinrich Greeven; trans. Mary Ling; New York: Charles Scribner's Sons, 1956) 111–12.

[64] In any case, the relationship between food- (and purity-)laws and social relationship should not be ignored. One should therefore resist seeing the connection between the vision and the Gentile issue as a forced one. Mark A. Plunkett ("Ethnocentricity and Salvation History in the Cornelius Episode (Acts 10:1–11:18)," *SBLSP* 24 [1985] 465–79) has further

conversion account of Cornelius therefore illustrates the breakdown of the barrier for Gentiles to be included into the community of the people of God as Gentiles.[65] The inclusion of Gentiles into the early Christian community is confirmed by the manifestations of the Holy Spirit in vss 44–48. The issue of purity that functions as one of the primary identity markers of the Jewish community is therefore overcome in the redefinition of the people of God.[66] Moreover, the transformation of the Isaianic vision can also be felt in statements that transcend the traditional understanding of the submission of the Gentiles in their participation in the community of the people of God. In a statement made by Peter, the universalistic concern is expressed through the affirmation of the impartiality of God:[67]

Ἐπ' ἀληθείας καταλαμβάνομαι ὅτι οὐκ ἔστιν προσωπολήμπτης ὁ θεός, ἀλλ' ἐν παντὶ ἔθνει ὁ φοβούμενος αὐτὸν καὶ ἐργαζόμενος δικαιοσύνην δεκτὸς αὐτῷ ἐστιν.

I truly understand that God shows no partiality, but in every nation anyone who fears him and does what is right is acceptable to him. (Acts 10:34–35)

While this statement does not deny the unique status of the people of God in the Lukan narrative, it should at least be considered as "a criticism of the Jewish theology of election."[68]

---

highlighted the issue of ethnocentricity in the Lukan use of the vision narrative although his distinction between purity and ethnocentric ethic is questionable.

[65] While Cornelius is introduced as a God-fearer (cf. φοβούμενος τὸν θεὸν, 10:2), he is portrayed as a Gentile throughout the account of his conversion. It is precisely his status as a Gentile that provides the context for both the vision and Peter's speech. See Wilson, *Gentiles and the Gentile Mission*, 176–77; and Jack T. Sanders, "Who is a Jew and Who is a Gentile in the Book of Acts?" *NTS* 37 (1991) 434–55. The question of Luke's understanding of phrases such as φοβούμενος τὸν θεὸν and σεβομένοι τὸν θεόν is a widely debated issue. See the discussion in Max Wilcox, "The 'God-Fearers' in Acts: A Reconsideration," *JSNT* 13 (1981) 102–22; and Ben Witherington, III, *The Acts of the Apostles: A Socio-Rhetorical Commentary* (Grand Rapids, MI: Eerdmans, 1998) 341–44.

[66] For a discussion of the significance of food-laws and the question of purity in general for community formation, see E. P. Sanders, *Judaism: Practice and Belief, 63 BCE–66 CE* (Philadelphia: Trinity Press International, 1992) 213–40.

[67] Jouette M. Bassler ("Luke and Paul on Impartiality," *Bib* 66 [1985] 548–51) argues that the Lukan conception of impartiality should be examined within the context of Greco-Roman universalism.

[68] François Bovon, "Israel, the Church and the Gentiles in the Twofold Work of Luke," in *New Testament Traditions and Apocryphal Narrative* (trans. Jane Haapiseva-Hunter; PTMS 36; Allison Park, PA: Pickwick, 1995) 87. Furthermore, Ronald E. Clements ("The Old Testament Background of Acts 10:34–35," in N. H. Keathley, ed., *With Steadfast Purpose* (Waco, TX: Baylor University, 1990] 203–16) argues that "the elevation of the idea of 'the fear of the LORD' (יְראַת יהוה) to this position where it has become the primary moral characterization of human conduct is a development that took place among the Jewish wisdom circles of the early post-exilic era" (209). He concludes that "the Petrine affirmation of Acts 10:34f marks a new departure from earlier Jewish thinking by the way in which it sets

The same emphasis can be found in another statement by Peter in 11:12: "The Spirit told me to go with them and not to make a distinction between them and us" (εἶπεν δὲ τὸ πνεῦμά μοι συνελθεῖν αὐτοῖς μηδὲν διακρίναντα). This summary statement reflects a distinct Lukan emphasis and interpretation of the Cornelius story.

The concluding statement in the conversion account of Cornelius also points in the same direction: "Then God has given even to the Gentiles the repentance that leads to life" (ἄρα καὶ τοῖς ἔθνεσιν ὁ θεὸς τὴν μετάνοιαν εἰς ζωὴν ἔδωκεν, Acts 11:18). In this verse, the fact that the Gentiles are included in the people of God as Gentiles is noted for it is stated that the Gentiles are "also" (καὶ) included in the true people of God.[69] One can therefore conclude that the lengthy account of the conversion of Cornelius (and those around him) presents a challenge to the conception of the superiority of the Jews in the new era of salvation.

The issues raised in the Cornelius story are further developed in the Lukan account of the Jerusalem Council in Acts 15. Luke's report of the meeting centers around the speeches of Peter (15:7–11) and James (15:13–21), the latter of which concludes with the "apostolic decree" (vss 19–20). A connection with the account of the conversion of Cornelius is explicitly made when the incidence is noted in both speeches (vss 7–9, 14). The conclusion reached in the Cornelius story in 11:12 is reiterated in 15:9 in Peter's statement concerning the astonishing work of God: "and in cleansing their hearts by faith he has made no distinction between them and us" (καὶ οὐθὲν διέκρινεν μεταξὺ ἡμῶν τε καὶ αὐτῶν, τῇ πίστει καθαρίσας τὰς καρδίας αὐτῶν). The reaffirmation of a certain kind of equality between Jews and Gentiles is made when the issue of purity is again raised with the assertion that God is the one who is able to provide "inner purity" for the Gentiles.[70] The phrase μεταξὺ ἡμῶν τε καὶ αὐτῶν ("between us and them") is striking in that both Jews and Gentiles are now understood as being equal parties before God. It is difficult to deny that this is a significant step beyond the relative status of the people of God and the nations in Isaiah.

The Gentiles who responded to the message of salvation are now explicitly identified as part of the people of God in the statement made by James: "Simeon has related how God first looked favorably on the Gentiles, to take from them a people for his name" (Συμεὼν ἐξηγήσατο καθὼς

already established truths about the importance of יהוה יְרֵאת above the traditions of covenant and divine election to which it was originally closely related" (216).

[69] Haenchen (*Acts of the Apostles*, 355) rightly concludes: "Once again, the formulation (τοῖς ἔθνεσιν — cf. 10.45 and 11.1) shows that what is happening is no negligible special case but a revolution of principle."

[70] Note the importance of the word καθαρίζω (10:15; 11:9; 15:9) and the related semantic group ἀκάθαρτος (10:14, 28; 11:8) and κοινός (10:14, 28; 11:8)/κοινόω (10:15; 11:9) in the discussion of the Gentile issue in Acts.

πρῶτον ὁ θεὸς ἐπεσκέψατο λαβεῖν ἐξ ἐθνῶν λαὸν τῷ ὀνόματι αὐτοῦ, 15:14). The surprising connection between "people" (λαὸν) and "Gentiles" (ἐθνῶν) in this definitive statement shows that Gentiles can now be considered part of the people of God.[71] Alongside the people of Israel, the believing Gentiles are now accepted in the New Exodus of Acts as Gentiles.[72] This naturally leads to the question of the law for the Gentile Christians. First of all, at the very beginning of the episode, the question of circumcision is raised by the claim of some: "Unless you are circumcised according to the custom of Moses, you cannot be saved" (ἐὰν μὴ περιτμηθῆτε τῷ ἔθει τῷ Μωϋσέως, οὐ δύνασθε σωθῆναι, 15:1). The negative portrayal of this position (cf. 15:24) and the conclusion reached by the council show that circumcision is no longer required for Gentile believers. Moving beyond this key issue, throughout Acts 15, the validity of the law for the salvation of the Gentiles is also questioned. The act of purification by God himself in Acts 15:9 and the acceptance of Gentiles as part of the people of God in 15:14 further confirm this understanding. In addition, one finds an emphasis on grace in contrast to other requirements as the means of salvation for both Jews and Gentiles in 15:10–11:

νῦν οὖν τί πειράζετε τὸν θεόν, ἐπιθεῖναι ζυγὸν ἐπὶ τὸν τράχηλον τῶν μαθητῶν ὃν οὔτε οἱ πατέρες ἡμῶν οὔτε ἡμεῖς ἰσχύσαμεν βαστάσαι; ἀλλὰ διὰ τῆς χάριτος τοῦ κυρίου Ἰησοῦ πιστεύομεν σωθῆναι καθ᾽ ὃν τρόπον κἀκεῖνοι.

Now therefore why are you putting God to the test by placing on the neck of the disciples a yoke that neither our ancestors nor we have been able to bear? On the contrary, we believe that we will be saved through the grace of the Lord Jesus, just as they will.

In this passage, the "yoke" is explicitly contrasted with "grace" by the adversative conjunction ἀλλά. The first part contains a criticism of the

---

[71] See Jacques Dupont, "Un peuple d'entre les nations (Actes 15.14)," *NTS* 31 (1985) 321–35. For the possible allusions to the Hebrew Bible, see also Jacques Dupont, "ΛΑΟΙ ΕΘΝΩΝ Acts 15:14," *NTS* 3 (1956–57) 47–50; and Nils A. Dahl, "'A People for His Name' (Acts XV. 14)," *NTS* 4 (1958) 319–27. In discussing the quotation from Amos 9:11–12 that follows (Acts 15:16–18), Royce Dickinson, Jr. ("The Theology of the Jerusalem Conference: Acts 15:1–35," *ResQ* 32 [1990] 77) has further argued that the conjunction καὶ in vs 17 should be considered as epexegetical and, therefore, the "redeemed Gentiles are not included in the remnant; they are the remnant."
[72] In comparing the role of the Gentiles in Acts and early Jewish traditions, Alan F. Segal ("Conversion and Universalism: Opposites that Attract," in Bradley H. McLean, ed., *Origins and Method: Towards a New Understanding of Judaism and Christianity: Essays in Honour of John C. Hurd* [JSNTSup 86; Sheffield: Sheffield Academic Press, 1993] 175) argues that in Acts, one finds a separation between salvation and conversion, one that is absent in early Jewish traditions. It is only with this separation that "some Gentiles can be saved *qua* Gentiles without conversion."

people of Israel who in general had failed to observe the law themselves.[73] The second part argues against the imposition of these demands on the Gentiles if not also on the Jews themselves.[74] While a systematic understanding of the law may not be extracted from either Acts 15 or even the entire narrative of Luke-Acts, the limitation of the salvific significance of the law is clearly present.[75]

In connection with the question of the law for Gentile believers, the nature and meaning of the apostolic decree also needs to be discussed:[76]

ἀλλὰ ἐπιστεῖλαι αὐτοῖς τοῦ ἀπέχεσθαι τῶν ἀλισγημάτων τῶν εἰδώλων καὶ τῆς πορνείας καὶ τοῦ πνικτοῦ καὶ τοῦ αἵματος·

---

[73] Questions have been raised concerning the exact meaning of the verse especially in light of evidence that contradicts the understanding of the law as a yoke in Jewish traditions. The contrast between law and grace has also raised questions in light of recent discussion of law and covenant in Second Temple Jewish traditions. See, in particular, E. P. Sanders, *Paul and Palestinian Judaism* (Philadelphia: Fortress, 1977) 419–22. In the context of Acts 15, however, there is no question that the law is portrayed as having no salvific significance for the Gentiles.

[74] Cf. Haenchen, *Acts of the Apostles*, 446: "the Gentile Christian Luke, who is speaking here, has lost sight of the continuing validity of the law for Jewish Christians (which he does not contest — cf. 21.21), because all that matters to him is to demonstrate Gentile Christian freedom from the law."

[75] A distinction between ecclesiological and soteriological functions of the law may be helpful here as noted by François Bovon, "La figure de Moïse dans l'œuvre de Luc," in Robert Martin-Achard et al., eds., *La Figure de Moïse: Ecriture et relectures* (Geneva: Labor et Fides, 1978) 50. See also the discussion in John Nolland, "A Fresh Look at Acts 15,10," *NTS* 27 (1980) 109–111. For Jacob Jervell (*Luke and the People of God* [Minneapolis: Augsburg, 1972] 141), "Luke has the most conservative outlook within the New Testament, because of his concern for the law as Israel's law, the sign of God's people." This view has been adequately answered in Craig L. Blomberg, "The Law in Luke-Acts," *JSNT* 22 (1984) 53–80; Stephen G. Wilson, *Luke and the Law* (SNTSMS 50; Cambridge: Cambridge University Press, 1983); and M. A. Seifrid, "Jesus and the Law in Acts," *JSNT* 30 (1987) 39–57.

[76] The textual problem surrounding the apostolic decree is well known and most have accepted the Alexandrian reading that prevents a strict ethical reading of the decree as evident in the Western textual tradition that contains the negative version of the golden rule. See, in particular, the discussion in E. Bammel, "Der Text von Apostelgeschichte 15," in J. Kremer, ed., *Les Actes des Apôtres: Traditions, rédaction, théologie* (BETL 48; Leuven: Leuven University Press, 1979) 439–46; J. Julius Scott, Jr., "Textual Variants of the 'Apostolic Decree' and their Setting in the Early Church," in Morris Inch and Ronald Youngblood, eds., *The Living and Active Word of God: Studies in Honor of Samuel J. Schultz* (Winona Lake, IN: Eisenbrauns, 1983) 171–83; and Bruce Metzger, *A Textual Commentary on the Greek New Testament* (2nd ed.; New York: United Bible Societies, 1994) 379–83. Cf. Charles K. Barrett, "The First Christian Moral Legislation," in M. Daniel Carroll R., David J. A. Clines, and Philip R. Davies, eds., *The Bible in Human Society: Essays in Honour of John Rogerson* (JSOTSup 200; Sheffield: Sheffield Academic Press, 1995) 58–66.

But we should write to them to abstain only from things polluted by idols and from fornication and from whatever has been strangled and from blood. (Acts 15:20)[77]

While some such as Stephen Wilson have suggested that the apostolic decree shows that "even among the Gentiles there should be some commitment to Mosaic principles even though there is no commitment to the law in the stricter and fuller sense,"[78] the context in which the apostolic decree is set prevents one from understanding it as a set of "laws" that have any salvific value for the Gentiles. Many have pointed to the laws concerning "strangers of the land" in Leviticus 17–18 as the possible context of the decree,[79] but the difference both in social context and in the details of the decree argue against an exact identification between the two.[80] Even if the Levitical background is to be accepted, in the context of Acts 15 the Levitical commands may simply be recalled to facilitate the interaction between Jews and Gentiles in the early Christian community. The recognition of the sociological function of the decree should prevent one from understanding it as a universal and absolute principle.

A more relevant context in which the apostolic decree should be examined is the polemic against pagan worship. Ben Witherington has recently provided a detailed defense of this position.[81] The mentioning of the idols at the very beginning of the decree provides the key to understanding it. As mentioned above,[82] the polemic against the idols of the nations plays a significant role in the narrative of Acts. The term πορνεία may point to sacred prostitution if not a general criticism of the morality of the Gentiles.[83] Furthermore, references to strangled animals and blood may point to the cultic practices of the Gentiles. Finally, the intended recipients of this decree suggests a setting beyond the land of Israel, a context that argues against the relevance of Leviticus 17–18 that was intended for foreigners living among the Jews in the

---

[77] Cf. 15:29 and 21:25.

[78] Wilson, *Luke and the Law*, 106.

[79] See, for example, Haenchen, *Acts of the Apostles*, 469; and Conzelmann, *Acts of the Apostles*, 118–19.

[80] After a detailed discussion, Wilson (*Luke and the Law*, 84–87) concludes: "Whether we are thinking of the original or the Lucan setting of the decree, a connection with Lev. 17–18 seems improbable" (87). This conclusion is based on the fact that the correspondence between the decree and the items in Leviticus 17–18 is far from exact; and there is no evidence that the Levitical commandments are applied to proselytes in the first century. Furthermore, the Mosaic rules are only applied to people residing in the land of Israel.

[81] Witherington, *Acts of the Apostles*, 461–67.

[82] See chapter six above.

[83] See also the discussion in Peder Borgen, "Catalogues of Vices, The Apostolic Decree, and the Jerusalem Meeting," in Jacob Neusner, Ernest S. Frerichs, Peder Borgen, and Richard Horsley, eds., *The Social World of Formative Christianity and Judaism: Essays in Tribute to Howard Clark Kee* (Philadelphia: Fortress, 1988) 126–41.

land of Israel. It seems probable, therefore, that the apostolic decree is intended to call Gentile believers to worship the one true God.[84]

The apostolic decree is therefore not another set of laws to be imposed on the Gentiles but a call to abandon their past behavior to worship the Lord of the early Christians. This reading is consistent with the emphasis of the Cornelius story in Acts 10–11 that points to the worship of the one God without noting the continuing relevance of the Mosaic laws. This is also consistent with the verse that immediately precedes the apostolic decree where the emphases on turning to God and the inappropriateness of imposing on the Gentiles can be found: "Therefore I have reached the decision that we should not trouble those Gentiles who are turning to God" (διὸ ἐγὼ κρίνω μὴ παρενοχλεῖν τοῖς ἀπὸ τῶν ἐθνῶν ἐπιστρέφουσιν ἐπὶ τὸν θεόν, 15:19).[85] Therefore, the apostolic decree should not be understood as a compromise[86] but an extension of the argument developed in the speeches of Peter and James. The Gentiles will be accepted into the community of the new people of God as Gentiles when they turn to the one true God, as the remainder of the narrative in Acts also confirms.

In the narrative of the conversion of Cornelius and the account of the Jerusalem Council, the impartiality of God becomes the central theme. Believing Gentiles can now be considered part of the people of God without having to be a lesser partner in the salvific program in Acts. This equality between Jews and Gentiles and the possibility of becoming part of the people of God without having to be circumcised represent the most striking aspects of the transformation of the Isaianic New Exodus in Acts.

---

[84] Some such as Alan Segal ("Conversion and Universalism," 184) have argued that the original intent of the decree is transformed through the hands of Luke and, therefore, "the history of the Apostolic Decree is incomplete as it stands now." This may point to the difficulties behind the search for the context of the decree although the intent of the decree as it appears in Acts 15 is clear.

[85] The notoriously difficult statement in 15:21 ("For in every city, for generations past, Moses has had those who proclaim him, for he has been read aloud every sabbath in the synagogues" [Μωϋσῆς γὰρ ἐκ γενεῶν ἀρχαίων κατὰ πόλιν τοὺς κηρύσσοντας αὐτὸν ἔχει ἐν ταῖς συναγωγαῖς κατὰ πᾶν σάββατον ἀναγινωσκόμενος]) may point to the preaching of the one God throughout the world. In light of the arguments in the speeches of Peter and James, it is difficult to understand the verse as pointing to the importance of the Mosaic law for the Gentiles. Daniel R. Schwartz ("The Futility of Preaching Moses (Acts 15,21)," *Bib* [1986] 276–81) has suggested the reading: since the Jews themselves failed to observe the law, to impose them on the Gentiles is a futile effort. This view is consistent with 15:10 that notes the failure of the Jews to observe the law. *Contra* Haenchen, *Acts of the Apostles*, 450: "from ancient times the law has been preached in the synagogues of every city, therefore the Gentiles must observe the four prohibitions which it imposes also on them."

[86] So Schneider, *Apostelgeschichte*, 2.184.

c. The Response of the Jews and the Mission to the Gentiles

A discussion of the Gentiles in Acts should conclude with the mentioning of the connection between the rejection by the Jews and the mission to the Gentiles. A move from a focus upon the deliverance of the Jews to a focus on the Gentiles can be seen from the three statements in Acts made in response to Jewish rejection of the gospel:

Ὑμῖν ἦν ἀναγκαῖον πρῶτον λαληθῆναι τὸν λόγον τοῦ θεοῦ· ἐπειδὴ ἀπωθεῖσθε αὐτὸν καὶ οὐκ ἀξίους κρίνετε ἑαυτοὺς τῆς αἰωνίου ζωῆς, ἰδοὺ στρεφόμεθα εἰς τὰ ἔθνη.

It was necessary that the word of God should be spoken first to you. Since you reject it and judge yourselves to be unworthy of eternal life, we are now turning to the Gentiles. (Acts 13:46)

Τὸ αἷμα ὑμῶν ἐπὶ τὴν κεφαλὴν ὑμῶν· καθαρὸς ἐγώ· ἀπὸ τοῦ νῦν εἰς τὰ ἔθνη πορεύσομαι.

Your blood be on your own heads! I am innocent. From now on I will go to the Gentiles. (Acts 18:6b)

γνωστὸν οὖν ἔστω ὑμῖν ὅτι τοῖς ἔθνεσιν ἀπεστάλη τοῦτο τὸ σωτήριον τοῦ θεοῦ· αὐτοὶ καὶ ἀκούσονται.

Let it be known to you then that this salvation of God has been sent to the Gentiles; they will listen. (Acts 28:28)

From these three statements, one cannot deny that a connection between the response of the Jews and the mission to the Gentiles is present in the narrative of Acts. This theme should be located within the Lukan scheme of the divine plan. As early as the speech of Simeon in the Lukan prologue, both the promise of salvation to the Gentiles (Luke 2:29–32) and the rejection by some among the people of Israel (Luke 2:34) have been announced. Furthermore, Luke's use of Scripture to frame the response of the Jews and the mission to the Gentiles[87] shows that the turn to the Gentiles is rooted in the wider framework of the Lukan New Exodus program.[88] Nevertheless, no

---

[87] The clearest example can be found in Acts 13:46–47 where the response of the Jews is connected with the Isaianic promise of salvation to the nations in Isa 49:6. Similarly, in Acts 28:26–28, the turn to the Gentiles is connected with the Isaianic polemic against the idolatrous people (Isa 6:9–10).

[88] For a discussion of the connection between the response of the Jews and the turn to the Gentiles, please also refer to chapter three above within the discussion of Acts 13:46–47 and 28:26–28. To suggest the existence of this connection does not, however, necessarily imply that the mission to the Jews has ended. See Robert C. Tannehill, "Rejection by Jews and Turning to Gentiles: The Pattern of Paul's Mission in Acts," *SBLSP* 25 (1986) 130–41; and Charles H. Talbert, "Once Again: The Gentile Mission in Luke-Acts," in Claus Bussmann and Walter Radl, eds., *Der Treue Gottes Trauen* (Freiberg: Herder, 1991)

matter how the exact relationship between the two is conceived, the connection between the response of the Jews and the mission to the Gentiles does present yet another aspect in the transformation of the Isaianic New Exodus in Acts. While the Isaianic program envisions the deliverance of the people of God and the eventual submission of the Gentiles to the God of Israel, the turn to the Gentiles "because of" or "in spite of" the rejection of the message of salvation by the Jews represents a surprising move beyond the Isaianic vision.[89]

In emphasizing the acceptance of the gospel message by the Jews in the early chapters of Acts, Jacob Jervell has suggested that it is not the rejection by the Jews but their reception of salvation that leads to the Gentile mission. He concludes: "It is more correct to say that only when Israel has accepted the gospel can the way to Gentiles be opened."[90] While Jervell is correct in emphasizing the significance of Jewish converts in Acts, the connection between the rejection by the Jews and the Gentile mission still needs to be recognized. Significantly, the narrative development in Acts reveals the major weakness of Jervell's thesis since the accounts of mass Jewish converts can only be found in the early chapters of Acts and the increased hostility of the Jewish audience is depicted in the latter half of the narrative.[91] The significance of the final and climactic announcement through the quotation from Isa 6:9–10 can only be appreciated when the connection between the Jewish rejection and the Gentiles mission is recognized. It is therefore impossible to deny the significance of the three repetitive statements that provide a principle for understanding the narrative even if one questions whether or not this principle should be understood as the center of Luke's

---

99–109. *Contra* Earl Richard, "The Divine Purpose: The Jews and the Gentile mission (Acts 15)," in Charles H. Talbert, ed., *Luke-Acts: New Perspectives from the Society of Biblical Literature Seminar* (New York: Crossroad, 1984) 197–99, the existence of a continuing mission to the Jews does not diminish the significance of the three statements that provide the hermeneutical framework in which the events are to be interpreted.

[89] One must admit, however, that the failure of some among the exiles to respond is already present; and the universal manifestation of the glory of God may be related to this failure as seen in passages such as 42:1–4 and 49:1–6. Cf. Paul-Eugène Dion, "L'universalisme religieux dans des différentes couches rédactionnelles d'Isaïe 40–55," *Bib* 51 (1970) 161–82. Nevertheless, the explicit connection that appears in Acts is absent in Isaiah.

[90] Jervell, *Luke and the People of God*, 55.

[91] For an account that takes note of the literary pattern and narrative progression of Acts, see Joseph B. Tyson, "The Jewish Public in Luke-Acts," *NTS* 30 (1984) 574–83. See also David L. Tiede, "Glory to thy People Israel," in Jacob Neusner, Ernest S. Frerichs, Peder Borgen, and Richard Horsley, eds., *The Social World of Formative Christianity and Judaism: Essays in Tribute to Howard Clark Kee* (Philadelphia: Fortress, 1988) 327–41.

conception of the relationship between the mission to the Jews and that to the Gentiles.[92]

7.4 Conclusion

In this chapter, I have shown that while both universalistic and particularistic emphases can be found in Isaiah, the submission of the nations within the universalistic program sufficiently characterized the Isaianic conception of the fate of the nations. In the narrative of Acts, however, the elevation of the status of the Gentiles is accomplished through (1) the primacy of and focus on the mission to the Gentiles as the center of the Lukan program; (2) the depiction of the impartiality of God and the soteriological equality among Jews and Gentiles; and (3) the correlation between the response of the Jews and the turn to the Gentiles. The focus on the Gentiles is therefore one of the most significant ways in which the Isaianic New Exodus has been transformed in Acts; and this transformation points to a rather different era in the history of salvation.

Excursus: Jews and Gentiles in the Final Age

As in the case of Isaiah, different understandings of the fate of the Gentiles at the end of times can be found in Second Temple Jewish traditions.[93]

---

[92] As suggested by Bovon ("Israel, the Church and the Gentiles in the Twofold Work of Luke," 89), the relationship between the Lukan community and the Jews can best be described as one of "polemical continuity." An adequate treatment of the question of anti-Semitism in Luke-Acts lies beyond the scope of this study. The complexity of the issue and the question of perspective should prevent one from simply equating the criticism that is directed against the unbelieving Jews with a blatant anti-Jewish polemic. See Marilyn Salmon, "Insider or Outsider? Luke's Relationship with Judaism," in Joseph B. Tyson, ed., *Luke-Acts and the Jewish People: Eight Critical Perspectives* (Minneapolis: Augsburg, 1988) 51–75; Luke Timothy Johnson, "The New Testament's Anti-Jewish Slander and the Conventions of Ancient Polemic," *JBL* 108 (1989) 419–441; Jon A. Weatherly, "The Jews in Luke-Acts," *TynBul* 40 (1989) 107–117; and Craig A. Evans, "Prophecy and Polemic: Jews in Luke's Scriptural Apologetic," in Craig A. Evans and James A. Sanders, *Luke and Scripture* (Minneapolis: Fortress, 1993) 171–211. Cf. Jack T. Sanders, *The Jews in Luke-Acts* (London: SCM, 1987).

[93] See the survey in E. P. Sanders, *Jesus and Judaism* (Philadelphia: Fortress, 1985) 213–18; and J. Julius Scott, Jr., *Customs and Controversies: Intertestamental Jewish Backgrounds of the New Testament* (Grand Rapids, MI: Baker, 1995) 347–52. The listing of positions in these helpful discussions can be further organized into theologically meaningful categories where their differences can be understood in their proper contexts. The different understandings concerning the fate of the Gentiles can be explained in light of the different

However, these traditions reflect more the contemporary conditions of the people of God than systematic constructions of the "doctrine" of the end-times.[94]

The most prominent expectations are of the eschatological destruction of the nations. This naturally correspond to the self-understanding of Israel as the oppressed people. In the *Psalms of Solomon*, the actions of the expected Davidic ruler are described:

> To shatter all their substance with an iron rod;
> To destroy the unlawful nations with the word of his mouth;
> At his warning the nations will flee from his presence;
> And he will condemn sinners by the thoughts of their hearts. (*Pss. Sol.* 17:24–25)

Condemnation at the time of judgment becomes the dominating theme in Second Temple literature.[95] The suffering of the people is translated into the expected annihilation of the enemies of Israel, a category at times generalized to include all nations.[96]

On the other hand, one finds expectation of the salvation of Gentiles. In the *Testament of Simeon*, for example, Gentiles will be saved together with Israel: "For the Lord will raise up from Levi someone as high priest and from Judah someone as king .... He will save all the gentiles and the tribe of Israel" (7.2). Similarly, in Tob 14.6, it is proclaimed that "the nations in the whole world will all be converted and worship God in truth." This is connected to other texts that reflect the belief in the eschatological pilgrimage of the Gentiles. In *Pss. Sol.* 17.31, for example, one reads that the Davidic ruler will prepare Jerusalem for "nations to come from the ends of the earth to see his glory."

---

expressions of the role of Israel when ancient promises are fulfilled. The center of these discussions always turns upon the issue of the people of God itself.

[94] I will limit myself to the discussion of eschatological expectations. For a discussion of relationship between Jews and Gentiles during the Second Temple period, see Shaye J. D. Cohen, *From the Maccabees to the Mishnah* (Philadelphia: Westminster, 1987) 27–59; and, more recently, the extensive discussion in Louis H. Feldman, *Jews and Gentiles in the Ancient World* (Princeton, NJ: Princeton University Press, 1993).

[95] See also Sir 36.7; Bar 4.25–35; *Jub.* 22.16–22; 24.27–33; *1 En.* 90.19; 91:9; *T. Mos.* 10.7; *2 Bar.* 39–40; and 1QM 12.12.

[96] In some texts, the distinction between the enemies of Israel and other Gentiles is made. In *Second Baruch*, for example, one notes that the Anointed One "will call all nations, and some of them he will spare, and others he will kill .... Every nation which has not known Israel and which has not trodden down the seed of Jacob will live" (72.2–4). Moreover, in depicting the destruction of the nations, these authors frequently emphasize that it was because of the sins of the nations that they are punished. The Qumran community justified its own existence by emphasizing this distinction between the righteous and the wicked (e.g., 1QS 3–4; 1QH 1, 4) although the distinction between Jews and Gentiles does not altogether disappear.

As in the case of Isa 2:2–4, these pilgrimage texts are often linked with the eschatological restoration of Israel.[97] They do not, however, provide a vision for unqualified blessings falling upon the nations. Gentiles will recognize the glory of the God of Israel, but it is doubtful whether they are expected to share the blessings of Israel as equal partners. Israel remains the center of eschatological blessings. In the second part of the passage quoted above (*Pss. Sol.* 17.31), the gifts that the nations will bring in their pilgrimage is "her (Jerusalem's) children who had been driven out." Furthermore, in other texts, the gentiles will serve Israel at the end of time: "Then I saw all the sheep that had survived as well as all the animals upon the earth and the birds in heaven, falling down and worshipping those sheep, making petition to them and obeying them in every respect" (*1 En.* 90.30). Israel (i.e. the sheep) will be worshipped by the Gentiles, those who have survived the destructive acts of God. When Israel remains at the center of eschatological hopes, the coexistence of texts that point to both the destruction and inclusion of Gentiles is not entirely surprising.[98]

In some texts, the eschatological "equality" of Jews and Gentiles is hinted at. This is most apparent in Hellenistic wisdom texts that betray a universal outlook. In Philo, for example, one finds an emphasis on the equality between proselytes and Jews (*Spec.* 1.51–52; 1.309). This, however, only applies to those who willingly join the existing community as converts.[99] The Lukan redefinition of the community of the people of God itself, so that Gentiles are

---

[97] For an argument stressing the importance of this tradition for understanding the Pauline mission, see Jacob Jervell, "Das gespaltene Israel und die Heidenvolker," *ST* 19 (1965) 68–96. The Lukan transformation of these Jewish traditions need to be noted, however.

[98] Even in texts where inclusion of Gentiles is noted, active efforts to seek converts does not play an important role. Whether this reflects the situation during the Second Temple period is a matter of debate. Arguing against the opinion of most, Scot McKnight (*A Light Among the Gentiles* [Minneapolis: Fortress, 1991]) presents evidence to show that Second Temple Judaism is not a "missionary religion." This conclusion is based on his definition of "missionary religion" as "a religion that self-consciously defines itself as a religion, one aspect of whose 'self-definition' is a mission to the rest of the world, or at least a large portion of that world" (4). McKnight's study is supported by A. Thomas Kraabel, "The Roman Diaspora: Six Questionable Assumptions," *JJS* 33 (1982) 445–64; and Shaye J. D. Cohen, "Adolf Harnack's 'The Mission and Expansion of Judaism': Christianity Succeeds Where Judaism Fails," in Birger A. Pearson, ed., *The Future of Early Christianity: Essays in Honor of Helmut Koester* (Minneapolis: Fortress, 1991) 163–69. In response, Feldman (*Jews and Gentiles*, 288–341) provides substantial evidence for Jewish missionary activities in the Second Temple period. The noted evidence, however, does not reflect a systematic missionary movement; and, if one accepts McKnight's definition, available evidence does not support the understanding of Second Temple Judaism(s) as a religion that considers missionary activity the core of its self-identity.

[99] Elsewhere in Philo, the destruction of the nations is noted (e.g., *Praem.* 16). In other authors, "equality" is sometimes depicted as equality in sin (e.g., *1 En.* 90.33).

accepted as Gentiles, lies beyond Philo's theological framework. Furthermore, Luke's argument from the "impartiality of God" is also unheard of in Second Temple Jewish traditions.[100]

---

[100] Even in early Christian circles, only Luke and Paul appeal to divine impartiality as justification for the inclusion of Gentiles. Jouette M. Bassler ("Luke and Paul on Impartiality," 546–52) argues, however, that the two authors have rather different understandings of divine impartiality. Bassler argues that unlike Paul, Luke appeals to the Greco-Roman ideal of impartiality based on virtues in his depiction of the conversion of Cornelius. Therefore, "in Acts' equivalent of Paul's new dispensation, the eschatological notion of justification is replaced by the tamed and historicized notion of acceptability, and merit is very much in evidence" (551). Even if Bassler's analysis of Acts 10 is acceptable, her conclusion is questionable in light of the wider program of Luke especially in his transformation of the Isaianic program.

Chapter 8

Conclusion

8.1 Summary

In this study, I have demonstrated the importance of the foundation story of ancient Israel as transformed in Isaiah for the narrative of Acts. Through the hermeneutical paradigm provided by the Isaianic New Exodus, Luke is able to present a meaningful and coherent "history" in his structuring of diverse traditional stories of the development of the early Christian movement. As the Exodus traditions are utilized in the construction of the Isaianic vision in the context of the rebuilding of the exilic community, so the Exodus traditions as transformed in the Isaianic corpus are evoked by Luke in the articulation of an identity claim in the development of the early Christian community.

The extended quotation of Isa 40:3–5 at the very beginning of the public ministry of Jesus provides the hermeneutic key through which the rest of the Lukan narrative is to be understood. This is best seen in the way Luke repeatedly uses the Isaianic way-terminology in Acts as a designation of the early Christian movement. This use of the symbol signals the establishment of a polemic claim concerning the identity of the early Christian movement as the true people of God. Furthermore, this quotation, taken from the prologue to Isaiah 40–55, points to the wider Isaianic program from which the author of the Lukan writings draws. The various themes highlighted in this Isaianic prologue are developed extensively in Isaiah 40–55, and they become the controlling motifs of the narrative of Acts.

Moving beyond the initial Isaianic quotation in Luke, I have provided a discussion of the significance of Isaiah in the narrative framework of the Lukan writings. First, two passages in Luke are examined (Luke 4:16–30; 24:44–49). The importance of Isaiah in them is highlighted, and both passages are demonstrated to be programmatic for the narrative of Acts. In Acts itself, I have suggested that Acts 1:8 provides a programmatic statement in Isaianic terms for the development of the narrative in Acts. The three categories signaled in Acts 1:8 ("Jerusalem," "Judea and Samaria," and "the ends of the earth") are to be understood in theopolitical terms; and these categories represent the three stages of the Isaianic program: the dawn of the era of salvation upon Jerusalem, the restoration of Israel, and the mission to the

Gentiles. In the critical turn of the narrative in Acts 13:46–47, Luke's focus upon the Gentiles is emphasized through the Isaianic quotation of Isa 49:6. Finally, the conclusion of the Lukan narrative in Acts 28:25–28 is again constructed around an Isaianic quotation. The significance of this quotation can be recognized only when it is examined together with the quotation of Isa 40:3–5 in Luke 3:4–6.

In the four subsequent chapters, I have discussed the motifs introduced in the Isaianic prologue to Isa 40:1–11: the restoration of Israel, the word of God, the anti-idol polemic, and the status of the nations/Gentiles. I have attempted to show how these Isaianic motifs also play a critical role in the narrative of Acts. Furthermore, I have demonstrated the significance of the Isaianic context for understanding these motifs as they are developed in Acts. In discussing the restoration program in both Isaiah and Acts, I have shown how this program lends unity to the various stories in the early chapters of Acts. From the reconstitution of the Twelve in Acts 1 to the concern for the outcasts in the story of the Ethiopian eunuch in Acts 8, the early chapters of Acts are best examined within the Isaianic hope of the restoration of the people of God. In discussing the role of the word of God in Acts, I have highlighted the often ignored emphasis of the traveling of the powerful word in the narrative of Acts. The goal of this journey is to create the "community of the word." In discussing the anti-idol polemic, I have demonstrated the repeated emphases on this motif throughout the narrative of Acts. This polemic serves to establish the unique lordship of Jesus within the early Christian community. Finally, in discussing the status of the nations/Gentiles in Isaiah and in Acts, I have demonstrated how the Isaianic vision has been transformed in the Lukan program. Unlike the Isaianic New Exodus, the New Exodus in Acts provides a striking vision of the soteriological equality of the Jews and the Gentiles.

In sum, through an examination of individual Isaianic quotations, the wider narrative framework of Acts, and the role of Isaianic motifs in the narrative of Acts, the significance of the Isaianic New Exodus behind the story of Acts can no longer be doubted. The influence of the Isaianic vision cannot be limited to isolated quotations and allusions. The entire Isaianic New Exodus program provides the structural framework for the narrative of Acts as well as the various emphases developed within this framework. The national story of the ancient Israelite tradition provides the foundation story through which the identity of the early Christian movement can be constructed.

8.2 Implications for the Study of the Lukan Use of Scripture

A more fundamental concern of this study is the understanding of the use of Scripture in the Lukan writings. The contributions of this study to the ongoing discussion can be briefly outlined.

First, the study of the importance of scriptural traditions behind the Lukan story should not be limited to an examination of individual quotations and allusions. The role of the scriptural story behind the pattern of the narrative also needs to be highlighted. An appreciation of the wider significance of scriptural traditions may supplement if not replace previous attempts to justify the existence of various Lukan passages by appealing to either editorial "carelessness" or excessive burden of the Lukan sources.

Second, the emphasis on the christological use of Scripture should be balanced by an emphasis on the ecclesiological significance of the appropriation of scriptural traditions. The concerns expressed in the later christological controversies should not be read back into the Lukan narrative without adequate justification. Furthermore, an emphasis on the typological use of Scripture that focuses primarily on individual figures of Israel's past should be balanced by an approach that emphasizes the broader story in which the individuals play a part.

This leads to the third area concerning the "role" of Scripture in the Lukan writings. The hermeneutical use of Scripture should be highlighted even when the significance of the proof-from-prophecy paradigm is affirmed. A more significant point is that the scriptural traditions should not be understood simply as "passive" entities in which individual parts can be used by various authors. The "active" role of scriptural traditions in the presentation of the Lukan story needs to be stressed. The contribution of Scripture in the selection and organization of traditional material has to be recognized in any attempt to perform either diachronic or synchronic analyses.

Fourth, the dichotomy of narrative and speech evident in numerous studies of the Lukan use of Scripture should be avoided. Many studies have concentrated on the role of Scripture in the construction of the Lukan speeches. The narrative has, however, been ignored. This may partly be due to an overemphasis on the christological use of Scripture that is evident in the Lukan speeches in Acts. The significance of Scripture behind various "stories" should also be emphasized.

Fifth, the transformation of the scriptural tradition within the Lukan writings has often been ignored. In many instances, the power of the text can only be appreciated in the way it goes beyond the scriptural paradigm from which it has been drawn. One should be reminded that in any use of "ancient" texts, the embedded meaning of the source text is both affirmed and qualified.

Therefore, in any examination of the use of Scripture in the Lukan writings, the investigation has to go beyond the simple identification of the source text.

Finally, the intimate connection between allusions and the sociological setting of these allusions also needs to be stressed. One should be aware of the possibility that certain scriptural passages are quoted precisely because they are also quoted by other competing communities. The polemical function of the use of Scripture should, therefore, be noted. In other words, the history of the use of similar scriptural traditions also needs to be considered. This realization points to the direction in which a further study of the Lukan use of Scripture might proceed.

8.3 Implications for the Study of the Theology and Narrative of Acts

The contribution of this study is not limited to the area of the Lukan use of Scripture. Its significance for understanding the wider issues in the theology and narrative of Acts should also be considered.

First, in recognizing the importance of scriptural traditions in the construction of the Lukan narrative, this study provides a possibility of reopening the discussion concerning the purpose of the Lukan writings. Moving beyond the concentration on the delay of the parousia, this study shows the significance of the concern for the identity of the early Christian community. No discussion concerning the purpose of the Lukan writings can avoid the question of the Lukan use of Scripture.

Second, recognizing the significance of the Isaianic New Exodus also forces one to reevaluate the structure of the narrative of Acts. Recognizing the theopolitical significance of Acts 1:8 in terms of the Isaianic program provides a starting point for any reexamination of the development of the Lukan narrative.

Third, this study also participates, albeit in a limited way, in the current debate concerning the role of the Jews in the Lukan writings. This study has suggested that the emphasis on the Gentile issue should be balanced by the emphasis on the restoration of Israel in the early chapters of Acts. On the other hand, the recognition of the transformation of the Isaianic vision in Acts should prevent one from concentrating solely on the early chapters when examining the question of the Jews in the Lukan writings. In short, both the continuity and the discontinuity with the past have to be recognized.

Fourth, the study of the journey of the word of God provides an opportunity to study the travel narrative in Acts from a fresh perspective. The circular journeys of Paul, among others, should not overshadow the linear journey of the word. When the role of the word in the travel narrative in Acts is recognized, the significance of the parallels with the travel of the Lukan Jesus in the central section of Luke can be addressed. More specifically, opening the discussion concerning the possible relationship between the Lukan Jesus in Luke and the word in Acts provides exciting opportunities for further study of Lukan christology.

Fifth, the focus on the anti-idol polemic provides a basis on which various seemingly unrelated confrontation stories in Acts can be examined. Furthermore, these stories should no longer be examined primarily within the context provided by Greco-Roman romance literature. Understanding these stories in light of the anti-idol polemic of the Jewish traditions forces one to reexamine the function of these stories especially since they constitute a significant part of the Lukan narrative.

Finally, the recent debate concerning the unity of Luke and Acts should also be reexamined considering the role the Isaianic New Exodus plays in the Lukan writings. The parallels between the portrayal of Jesus in Luke and the word in Acts affirm the narrative unity of the two works. More importantly, the existence of the wider Isaianic story behind the Lukan writings allows one to consider an understanding of the Lukan writings in terms of their "scriptural unity." While the New Exodus program is introduced in Luke where the coming of the salvation of God is depicted in Isaianic terms, the further development of the Isaianic program can only be found in the narrative of Acts. Without probing further into the significance of the Isaianic program in the first volume of the Lukan writings, one can at least affirm that the same scriptural "story" underlies the two volumes of the Lukan writings. The role of Isaiah in Luke should be reexamined; and the debate concerning the unity of Luke-Acts cannot be considered a closed one.

All these only reaffirm the contention that the study of Lukan theology cannot be separated from the study of the use of Scripture in the Lukan writings. A study of one promises to illuminate aspects of the study of the other.

Bibliography

Adams, Percy. *Travel Literature and the Evolution of the Novel.* Lexington, KY: University Press of Kentucky, 1983.

Aejmelaeus, L. *Die Rezeption der Paulusbriefe in der Miletrede (Apg. 20:18–35).* Helsinki: Academia Scientiarum Fennicae, 1987.

Aitken, Kenneth T. "Hearing and Seeing: Metamorphoses of a Motif in Isaiah 1–39," in Philip R. Davies and David J. A. Clines, eds., *Among the Prophets: Language, Image and Structure in the Prophetic Writings*, 12–41. JSOTSup 144. Sheffield: JSOT Press, 1993.

Aletti, Jean-Noël. "Jésus à Nazareth (Lc 4, 16–30): Prophétie Écriture et Typologie," *À Cause de l'Évangile: Études sur les Synoptiques et les Actes: Offertes au P. Jacques Dupont, O. S. B. à l'occasion de son 70ᵉ anniversaire*, 431–51. Paris: Cerf, 1985.

Alexander, Loveday C. A. "'In Journeying Often': Voyaging in the Acts of the Apostles and in Greek Romance," in Christopher M. Tuckett, ed., *Luke's Literary Achievement*, 17–49. Sheffield: Sheffield Academic Press, 1995.

___. *The Preface to Luke's Gospel: Literary Convention and Social Context in Luke 1.1–4 and Acts 1.1.* SNTSMS 78. Cambridge: Cambridge University Press, 1993.

Allen, O. Wesley, Jr. *The Death of Herod: The Narrative and Theological Function of Retribution in Luke-Acts.* Atlanta, GA: Scholars Press, 1997.

Allison, Dale C., Jr. *The New Moses: A Matthean Typology.* Minneapolis: Fortress, 1993.

Anderson, Bernhard W. *Creation Versus Chaos: The Reinterpretation of Mythical Symbolism in the Bible.* New York: Association Press, 1967.

___. "Exodus and Convenant in Second Isaiah and Prophetic Tradition," in F. M. Cross, W. E. Lemke, and P. D. Miller, Jr., eds., *Magnalia Dei: The Mighty Acts of God*, 339–60. New York: Doubleday, 1976.

___. "Exodus Typology in Second Isaiah," in B. W. Anderson and W. Harrelson, eds., *Israel's Prophetic Heritage: Essays in Honor of James Muilenburg*, 177–95. New York: Harper, 1962.

Ashby, Godfrey. "The Chosen People: Isaiah 40–55," *JTSA* 64 (1988) 34–38.

Bachmann, Michael. *Jerusalem und der Tempel: Die geographisch-theologischen Elemente in der lukanischen Sicht des jüdischen Jultzentrums.* BWANT 109. Stuttgart: Kohlhammer, 1980.

Balentine, George. L. "Death of Jesus as a New Exodus," *RevExp* 59 (1962) 27–44.

Baltzer, Klaus. "Liberation from Debt Slavery After the Exile in Second Isaiah and Nehemiah," in Patrick D. Miller, Jr., Paul D. Hanson, and S. Dean McBride, eds., *Ancient Israelite Religion: Essays in Honor of Frank Moore Cross*, 477–84. Philadelphia: Fortress, 1987.

___. "The Meaning of the Temple in the Lukan Writings," *HTR* 58 (1965) 263–77.

Bammel, Ernst. "Der Text von Apostelgeschichte 15," in Jacob Kremer, ed., *Les Actes des Apôtres: Traditions, rédaction, théologie*, 439–46. BETL 48. Leuven: Leuven University Press, 1979.

___. "πτωχός, πτωχεία, πτωχεύω," *TDNT* 6 (1968) 885–915.

Barrett, Charles K. *A Critical and Exegetical Commentary on the Acts of the Apostles*, 2 vols. ICC. Edinburgh: T & T Clark, 1994, 1998.

___. *Luke the Historian in Recent Study.* London: Epworth, 1961.

___. "Paul's Address to the Ephesian Elders," in Jacob Jervell and Wayne A Meeks, ed., *God's Christ and His People*, 107–21. Oslo: Universitetsforlaget, 1977.

___. "The First Christian Moral Legislation," in M. Daniel Carroll R., David J. A. Clines and Philip R. Davies, eds., *The Bible in Human Society: Essays in Honour of John Rogerson*, 58–66. JSOTSup 200. Sheffield: Sheffield Academic Press, 1995.

___. "The Gentile Mission as an Eschatological Phenomenon," in W. Hulitt Gloer, ed., *Eschatology and the New Testament: Essays in Honor of George Raymond Beasley-Murray*, 65–75. Peabody, MA: Hendrickson, 1988.

___. "The Third Gospel as a Preface to Acts? Some Reflections," in Frans van Segbroeck, Christopher M. Tuckett, Gilbert van Belle and J. Verheyden, eds., *The Four Gospels: Festschrift Frans Neirynck*, vol. 2, 1451–66. BETL 100. Leuven: Peeters, 1992.

Barstad, Hans M. *A Way in the Wilderness: The "Second Exodus" in the Message of Second Isaiah*. Manchester: University of Manchester Press, 1989.

Bascom, Robert A. "Preparing the Way — Midrash in the Bible," in Philip C. Stine, ed., *Issues in Bible Translation*, 221–46. London: United Bible Societies, 1988.

Bassler, Jouette M. "Luke and Paul on Impartiality," *Bib* 66 (1985) 546–52.

Batto, Bernard F. *Slaying the Dragon: Mythmaking in the Biblical Tradition*. Louisville, KY: Westminster/John Knox, 1992.

Bauckham, Richard. *God Crucified: Monotheism and Christology in the New Testament*. Grand Rapids, MI: Eerdmans, 1999.

___, ed. *The Gospels for All Christians: Rethinking the Gospel Audiences*. Grand Rapids, MI: Eerdmans, 1998.

___, ed. *The Book of Acts in its Palestinian Setting*. Grand Rapids, MI: Eerdmans, 1995.

Bauernfeind, O. "μάταιος," *TDNT* 4 (1967) 519–22.

Baumgarten, Joseph M. "The Duodecimal Courts of Qumran, the Apocalypse, and the Sanhedrin," *JBL* 95 (1976) 59–78.

Beale, Gregory K. "An Exegetical and Theological Consideration of the Hardening of Pharaoh's Heart in Exodus 4–14 and Romans 9," *TrinJ* 5 (1984) 129–54.

___. "Isaiah vi 9–13: A Retributive Taunt Against Idolatry," *VT* 41 (1991) 257–78.

Beaudet, Roland. "La typologie de l'Exode dans le Second-Isaie," *LavalTPh* 19 (1963) 12–21.

Beavis, Mary A. *Mark's Audience: The Literary and Social Setting of Mark 4.11–12*. JSNTSup 33. Sheffield: JSOT Press, 1989.

Beck, B. E. "The Common Authorship of Luke and Acts," *NTS* 23 (1977) 346–52.

Becker, Uwe. *Jesaja — von der Botschaft zum Buch*. Göttingen: Vandenhoeck & Ruprecht, 1997.

Beecher, Willis J. "Torah: A Word-Study in the Old Testament," *JBL* 24 (1905) 1–16.

Beentjes, Pancratius C. "Wisdom of Solomon 3,1–4,19 and the Book of Isaiah," in J. van Ruiten and M. Vervenne, eds., *Studies in the Book of Isaiah: Festschrift Willem A. M. Beuken*, 413–20. BETL 132. Leuven: Leuven University Press, 1997.

Begg, Christopher T. "Babylon in the Book of Isaiah," in J. Vermeylen, ed., *The Book of Isaiah — Le Livre d'Isaïe. Les oracles et leurs relectures. Unité et complexité de l'ouvrage*, 121–25. BETL 81. Leuven: Leuven University Press, 1989.

___. "Foreigners in Third Isaiah," *TBT* 23 (1985) 90–108.

Bellinger, William H., Jr. "The Psalms and Acts: Reading and Rereading," in N. H. Keathley, ed., *With Steadfast Purpose*, 127–43. Waco, TX: Baylor University, 1990.

___, and William R. Farmer, eds. *Jesus and the Suffering Servant: Isaiah 53 and Christian Origins*. Harrisburg, PA: Trinity Press International, 1998.

Bellinzoni, Arthur, ed. *The Two-Source Hypothesis: A Critical Appraisal*. Macon, GA: Mercer, 1985.

Benoit, Pierre. "Some Notes on the 'Summaries' in Acts 2, 4, 5," *Jesus and the Gospel*, vol. 2, 95–103. Trans. B. Weatherhead. New York: Seabury, 1974.

Bergholz, Thomas. *Der Aufbau des lukanischen Doppelwerkes: Untersuchungen zum formallisterarischen Charakter von Lukas-Evangelium und Apostelgeschichte.* Frankfurt am Main/New York: Peter Lang, 1995.

Best, Ernst. "Acts XIII. 1–3," *JTS* 11 (1960) 344–48.

Betori, Giuseppe. "Luke 24:47: Jerusalem and the Beginning of the Preaching to the Pagans in the Acts of the Apostles," in Gerald O'Collins and Gilberto Marconi, eds., *Luke and Acts*, 103–20, 235–43. Trans. Matthew J. O'Connell. New York: Paulist, 1993.

Betz, Hans. "Jesus as Divine Man," in F. Thomas Trotter, ed., *Jesus and the Historian: Essays Written in Honor of Ernest Cadman Colwell*, 114–33. Philadelphia: Westminster, 1968.

Betz, Otto. "Jesus and Isaiah 53," in William H. Bellinger, Jr., and William R. Farmer, eds., *Jesus and the Suffering Servant: Isaiah 53 and Christian Origins*, 70–87. Harrisburg, PA: Trinity Press International, 1998.

———. "The Concept of the so-called 'Divine Man' in Mark's Christology," in David E. Aune, ed., *Studies in New Testament and Early Christian Literature: Essays in Honor of Allen P. Wikgren*, 229–40. NovTSup 33. Leiden: Brill, 1972.

Beuken, W. A. M. "An Example of the Isaianic Legacy of Trito-Isaiah," in J. W. van Henten et al., eds., *Tradition and Re-Interpretation in Jewish and Early Christian Literature: Essays in Honour of Jurgen C. H. Lebram*, 48–64. Leiden: Brill, 1986.

———. "Mispat: The First Servant Song and its Context," *VT* 22 (1972) 1–30.

———. "Servant and Herald of Good Tidings. Isaiah 61 as an Interpretation of Isaiah 40–55," in J. Vermeylen, ed., *The Book of Isaiah — Le Livre d'Isaïe. Les oracles et leurs relectures. Unité et complexité de l'ouvrage*, 411–42. BETL 81. Leuven: Leuven University Press, 1989.

———. "The Main Theme of Trito-Isaiah 'The Servants of Yahweh'," *JSOT* 47 (1990) 67–87.

Bieler, Ludwig. ΘΕΙΟΣ ANHP: *Das Bild des "göttlichen Menschen" in Spätantike und Frühchristentum*, 2 vols. Darmstadt: Wissenschaftliche Buchgesellschaft, 1976.

Blair, Edward P. "Paul's Call to the Gentiles Mission," *BR* 10 (1965) 19–32.

Blank, Sheldon. "Studies in Deutero-Isaiah," *HUCA* 15 (1940) 1–46.

Blenkinsopp, Joseph. "Scope and Depth of the Exodus Tradition in Deutero-Isaiah, 40–55," *Dynamism of Biblical Tradition*, 41–50. Concilium 20. New York: Paulist, 1967.

———. "Second Isaiah — Prophet of Universalism," *JSOT* 41 (1988) 83–103.

Blomberg, Craig L. "Midrash, Chiasmus, and the Outline of Luke's Central Section," in R. T. France and David Wenham, eds., *Gospel Perspectives. III. Studies in Midrash and Historiography*, 217–59. Sheffield: JSOT Press, 1983.

———. "The Law in Luke-Acts," *JSNT* 22 (1984) 53–80.

Bock, Darrell L. "Jesus as Lord in Acts and in the Gospel Message," *BSac* 143 (1986) 146–54.

———. *Luke*, 2 vols. BECNT 3A & 3B. Grand Rapids, MI: Baker, 1994–96.

———. *Proclamation from Prophecy and Pattern: Lucan Old Testament Christology.* JSNTSup 12. Sheffield: Sheffield Academic Press, 1987.

Boismard, Marie-Émile. "Le 'Concile' de Jérusalem (Act 15,1–33): Essai de critique littéraire," *EthL* 64 (1988) 433–40.

———, and Arnaud Lamouille. *Les Actes des deux Apôtres, III: Analyses Littéraires.* Paris: Gabalda, 1990.

Bonnard, Pierre E. *Le Second Isaïe, son disciple et leurs éditerus.* SB. Paris: Gabalda, 1972.

Bonz, Marianne Palmer. "The Best of Times, the Worst of Times: Luke-Acts and Epic Tradition." Th.D. diss., Harvard Divinity School, 1996.

Borgen, Peder. "Catalogues of Vices, The Apostolic Decree, and the Jerusalem Meeting," in Jacob Neusner, Ernest S. Frerichs, Peder Borgen, and Richard Horsley, eds., *The Social World of Formative Christianity and Judaism: Essays in Tribute to Howard Clark Kee*, 126–41. Philadelphia: Fortress, 1988.

———. "From Paul to Luke: Observations toward Clarification of the Theology of Luke-Acts," *CBQ* 31 (1969) 168–82.

258   *Bibliography*

___. "Philo, Luke and Geography," *Paul Preaches Circumcision and Pleases Men and Other Essays on Christian Origins*, 59–71. Norway: TAPIR, 1983.

Bovon, François. *Das Evangelium nach Lukas: 1. Teilband Lk 1,1–9,50*. EKK III/1. Zürich: Benziger Verlag, 1989.

___. *Das Evangelium nach Lukas: 2. Teilband Lk 9,51–14,35*. EKK III/2. Zürich: Benziger Verlag, 1996.

___. *De Vocatione Gentium: Histoire de l'interprétation d'Act. 10,1–11,18 dans les six premier siècles*. BGBE 8. Tübingen: Mohr Siebeck, 1967.

___. "'How well the Holy Spirit Spoke Through the Prophet Isaiah to Your Ancestors!' (Acts 28:25)," *New Testament Traditions and Apocryphal Narrative*, 43–50. Trans. Jane Haapiseva-Hunter. PTMS 36. Allison Park, PA: Pickwick, 1995.

___. "Israel, the Church and the Gentiles in the Twofold Work of Luke," *New Testament Traditions and Apocryphal Narrative*, 81–95. Trans. Jane Haapiseva-Hunter. PTMS 36. Allison Park, PA: Pickwick, 1995.

___. "La figure de Moïse dans l'œuvre de Luc," in Robert Martin-Archard et al., eds., *La Figure de Moïse: Ecriture et relectures*, 47–65. Geneva: Labor et Fides, 1978.

___. *Luke the Theologian: Thirty-Three Years of Research (1950–1983)*. Trans. K. McKinney. PTMS 12. Allison Park, PA: Pickwick, 1987.

___. "Studies in Luke-Acts: Retrospect and Prospect," *HTR* 85 (1992) 175–96.

___. "The Effect of Realism and Prophetic Ambiguity in the Works of Luke," *New Testament Traditions and Apocryphal Narrative*, 97–104. Trans. Jane Haapiseva-Hunter. PTMS 36. Allison Park, PA: Pickwick, 1995.

___. "Tradition et rédaction en Actes 10,1–11,18," *ThZ* 26 (1970) 22–45.

Brassey, Paul Del. "Metaphor and the Incomparable God in Isaiah 40–55." Th.D. diss., Harvard University, 1997.

Brawley, Robert L. *Luke-Acts and the Jews: Conflict, Apology, and Conciliation*. SBLMS 33. Atlanta, GA: Scholars, 1987.

Brent, Allen. "Luke-Acts and the Imperial Cult in Asia Minor," *JTS* 48 (1997) 411–38.

Brewer, David Instone. *Techniques and Assumptions in Jewish Exegesis before 70 CE*. TSAJ 30. Tübingen: Mohr Siebeck, 1992.

Brinkman, John. A. "The Literary Background of the 'Catalogue of the Nations'," *CBQ* 25 (1963) 418–27.

Brodie, Thomas L. *Luke the Literary Interpreter: Luke-Acts as a Systematic Rewriting and Updating of the Elijah-Elisha Narrative*. Rome: Pontifical University of St. Thomas Aquinas, 1987.

___. "Luke-Acts as an imitation and emulation of the Elijah-Elisha narrative," in Earl Richard, ed., *New Views on Luke and Acts*, 78–85. Collegeville, MN: Liturgical Press, 1990.

___. "The Departure for Jerusalem (Luke 9:51–56) and a Rhetorical Imitation of Elijah's Departure for the Jordan (2 Kgs 1:1–2:6)," *Bib* 70 (1989) 96–109.

___. "Towards Unraveling the Rhetorical Imitation of Sources in Acts: 2 Kgs 5 as one component of Acts 8:9–40," *Bib* 67 (1986) 41–67.

Brooke, George J. "Isaiah 40:3 and the Wilderness Community," in George J. Brooke, ed., *New Qumran Texts and Studies: Proceedings of the First Meeting of the International Organization for Qumran Studies, Paris 1992*, 117–32. STDJ 15. Leiden: Brill, 1994.

Brosend, Wm. F., II. "The Means of Absent Ends," in Ben Witherington, III, ed., *History, Literature, and Society in the Book of Acts*, 348–62. Cambridge: Cambridge University Press, 1996.

Brown, Raymond. *The Gospel According to John*. AB 29 & 29A. Garden City, NJ: Doubleday, 1966, 1970.

Brown, Schuyler. *Apostasy and Perseverance in the Theology of Luke*. Rome: Biblical Institute Press, 1969.

Broyles, Craig C., and Craig A. Evans, eds., *Writing and Reading the Scroll of Isaiah: Studies of an Interpretive Tradition, vol. 2*. Leiden: Brill, 1997.
Bruce, F. F. *The Acts of the Apostles*. 3rd ed. Grand Rapids, MI: Eerdmans, 1990.
___. "The Acts of the Apostles: Historical Record or Theological Reconstruction?" *ANRW* 2.25.3 (1985) 2569–603.
___. "Chronological Questions in the Acts of the Apostles," *BJRL* 68 (1986) 273–95.
___. "The Apostolic Decree of Acts 15," in Wolfgang Schrage, ed., *Studien zum Text und zur Ethik des Neuen Testaments: Festschrift zum 80. Geburtstag von Heinrich Greeven*, 115–24. Berlin/New York: Walter de Gruyter, 1986.
___. "The Davidic Messiah in Luke-Acts," in Gary A. Tuttle, ed., *Biblical and Near Eastern Studies: Essays in Honor of William Sanford LaSor*, 7–17. Grand Rapids, MI: Eerdmans, 1978.
Buchanan, George Wesley. *Introduction to Intertextuality*. Lewiston, NY: Mellen, 1994.
___. "Isaianic Midrash and the Exodus," in Craig A. Evans and James A. Sanders, eds., *The Function of Scripture in Early Jewish and Christian Tradition*, 89–109. JSNTSup 154. Sheffield: Sheffield Academic Press, 1998.
___. "The Word of God and the Apocalyptic Vision," *SBLSP* 14 (1978) 183–92.
Büchsel, Friedrich. "παλιγγενεσία," *TDNT* 1 (1964) 686–89.
Buckwalter, H. Douglas. *The Character and Purpose of Luke's Christology*. SNTSMS 89. Cambridge: Cambridge University Press, 1996.
Bultmann, Rudolf. *The History of the Synoptic Tradition*. Trans. John Marsh. New York: Harper & Row, 1963.
Burchard, Christoph. "A Note on 'PHMA in JosAs 17:1 f.; Luke 2:15, 17; Acts 10:37," *NovT* 27 (1985) 281–95.
Burfeind, Carsten. "Paulus muß nach Rom. Zur politischen Dimension der Apostelgeschichte," *NTS* 46 (2000) 75–91.
Buss, Matthäus Franz-Josef. *Die Missionspredigt des Paulus im pisidischen Antiochien: Analyse von Apg 13, 16–41 im Hinblick auf die literarische und thematische Einheit der Paulusrede*. Stuttgart: Verlag Katholisches Bibelwerk, 1980.
Buzzard, Anthony. "Acts 1:6 and the Eclipse of the Biblical Kingdom," *EvQ* 66 (1994) 197–215.
Cadbury, Henry J. "Commentary on Luke's Preface," in F. J. Foakes Jackson and Kirsopp Lake, eds., *The Beginnings of Christianity, Part I: The Acts of the Apostles*, vol. 2, 489–510. London: Macmillan, 1922.
___. "Names for Christians and Christianity in Acts," in F. J. Foakes Jackson and Kirsopp Lake, eds., *The Beginnings of Christianity, Part I: The Acts of the Apostles*, vol. 5, 375–92. London: Macmillan, 1933.
___. *The Book of Acts in History*. New York: Harper and Brothers, 1955.
___. "The Knowledge Claimed in Luke's Preface," *Expositor* 8 (1922) 401–20.
___. *The Making of Luke-Acts*. New York: Macmillan, 1927.
___. "The Speeches in Acts," in Kirsopp Lake and Henry J. Cadbury, eds., *The Beginnings of Christianity*, vol. 5, 402–27. London: Macmillan, 1933.
___. *The Style and Literary Method of Luke*. New York: Klaus, 1969.
Cambe, M. "La χάρις chez saint Luc," *RB* 70 (1963) 193–207.
Cambier, Jules. "Le voyage de S. Paul à Jérusalem en Act. IX, 26ss. et le schéma missionaire théologique de S. Luc," *NTS* 8 (1961–62) 249–57.
Cancik, Hubert. "The History of Culture, Religion, and Institutions in Ancient Historiography: Philological Observations Concerning Luke's History," *JBL* 116 (1997) 673–95.
Cannawurf, E. "The Authenticity of Micah IV 1–4," *VT* 13 (1963) 26–33.
Carmignac, Jean. "Les citations de l'Ancien Testament dans 'La Guerre des fils de lumière contre les fils de ténèbres'," *RB* 63 (1956) 234–60, 375–90.

Carr, David McLain, "Isaiah 40:1–11 in the Context of the Macrostructure of Second Isaiah," in Walter R. Bodine, ed., *Discourse Analysis of Biblical Literature*, 52–64. Alpharetta, GA: Scholars Press, 1996.

Carroll, John T. *Response to the End of History: Eschatology and Situation in Luke-Acts.* SBLDS 92. Atlanta, GA: Scholars Press, 1988.

___. "The Uses of Scriptures in Acts," *SBLSP* 29 (1990) 512–28.

Carroll, Robert P. *Jeremiah: A Commentary.* OTL. Philadelphia: Westminster, 1986.

Casey, Maurice. "Where Wright is Wrong: A Critical Review of N. T. Wright's *Jesus and the Victory of God*," *JSNT* 69 (1998) 95–103.

Cassuto, Umberto. "On the Formal and Stylistic Relationship between Deutero-Isaiah and Other Biblical Writers," *Biblical and Oriental Studies, I, Bible*, 149–60. Jerusalem: Magnees, 1973.

Causse, Antonin. "Le pèlerinage à Jérusalem et la première Pentecôte," *RHPhR* 20 (1940) 120–41.

Chance, J. Bradley. *Jerusalem, the Temple, and the New Age in Luke-Acts.* Macon, GA: Mercer University Press, 1988.

Charlesworth, James H. "From Messianology to Christology: Problems and Prospects," in James H. Charlesworth, ed., *The Messiah*, 3–35. Minneapolis: Fortress, 1992.

___. "Intertextuality: Isaiah 40:3 and the Serek ha-Yahad," in Craig A. Evans and Shemaryahu Talmon, eds., *The Quest for Context and Meaning: Studies in Biblical Intertextuality in Honor of James A. Sanders*, 197–224. Leiden: Brill, 1997.

___. "The Jewish Roots of Christology: The Discovery of the Hypostatic Voice," *SJT* 39 (1986) 19–41.

___ et al., eds. *The Dead Sea Scrolls: Hebrew, Aramaic, and Greek Texts with English Translations.* 2 vols. Tübingen: Mohr Siebeck, 1994, 1995.

Charpentier, Etienne. *Jeunesse du Vieux Testament.* Paris: Fayard, 1963.

Childs, Brevard S. *Old Testament Theology in a Canonical Context.* Philadelphia: Fortress, 1985.

___. *The Book of Exodus.* OTL. Louisville, KY: Westminster, 1974.

Chilton, Bruce D. *A Galilean Rabbi and His Bible: Jesus' Use of the Interpreted Scripture of His Time.* Wilmington, DE: Michael Glazier, 1984.

___. "Announcement in Nazara," in R. T. France and D. Wenham, eds., *Gospel Perspectives II*, 147–72. Sheffield: JSOT Press, 1981.

___. *God in Strength: Jesus' Announcement of the Kingdom.* Freistadt: Plöchl, 1979.

___. "Jesus and the Repentance of E. P. Sanders," *TynBul* 39 (1988) 1–18.

___. "Recent and Prospective Discussion of *Memra*," in J. Neusner, E. S. Frerichs and N. M. Sarna, eds., *From Ancient Israel to Modern Judaism, vol. 2*, 119–37. BJS 173. Atlanta, GA: Scholars Press, 1989.

___. *The Glory of Israel: The Theology and Provenience of the Isaiah Targum.* JSOTSup 23. Sheffield: JSOT Press, 1983.

___. *The Isaiah Targum: Introduction, Translation, Apparatus and Notes.* ArBib 11. Wilmington, DE: Michael Glazier, 1987.

___. "Typologies of *memra* and the fourth Gospel," in Paul V. M. Flesher, ed., *Targum Studies, Vol. One: Textual and Contextual Studies in the Pentateuchal Targums*, 89–100. Atlanta, GA: Scholars, 1992.

Chung, Yun Lak. "'The Word of God' in Luke-Acts: A Study in Lukan Theology." Ph.D. diss., Emory University, 1995.

Clarke, William K. L. "The Use of the Septuagint in Acts," in F. J. Foakes Jackson and Kirsopp Lake, eds., *The Beginnings of Christianity*, vol. 2.1, 66–105. London: Macmillan, 1922.

Clements, Ronald E. "A Light to the Nations: A Central Theme of the Book of Isaiah," in James W. Watts and Paul R. House, eds., *Forming Prophetic Literature: Essays on Isaiah and the Twelve in Honor of John D. W. Watts*, 57–69. Sheffield: Sheffield Academic Press, 1996.

___. "Beyond Tradition-History: Deutero-Isaianic Development of First Isaiah's Themes," *JSOT* 31 (1985) 95–113.

___. *Isaiah 1–39*. NCBC. London: Marshall, Morgan & Scott, 1980.

___. "Patterns in the Prophetic Canon: Healing the Blind and the Lame," in Gene M. Tucker, David L. Petersen, and Robert R. Wilson, eds., *Canon, Theology, and Old Testament Interpretation: Essays in Honor of Brevard S. Childs*, 189–200. Philadelphia: Fortress, 1988.

___. "The Old Testament Background of Acts 10:34–35," in N. H. Keathley, ed., *With Steadfast Purpose*, 203–16. Waco, TX: Baylor University, 1990.

___. "The Prophecies of Isaiah and the Fall of Jerusalem in 587 B.C.," *VT* 30 (1980) 421–36.

___. "Zion as Symbol and Political Reality: A Central Isaianic Question," in J. van Ruiten and M. Vervenne, eds. *Studies in the Book of Isaiah: Festschrift Willem A. M. Beuken*, 3–17. Leuven: Leuven University Press, 1997.

Clifford, Richard J. *Fair Spoken and Persuading: An Interpretation of Second Isaiah*. New York: Paulist, 1984.

___. "Isaiah 55: Invitation to a Feast," in Carol L. Meyers and M. O'Connor, eds., *The Word of the Lord Shall Go Forth: Essays in Honor of David Noel Freedman in Celebration of His Sixtieth Birthday*, 27–35. Winona Lake, IN: Eisenbrauns, 1983.

___. "The Function of Idol Passages in Second Isaiah," *CBQ* 42 (1980) 450–64.

Coggins, Richard J. "The Samaritans and Acts," *NTS* 28 (1982) 423–34.

Cohen, Shaye J. D. "Adolf Harnack's 'The Mission and Expansion of Judaism': Christianity Succeeds Where Judaism Fails," in Birger A. Pearson, ed., *The Future of Early Christianity: Essays in Honor of Helmut Koester*, 163–69. Minneapolis: Fortress, 1991.

___. *From the Maccabees to the Mishnah*. Philadelphia: Westminster, 1987.

Collins, John J. *Between Athens and Jerusalem: Jewish Identity in the Hellenistic Diaspora*. 2nd ed. Grand Rapids, MI: Eerdmans, 2000.

___. "Cosmos and Salvation: Jewish Wisdom and Apocalyptic in the Hellenistic Age," *HR* 17 (1977) 121–142.

___. *Jewish Wisdom in the Hellenistic Age*. OTL. Louisville, KY: Westminster/John Knox, 1997.

___. "Prophecy and Fulfillment in the Qumran Scrolls," *JETS* 30 (1987) 257–78.

___. *The Scepter and the Star: The Messiahs of the Dead Sea Scrolls and Other Ancient Literature*. New York: Doubleday, 1995.

Conrad, Edgar W. "Community as King in Second Isaiah," in James T. Butler, Edgar W. Conrad, and Ben C. Ollenburger, eds., *Understanding the Word: Essays in Honor of Bernhard W. Anderson*, 99–111. JSOTSup 37. Sheffield: JSOT Press, 1985.

___. *Fear Not Warrior*. BJS 75. Chico, CA: Scholars, 1985.

___. *Reading Isaiah*. Minneapolis: Fortress, 1991.

___. "The Fear Not Oracles in Second Isaiah," *VT* 34 (1984) 126–52.

Conzelmann, Hans. *Acts of the Apostles: A Commentary on the Acts of the Apostles*. Trans. James Limburg, A. Thomas Kraabel, and Donald H. Juel. Hermeneia. Philadelphia: Fortress, 1987.

___. *History of Primitive Christianity*. Trans. John E. Steely. Nashville: Abingdon, 1973.

___. *The Theology of St. Luke*. Trans. Geoffrey Buswell. 2nd ed. New York: Harper & Row, 1960.

___. "χάρις, χαρίζομαι, χαριτόω, ἀχάριστος, (A. Profane Greek)," *TDNT* 9 (1974) 373–76.

Cosgrove, Charles H. "The Divine ΔΕΙ in Luke-Acts: Investigations into the Lukan Understanding of God's Providence," *NovT* 26 (1984) 168–90.

Crockett, L. C. "Luke iv 16–30 and the Jewish Lectionary Cycle: A Word of Caution," *JJS* 17 (1966) 13–46.

262 *Bibliography*

Cross, Frank M. *Canaanite Myth and Hebrew Epic: Essays in the History of the Religion of Israel.* Cambridge, MA: Harvard University Press, 1973.
___. "The Council of Yahweh in Second Isaiah," *JNES* 12 (1953) 274–77.
___. "The Redemption of Nature," *PSB* 10.2 (1986) 94–104.
Culler, Jonathan. *The Pursuit of Signs: Semiotics, Literature, Deconstruction.* Ithaca: Cornell, 1981.
Dahl, Nils A. "'A People for His Name' (Acts XV. 14)," *NTS* 4 (1958) 319–27.
___. *Das volk Gottes.* Norske Videnskapsakad Skrifter 1941/1. Oslo: Jacob Dybwad, 1941.
___. "The Purpose of Luke-Acts," *Jesus in the Memory of the Early Church,* 87–98. Minneapolis: Augsburg Fortress, 1976.
___. "The Story of Abraham in Luke-Acts," in Leander E. Keck and J. Louis Martyn, eds., *Studies in Luke-Acts: Essays Presented in Honor of Paul Schubert,* 139–59. Nashville: Abingdon, 1966.
Davidson, Robert. "Universalism in Second Isaiah," *SJT* 16 (1963) 166–85.
Davies, Graham I. "The Destiny of the Nations in the Book of Isaiah," in J. Vermeylen, ed., *The Book of Isaiah — Le Livre d'Isaïe. Les oracles et leurs relectures. Unité et complexité de l'ouvrage,* 93–120. BETL 81. Leuven: Leuven University Press, 1989.
___. "The Wilderness Itineraries: A Comparative Study," *TB* 25 (1974) 46–81.
Davies, Philip. "The Ending of Acts," *ExpTim* 94 (1983) 334–35.
Davies, Philip R. "God of Cyrus, God of Israel: Some Religio-Historical Reflections on Isaiah 40–55," in J. Davies, G. Harvey, and W. G. E. Watson, eds., *Words Remembered, Texts Renewed: Essays in Honour of John F. A. Sawyer,* 207–25. Sheffield: Sheffield Academic Press, 1995.
Davies, William D. *The Gospel and the Land: Early Christianity and Jewish Territorial Doctrine.* Berkeley: University of California Press, 1974.
___. *Paul and Rabbinic Judaism.* London: SPCK, 1955.
___, and Dale C. Allison, Jr. *The Gospel According to Saint Matthew,* 3 vols. ICC. Edinburgh: T & T Clark, 1988–97.
Davis, Carl Judson. *The Name and Way of the Lord: Old Testament Themes, New Testament Christology.* JSNTSup 129. Sheffield: Sheffield Academic Press, 1996.
de Boer, Pieter A. H. *Second Isaiah's Message.* OTS 11. Leiden: Brill, 1956.
de la Potterie, Ignace. "The Anointing of Christ," in Leo J. O'Donovan, ed., *Word and Mystery: Biblical Essays on the Person and Mission of Christ,* 155–84. New York: Newman, 1968.
Decock, Paul B. "The Understanding of Isaiah 53: 7–8 in Acts 8:32–33," *Neot* 14 (1981) 111–33.
Denova, Rebecca I. *The Things Accomplished Among Us: Prophetic Tradition in the Structural Pattern of Luke-Acts.* JSNTSup 141. Sheffield: Sheffield Academic Press, 1997.
Des Places, Édouard. "Actes 17,27," *Bib* 48 (1967) 1–6.
___. "Actes 17,30–31," *Bib* 52 (1971) 526–34.
Dibelius, Martin. *From Tradition to Gospel.* New York: Scribner, 1965.
___. *Studies in the Acts of the Apostles.* Ed. Heinrich Greeven. Trans. Mary Ling. New York: Scribner, 1956.
___, and Hans Conzelmann. *The Pastoral Epistles.* Trans. Philip Buttolph and Adela Yarbro. Hermeneia. Philadelphia: Fortress, 1972.
Dickinson, Royce, Jr. "The Theology of the Jerusalem Conference: Acts 15:1–35," *ResQ* 32 (1990) 65–83.
Dillon, Richard J. "Easter Revelation and Mission Program in Luke 24:46–48," in Daniel Durken, ed., *Sin, Salvation, and the Spirit: Commemorating the Fiftieth Year of The Liturgical Press,* 240–70. Collegeville, MN: Liturgical Press, 1979.
___. *From Eye-Witnesses to Ministers of the Word: Tradition and Composition in Luke 24.* AnBib 82. Rome: Pontifical Biblical Institute, 1978.

___. "The Prophecy of Christ and His Witnesses According to the Discourses in Acts," *NTS* 32 (1986) 544–56.

Dion, Paul-Eugène. "Les chants du Serviteur de Yahweh et quelques passages apparentés d'Is 40–55. Un essai sur leur limites précises et sur leurs origines respectives," *Bib* 51 (1970) 17–38.

___. "L'universalisme religieux dans les différentes couches rédactionelles d'Isaïe 40–55," *Bib* 51 (1970) 161–82.

___. "The 'Fear Not' Formula and Holy War," *CBQ* 32 (1970) 565–70.

Dodd, C. H. *According to the Scriptures: The Sub-Structure of New Testament Theology.* London: Nisbet, 1952.

___, "The Fall of Jerusalem and the 'Abomination of Desolation'," *JRS* 37 (1947) 47–54.

Donahue, John R. "Redaction Criticism: Has the *Hauptstrasse* Become a *Sackgasse*?" in Elizabeth S. Malbon and Edgar V. McKnight, eds., *The New Literary Criticism and the New Testament*, 27–57. Sheffield: Sheffield Academic Press, 1994.

Dozeman, Thomas B. *God at War: Power in the Exodus Tradition.* New York: Oxford University Press, 1996.

Drury, John. *Tradition and Design in Luke's Gospel: A Study of Early Christian Historiography.* Atlanta, GA: John Knox, 1976.

Dumbrell, William J. "The Purpose of the Book of Isaiah," *TynBul* 36 (1985) 111–28.

Duncan, Robert L. "The Logos: From Sophocles to the Gospel of John," *Christian Scholar's Review* 9 (1979) 121–30.

Dunn, James D. G. "ΚΥΡΙΟΣ in Acts," in *The Christ and the Spirit: Vol. 1 Christology,* 241–53. Grand Rapids, MI: Eerdmans, 1998.

Dupont, Jacques. "La conclusion des Actes et son rapport à l'ensemble de l'ouvrage de Luc," in J. Kremer, ed., *Les Actes des Apôtres: Traditions, rédaction, théologie,* 359–404. BETL 48. Leuven: Leuven University Press, 1979.

___. "La Mission de Paul d'après Actes 26.16–23 et la Mission des Apôtres d'après Luc 24.44–9 et Actes 1.8," in M. D. Hooker and S. G. Wilson, eds., *Paul and Paulinism: Essays in Honor of C. K. Barrett,* 290–301. London: SPCK, 1982.

___. "La portée christologique de l'évangélisation des nations d'après Lc 24,47," in Joachim Gnilka, ed., *Neues Testament und Kirche: Für Rudolf Schnackenburg,* 125–43. Freiburg: Herder, 1974.

___. "La question du plan des Actes de Apôtres à la lumière d'un texte de Lucien de Samosate," *NovT* 21 (1979) 220–31.

___. "ΛΑΟΙ 'ΕΘΝΩΝ Acts 15:14," *NTS* 3 (1956–57) 47–50.

___. *Le discours de Milet: Testament pastoral de Paul Actes 20, 18–36.* Paris: Cerf, 1962.

___. "Le douzième apôtre (Actes 1:15–26): À propos d'une explication récente," in William C. Weinrich, ed., *The New Testament Age: Essays in Honor or Bo Reicke,* vol. 1, 139–45. Macon, GA: Mercer University Press, 1984.

___. "Le salut des gentils et la signification théologique du livre des Actes," *NTS* 6 (1959–60) 132–55.

___. "'Le Seigneur de tous' (Ac 10:36; Rm 10:12): Arrière-fond scripturaire d'une formule christologique," in Gerald F. Hawthorne and Otto Betz, eds., *Tradition and Interpretation in the New Testament: Essays in Honor of E. Earle Ellis for His 60th Birthday,* 229–36. Grand Rapids, MI: Eerdmans, 1987.

___. "Notes sur les Actes des Apôtres," *RB* 62 (1955) 45–59.

___. *Nouvelles Études sur les Actes des Apôtres.* LD 118. Paris: Cerf, 1984.

___. *The Salvation of the Gentiles: Studies in the Acts of the Apostles.* Trans. J. R. Keating. New York: Paulist, 1979.

___. *The Sources of Acts: The Present Position.* Trans. Kathleen Pond. New York: Herder and Herder, 1964.

___. "Un peuple d'entre les nations (Actes 15.14)," *NTS* 31 (1985) 321–35.

Egelkraut, Helmuth L. *Jesus' Mission to Jerusalem: A Redaction-Critical Study of the Travel Narrative in the Gospel of Luke, Lk. 9:51–19:48.* Frankfurt am Main/New York: Peter Lang, 1976.

Eichrodt, Walther. *Theology of the Old Testament,* 2 vols. Trans. J. A. Baker. Philadelphia: Westminster, 1967.

Eissfeldt, Otto. "The Promises of Grace to David in Isaiah 55:1–5," in Bernhard W. Anderson and Walter Harrelson, eds., *Israel's Prophetic Heritage: Essays in Honor of James Muilenburg,* 196–207. New York: Harper & Brothers, 1962.

Ellis, E. Earle. "'The End of the Earth' (Acts 1:8)," *BBR* 1 (1991) 123–32.

___. *The Making of the New Testament Documents.* BibInt 39. Leiden: Brill, 1999

___. *The Old Testament in Early Christianity: Canon and Interpretation in the Light of Modern Research.* WUNT 54. Tübingen: Mohr Siebeck, 1991.

Esser, Hans-Helmut. "χάρις," *NIDNT* 2 (1986) 115–24.

Evans, Christopher F. "The Central Section of St. Luke's Gospel," in Dennis E. Nineham, ed., *Studies in the Gospels: Essays in Honor of R. H. Lightfoot,* 37–53. Oxford: Basil Blackwell, 1955.

Evans, Craig A. "From Gospel to Gospel: The Function of Isaiah in the New Testament," in Craig C. Broyles and Craig A. Evans, eds., *Writing and Reading the Scroll of Isaiah: Studies of an Interpretive Tradition, vol. 2,* 651–91. Leiden: Brill, 1997.

___. "Jesus and the Continuing Exile of Israel," in Carey C. Newman, *Jesus and the Restoration of Israel: A Critical Assessment of N. T. Wright's Jesus and the Victory of God,* 77–100. Downers Grove, IL: InterVarsity Press, 1999.

___. "Jesus and the Spirit: On the Origin and Ministry of the Second Son of God," in Craig A. Evans and James A. Sanders, *Luke and Scripture: The Functions of Sacred Tradition in Luke-Acts,* 26–45. Minneapolis: Fortress, 1993.

___. "On the Isaianic Background of the Sower Parable," *CBQ* 47 (1985) 464–68.

___. "Prophecy and Polemic: Jews in Luke's Scriptural Apologetic," in Craig A. Evans and James A Sanders, eds., *Luke and Scripture,* 171–211. Minneapolis: Fortress, 1993.

___. "Source, Form and Redaction Criticism: The 'Traditional' Methods of Synoptic Interpretation," in S. E. Porter and D. Tombs, eds., *Approaches to New Testament Study,* 17–45. Sheffield: Sheffield Academic Press, 1995.

___. *To See and Not Perceive: Isaiah 6:9–10 in Early Jewish and Christian Interpretation.* Sheffield: Sheffield Academic Press, 1989.

___. *Word and Glory: On the Exegetical and Theological Background of John's Prologue.* Sheffield: JSOT Press, 1993.

___, and James A. Sanders. *Luke and Scripture: The Function of Sacred Tradition in Luke-Acts.* Minneapolis: Fortress, 1993.

Feiler, Paul F. "Jesus the Prophet: The Lucan Portrayal of Jesus as the Prophet like Moses." Ph.D. diss., Princeton Theological Seminary, 1986.

Fekkes, Jan, III. *Isaiah and Prophetic Traditions in the Book of Revelation: Visionary Antecedents and their Development.* JSNTSup 93. Sheffield: JSOT Press, 1994.

Feldman, Louis H. *Jews and Gentiles in the Ancient World.* Princeton, NJ: Princeton University Press, 1993.

___. "The Concept of Exile in Josephus," James M. Scott, ed., *Exile: Old Testament, Jewish, and Christian Conceptions,* 145–72. JSJSup 56. Leiden: Brill, 1997.

Ferguson, Everett. "Canon Muratori: Date and Provenance," *Studia Patristica* 18 (1982) 677–83.

___. "'When You Come Together': *Epi To Auto* in Early Christian Literature," *ResQ* 16 (1973) 202–8.

Filson, Floyd V. "The Journey Motif in Luke-Acts," in W. Ward Gasque and Ralph P. Martin, eds., *Apostolic History and the Gospel: Biblical and Historical Essays Presented to F. F. Bruce on his 60th Birthday,* 68–77. Grand Rapids, MI: Eerdmans, 1970.

Fishbane, Michael. "The 'Exodus' Motif: The Paradigm of Historical Renewal," *Text and Texture: Close Readings of Selected Biblical Texts*, 121–40. New York: Schocken Books, 1979.

Fisher, Robert W. "The Herald of Good News in Second Isaiah," in Jared J. Jackson and Martin Kessler, eds., *Rhetorical Criticism: Essays In Honor of James Muilenburg*, 117–32. PTMS 1. Pittsburgh: Pickwick, 1974.

Fitzmyer, Joseph A. "David, 'Being Therefore a Prophet' ... (Acts 2:30)," *CBQ* 34 (1972) 332–39.

____. *Essays on the Semitic background of the New Testament.* Missoula, MT: Scholars Press, 1974.

____. "Further Light on Melchizedek from Qumran Cave 1," *JBL* 86 (1967) 25–41.

____. "Jewish Christianity in Acts in Light of the Qumran Scrolls," in Leander E. Keck and J. Louis Martyn, eds., *Studies in Luke-Acts*, 233–57. Nashville: Abingdon, 1966.

____. *Luke the Theologian: Aspects of his Teaching.* Mahwah, NJ: Paulist, 1989.

____. *The Acts of the Apostles.* AB31. New York: Doubleday, 1997.

____. *The Gospel According to Luke*, 2 vols. AB 28 & 28A. Garden City, NJ: Doubleday, 1981–85.

Foerster, Werner. "κλῆρος," *TDNT* 3 (1965) 758–64.

Fohrer, Georg. *Das Buch Jesaja: Kapitel 40–66*, vol. 3. ZBK. Zürich: Zwingli, 1964.

Forsyth, Neil. *The Old Enemy: Satan and the Combat Myth.* Princeton, NJ: Princeton University Press, 1987.

Fossum, Jarl E. *The Name of God and the Angel of the Lord: Samaritan and Jewish Concepts of Intermediation and the Origin of Gnosticism.* WUNT 36. Tübingen: Mohr Siebeck, 1985.

Frankemölle, Hubert. "Jesus als deuterojesajanischer Freudenbote?" in H. Fankemölle und K. Kertelge, eds., *Vom Urchristentum zu Jesus. FS. Joachim Gnilka zum 60 Geburtstag*, 34–67. Breisgau, Basel, Wein: Herder, 1989.

Franklin, Eric. *Christ the Lord: A Study in the Purpose and Theology of Luke-Acts.* London: SPCK, 1975.

Freedman, David Noel. "The Structure of Isaiah 40:1–11," in Edgar W. Conrad and Edward G. Newing, eds., *Perspectives on Language and Text: Essays and Poems in Honor of Francis I. Andersen's Sixtieth Birthday*, 167–93. Winona Lake, IN: Eisenbrauns, 1987.

Fusco, Vittorio. "Luke-Acts and the Future of Israel," *NovT* 38 (1996) 1–17.

____. "'Point of View' and 'Implicit Reader' in Two Eschatological Texts: Lk 19,11–28; Acts 1,6–8," in Frans van Segbroeck, Christopher M. Tuckett, Gilbert van Belle, and J. Verheyden, eds., *The Four Gospels: Festschrift Frans Neirynck*, vol. 2, 1677–96. BETL 100. Leuven: Leuven University Press, 1992.

Gafni, Isaiah M. *Land, Centre, and Diaspora: Jewish Constructs in Late Antiquity.* JSPSup 21. Sheffield: Sheffield Academy Press, 1997.

Gager, John G. "Jews, Gentiles, and Synagogues in the Book of Acts," *HTR* 79 (1986) 91–99.

Garrett, Susan R. "Exodus from Bondage: Luke 9:31 and Acts 12:1–24," *CBQ* 52 (1990) 656–80.

____. *The Demise of the Devil: Magic and the Demonic in Luke's Writings.* Minneapolis: Fortress, 1989.

Gärtner, Bertil E. *The Areopagus Speech and Natural Revelation.* Uppsala: C. W. K. Gleerup, 1955.

Gasque, W. Ward. *A History of the Criticism of the Acts of the Apostles.* Grand Rapids, MI: Eerdmans, 1975.

Gaventa, Beverly R. "The Overthrown Enemy: Luke's Portrait of Paul," *SBLSP* 24 (1985) 439–49.

Gelston, Anthony. "Isaiah 52:13–53:12 — An Eclectic Text and a Supplementary Note on the Hebrew Manuscript Kennicott 96," *JSS* 35 (1990) 187–211.

____. "The Missionary Message of Second Isaiah," *SJT* 18 (1965) 308–18.

___. "Universalism in Second Isaiah," *JTS* 43 (1992) 377–98.

Gilbert, Maurice. *La Critique des dieux dans le Livre de la Sagesse.* AnBib 53. Rome: Biblical Institute Press, 1973.

Gill, David H. "Observations on the Lukan Travel Narrative and Some Related Passages," *HTR* 63 (1970) 199–221.

___, and Conrad Gempf, eds. *The Book of Acts in its Graeco-Roman Setting.* Grand Rapids, MI: Eerdmans, 1994.

Gnilka, Joachim. *Der Verstockung Israels: Isaias 6, 9–10 in der Theologie der Synoptiker.* SANT 3. Münich: Kösel, 1961.

Göllner, Reinhard. "Der 'Weg' christlichen Glaubens Perspektiven lukanischer Theologie," in Michael Albus, ed., *Der dreieine Gott und die eine Menschheit,* 199–215. Wein: Herder, 1989.

Gosse, Bernard. "Isaïe 52,13–53,12 et Isaïe 6," *RB* 98 (1991) 537–43.

___. "Michée 4,1–5, Isaïe 2,1–5 et les rédacteurs finaux du livre d'Isaïe," *ZAW* 105 (1993) 98–102.

Gottwald, Norman K. *All the Kingdoms of the Earth: Israelite Prophecy and International Relations in the Ancient Near East.* New York: Harper & Row, 1964.

Goulder, Michael D. *The Evangelists' Calendar: A Lectionary Explanation of the Development of Scripture.* London: SPCK, 1978.

___. *Type and History in Acts.* London: SPCK, 1964.

Grappe, Christian. "Le logion des douze trônes: Eclairages intertestamentaires," in Marc Philonenko, ed., *Le Trône de Dieu,* 204–12. Tübingen: Mohr Siebeck, 1993.

Green, Joel B. "The Problem of a Beginning: Israel's Scripture in Luke 1–2," *BBR* 4 (1994) 1–25.

Grelot, Pierre. *Les Poèmes du Serviteur. De la lecture critique a l'herméneutique.* LD 103. Paris: Cerf, 1981.

___. "Note sur Actes, XIII, 47," *RB* 88 (1981) 368–72.

Grether, Oskar. *Name und Wort Gottes im Alten Testament.* BZAW 64. Giessen: Töpelmann, 1934.

Grimm, W. *Weil ich dich liebe: Die Verkündigung Jesu und Deuterojesaja.* ANTJ 1. Frankfurt am Main/New York: Peter Lang, 1981.

Grogan, Geoffrey W. "The Light and the Stone: A Christological Study in Luke and Isaiah," in Harold H. Rowdon, ed., *Christ the Lord: Studies in Christology Presented to Donald Guthrie,* 151–67. Leicester: InterVarsity Press, 1982.

Grumm, Meinert H. "Another Look at Acts," *ExpTim* 96 (1985) 333–37.

Grundmann, Walter. "δεῖ, δέον ἐστί," *TDNT* 2 (1964) 21–25.

___. "Der Bergpredigt nach der Lukasfassung," *StEv* 1 (1957) 180–9.

___. "Fragen der Komposition des lukanischen 'Reiseberichtes'," *ZNW* 50 (1959) 252–70.

Guenther, Heinz O. *The Footprints of Jesus' Twelve in Early Christian Traditions: A Study in the Meaning of Religious Symbolism.* Frankfurt am Main/New York: Peter Lang, 1985.

Gundry, Robert H. *Mark: A Commentary on His Apology for the Cross.* Grand Rapids, MI: Eerdmans, 1993.

___. *The Use of the Old Testament in St. Matthew's Gospel.* NovTSup 18. Leiden: Brill, 1967.

Gunn, David M. "Deutero-Isaiah and the Flood," *JBL* 94 (1976) 493–508.

Haarbeck, H. et al. "Word," *NIDNTT* 3 (1986) 1078–145.

Haenchen, Ernst. "Judentum und Christentum in der Apostelgeschichte," *ZNW* 54 (1963) 155–87.

___. *The Acts of the Apostles: A Commentary.* Trans. R. McL. Wilson. Oxford: Basil Blackwell, 1971.

___. "Tradition und Komposition in der Apostelgeschichte," *ZTK* 52 (1955) 205–25.

Hafemann, Scott J. "Paul and the Exile of Israel in Galatians 3–4," in James M. Scott, ed., *Exile: Old Testament, Jewish, and Christian Conceptions*, 329–71. JSJSup 56. Leiden: Brill, 1997.

Hahneman, Geoffrey M. *The Muratorian Fragment and the Development of the Canon* Oxford: Clarendon, 1992.

Halas, Roman. "The Universalism of Isaias," *CBQ* 12 (1950) 162–70.

Hamlin, E. John. "Deutero-Isaiah's Reinterpretation of the Exodus in the Babylonian Twilight," *Proceedings: Eastern Great Lakes and Midwest Biblical Societies* 11 (1991) 75–80.

Hamm, Dennis. "Paul's Blindness and its Healing: Clues to Symbolic Intent (Acts 9, 22 and 26)," *Bib* 71 (1990) 63–72.

___. "Sight to the Blind: Vision as Metaphor in Luke," *Bib* 67 (1986) 457–77.

Hanson, Paul D. *Isaiah 40–66*. Interpretation. Louisville, KY: John Knox Press, 1995.

___. *The Dawn of the Apocalyptic*. Rev. ed. Philadelphia: Fortress, 1979.

Harris, J. R. *Testimonies*, 2 vols. Cambridge: Cambridge University Press, 1920.

Harvey, Graham. *The True Israel: Uses of the Names Jew, Hebrew and Israel in Ancient Jewish and Early Christian Literature*. Leiden: Brill, 1996.

Hasel, Gerhard F. *The Remnant: The History and Theology of the Remnant Idea from Genesis to Isaiah*. Berrien Springs, MI: Andrews University Press, 1974.

Hays, Richard B. *Echoes of Scripture in the Letters of Paul*. New Haven, CT: Yale University Press, 1989.

___. "'Who Has Believed Our Message?' Paul's Reading of Isaiah," *SBLSP* 37 (1998) 205–25.

Hayward, Robert C. T. *Divine Name and Presence: The Memra*. Totowa, NJ: Allandheld, Osmund & Co., 1981.

Hazelton, Juan S. "Aspectos de la cristologia de Lucas revelados por su uso del término 'Logos'," *Cuadernos de Teologia* 2 (1972) 124–38.

Hedrick, Charles W. "Paul's Conversion/Call: A Comparative Analysis of the Three Reports in Acts," *JBL* 100 (1981) 415–32.

Helyer, Larry R. "Luke and the Restoration of Israel," *JETS* 36 (1993) 317–29.

Hemer, Colin J. "First Person Narrative in Acts 27–28," *TynBul* 36 (1985) 79–109.

___. *The Book of Acts in the Setting of Hellenistic History*. WUNT 49. Tübingen: Mohr Siebeck, 1989.

Hengel, Martin. *Acts and the History of Earliest Christianity*. Trans. John Bowden. Philadelphia: Fortress, 1980.

___. *Between Jesus and Paul: Studies in the Earliest History of Christianity*. Philadelphia: Fortress, 1983.

___. *Earliest Christianity*. Trans. John Bowden. London: SCM Press, 1986.

___. "Kerygma oder Geschichte," *TQ* 151 (1971) 323–36.

___, and Anna Maria Schwemer, *Paulus zwischen Damaskus und Antiochien: Die unbekannten Jahre des Apostels*. WUNT 108. Tübingen: Mohr Siebeck, 1998.

Henne, P. "La datation du canon de Muratori," *RB* 100 (1993) 54–75.

Hill, C. E. "The Debate Over the Muratorian Fragment and the Development of the Canon," *WTJ* 57 (1995) 437–52.

Hobart, W. K. *The Medical Language of St. Luke*. Dublin: Hodges, Figgis, 1882.

Holladay, William L. *Jeremiah 1: A Commentary on the Book of the Prophet Jeremiah Chapters 1–25*. Hermeneia. Philadelphia: Fortress, 1986.

Hollenberg, D. E. "Nationalism and 'The Nations' in Isaiah XL–LV," *VT* 19 (1969) 21–36.

Holmgren, Fredrick C. "Isaiah 2.1–5," *Int* 51 (1997) 61–64.

Holter, Knut. *Second Isaiah's Idol-Fabrication Passages*. Frankfurt am Main/New York: Peter Lang, 1995.

Holtz, Traugott. *Untersuchungen über die alttestamentlichen Zitate bei Lukas*. TU 104. Berlin: Akademie-Verlag, 1968.

Hooker, Morna D. "Did the Use of Isaiah 53 to Interpret His Mission Begin with Jesus?" in William H. Bellinger, Jr., and William R. Farmer, *Jesus and the Suffering Servant: Isaiah 53 and Christian Origins*, 88–103. Harrisburg, PA: Trinity Press International, 1998.

___. *Jesus and the Servant: The Influence of the Servant Concept of Deutero-Isaiah in the New Testament*. London: SPCK, 1959.

Horbury, William. "The Twelve and the Phylarchs," *NTS* 32 (1986) 503–27.

Horsley, G. H. R., *New Documents Illustrating Early Christianity: A Review of the Greek Inscriptions and Papyri published in 1977*. Sydney, Australia: Macquarie University Ancient History Documentary Research Centre, 1982.

Horsley, Richard A., and John S. Hanson, *Bandits, Prophets, and Messiahs: Popular Movements at the Time of Jesus*. San Francisco: Harper & Row, 1985.

Houlden, James L. "The Purpose of Luke," *JSNT* 21 (1984) 53–65.

Hugenberger, Gordon P. "The Servant of the Lord in the 'Servant Songs' of Isaiah: A Second Moses Figure," in P. E. Satterthwaite, R. S. Hess, G. J. Wenham, eds., *The Lord's Anointed*, 105–40. Carlisle: Paternoster, 1995.

Isaac, E. "1 (Ethiopic Apocalypse of) Enoch," in James H. Charlesworth, ed., *The Old Testament Pseudepigrapha*, 1.5–100. Garden City, NY: Doubleday, 1983.

Jackson, F. J. Foakes, and Kirsopp Lake, eds. *The Beginnings of Christianity*, 5 vols. London: Macmillan, 1920–33.

Jaeger, Werner. *The Theology of the Early Greek Philosophers*. Oxford: Clarendon, 1947.

Janowski, Bernd, and Peter Stuhlmacher, *Der leidende Gottesknecht: Jesaja 53 und seine Wirkungsgeschichte, mit einer Bibliographie zu Jes 53*. FAT 14. Tübingen: Mohr Siebeck, 1996.

Jeremias, Joachim. *Jesus' Promise to the Nations*. Trans. S. H. Hooke. Philadelphia: Fortress, 1982.

Jervell, Jacob. "Das gespaltene Israel und die Heidenvolker," *ST* 19 (1965) 68–96.

___. *Die Apostelgeschichte*. KEK 17. Göttingen: Vandenhoeck & Ruprecht, 1998.

___. *Luke and the People of God*. Minneapolis: Augsburg, 1972.

___. "Paul in the Acts of the Apostles: Tradition, History, Theology," in Jacob Kremer, ed., *Les Actes des Apôtres: Traditions, rédaction, théologie*, 297–306. BETL 48. Leuven: Leuven University Press, 1979.

___. "The Church of Jews and God-Fearers," in Joseph B. Tyson, ed., *Luke-Acts and the Jewish People: Eight Critical Perspectives*, 11–20. Minneapolis: Augsburg, 1988.

___. *The Theology of the Acts of the Apostles*. Cambridge: Cambridge University Press, 1996.

___. *The Unknown Paul: Essays on Luke-Acts and Early Christian History*. Minneapolis: Augsburg, 1984.

Johnson, Dennis E. "Jesus Against the Idols: The Use of Isaianic Servant Songs in the Missiology of Acts," *WTJ* 52 (1990) 343–53.

Johnson, Luke Timothy. *The Acts of the Apostles*. Collegeville, MN: Liturgical Press, 1992.

___. *The Literary Function of Possessions in Luke-Acts*. SBLDS 39. Missoula, MT: Scholars Press, 1977.

___. "The New Testament's Anti-Jewish Slander and the Conventions of Ancient Polemic," *JBL* 108 (1989) 419–441.

Kaiser, Otto. *Isaiah 1–12: A Commentary*. Trans. John Bowden. 2nd ed. OTL. Philadelphia: Westminster, 1983.

Kaiser, Walter C., Jr. "The Promise of God and the Outpouring of the Holy Spirit: Joel 2:28–32 and Acts 2:16–21," in Morris Inch and Ronald Youngblood, eds., *The Living and Active Word of God: Studies in Honor of Samuel J. Schultz*, 109–22. Winona Lake, IN: Eisenbrauns, 1983.

___. "The Promise to David in Psalm 16 and Its Application in Acts 2:25–33 and 13:32–37," *JETS* 23 (1980) 219–29.

___. "The Unfailing Kindness Promised to David: Isaiah 55.3," *JSOT* 45 (1989) 91–98.

Keck, Leander E., and James Louis Martyn, eds. *Studies in Luke-Acts*. Philadelphia: Fortress Press, 1966.

Kee, Howard Clark. *Who are the People of God? Early Christian Models of Community*. New Haven, CT: Yale University Press, 1997.

Kiesow, Klaus. *Exodustexte im Jesajabuch: Literarkritische und motivgeschichtliche Analysen*. Göttingen: Vandenhoeck & Ruprecht, 1979.

Kilgallen, John J. "Acts 13, 38–39: Culmination of Paul's Speech in Pisidia," *Bib* 69 (1988) 480–506.

___. "Persecution in the Acts of the Apostles," in Gerald O'Collins and Gilberto Marconi, ed., *Luke and Acts*, 143–60, 245–50. Trans. Matthew J. O'Connell. New York: Paulist, 1993.

___. *The Stephen Speech*. AnBib 67. Rome: Biblical Institute Press, 1976.

Kilpatrick, George Dunbar. "ΛΑΟΙ at Luke II. 31 and Acts IV. 25, 27," *JTS* 16 (1965) 127.

___. "Some Quotations in Acts," *Les Actes des Apôtres: Traditions, rédaction théologie*, ed. Jacob Kremer, 81–97. BETL 48. Leuven: Leuven University Press, 1979.

Kim, Seyoon. *The Son of Man as the Son of God*. WUNT 30. Tübingen: Mohr Siebeck, 1983.

Knibb, Michael A., "Isaianic Traditions in the Apocrypha and Pseudepigrapha," in Craig C. Broyles and Craig A. Evans, eds., *Writings and Reading the Scroll of Isaiah: Studies of an Interpretive Tradition, vol. 2*, 633–50. Leiden: Brill, 1997.

___. "Isaianic Traditions in the Book of Enoch," in John Barton and David J. Reimer, eds., *After the Exile: Essays in Honour of Rex Mason*, 217–29. Macon, GA: Mercer University Press, 1996.

___. "The Exile in the Literature of the Intertestamental Period," *HeyJ* 17 (1976) 253–72.

Knox, John. *Marcion and the New Testament: An Essay in the Early History of the Canon*. Chicago: University of Chicago Press, 1942.

Koch, Klaus. "Die Stellung des Kyros im Geschichtsbild Deuterojesajas und ihre überlieferungs-geschichtliche Verankerung," *ZAW* 84 (1972) 352–56.

___. "Messias und Sündenvergebung in Jesaja 53 — Targum," *JSJ* 3 (1972) 117–48.

___. "The Language of Prophecy: Thoughts on the Macrosyntax of the *debar* YHWH and Its Semantic Implications in the Deuteronomistic History," in H. T. C. Sun, K. L. Eades, J. M. Robinson, and G. I. Moller, eds., *Problems in Biblical Theology: Essays in Honor of Rolf Knierim*, 210–221. Grand Rapids, MI: Eerdmans, 1997.

Kodell, Jerome. "'The Word of God Grew': The Ecclesial Tendency of Λόγος in Acts 6,7; 12,24; 19,20," *Bib* 55 (1974) 505–19.

Koester, Helmut. *Ancient Christian Gospels: Their History and Development*. Philadelphia: Trinity Press International, 1990.

___. "ὑπόστασις," *TDNT* 8 (1972) 572–89.

___. "Writings and the Spirit: Authority and Politics in Ancient Christianity," *HTR* 84 (1991) 353–72.

Koet, Bart J. *Five Studies on Interpretation of Scripture in Luke-Acts*. SNTA 14. Leuven: Leuven University Press, 1989.

Kosmala, Hans. *Hebräer — Essener — Christen*. SPB 1. Leiden: Brill, 1959.

Kraabel, A. Thomas. "The Roman Diaspora: Six Questionable Assumptions," *JJS* 33 (1982) 445–64.

Kratz, Reinhard Gregor. "Der Anfang des Zweiten Jesaja in Jes 40,1f. und seine literarischen Horizonte," *ZAW* 105 (1993) 400–19.

Kremer, Jacob, ed. *Les Actes des Apôtres: Traditions, Redaction, Théologie*. BETL 48. Leuven: Leuven University Press, 1977.

Kristeva, Julia. *Revolution in Poetic Language*. Trans. Margaret Waller. New York: Columbia University Press, 1984.

Kugel, James L. *Traditions of the Bible: A guide to the Bible As It Was at the Start of the Common Era*. Cambridge, MA: Harvard University Press, 1998.

___. "Two Introductions to Midrash," in Geoffrey H. Hartman and Sanford Budick, eds., *Midrash and Literature*, 77–103. New Haven, CT: Yale University Press, 1985.

Külling, Heinz. *Geoffenbartes Geheimnis: Eine Auslegung von Apostelgeschichte 17, 16–34.* Zürich: Theologischer Verlag, 1993.

Kurz, William S. *Reading Luke-Acts: Dynamics of Biblical Narrative.* Louisville, KY: Westminster/John Knox, 1993.

Laato, Antti. "The Composition of Isaiah 40–55," *JBL* 109 (1990) 207–228.

Labuschagne, C. J. *The Incomparability of Yahweh in the Old Testament.* Leiden: Brill, 1966.

Lack, Rémi. *La symbolique du livre d'Isaïe.* AnBib 59. Rome: Biblical Institute Press, 1973.

Lane, Thomas J. *Luke and the Gentile Mission: Gospel Anticipates Acts.* Frankfurt am Main/New York: Peter Lang, 1996.

Lane, William L. *The Gospel According to Mark.* NICNT. Grand Rapids, MI: Eerdmans, 1974.

___. "Times of Refreshment: A Study of Eschatological Periodization in Judaism and Christianity." Th.D. diss., Harvard Divinity School, 1962.

Lee, Stephen. "Power not Novelty: The Connotations of ברא in the Hebrew Bible," in A. Graeme Auld, ed., *Understanding Poets and Prophets: Essays in Honour of George Wishart Anderson*, 199–212. Sheffield: JSOT Press, 1993.

Leske, Adrian M. "Isaiah and Matthew: The Prophetic Influence in the First Gospel: A Report on Current Research," in William H. Bellinger, Jr., and William R. Farmer, *Jesus and the Suffering Servant: Isaiah 53 and Christian Origins*, 152–69. Harrisburg, PA: Trinity Press International, 1998.

___. "The Influence of Isaiah on Christology in Matthew and Luke," in William R. Farmer, ed., *Crisis in Christology: Essays in Quest of Resolution*, 241–69. Livonia, MI: Dove, 1995.

Levenson, Jon D. *Creation and the Persistence of Evil.* New York: Harper & Row, 1988.

___. *Sinai and Zion.* Minneapolis, MN: Winston, 1985.

Lindars, Barnabas. "Good Tidings to Zion: Interpreting Deutero-Isaiah Today," *BJRL* 68 (1986) 473–97.

___. "The Old Testament and Universalism in Paul," *BJRL* 69 (1987) 511–27.

Lindblom, Johannes. *The Servant Songs in Deutero-Isaiah: A New Attempt to Solve an Old Problem.* Lund: G. W. K. Gleerup, 1951.

Litke, Wayne Douglas. "Luke's Knowledge of the Septuagint: A Study of the Citations in Luke-Acts." Ph.D. diss., McMaster University, 1993.

Loewenstamm, Samuel E. *The Evolution of the Exodus Tradition.* Trans. Baruch J. Schwartz. Jerusalem: Magnes Press, 1992.

Lohfink, Gerhard. *Die Sammlung Israels: Eine Untersuchung zur lukanischen Ekklesiologies.* Munich: Kösel, 1975.

Loisy, Alfred. *Les Actes des Apôtres.* Paris: E. Nourry, 1920.

Lüdemann, Gerd. *Early Christianity according to the Traditions in Acts: A Commentary.* Trans. J. Bowden. Philadelphia: Fortress, 1989.

Ludwig, Theodore M. "The Traditions of the Establishing of the Earth in Deutero-Isaiah," *JBL* 92 (1973) 345–57.

Lyonnet, Stanislas. "'La Voie' dans les Actes des apôtres," *RechSR* 69 (1981) 149–64.

Machinist, Peter. "Assyria and its Image in the First Isaiah," *JAOS* 103 (1983) 719–37.

Maddox, Robert. *The Purpose of Luke-Acts.* Edinburgh: T. & T. Clark, 1982.

Malherbe, Abraham J. "'Not in a Corner': Early Christian Apologetic in Acts 26:26," *SecCent* 5 (1985–1986) 193–210.

Malina, Bruce J. and Jerome H. Neyrey. "First-Century Personality: Dyadic, Not Individualistic," in Jerome H. Neyrey, ed., *The Social World of Luke-Acts: Models for Interpretation*, 67–96. Peabody, MA: Hendrickson, 1991.

Maloney, Linda M. *"All that God had Done with Them": The Narration of the Works of God in the Early Christianity as Described in the Acts of the Apostles.* Frankfurt am Main/New York: Peter Lang, 1991.

Mánek, Jindrich. "The New Exodus in the Books of Luke," *NovT* 2 (1957) 8–23.

Mann, Thomas W. *Divine Presence and Guidance in Israelite Traditions: The Typology of Exaltation.* Baltimore: John Hopkins University Press, 1977.

Marcus, Joel. "Entering into the Kingly Power of God," *JBL* 107 (1988) 663–75.

___. "Mark and Isaiah," in A. B. Beck, A. H. Bartelt, P. R. Raabe, and C. A. Franke, eds., *Fortunate the Eyes that See: Essays in Honor of David Noel Freedman in Celebration of His Seventieth Birthday,* 449–66. Grand Rapids, MI: Eerdmans, 1995.

___. *The Way of the Lord: Christological Exegesis of the Old Testament in the Gospel of Mark.* Louisville, KY: Westminster/John Knox, 1992.

Marguerat, Daniel. "Saul's Conversion (Acts 9, 22, 26) and the Multiplication of Narrative in Acts," in Christopher M. Tuckett, ed., *Luke's Literary Achievement,* 127–55. JSNTSup 116. Sheffield: Sheffield Academic Press, 1995.

___. Daniel Marguerat, "The Enigma of the Silent Closing of Acts (28:16–31)," in David P. Moessner, ed., *Jesus and the Heritage of Israel: Luke's Narrative Claim upon Israel's Legacy,* 284–304. Harrisburg, PA: Trinity Press International, 1999.

Marshall, I. Howard. *Luke: Historian and Theologian.* 2nd ed. Grand Rapids, MI: Zondervan, 1989.

___. *The Acts of the Apostles.* TNTC. Grand Rapids, MI: Eerdmans, 1980.

___. *The Gospel of Luke: A Commentary on the Greek Text.* NIGTC. Grand Rapids, MI: Eerdmans, 1978.

Marx, W. "Luke, the Physician, Re-examined," *ExpTim* 91 (1980) 168–72.

März, Claus P. *Das Wort Gottes bei Lukas: Die lukanische Worttheologie als Frage an die neuere Lukasforschung.* EThSt 11. Leipzig: St. Benno-Verlag, 1974.

Masson, Charles. "La reconstitution du collège des douze d'après Actes 1:15–26," *RThPh* 5 (1955) 193–201.

Mauchline, John. "Implicit Signs of a Persistent Belief in the Davidic Empire," *VT* 20 (1970) 287–303.

McCasland, Selby Vernon. "Signs and Wonders," *JBL* 76 (1957) 149–52.

___. "The Way," *JBL* 77 (1958) 222–30.

McKenzie, John L. *Second Isaiah.* AB 20. Garden City: Doubleday, 1968.

___. "The Word of God in the Old Testament," *TS* 21 (1960) 183–206.

McKnight, Scot. *A Light Among the Gentiles.* Minneapolis: Fortress, 1991.

McLaughlin, John L. "Their Hearts were Hardened: The Use of Isaiah 6,9–10 in the Book of Isaiah," *Bib* 75 (1994) 1–25.

Méhat, A. "'Apocatastase': Origène, Clément d'Alexandre, Act. 3,21," *VC* 10 (1956) 196–214.

Melugin, Roy F. "Israel and the Nations in Isaiah 40–55," in H. T. C. Sun, K. L. Eades, J. M. Robinson, and G. I. Moller, eds., *Problems in Biblical Theology: Essays in Honor of Rolf Knierim,* 249–64. Grand Rapids, MI: Eerdmans, 1997.

___. *The Formation of Isaiah 40–55.* BZAW 141. Berlin/New York: Walter de Gruyter, 1976.

___, and Marvin A. Sweeney, eds. *New Visions of Isaiah.* JSOTSup 214. Sheffield: Sheffield Academic Press, 1996.

Menoud, Philippe H. "Le plan des Actes des Apôtres," *NTS* 1 (1954) 44–51.

___. "The Additions to the Twelve Apostles According to the Book of Acts," in *Jesus Christ and the Faith: A Collection of Studies by Philippe H. Menoud,* 133–48. Trans. Eunice M. Paul. Pittsburgh, PA: Pickwick, 1978.

Menzies, Robert P. *The Development of Early Christian Pneumatology with Special Reference to Luke-Acts.* Sheffield: JSOT Press, 1991.

Mettinger, T. N. D. *A Farewell to the Servant Songs: A Critical Examination of an Exegetical Axiom.* Scripta Minora. Lunk: CWK Gleerup, 1983.

Metzger, Bruce M. *A Textual Commentary on the Greek New Testament*. 2nd ed. New York: United Bible Societies, 1994.

___. "Ancient Astrological Geography and Acts 2:9–11," in W. Ward Gasque and Ralph P. Martin, eds., *Apostolic History and the Gospel: Biblical and Historical Essays Presented to F. F. Bruce on his 60th Birthday*, 123–33. Grand Rapids, MI: Eerdmans, 1970.

Michaelis, Wilhelm. "κράτος (θεοκρατία)," *TDNT* 9 (1974) 905–10.

___. "ὁδός," *TDNT* 5 (1967) 42–114.

Miesner, Donald R. "The Circumferential Speeches of Luke-Acts," *SBLSP* 14 (1978) 2.223–37.

___. "The Missionary Journeys Narrative: Patterns and Implications," in Charles H. Talbert, ed., *Perspectives on Luke-Acts*, 199–214. Edinburgh: T. & T. Clark, 1978.

Milikowsky, Chaim. "Notions of Exile, Subjugation and Return in Rabbinic Literature," in James M. Scott, ed., *Exile: Old Testament, Jewish, and Christian Conceptions*, 265–96. JSJSup 56. Leiden: Brill, 1997.

Minear, Paul S. "Dear Theo. The Kerygmatic Intention and Claim of the Book of Acts," *Int* 27 (1973) 131–50.

___. *Images of the Church in the New Testament*. Philadelphia: Westminster Press, 1960.

___. "Logos Affiliations in Johannine Thought," in Robert F. Berkey and Sarah A. Edwards, eds., *Christology in Dialogue*, 142–56. Cleveland, OH: Pilgrim, 1993.

___. "Luke's Use of the Birth Stories," in Leander E. Keck and J. Louis Martyn, eds., *Studies in Luke-Acts: Essays Presented in Honor of Paul Schubert*, 111–30. Nashville: Abingdon, 1966.

Miyoshi, Michi. *Der Anfang des Reiseberichts Lk 9,51–10,24: Eine redaktion-geschichtliche Untersuchung*. AnBib 60. Rome: Biblical Institute Press, 1974.

Moessner, David P. "'Eyewitnesses,' 'Informed Contemporaries,' and 'Unknowing Inquirers': Josephus' Criteria for Authentic Historiography and the Meaning of ΠΑΡΑΚΟΛΟΥΘΕΩ," *NovT* 38 (1996) 105–22.

___. "Ironic Fulfillment of Israel's Glory," in J. B. Tyson, ed., *Luke-Acts and the Jewish People: Eight Critical Perspectives*, 35–50. Minneapolis, MN: Augsburg, 1988.

___. *Lord of the Banquet: The Literary and Theological Significance of the Lukan Travel Narrative*. Minneapolis: Fortress, 1989.

___. "Paul and the Pattern of the Prophet like Moses in Acts," *SBLSP* 22 (1983) 203–12.

___. "Paul in Acts: Preacher of Eschatological Repentance to Israel," *NTS* 34 (1988) 96–104.

___. "The Appeal and Power of Poetics (Luke 1:1–4): Luke's Superior Credentials (παρηκολουθηκότι), Narrative Sequence (καθεξῆς), and Firmness of Understanding (ἡ ἀσφάλεια) for the Reader," in David P. Moessner, ed., *Jesus and the Heritage of Israel: Luke's Narrative Claim upon Israel's Legacy*, 84–123. Harrisburg, PA: Trinity Press International, 1999.

Moore, Carey A. *Daniel, Esther and Jeremiah: The Additions*. AB 44. Garden City: NY: Doubleday, 1977.

Morgenstern, Julian. "Deutero-Isaiah's Terminology for Universal God," *JBL* 62 (1943) 269–80.

Moule, C. F. D. "Fulfillment-Words in the New Testament: Use and Abuse," *NTS* 14 (1967–68) 293–320.

Munck, Johannes. *Paul and the Salvation of Mankind*. Trans. F. Clarke. Atlanta, GA: John Knox, 1977.

Mußner, Franz. "Die Idee der Apokatastasis in der Apostelgeschichte," in Heinrich Groß and Franz Mußner, eds., *Lex tua veritas: Festschrift für Hubert Junker zur Vollendung des siebzigsten Lebensjahres am 8. August 1961*, 293–306. Trier: Paulinus-Verlag, 1961.

Neirynck, Frans. "Ac 10,36–43 et l'Évangile," *EthL* 60 (1984) 109–17.

___. "Acts 10,36a τὸν λόγον ὅν," *EthL* 60 (1984) 118–23.

___. "Le texte des Actes des Apôtres et les caracteristiques stylistiques lucaniennes," *EthL* 61 (1985) 304–39.

Nelson, Edwin S. "Paul's First Missionary Journey as Paradigm: A Literary-Critical Assessment of Acts 13–14." Ph.D. diss., Boston University, 1982.

Neudorfer, Heinz-Werner. *Die Apostelgeschichte des Lukas.* Neuhausen-Stuttgart: Hänssler, 1986.

Neufeld, Tom Yoder. *Put on the Armour of God: The Divine Warrior from Isaiah to Ephesians.* JSNTSup 140. Sheffield: Sheffield Academic Press, 1997.

Nickelsburg, George W. E. "Reading the Hebrew Scriptures in the First Century: Christian Interpretations in Their Jewish Context," *WW* 3 (1983) 238–50.

_____. *Resurrection, Immortality, and Eternal Life in Intertestamental Judaism.* HTS 26. Cambridge, MA: Harvard University Press, 1972.

_____. "Stories of Biblical and Early Post-Biblical Times," in Michael E. Stone, ed., *Jewish Writings of the Second Temple Period,* 33–87. CRINT 2.2. Philadelphia: Fortress, 1984.

Niehoff, Maren R. "Philo's Views on Paganism," in Graham N. Stanton and Guy S. Stroumsa, eds., *Tolerance and Intolerance in Early Judaism and Christianity,* 135–58. Cambridge: Cambridge University Press, 1998.

Nielsen, Kirsten. "Is 6:1–8:18 as Dramatic Writing," *StTh* 40 (1986) 1–16.

Nixon, Robin E. *The Exodus and the New Testament.* London: Tyndale, 1963.

Nolland, John. "A Fresh Look at Acts 15.10," *NTS* 27 (1980) 105–15.

_____. "Classical and Rabbinic Parallels to 'Physician, Heal Yourself' (Lk. IV.2)," *NovT* 21 (1979) 193–209.

_____. *Luke,* 3 vols. WBC 35a–c. Dallas, TX: Word, 1989–1993.

_____. "Luke's Readers — A Study of Luke 4.22–8; Acts 13.46; 18.6; 28:28 and Luke 21:5–36." Ph.D. diss., University of Cambridge, 1977.

_____. "Words of Grace (Luke 4:22)," *Bib* 84 (1984) 44–60.

Noorda, Sijbolt J. "'Cure Yourself Doctor!' (Luke 4:23). Classical Parallels to an Alleged Saying of Jesus," in J. Delobel, ed., *Logia: Les Paroles de Jésus — The Sayings of Jesus. Mémorial Joseph Coppens,* 459–67. BETL 59. Leuven: Leuven University Press, 1982.

North, Christopher R. *The Suffering Servant in Deutero-Isaiah: An Historical and Critical Study.* London: Oxford University Press, 1948.

O'Neill, John C. "The Six Amen Sayings in Luke," *JTS* 10 (1959) 1–9.

_____. *The Theology of Acts in its Historical Setting.* 2nd ed. London: SPCK, 1970.

O'Reilly, Leo. *Word and Sign in the Acts of the Apostles: A Study in Lucan Theology.* AnGr 82. Rome: Editrice Pontifica Universita Gregorians, 1987.

O'Toole, Robert F. "Acts 2:30 and the Davidic Covenant of Pentecost," *JBL* 102 (1983) 245–58.

_____. "Parallels between Jesus and His Disciples in Luke-Acts: A Further Study," *BZ* 27 (1983) 195–212.

_____. *The Unity of Luke's Theology: An Analysis of Luke-Acts.* GNS 9. Wilmington, DE: Michael Glazier, 1984.

Oepke, Albrecht. "ἀποκαθίστημι, ἀποκατάστασις," *TDNT* 1 (1964) 387–93.

Orlinsky, Harry M. "'Israel' in Isa. XLIX, 3: A Problem in the Methodology of Textual Criticism," in N. Avigad, M. Avi-Yonah, H. Z. Hirschberg, and B. Mazar, eds., *E. L. Sukenik Memorial Volume (1889–1953),* 42–45. Jerusalem: Israel Exploration Society, 1967.

_____. "The So-Called 'Servant of the Lord' and 'Suffering Servant' in Second Isaiah," in N. H. Snaith and H. M. Orlinsky, *Studies on the Second Part of the Book of Isaiah,* 3–133. VTSup 14. Leiden: Brill, 1967.

Overholt, T. W. "The Falsehood of Idolatry: An Interpretation of Jeremiah x.1–16," *JTS* 16 (1965) 1–16.

Pao, David W. "Review of Rebecca Denova, *The Things Accomplished Among Us,*" *TLZ* 124.4 (1999) 400–01.

274   *Bibliography*

___. "The Genre of the Acts of Andrew," *Apocrypha: Revue Internationale des Littératures Apocryphes* 6 (1995) 179–202.

Parker, James, III. *The Concept of Apokatastasis in Acts: A Study in Primitive Christian Theology.* Austin, TX: Schola Press, 1978.

Parsons, Mikeal C. "Isaiah 53 in Acts 8: A Reply to Professor Morna Hooker," in William H. Bellinger, Jr., and William R. Farmer, eds., *Jesus and the Suffering Servant: Isaiah 53 and Christian Origins,* 104–19. Harrisburg, PA: Trinity Press International, 1998.

___. *The Departure of Jesus in Luke-Acts: The Ascension Narratives in Context.* Sheffield: JSOT Press, 1987.

___. "The Narrative Unity of Luke and Acts," in Mikeal C. Parsons and Richard I. Pervo, *Rethinking the Unity of Luke and Acts,* 45–83. Minneapolis, MN: Fortress, 1993.

___. "The Unity of the Lukan Writings: Rethinking *the Opinio Communis,*" in Naymond H. Keathley, ed., *With Steadfast Purpose: Essays on Acts in Honor of Henry Jackson Flanders, Jr.,* 29–53. Waco, TX: Baylor University, 1990.

___, and Richard I. Pervo. *Rethinking the Unity of Luke and Acts.* Minneapolis: Fortress, 1993.

Patrick, Dale A. "Epiphanic Imagery in Second Isaiah's Portrayal of a New Exodus," *HAR* 8 (1984) 125–41.

Penney, John Michael. *The Missionary Emphasis of Lukan Pneumatology.* JPTSS 12. Sheffield: Sheffield Academic Press, 1997.

Perrin, Norman. "The Interpretation of the Gospel of Mark," *Int* 30 (1976) 115–24.

Perrot, Charles. *La lecture de la Bible dans la synagogue: Les anciennes lectures palestiniennes du Shabbat et des fêtes.* Hildesheim: Gerstenberg, 1973.

Pervo, Richard J. *Profit with Delight: The Literary Genre of the Acts of the Apostles.* Philadelphia: Fortress Press, 1987.

___. "Social and Religious Aspects of the 'Western' Text," in Dennis E. Groh and Robert Jewett, eds., *The Living Text: Essays in Honor of Ernest W. Saunders,* 229–41. New York: University Press of America, 1985.

Pesch, Rudolf. *Die Apostelgeschichte,* 2 vols. EKK 5. Zürich: Benziger Verlag, 1986.

Petersen, Norman R. *Literary Criticism for New Testament Critics.* Philadelphia: Fortress, 1978.

Plümacher, Eckhard. "Wirklichkeitserfahrung und Geschichtsschreibung bei Lukas: Erwägungen zu den Wir-Stücken der Apostelgeschichte," *ZNW* 68 (1977) 2–22.

Plunkett, Mark A. "Ethnocentricity and Salvation History in the Cornelius Episode (Acts 10:1–11:18)," *SBLSP* 24 (1985) 465–79.

Pomykala, Kenneth. *The Davidic Dynasty Tradition in Early Judaism: Its History and Significance for Messianism.* Atlanta, GA: Scholars, 1995.

Ponizy, Bogdan. "Logos in the Book of Wisdom 18:14–16," in M. Augustin and K.-D. Schunck, *"Dort ziehen Schiffe dahin ...": Collected Communications to the XIVth Congress of the International Organization for the Study of the Old Testament, Paris 1992,* 169–77. Frankfurt am Main/New York: Peter Lang, 1996.

Porter, Stanley E. *The Paul of Acts: Essays in Literary Criticism, Rhetoric, and Theology.* WUNT 115. Tübingen: Mohr Siebeck, 1999.

___. "The 'We' Passages," in David W. J. Gill and Conrad Gempf, eds., *The Book of Acts in its First Century Setting,* 545–74. Grand Rapids, MI: Eerdmans, 1994.

___, and David Tombs. *Approaches to New Testament Study.* Sheffield: Sheffield Academic Press, 1995.

Praeder, Susan M. "The Problem of First Person Narration in Acts," *NovT* 29 (1987) 193–218.

Preuss, Horst Dietrich. *Deuterojesaja: Eine Einführung in seine Botschaft.* Neukirchen: Neukirchener Verlag, 1976.

___. *Old Testament Theology,* 2 vols. Louisville, KY: Westminster/John Knox, 1995.

___. *Verspottung fremder Religionen im Alten Testament.* BWANT 92. Stuttgart: W. Kohlhammer, 1971.

Priest, J. "Testament of Moses," in James H. Charlesworth, ed., *The Old Testament Pseudepigrapha*, 1.919–34. Garden City, NY: Doubleday, 1983.

Prior, Michael. *Jesus the Liberator: Nazareth Liberation Theology (Luke 4:16–30)*. Sheffield: Sheffield Academic Press, 1996.

Procksch, Otto. "λέγω (C. The Word of God in the Old Testament)," *TDNT* 4 (1967) 91–100.

Puskas, Charles B. "The Conclusion of Luke-Acts: An Investigation of the Literary Function and Theological Significance of Acts 28:16–31." Ph.D. diss., St. Louis University, 1980.

Ramsay, William M. *St. Paul the Traveller and the Roman Citizen*. London: Hodder & Stoughton, 1897.

Rapske, Brian. "Acts, Travel and Shipwreck," in David W. J. Gill and Conrad Gempf, eds., *The Book of Acts in Its Graeco-Roman Setting*, 1–47. Grand Rapids, MI: Eerdmans, 1994.

———. *The Book of Acts and Paul in Roman Custody*. Grand Rapids, MI: Eerdmans, 1994.

Ravens, David. *Luke and the Restoration of Israel*. Sheffield: Sheffield Academic Press, 1995.

Ray, Jerry Lynn. *Narrative Irony in Luke-Acts: The Paradoxical Interaction of Prophetic Fulfillment and Jewish Rejection*. New York: Edwin Mellen, 1996.

Reardon, Bryan P. "The Greek Novel," *Phoenix* 23 (1966) 291–309.

———. *The Form of Greek Romance*. Princeton: Princeton University Press, 1991.

Reicke, Bo. "Die Mahlzeit mit Paulus auf den Wellen des Mittelmeers Act. 27,33–38," *ThZ* 4 (1948) 401–410.

———. "Jesus in Nazareth — Lk 4, 14–30," in Horst Baly and Siegfried Schulz, eds., *Das Wort und die Wörter. FS Gerhard Friedrich*, 47–55. Stuttgart: W. Kohlhammer, 1973.

Reim, G. "Targum und Johannesevangelium," *BZ* 27 (1983) 1–13.

Reinhardt, Wolfgang. *Das Wachstum des Gottesvolkes: Untersuchungen zum Gemeindewachstum im lukanischen Doppelwerk auf dem Hintergrund des Alten Testaments: Mit zwei Schaubildern und vier Tabellen*. Göttingen: Vandenhoeck & Ruprecht, 1995.

Renaud, Bernard. *La formation du livre de Michée*. Paris: Gabalda, 1977.

Rendtorff, Rolf. "Jesaja 6 im Rahmen der Komposition des Jesajabuches," in J. Vermeylen, ed., *The Book of Isaiah — Le Livre d'Isaïe. Les oracles et leurs relectures. Unité et complexité de l'ouvrage*, 73–82. BETL 81. Leuven: Leuven University Press, 1989.

———. "Zur Komposition des Buches Jesaja," *VT* 34 (1984) 295–320.

Rengstorf, Karl H. *Das Evangelium nach Lukas*. Göttingen: Vandenhoeck & Ruprecht, 1966.

———. "The Election of Matthias," in W. Klassen and G. F. Snyder, eds., *Current Issues in New Testament Interpretation: Essays in Honor of Otto A. Piper*, 178–92. New York: Harper, 1962.

Repo, E. *Der 'Weg' als Selbstbezeichnung des Urchristentums*. Helsinki: Suomalainen Tiedeakatemia, 1964.

Rese, Martin. *Alttestamentliche Motive in der Christologie des Lukas*. StNT 1. Gütersloh: Gütersloher Verlagshaus, 1969.

———. "Die Funktion der alttestamentlichen Zitate und Anspielungen in den Reden der Apostelgeschichte," in Jacob Kremer, ed., *Les Actes des Apôtres: Traditions, rédaction théologie*, 61–79. BETL 48. Leuven: Leuven University Press, 1979.

Richard, Earl. *Acts 6:1–8:4: The Author's Method of Composition*. SBLDS 41. Missoula, MT: Scholars Press, 1978.

———. "The Divine Purpose: The Jews and the Gentile Mission (Acts 15)," in Charles H. Talbert, ed., *Luke-Acts: New Perspectives from the Society of Biblical Literature Seminar*, 188–209. New York: Crossroad, 1984.

———. "The Old Testament in Acts: Wilcox's Semitisms in Retrospect," *CBQ* 42 (1980) 330–41.

Ringgren, Helmer. *Word and Wisdom*. Lund: Haken Ohlssons Boktrycheri, 1947.

Rissi, Matthias. "Der Aufbau des vierten Evangeliumss," *NTS* 29 (1983) 48–54.

Robbins, Vernon K. "The Social Location of the Implied Author of Luke-Acts," in J. H. Neyrey, ed., *The Social World of Luke Acts: Models for Interpretation*, 305–32. Peabody: Hendrickson, 1991.

___. "The We-Passages in Acts and Ancient Sea Voyages," *BR* 20 (1975) 5–18.

Robinson, William C., Jr. "The Theological Context for Interpreting Luke's Travel Narrative (9:51ff)," *JBL* 79 (1960) 20–31.

___. "The Way of the Lord: A Study of History and Eschatology in the Gospel of Luke." Dr.Theol. diss., University of Basel, 1960.

Rofé, Alexander. "How is the Word Fulfilled? Isaiah 55:6–11 within the Theological Debate of its Time," in Gene M. Tucker, David L. Petersen, and Robert R. Wilson, eds., *Canon, Theology, and Old Testament Interpretation: Essays in Honor of Brevard S. Childs*, 246–61. Philadelphia: Fortress, 1988.

___. "Isaiah 59:19 and Trito-Isaiah's Vision of Redemption," in J. Vermeylen, ed., *The Book of Isaiah — Le Livre d'Isaïe. Les oracles et leurs relectures. Unité et complexité de l'ouvrage*, 407–10. BETL 81. Leuven: Leuven University Press, 1989.

Roloff, Jurgen. *Die Apostelgeschichte*. NTD 5. Göttingen: Vandenhoeck & Ruprecht, 1988.

Ropes, J. H. *The Beginnings of Christianity. Vol. 3: The Text of Acts*. Ed. F. J. Foakes Jackson and Kirsopp Lake. London: Macmillan, 1926.

Roth, Wolfgang M. W. "For Life, He Appeals to Death (Wis 13:18): A Study of Old Testament Idol Parodies," *CBQ* 37 (1975) 21–47.

Sacon, Kiyoshi Kinoshita. "Isaiah 40:1–11: A Redactional-Critical Study," in Jared J. Jackson and Martin Kessler, eds., *Rhetorical Criticism: Essays In Honor of James Muilenburg*, 99–116. PTMS 1. Pittsburgh: Pickwick, 1974.

Salmon, Marilyn. "Insider or Outsider? Luke's Relationship with Judaism," in Joseph B. Tyson, ed., *Luke-Acts and the Jewish People: Eight Critical Perspectives*, 51–75. Minneapolis: Augsburg, 1988.

Sanders, E. P. *Jesus and Judaism*. Philadelphia: Fortress, 1985.

___. "Jesus and the Kingdom: The Restoration of Israel and the New People of God," in E. P. Sanders, ed., *Jesus, the Gospels, and the Church: Essays in Honor of William R. Farmer*, 225–39. Macon, GA: Mercer University Press, 1987.

___. *Judaism: Practice and Belief, 63 BCE–66 CE*. Philadelphia: Trinity Press International, 1992.

___. *Paul and Palestinian Judaism*. Philadelphia: Fortress, 1977.

Sanders, Jack T. "The Jewish People in Luke-Acts," in J. B. Tyson, ed., *Luke-Acts and the Jewish People: Eight Critical Perspectives*, 51–75. Minneapolis: Augsburg, 1988.

___. *The Jews in Luke-Acts*. London: SCM, 1987.

___. "Who is a Jew and Who is a Gentile in the Book of Acts?" *NTS* 37 (1991) 434–55.

Sanders, James A. "From Isaiah 61 to Luke 4," in J. Neusner, ed., *Christianity, Judaism and Other Greco-Roman Cults: Studies for Morton Smith at Sixty*. 1.75–106. Leiden: Brill, 1975.

___. *From Sacred Story to Sacred Text*. Philadelphia: Fortress, 1987.

___. "Isaiah in Luke," *Int* 36 (1982) 144–55.

___. "The Salvation of the Jews in Luke-Acts," in Charles H. Talbert, ed., *Luke-Acts: Perspectives from the Society of Biblical Literature Seminar*, 104–17. New York: Crossroad, 1984.

Sawyer, John F. A. *The Fifth Gospel: Isaiah in the History of Christianity*. Cambridge: Cambridge University Press, 1996.

Schlatter, Adolf. *The Church in the New Testament Period*. Trans. P. Levertoff. London: SPCK, 1961.

Schlier, Heinrich. "αἵρεσις," *TDNT* 1 (1964) 180–84.

Schlosser, Jacques. "Moïse, serviteur du kérygme apostolique d'après Ac 3,22–29," *RevScRel* 61 (1987) 17–31.

Schmidt, W. H. "דָּבָר," *TDOT* 3 (1978) 84–125.
Schmitt, J. "L'Église de Jérusalem ou la 'restauration' d'Israel d'aprés les cinq premiers chapitres des Actes," *RevScRel* 27 (1953) 209–18.
Schmitz, Otto, and Gustav Stählin. "παρακαλέω, παράκλησις," *TDNT* 5 (1967) 773–800.
Schnackenburg, Rudolf. *God's Rule and Kingdom.* New York: Herder and Herder, 1963.
Schneck, R. *Isaiah in the Gospel of Mark, I–VIII.* Bibal Dissertation Series 1. Berkeley: Bibal, 1994.
Schneider, Gerhard. *Die Apostelgeschichte,* 2 vols. Freiburg: Herder, 1980–82.
Scholes, Robert E., and Robert Kellogg. *The Nature of Narrative.* New York: Oxford University Press, 1968.
Schoors, Antoon. *I am God Your Saviour.* VTSup 24. Leiden: Brill, 1973.
___. "Les choses antérieures et lest choses nouvelles dans les oracles deutéro-isaïens," *EthL* 40 (1964) 19–47.
Schreck, Christopher J. "The Nazareth Pericope: Luke 4.16–30 in Recent Study," in Frans Neirynck, ed., *L'Evangile de Luc — The Gospel of Luke,* 399–471. BETL 32. Leuven: Leuven University Press, 1989.
Schrenk, Gottlob. "γραφή," *TDNT* 1 (1964) 749–61.
Schubert, Paul. "The Final Cycle of Speeches in the Book of Acts," *JBL* 87 (1968) 1–16.
___. "The Place of the Areopagus Speech in the Composition of Acts," in J. C. Rylaardsdam, ed., *Transitions in Biblical Scholarship,* 235–61. Chicago: University of Chicago Press, 1968.
___. "The Structure and Significance of Luke 24," in W. Eltester, ed., *Neutestamentliche Studien für Rudolf Bultmann,* 165–88. Berlin: Alfred Töpelmann, 1954.
Schultz, Richard. "The King in the Book of Isaiah," in P. E. Satterthwaite, R. S. Hess, G. J. Wenham, eds., *The Lord's Anointed,* 141–65. Carlisle: Paternoster, 1995.
Schürmann, Heinz. *Das Lukasevangelium,* vol. 1–2.1. HKNT 3. Freiburg: Herder, 1969, 1994.
Schwartz, Daniel R. "The End of the ΓΗ (Acts 1:8): Beginning or End of the Christian Vision?" *JBL* 105 (1986) 669–676.
___. "The End of the Line: Paul in the Canonical Book of Acts," in William S. Babcock, ed., *Paul and the Legacies of Paul,* 3–24. Dallas: Southern Methodist University Press, 1990.
___. "The Futility of Preaching Moses (Acts 15,21)," *Bib* (1986) 276–81.
Scott, J. Julius, Jr. *Customs and Controversies: Intertestamental Jewish Backgrounds of the New Testament.* Grand Rapids, MI: Baker, 1995.
___. "Textual Variants of the 'Apostolic Decree' and their Setting in the Early Church," in Morris Inch and Ronald Youngblood, eds., *The Living and Active Word of God: Studies in Honor of Samuel J. Schultz,* 171–83. Winona Lake, IN: Eisenbrauns, 1983.
Scott, James M, ed. *Exile: Old Testament, Jewish, and Christian Conceptions.* JSJSup 56. Leiden: Brill, 1997.
___. "Luke's Geographical Horizon," in D. W. J. Gill and C. Gempf, eds., *The Book of Acts in its Graeco-Roman Setting,* 483–544. Grand Rapids, MI: Eerdmans, 1994.
___. "Philo and the Restoration of Israel," *SBLSP* 34 (1995) 553–75.
___. "The Use of Scripture in 2 Corinthians 6.16c–18 and Paul's Restoration Theology," *JSNT* 56 (1994) 73–99.
Scott, R. B. Y. "The Relation of Isaiah, Chapter 35, to Deutero-Isaiah," *AJSL* 52 (1935–36) 178–91.
Seager, A. "Ancient Synagogue Architecture: An Overview," J. Gutmann, ed., *Ancient Synagogues: The State of Research,* 39–43. Chico, CA: Scholars Press, 1981.
Seccombe, David P. "Luke and Isaiah," *NTS* 27 (1981) 252–59.
___. *Possessions and the Poor in Luke-Acts.* Linz: SNTU, 1982.
Seely, David Rolph. "The Image of the Hand of God in the Exodus Traditions." Ph.D. diss., University of Michigan, 1990.

___. "The Raised Hand of God as an Oath Gesture," in Astrid B. Beck, Andrew H. Bartelt, Paul R. Raabe, and Chris A. Franke, eds., *Fortunate the Eyes That See: Essays in Honor of David Noel Freedman in Celebration of His Seventieth Birthday*, 411–21. Grand Rapids, MI: Eerdmans, 1995.

Segal, Alan F. "Conversion and Universalism: Opposites that Attract," in Bradley H. McLean, ed., *Origins and Method: Towards a New Understanding of Judaism and Christianity: Essays in Honour of John C. Hurd*, 162–89. JSNTSup 86. Sheffield: Sheffield Academic Press, 1993.

Seifrid, M. A. "Jesus and the Law in Acts," *JSNT* 30 (1987) 39–57.

Seitz, Christopher R. "How is the Prophet Isaiah Present in the Latter Half of the Book? The Logic of Chapters 40–66 within the Book of Isaiah," *JBL* 115 (1996) 219–40.

___. "The Divine Council: Temporal Transition and New Prophecy in the Book of Isaiah," *JBL* 109 (1990) 229–47.

___. *Zion's Final Destiny: The Development of the Book of Isaiah.* Minneapolis: Fortress, 1991.

Sheeley, Steven M. "Getting into the Act(s): Narrative Presence in the 'We' Sections," *PRSt* 26 (1999) 203–20.

___. *Narrative Asides in Luke-Acts.* Sheffield: Sheffield Academic Press, 1992.

Shepherd, William H., Jr. *The Narrative Function of the Holy Spirit as a Character in Luke-Acts.* SBLDS 43. Atlanta, GA: Scholars, 1994.

Shin, Gabriel K.-S. *Die Ausrufung des endgültigen Jubeljahres durch Jesus in Nazareth: Eine historisch-kritische Studie zu Lk 4,16–30.* Europäische Hochschulschriften 23.378. Frankfurt am Main/New York: Peter Lang, 1989.

Siker, Jeffrey S. *Disinheriting the Jews: Abraham in Early Christian Controversy.* Louisville, KY: Westminster/John Knox, 1991.

___. "'First to the Gentiles': A Literary Analysis of Luke 4:16–30," *JBL* 111 (1992) 73–90.

Simian-Yofre, Horacio. "Exodo en Deuteroisaias," *Bib* 61 (1980) 530–53.

Skehan, Patrickt W. *Studies in Israelite Poetry and Wisdom.* CBQMS 1. Washington, DC: Catholic Biblical Association of America, 1971.

Sloan, Robert B. *The Favorable Year of the Lord: A Study of Jubilary Theology in the Gospel of Luke.* Austin, TX: Schola Press, 1977.

___. "'Signs and Wonders': A Rhetorical Clue to the Pentecost Discourse," in N. H. Keathley, ed., *With Steadfast Purpose*, 145–62. Waco, TX: Baylor University, 1990.

Snaith, Norman H. "Isaiah 40–66: A Study of the Teaching of the Second Isaiah and Its Consequences," in N. H. Snaith and H. M. Orlinksy, eds., *Studies on the Second Part of the Book of Isaiah*, 137–264. VTSup 14. Leiden: Brill, 1967.

___. "The Servant of the Lord in Deutero-Isaiah," in H. H. Rowley, ed., *Studies in Old Testament Prophecy Presented to Professor Theodore H. Robinson by the Society for Old Testament Study on his Sixty-Fifth Birthday, August 9th, 1946*, 187–200. Edinburgh: T. & T. Clark, 1950.

Snodgrass, Klyne R. "Streams of Tradition Emerging from Isaiah 40:1–5 and their Adaptation in the New Testament," *JSNT* 8 (1980) 24–45.

Soards, Marion L. *The Speeches in Acts: Their Content, Context, and Concerns.* Louisville, KY: Westminster/John Knox, 1994.

Söder, Rosa. *Die apokryphen Apostelgeschichten und die romanhafte Literatur der Antike.* Stuttgart: W. Kohlhammer Verlag, 1932.

Sommer, Benjamin D. *A Prophet Reads Scripture: Allusion in Isaiah 40–66.* Stanford, CA: Stanford University Press, 1998.

Spencer, Franklin Scott. "The Ethiopian Eunuch and His Bible: A Social-Science Analysis," *BTB* 22 (1992) 155–65.

___. *The Portrait of Philip in Acts: A Study of Role and Relations.* Sheffield: Sheffield Academic Press, 1992.

Spencer, Richard A., ed., *Orientation by Disorientation: Studies in Literary Criticism and Biblical Literary Criticism Presented in Honor of William A. Beardslee*. Pittsburgh: Pickwick, 1980.

Spykerboer, Hendrik C. "Isaiah 55:1–5: The Climax of Deutero-Isaiah: An Invitation to Come to the New Jerusalem," in J. Vermeylen, ed., *The Book of Isaiah — Le Livre d'Isaïe. Les oracles et leurs relectures. Unité et complexité de l'ouvrage*, 357–59. BETL 81. Leuven: Leuven University Press, 1989.

___. *The Structure and Composition of Deutero-Isaiah: With Special Reference to the Polemics against Idolatry*. Franeker, Netherlands: T. Wever, 1976.

Squires, John T. *The Plan of God in Luke-Acts*. SNTSMS 76. Cambridge: Cambridge University Press, 1993.

Stade, B. "Bemerkungen zu vorstehendem Aufsatze," *ZAW* 4 (1884) 291–97.

___. "Deuterozacharja: Eine kritische Studie, II," *ZAW* 1 (1881) 151–72.

Stählin, Gustav. *Die Apostelgeschichte*. NTD 5. Göttingen, 1966.

___. "Tὸ πνεῦμα 'Ιησοῦ (Apostelgeschichte 16:7)," in Barnabas Lindars and Stephen S. Smalley, eds., *Christ and Spirit in the New Testament*, 229–52. Cambridge: Cambridge University Press, 1973.

Stanley, Christopher D. "The Importance of 4QTanhumim (4Q176)," *RevQum* 15 (1992) 569–82.

___. *Paul and the Language of Scripture: Citation Technique in the Pauline Epistles and Contemporary Literature*. SNTSMS 74. Cambridge: Cambridge University Press, 1992.

___. "The Importance of 4QTanhumim (4Q176)," *RevQ* 15 (1992) 589–92.

Stanton, Graham. "Stephen in Lucan Perspective," *StudBib* 3 (1978) 345–60.

Stendahl, Krister. *Paul among Jews and Gentiles*. Philadelphia: Fortress, 1976.

___. *The School of St. Matthew and Its Use of the Old Testament*. Second Edition. Philadelphia: Fortress, 1968.

Stenning, J. F., ed. *The Targum of Isaiah*. Oxford: Clarendon, 1949.

Steyn, Gert Jacobus. *Septuagint Quotations in the Context of the Petrine and Pauline Speeches of the Acta Apostolorum*. CBET 12. Kampen: Pharos, 1995.

Stoops, Robert F., Jr. "Riot and Assembly: The Social Context of Acts 19:23–41," *JBL* 108 (1989) 73–91.

Storm, Hans-Martin. *Die Paulusberufung nach Lukas und das Erbe der Propheten*. Frankfurt am Main/New York: Peter Lang, 1995.

Strange, W. A. *The Problem of the Text of Acts*. SNTSMS 71. Cambridge: Cambridge University Press, 1992.

___. "The Sons of Sceva and the Text of Acts 19:14," *JTS* 38 (1987) 97–106.

Strauss, Mark L. *The Davidic Messiah in Luke-Acts: The Promise and Its Fulfillment in Lukan Christology*. JSNTSup 110. Sheffield: Sheffield Academic Press, 1995.

Strelan, Rick. *Paul, Artemis, and the Jews in Ephesus*. Berlin/New York: Walter de Gruyter, 1996.

Strom, Mark R. "An Old Testament Background to Acts 12.20–23," *NTS* 32 (1986) 289–92.

Stuart, Douglas. "The Sovereign's Day of Conquest," *BASOR* 221 (1976) 159–64.

Stuhlmacher, Peter. *Die paulinische Evangelum: 1 Vorgeschichte*. FRLANT 95. Göttingen: Vandenhoeck & Ruprecht, 1968.

Stuhlmueller, Carroll. *Creative Redemption in Deutero-Isaiah*. Rome: Pontifical Biblical Institute, 1970.

___. "Deutero-Isaiah: Major Transitions in the Prophet's Theology and in Contemporary Scholarship," *CBQ* 42 (1980) 1–29.

___. "The Painful Cost of Great Hopes: The Witness of Isaiah 40–55," in Daniel Durken, ed., *Sin, Salvation, and the Spirit: Commemorating the Fiftieth Year of The Liturgical Press*, 146–62. Collegeville, MN: Liturgical Press, 1979.

Sundberg, Albert, Jr. "Canon Muratori: A Fourth-Century List," *HTR* 66 (1973) 1–41.

Swartley, Willard M. *Israel's Scripture Traditions and the Synoptic Gospels: Story Shaping Story.* Peabody, MA: Hendrickson, 1994.
___. *Mark: The Way for All Nations.* Scottdale, PA: Herald Press, 1979.
___. "The Structural Function of the Term 'Way' (*Hodos*) in Mark's Gospel," in William Klassen, ed., *The New Way of Jesus: Essays Presented to Howard Charles,* 73–86. Newton, KS: Mennonite Press, 1980.
Sweeney, Marvin A. *Isaiah 1–4 and the Post-Exilic Understanding of the Isaianic Tradition.* BZAW 171. Berlin/New York: Walter de Gruyter, 1983.
___. *Isaiah 1–39 with an Introduction to the Prophetic Literature.* FOTL 16. Grand Rapids, MI: Eerdmans, 1996.
Talbert, Charles H. "Biographies of Philosophers and Rulers in Mediterranean Antiquity," *ANRW* 2.16.2 (1978) 1619–51.
___. *Literary Patterns, Theological Themes and the Genre of Luke-Acts.* SBLMS 20. Missoula, MT: Scholars Press, 1974.
___. "Luke-Acts," in Eldon J. Epp and George W. MacRae, eds., *The New Testament and Its Modern Interpreters,* 297–320. Philadelphia: Fortress, 1989.
___. "Once Again: The Gentile Mission in Luke-Acts," in Claus Bussmann and Walter Radl, eds., *Der Treue Gottes Trauen,* 99–109. Freiberg: Herder, 1991.
___. "Promise and Fulfillment in Lucan Theology," in Charles H. Talbert, ed., *Luke-Acts: New Perspectives from the Society of Biblical Literature Seminar,* 91–103. New York: Crossroad, 1984.
___. *Reading Acts: A Literary and Theological Commentary on The Acts of the Apostles.* New York: Crossroad, 1997.
___. *Reading Luke: A Literary and Theological Commentary on the Third Gospel.* New York: Crossroad, 1982.
___. "Shifting Sands: The Recent Study of the Gospel of Luke," *Int* 30 (1976) 381–95.
___. "The Place of the Resurrection in the Theology of Luke," *Int* 46 (1992) 19–30.
___. "The Way of the Lukan Jesus: Dimension of Lukan Spirituality," *PRSt* 9 (1982) 237–49.
Talmon, Shemaryahu. "Between the Bible and the Mishna," *The World of Qumran from Within: Collected Studies,* 11–52. Leiden: Brill, 1989.
___. "The Community of the Renewed Covenant: Between Judaism and Christianity," in Eugene Ulrich and James Vanderkam, eds., *The Community of the Renewed Covenant,* 3–24. Notre Dame, IN: University of Notre Dame Press, 1994.
___. "The 'Desert Motif' in the Bible and in Qumran Literature," in A. Altmann, ed., *Biblical Motifs,* 31–63. Cambridge, MA: Harvard University Press, 1966.
Tannehill, Robert C. "Rejection by Jews and Turning to Gentiles: The Pattern of Paul's Mission in Acts," *SBLSP* 25 (1986) 130–41.
___. "The Mission of Jesus according to Luke IV.16–30," in W. Eltester, ed., *Jesus in Nazareth,* 51–75. Berlin/New York: Walter de Gruyter, 1972.
___. *The Narrative Unity of Luke-Acts: A Literary Interpretation,* 2 vols. Foundations and Facets. Philadelphia: Fortress Press, 1986, 1990.
Thiessens, Werner. *Christen in Ephesos: Die historische und theologische Situation in vorpaulinischer und paulinischer Zeit und zur Zeit der Apostelgeschichte und der Pastoralbriefe.* Tübingen: Francke, 1995.
Thornton, Claus-Jürgen. *Der Zeuge des Zeugen, Lukas als Historiker der Paulusreisen.* WUNT 56. Tübingen: Mohr Siebeck, 1991.
Thornton, T. C. G. "To the End of the Earth: Acts 1:8," *ExpTim* 89 (1977–78) 374–75.
Tiede, David L. "Acts 1:6–8 and the Theo-Political Claims of Christian Witness," *WW* 1 (1982) 41–51.
___. "Glory to thy People Israel," in Jacob Neusner, Ernest S. Frerichs, Peder Borgen and Richard Horsley, eds., *The Social World of Formative Christianity and Judaism: Essays in Tribute to Howard Clark Kee,* 327–41. Philadelphia: Fortress, 1988.
___. *Prophecy and History in Luke-Acts.* Philadelphia: Fortress, 1980.

___. "The Exaltation of Jesus and the Restoration of Israel in Acts 1," *HTR* 79 (1986) 278–86.

Tomasino, Anthony J. "Isaiah 1:1–2:4 and 63–66, and the Composition of the Isaianic Corpus," *JSOT* 57 (1993) 81–98.

Torrey, C. C. *The Second Isaiah: A New Interpretation.* New York: Charles Scribner's Sons, 1928,

Townsend, John T. "Missionary Journeys in Acts and European Missionary Societies," *SBLSP* 24 (1985) 433–37.

___. "The Contributions of John Knox to the Study of Acts: Some Further Notations," in Mikeal C. Parsons and Joseph B. Tyson, eds., *Cadbury, Knox, and Talbert: American Contributions to the Study of Acts,* 81–9. Atlanta, GA: Scholars Press, 1992.

___. "The Date of Luke-Acts," in Charles H. Talbert, ed., *Luke-Acts: New Perspectives from the Society of Biblical Literature Seminar,* 47–62. New York: Crossroad, 1984.

Trocmé, Etienne. *Le 'Livre des Actes' et l'histoire.* Paris: Presses Universitaires de France, 1957.

Tsevat, Matitiahu. "The Prohibition of Divine Images According to the Old Testament," in M. Augustin and K.-D. Schunck, eds., *Wünschet Jerusalem Frieden: Collected Communications to the XIIth Congress of the International Organization for the Study of the Old Testament, Jerusalem 1986,* 211–20. Frankfurt am Main/New York: Peter Lang, 1988.

Tuckett, Christopher M., "Luke 4,16–30, Isaiah and Q," in J. Delobel, ed., *Logia: Les Paroles de Jésus — The Sayings of Jesus. Mémorial Joseph Coppens,* 343–54. BETL 59. Leuven: Leuven University Press, 1982.

___, ed. *Luke's Literary Achievement: Collected Essays.* Sheffield: Sheffield Academic Press, 1995.

Turner, Max M. "Jesus and the Spirit in Lucan Perspective," *TynBul* 32 (1981) 3–42.

___. *Power from on High. The Spirit in Israel's Restoration and Witness in Luke-Acts.* Sheffield: Sheffield Academic Press, 1996.

___. "The Spirit and the Power of Jesus' Miracles in the Lucan Conception," *NovT* 33 (1991) 124–52.

Tyson, Joseph B. *Images of Judaism in Luke-Acts.* Columbia, SC: University of South Carolina Press, 1992.

___. "John Knox and the Acts of the Apostles," in Mikeal C. Parsons and Joseph B. Tyson, eds., *Cadbury, Knox, and Talbert: American Contributions to the Study of Acts,* 55–80. Atlanta, GA: Scholars Press, 1992.

___, ed. *Luke-Acts and the Jewish People: Eight Critical Perspectives.* Minneapolis: Augsburg, 1988.

___. "The Gentile Mission and the Authority of Scripture in Acts," *NTS* 33 (1987) 619–31.

___. "The Jewish Public in Luke-Acts," *NTS* 30 (1984) 574–83.

___. "The Problem of Jewish Rejection in Acts," in Joseph B. Tyson, ed., *Luke-Acts and the Jewish People: Eight Critical Perspectives,* 124–37. Minneapolis: Augsburg, 1988.

van de Sandt, Hubertus. "An Explanation of Acts 15.6–21 in the Light of Deuteronomy 4.29–35 (LXX)," *JSNT* 46 (1992) 73–97.

___. "The Fate of the Gentiles in Joel and Acts 2: An Intertextual Study," *EThL* 66 (1990) 56–77.

___. "The Quotations in Acts 13:32–52 as a Reflection of Luke's LXX Interpretation," *Bib* 75 (1994) 26–58.

van der Horst, Pieter W. "Hellenistic Parallels to the Acts of the Apostles (2.1–47)," *JSNT* 25 (1985) 49–60.

___. "The Unknown God (Acts 17:23)," in R. van den Broek, T. Baarda, and J. Mansfeld, eds., *Knowledge of God in the Graeco-Roman World,* 19–42. Leiden: Brill, 1988.

van Ruiten, J. and M. Vervenne, eds. *Studies in the Book of Isaiah: Festschrift Willem A. M. Beuken.* Leuven: Leuven University Press, 1997.

van Unnik, Willem C. "Der Ausdruck'ΕΩΣ 'ΕΣΧΑΤΟΥ ΤΗΣ ΓΗΣ (Apostelgeschichte I 8) und sein Alttestamentlicher Hintergrund," *Sparsa Collecta: The Collected Essays of W. C. van Unnik*, 1.386–401. NovTSup 30. Leiden: Brill, 1973.

___. "Luke-Acts, A Storm Center in Contemporary Scholarship," in Leander Keck and J. Louis Martyn, eds., *Studies in Luke-Acts*, 15–32. Nashville: Abingdon, 1966.

___. "The Christian's Freedom of Speech in the New Testament," *Sparsa Collecta: The Collected Essays of W. C. van Unnik*, 2.269–89. NovTSup 30. Leiden: Brill, 1980.

van Winkle, D. W. "The Relationship of the Nations to Yahweh and to Israel in Isaiah xl–lv," *VT* 35 (1985) 446–58.

Verheyden, Joseph. "The Unity of Luke-Acts: What Are We Up To?" in J. Verheyden, ed., *The Unity of Luke-Acts*, 3–56. Leuven: Leuven University Press, 1999.

Via, E. Jane, "An Interpretation of Acts 7:35–37 from the Perspective of Major Themes in Luke-Acts," *SBLSP* 14.2 (1978) 209–22.

Vielhauer, P. "On the 'Paulinism' of Acts," in Leander E. Keck and J. Louis Martyn, eds., *Studies in Luke-Acts: Essays Presented in Honor of Paul Schubert*, 33–50. Nashville: Abingdon, 1966.

Völkel, Martin. "όδός," *EDNT* 2 (1991) 491–93.

von Rad, Gerhard. *God at Work in Israel*. Trans. John H. Marks. Nashville: Abingdon, 1980.

___. *Holy War in Ancient Israel*. Trans. B. Ollenburger. Grand Rapids, MI: Eerdmans, 1991.

___. *Old Testament Theology, vol. II: The Theology of Israel's Prophetic Traditions*. Trans. D. M. G. Stalker. New York: Harper & Row, 1965.

___. "The City on the Hill," *The Problem of the Hexateuch and Other Essays*, 232–42. Trans. E. W. Trueman Dicken. New York: McGraw-Hill, 1966.

___. *Wisdom in Israel*. Trans. James D. Marton. Nashville: Abingdon, 1972.

Wagner, J. Ross, Jr. "'Who Has Believed Our Message?': Paul and Isaiah 'In Concert' in the Letter to the Romans." Ph.D. diss., Duke University, 1999.

Wainwright, Arthur W. "Luke and the Restoration of the Kingdom to Israel," *ExpTim* 89 (1977) 76–79.

Walker, William O., Jr. "Acts and the Pauline Corpus Reconsidered," *JSNT* 24 (1985) 3–23.

Wall, Robert W. "Peter, 'Son' of Jonah: The Conversion of Cornelius in the Context of Canon," *JSNT* 29 (1987) 79–80.

___. "Successors to 'the Twelve' According to Acts 12:1–17," *CBQ* 53 (1991) 628–43.

Watson, Alan. *The Trial of Stephen: The First Christian Martyr*. Athens, GA: University of Georgia Press, 1996.

Watts, James W. *Forming Prophetic Literature: Essays on Isaiah and the Twelve in Honor of John D. W. Watts*. JSOTSup 235. Sheffield: Sheffield Academic Press, 1996.

___. "The Remnant Theme: A Survey of New Testament Research, 1921–1987," *PRSt* 15 (1988) 109–29.

Watts, John D. W. *Isaiah 1–33, Isaiah 34–66*. WBC 24, 25. Waco, TX: Word, 1985, 1987.

Watts, Rikki E. "Consolation or Confrontation? Isaiah 40–55 and the Delay of the New Exodus," *TynBul* 41 (1990) 31–59.

___. *Isaiah's New Exodus and Mark*. WUNT 2.88. Tübingen: Mohr Siebeck, 1997.

Weatherly, Jon A. "The Jews in Luke-Acts," *TynBul* 40 (1989) 107–117.

Wegner, Paul D. *An Examination of Kingship and Messianic Expectation in Isaiah 1–35*. Lewiston, NY: Mellen, 1992.

Wehnert, Jürgen. *Die Reinheit des "christlichen Gottesvolkes" aus Juden und Heiden: Studien zum historischen und theologischen Hintergrund des sogenannten Aposteldekrets*. Göttingen: Vandenhoeck & Ruprecht, 1997.

___. *Die Wir-Passagen der Apostelgeschichte: Ein lukanisches Stilmittel aus jüdischer Tradition*. GTA 40. Göttingen: Vandenhoeck & Ruprecht, 1989.

Weinert, Francis D. "Luke, Stephen, and the Temple in Luke-Acts," *BTB* 17 (1987) 88–90.
Weiser, Alfons. *Die Apostelgeschichte. Kapitel 1–12.* ÖTKzNT 5/1. Gütersloh: Gütersloher Verlagshaus, 1981.
___. *Die Apostelgeschichte. Kapitel 13–28.* ÖTKzNT 5/2. Gütersloh: Gütersloher Verlagshaus, 1985.
___. "Die Nachwahl des Mattias (Apg 1,15–26). Zur Rezeption und Deutung urchristlicher Geschichte durch Lukas," in G. Dautzenberg, Helmut Merklein, and Karlheinz Müller, eds., *Zur Geschichte des Urchristentums,* 97–110. QD 87. Freiburg: Herder, 1979.
Wenham, John. "The Identification of Luke," *EvQ* 63 (1991) 3–44.
Westermann, Claus. *Elements of Old Testament Theology.* Trans. Douglas W. Stott. Atlanta, GA: John Knox Press, 1982.
___. *Isaiah 40–66: A Commentary.* Trans. David M. G. Stalker. OTL. Philadelphia: Westminster, 1969.
___. *Sprache und Struktur der Prophetie Deuterojesajas.* Calwer Theologische Monographien 11. Stuttgart: Calwer, 1981.
Whybray, R. N. *Isaiah 40–66.* NCBC. Grand Rapids, MI: Eerdmans, 1975.
Widengren, Geo. "Yahweh's Gathering of the Dispersed," in W. B. Barrick and J. R. Spencer, eds., *In the Shelter of Elyon: Essays on Ancient Palestinian Life and Literature in Honor of G. W. Ahlström,* 227–45. JSOTSup 31. Sheffield: Sheffield Academic Press, 1984.
Wikenhauser, Alfred. *Die Apostelgeschichte.* RNT 5. Regensburg: F. Pustet, 1961.
Wiklander, Bertil. *Prophecy as Literature: A Text-Linguistic and Rhetorical Approach to Isaiah 2–4.* Uppsala: CWK Gleerup, 1984.
Wilckens, Ulrich. *Die Missionsreden der Apostelgeschichte. Form- und traditions-geschichtliche Untersuchungen.* WMANT 5. Neukirchen: Neukirchener Verlag, 1974.
Wilcox, Max. "The 'God-Fearers' in Acts: A Reconsideration," *JSNT* 13 (1981) 102–22.
___. "The Judas-Tradition in Acts I. 15–26," *NTS* 19 (1973) 438–52.
___. *The Semitisms of Acts.* Oxford: Clarendon, 1965.
Wilcox, Peter, and David Paton-Williams. "The Servant Songs in Deutero-Isaiah," *JSOT* 42 (1988) 79–102.
Wildberger, Hans. "Die Völkerwallfahrt zum Zion: Jes. II 1–5," *VT* 7 (1957) 62–81.
___. *Isaiah 1–12: A Commentary.* Trans. T. H. Trapp. Minneapolis: Fortress, 1991.
___. "Jesajas Verständnis der Geschichte," *VTSup* 9 (1962) 83–117.
Wilk, Florian. *Die Bedeutung des Jesajabuches für Paulus.* FRLANT 179. Göttingen: Vandenhoeck & Ruprecht, 1998.
Wilken, Robert L. "*In novissimis diebus*: Biblical Promises, Jewish Hopes and Early Christian Exegesis," *JECS* 1 (1993) 1–19.
Willey, Patricia Tull. *Remember the Former Things: The Recollection of Previous Texts in Second Isaiah.* SBLDS 161. Atlanta, GA: Scholars, 1997.
Williamson, Hugh G. M. "First and Last in Isaiah," in H. A. McKay and D. J. A. Clines, eds., *Of Prophets' Visions and the Wisdom of the Sages: Essays in Honour of R. Norman Whybray on his Seventieth Birthday,* 95–108. JSOTSup 162. Sheffield: Sheffield Academic Press, 1993.
___. "Isaiah 40,20 — A Case of Not Seeing the Wood for the Trees," *Bib* 67 (1986) 1–19.
___. *The Book Called Isaiah: Deutero-Isaiah's Role in Composition and Redaction.* Oxford: Clarendon, 1994.
Willis, John T. "Isaiah 2:2–5 and the Psalms of Zion," in Craig C. Broyles and Craig A. Evans, eds., *Writing and Reading the Scroll of Isaiah: Studies of an Interpretive Tradition,* vol. 1, 295–316. Leiden: Brill, 1997.
Wills, Lawrence M. "The Depiction of the Jews in Acts," *JBL* 110 (1991) 631–54.
___. *The Jew in the Court of the Foreign King.* HDR 26. Minneapolis: Fortress, 1990.
Wilshire, Leland E. "Was Canonical Luke Written in the Second Century?—A Continued Discussion," *NTS* (1973–74) 246–53.
Wilson, Andrew. *The Nations in Deutero-Isaiah.* Lewiston, NY: Edwin Mellen, 1986.

Wilson, Robert R. "The Hardening of Pharaoh's Heart," *CBQ* 41 (1979) 18–36.
Wilson, Stephen G. *The Gentiles and the Gentile Mission in Luke-Acts.* SNTSMS 23. Cambridge: Cambridge University Press, 1973.
___. *Luke and the Law.* SNTSMS 50. Cambridge: Cambridge University Press, 1983.
Wingren, G. "'Weg', 'Wanderung' und verwandte Begriffe," *ST* 3 (1951) 111–23.
Winston, David. *Logos and Mystical Theology in Philo of Alexandria.* Cincinnati: Hebrew Union College, 1985.
___. *The Wisdom of Solomon.* AB 43. Garden City, NY: Doubleday, 1979.
Winter, Bruce W. "On Introducing Gods to Athens: An Alternative Reading of Acts 17:18–20," *TynBul* 47 (1996) 71–90.
___, and Andrew D. Clarke, *The Book of Acts in its Ancient Literary Setting.* Grand Rapids, MI: Eerdmans, 1993.
Witherington, Ben, III. *Conflict and Community in Corinth.* Grand Rapids, MI: Eerdmans, 1995.
___. *Jesus the Sage: The Pilgrimage of Wisdom.* Minneapolis: Fortress, 1994.
___. *The Acts of the Apostles: A Socio-Rhetorical Commentary.* Grand Rapids, MI: Eerdmans, 1998.
Wolfson, H. A. *Philo.* Cambridge, MA: Harvard University Press, 1947.
Wolter, Michael. "Israel's Future and the Delay of the Parousia, According to Luke," in David P. Moessner, ed., *Jesus and the Heritage of Israel: Luke's Narrative Claim upon Israel's Legacy,* 307–24. Harrisburg, PA: Trinity Press International, 1999.
Wright, G. Ernest. "Introduction," *Joshua: A New Translation with Notes and Commentary.* AB 6. New York: Doubleday, 1982.
___. *The Old Testament and Theology.* New York: Harper & Row, 1969.
Wright, N. T. *The New Testament and the People-of God.* London: SPCK, 1992.
___. "The Servant and Jesus: The Relevance of the Colloquy for the Current Quest for Jesus," in William H. Bellinger, Jr., and William R. Farmer, eds., *Jesus and the Suffering Servant: Isaiah 53 and Christian Origins,* 281–97. Harrisburg, PA: Trinity Press International, 1998.
Wright, R. B. "Psalms of Solomon," in James H. Charlesworth, ed., *The Old Testament Pseudepigrapha,* 2.639–70. Garden City, NY: Doubleday, 1985.
Wycherley, R. E. "St. Paul at Athens," *JTS* 19 (1968) 619–21.
Yadin, Yigael. *The Scroll of the War of the Sons of Light Against the Sons of Darkness.* Trans. B. Rabin and C. Rabin. London: Oxford University Press, 1962.
York, John O. *The Last, Shall Be First: The Rhetoric of Reversal in Luke.* JSNTSup 46. Sheffield: JSOT Press, 1991.
Ziegler, Joseph. *Isaias.* 3rd ed. Septuaginta 14. Göttingen: Vandenhoek & Ruprecht, 1983.
___. *Untersuchungen zur Septuaginta des Buches Isaias.* AltAb 12.3. Münster: Aschendorffschen, 1934.
Zillessen, Alfred. "Der alte und der neue Exodus," *ARW* 30 (1903) 289–304.
Zimmerli, Walther. "Der 'neue Exodus' in der Verkündigung der beiden großen Exilspropheten," *Gottes Offenbarung: Gesammelte Aufsätze zum Alten Testament,* 192–204. ThB 19. Munich: C. Kaiser, 1963.
___. "Jahwes Wort bei Deuterojesaja," *VT* 32 (1982) 104–24.
___, and Joachim Jeremias. *The Servant of God.* Rev. ed. London: SCM, 1965.
Zingg, Paul. *Das Wachsen der Kirche. Beiträge zur Frage der lukanischen Redaktion und Theologie.* Göttingen: Vandenhoeck & Ruprecht, 1974.
Zmijewski, Josef. *Die Apostelgeschichte.* Regensburg: Pustet, 1994.
Zweck, Dean. "The Exordium of the Areopagus Speech, Acts 17.22, 23," *NTS* 35 (1989) 94–103.

Index of Ancient Sources

1. Old Testament

2. New Testament

3. Apocrypha and Pseudepigrapha

4. Other Ancient Writings

Index of Authors

Subject Index